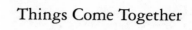

Things Come Together

ROBERT I. ROTBERG

Things Come Together

Africans Achieving Greatness

in the Twenty-First Century

OXFORD
UNIVERSITY PRESS

OXFORD
UNIVERSITY PRESS

Oxford University Press is a department of the University of Oxford. It furthers
the University's objective of excellence in research, scholarship, and education
by publishing worldwide. Oxford is a registered trade mark of Oxford University
Press in the UK and certain other countries.

Published in the United States of America by Oxford University Press
198 Madison Avenue, New York, NY 10016, United States of America.

Library of Congress Cataloging-in-Publication Data
Names: Rotberg, Robert I., author.
Title: Things come together: Africans achieving greatness in the
twenty-first century / Robert I. Rotberg.
Other titles: Africans achieving greatness in the twenty-first century
Description: New York: Oxford University Press, [2020] | Includes index.
Identifiers: LCCN 2019042471 (print) | LCCN 2019042472 (ebook) |
ISBN 9780190942540 (hardback) | ISBN 9780190942564 (epub) | ISBN 9780190942571
Subjects: LCSH: Africa—Politics and government—21st century. |
Africa—Economic conditions—21st century. | Africa—Social conditions—21st century.
Classification: LCC DT30.5 .R675 2020 (print) | LCC DT30.5 (ebook) | DDC 960.3/3—dc23
LC record available at https://lccn.loc.gov/2019042471
LC ebook record available at https://lccn.loc.gov/2019042472

9 8 7 6 5 4 3 2 1

Printed by Sheridan Books, Inc., United States of America

for
Joanna
beloved enduring sustainer
intrepid mother of three
friend of Africa

CONTENTS

TABLES AND FIGURES

TABLES

FIGURES

PREFACE

A FRICA WAS FALLING apart. But now it is coming together, and
  Africa and Africans are achieving greatness. This century is thus significant for every African. But it is a century not without consummate
challenges to match each and every major opportunity. This book extols
the opportunities and explains the challenges. Founded on a lifetime of intense scholarly and participatory involvement and an intimate acquaintance with many of its myriad peoples, this volume provides an in-depth but
accessible examination of who and what is African. It discusses the massive impact on Africa of population surges and the coming youth bulge
(recurring themes throughout the volume), the impact of climate heating
and consternation on African development, and the overriding roles of leadership and governance in determining African progress. This book further
analyzes Africa's distinctive economic trajectories and the curse of corruption,
the pervasive role of China in helping to strengthen Africa, the continent's
many battles with terrorists and internal insurgents, educational and public
health advances and challenges, the newest technological fixes that assist
Africa's drive to greatness, and—finally— the catastrophic loss of Africa's
animals to Asian-driven poaching, habitat loss, and human population pressure. A concluding chapter focuses on the resilience of Africa and its peoples
as they accomplish greatness. It explains my optimistic assessment of Africa's
future despite the mighty waves that lie immediately athwart the African

ship of state and powerfully threaten (as the following chapters enumerate) to disturb its smooth passage across the turbulent seas of African endeavor.

This book owes its inception to long-ago formative interactions. When I persuaded Tom Mboya, Kenya's charismatic up-and-coming young political leader, to speak at the University of Oxford in 1958—well before Jomo Kenyatta was released from detention—I could not have anticipated that the next sixty-plus years of my professional life would be devoted wholeheartedly and pleasurably to pursuing many of the important questions of anti-colonialism, emerging nationalism, governance, corrupt practices, and human and economic development in Africa—themes that Mboya articulated so well, and so early, and that Chinua Achebe limned in his magisterial *Things Fall Apart* (1959).

I interviewed Kenneth Kaunda, later president of Zambia for twenty-seven tumultuous years, in 1959 in Lusaka, just before he was arrested for agitating for national independence and against the Federation of Rhodesia and Nyasaland. My subsequent article about him in the *New York Times* introduced Kaunda to an international audience; what followed was a long involvement with Zambia and with many of the founders of its long dominant political party.

Likewise, I met Oliver Tambo in 1961, after first visiting apartheid-ridden South Africa and well before I was banned from white-ruled South Africa in 1972 for being involved with anti-apartheid activity there and for bringing freedom fighter Robert Sobukwe to tea in Kimberley. At about the same time, I was engaged with African attempts to oppose white rule in Rhodesia. The latter bastion of segregation barred my entrance from 1972 to 1980, when regime change occurred and Zimbabwe arose.

Both of those harsh cases, together with a participatory and scholarly engagement with nearly all of the other countries of the African continent south of the Sahara, indicate the extent to which this book draws on a lasting concern for the welfare and the fate of the many peoples of Africa. Over the course of a professional lifetime, I have written books and articles about many African countries and their political problems and solutions, created the Index of African Governance to measure how well governments in Africa deliver political goods to their citizens and taxpayers, lectured in Africa as well as at home, testified in Congress, taught an array of promising and now senior African politicians and executives, published numerous opinion pieces in major newspapers here and abroad, and kept as close an eye as a frequent visitor could do on the maturing vicissitudes of Africa.

Later, when Rebecca, my eldest daughter, was in the Peace Corps, I joined her in the very heart of the African continent—in Bria in the Central African

Republic, riding in the dusk on the back of her motorcycle the 105 miles from Bambari. (Nicola, another daughter, learned to crawl in Lusaka.) Visiting midwives with her and being in a village and speaking with villagers in the pulsating heart of Africa (not for the first time) supremely complemented my usual interactions with politically focused participants in the continent's cities. Africa in its full majesty, after all, represents the lives, aspirations, and interests of peoples of sometimes starkly disparate backgrounds and experiences—of rural persons subsisting far from roads and sources of water and power and of urban residents jostling with one another to achieve fame and fortune in some of our planet's largest and most congested urban conglomerations.

This book thus has roots deeply implanted into the enriching soils of Africa. It shares Africa's abiding greatness, its trajectory of development, and its several immediate and long-term challenges with readers who seek knowledge of where Africa, especially but not exclusively, sub-Saharan Africa, has come from and where it is going. In this book readers will find a discussion of Africa in all of its considerable breadth and depth. They will learn that there is no single thing called Africa; instead, there are many Africas, with countries sharing characteristics that might be geographical, ethnic, religious, and linguistic, but also embodying major distinctions and deep kinds of separation, even estrangement.

In the chapters that follow, readers will learn about those differences (and about similarities)—about distinctly singular methods of governing, providing schooling and health care, and treating the four cardinal human rights principles of speech, media, assembly, and religion; about despotism and democracy; and about how Africa embraces modern technology and seems poised to leapfrog many early advances pioneered elsewhere. Readers will also learn about the movements of terror and the sometimes accompanying insurgencies that are ripping Africa apart and making it extremely difficult for Africans, especially middle class Africans, to enhance their personal prosperity, attain more and better schooling, and join the march of progress that is engaging Asia and other parts of today's world.

Some of the contents of this book should alarm readers. Africa's population is exploding to such an extent that its 1.3 billion number today will become 2.5 billion by 2050 and as much as 3.6 million by the end of the century—more than doubling and tripling its current modest total people density. Soon Africa will be the globe's second most populous continent, after Asia. Three African countries will be among the ten most populous in the world, whereas only one is in that category today. Likewise, youth numbers will soar, large cities and small towns will double and triple in size, women will grow less fecund (but not rapidly enough), potable water will be rare, sanitation scarce, and electric power generating capacities will remain far below regional requirements.

Some countries will be much better governed than others, and some political leaders will be far more energetic and responsible, and much more dedicated to the national interest of their citizens and taxpayers than those who now rule these small and large states. This book appropriately emphasizes the importance of good leadership and good, measurable, governance for Africa and Africans. Some states will stay divided, ethnicized, and in civil conflict. Others will abandon, or at least reduce, the practice of corruption, especially at the grand level that today encumbers so many states, both north and south. Some will even be able to stanch the practice of poaching that is now decimating elephant, rhinoceros, giraffe, lion, and pangolin numbers by providing incentives sufficient at the rural level to transform poachers into wildlife rangers. Things are indeed coming together, if gradually and not always in equal measure across fifty-four countries.

Africa today is an integral part of the global village in a manner, and in a fullness, that has hitherto not been possible—or even necessarily desired—by the many component peoples of Africa. Yet, there are still immense distances to travel; movements of migrants to whom to give greater opportunities, and thus incentives to stay rather than to flee; hordes of young people anxious for well-paying jobs; foreign investors to seek; issues of urban sanitation to resolve; infectious diseases to conquer; deficiencies of electricity to end; and a dozen wars to terminate peacefully. Two chapters indicate how significant China's own prosperity and its foreign policy interests are to the future of the peoples of the African continent. Russia and India are also important players, along with Europe and the United States.

Africa is not exactly where it wants to be in terms of sustainable growth and consummate progress, but it is well positioned to succeed in ways that were never possible before now. This book's twelve chapters discuss, as thoroughly and candidly as possible, what has been accomplished and what still needs to be done. I try not to mince words.

As should be apparent from the opening paragraphs of this preface, *Things Come Together* emerges from deep wells of affection, respect, compassion, and involvement in Africa and with Africans. It is realistic, too, and appropriately skeptical of those who romanticize an Africa that hardly needs or wants to be romanticized. Thus, readers should recognize some of the seamy as well as the uplifting qualities of Africa. Sugar coating is neither appropriate nor desired by those inside and outside Africa who want to see Africans achieve enduring and uplifting betterment .

Africans will achieve greatness on their own terms and in their own several ways. A few of Africa's many countries will get there first. Others will follow, and some will struggle for decades—especially with the onrush of large people numbers—to catch up to their peers. This book provides a comprehensive framework for understanding what African leaders and governments are trying to accomplish, and a strong basis on which readers can follow their very different paths to the same positive common end. Things do come together.

—R. I. R.
13 February 2020

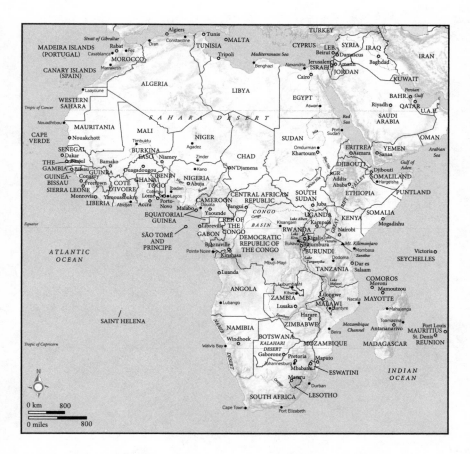

United States Central Intelligence Agency. *Africa*. Washington, DC: Central Intelligence Agency, 2012. Map. https://www.loc.gov/item/2014588822/.

Redrawn, updated, and modified for this book by George Chakvetadze.

1 | Africa The Diverse: Proliferating Peoples, Congested Cities, Colliding Faiths

A FRICA IS A continent, not a country. Indeed, with more political jurisdictions than any other continental land mass, more landlocked states, fewer navigable rivers, more separated deserts, and vastly more distinct peoples and languages than any other continent, Africa only by straining at definitions can be considered a single identity.

Africa stretches from the Arab-dominated borders of the Mediterranean Sea to the Atlantic and Indian Ocean waters lapping South Africa and from the West African bulge of the continent—where Senegal and Liberia jut out toward Brazil—across humid low-lying cities and villages, semi-deserts, and the Sahel, toward the easternmost promontory of Somalia. South of that lengthy territorial sweep west to east across the continent's shoulders is the low-lying Congo basin, encircled by that great river; major interior fresh-water lakes such as Victoria and Tanzania; the Great Rift Valley that plunges southward from the Red Sea to Lake Malawi and beyond; and the coastal lit-toral states of Kenya and Tanzania that face toward distant Asia.

Then there are the islands, the rocky smaller outposts in the Atlantic, and their mostly larger analogues in the Indian Ocean. Additionally, off the continent's southeastern coast lies Madagascar, the fourth largest island in the world and the home of unique fauna, unique avifauna, unique flora, and African peoples and languages that are Indonesian in their origin and unique to the island. Even the music and musical instruments of Madagascar's highland peoples are derived from Indonesia, if now also diffused across mainland Africa from southeast to northwest.

Just as Madagascar has strong early ties to Sumatra and Southeast Asia and mainland African coastal regions to its northwest experienced lasting economic and social ties to South Asia, Persia, and the Arabian Peninsula, in historic eras the main sub-Saharan African empires themselves were always tied to the northern (Roman and then Arab) cities and coasts by trade in salt, gold, ivory, and slaves. Likewise the Atlantic-facing lands up and down that coast were linked first to Portugal and other European seafaring nations by commercial trade, and then to the Americas by the odious trans-Atlantic slave trade, which also convulsed the interior and had its unfortunate echo in the easternmost side of the continent.

Africa, and especially what is now designated as sub-Saharan Africa, was never as isolated as the early mapmakers assumed. Much, but not all, of Africa—even the most remote parts of its interior—were from early times in at least indirect contact through commerce or conflict with other parts of the globe. Except for the very early indigenous languages and writing in what is now Ethiopia and northern Sudan, the spread of Arabic from the north and east, and a few local tongues that were written before the European conquest, many sections of sub-Saharan Africa largely lacked the convenience of written languages before the eighteenth and nineteenth centuries (when missionaries arrived).[1] Nevertheless, sub-Saharan Africa possessed thriving orally transmitted cultures and languages, and rich musical and artistic heritages. At the same time, the peoples of sub-Saharan Africa were heterodox, their many languages no more mutually intelligible than Finnish and Swedish or Russian and French. Thus there were always many Africas, never a single Africa or even a single sub-Saharan Africa.

Even Africa's staple food preferences varied and vary greatly. Many of the peoples of the western areas rely on rice and real yams. Moving southward and eastward, many societies prefer white maize and cassava (manioc or tapioca)—both imports from the Americas—consumed several times a day as a stiff porridge (occasionally with a meat or vegetable relish). Ugandans live off varieties of the abundant banana, and plantains. The Malagasy of Madagascar prefer rice, the Sudanese *fuul*, a paste of fava beans. Some pastoral peoples rely on milk and blood from their cattle. Nearly all Africans, if they can afford it, eat the meat of domesticated cattle, goats, and sheep. A minority even attempt to subsist on bushmeat culled from the monkeys and primates of the forest or the larger animals (mostly ungulates) of the savannah. Those who live near water dote on fish of both seagoing and freshwater variety.

The growth of these crops, and the herds of livestock on which so many Africans of very different backgrounds depend to sustain themselves, in turn is not viable without steady supplies of rainwater. Irrigation in sub-Saharan Africa is rare; African farmers and herdsmen perforce rely in the east on the monsoons that usually bring abundant downpours for five or six months, followed by winters (south of the Equator) that are dry everywhere but in the far south (near Cape Town), which has a Mediterranean climate that still suffers from arid spells. The rains of the interior and the west coast are all governed by the inter-tropical convergence system that, alas, is weakening as a result of climate change and global warming. Hitherto, tropical moist oceanic air reliably moved from the Atlantic and Indian Oceans toward an equatorial low-pressure zone in the center of Africa, producing steady rains. That reliability is now no longer assured.

The new Africa cannot expect the steady moisture of decades past. Now there are floods in lands that were dry, and recurring droughts in places rarely without abundant water in the past. Changes in atmospheric circulation patterns have caused and will in future cause weather systems to stall. As much as 92 percent of sub-Saharan Africa beyond the humid tropical belt now has too little water most of the time, or much too much episodically. Torrential rains, flooding, and landslides engulfed large sections of western Kenya and eastern Uganda on an unprecedented scale in late 2019. The massive cyclones earlier in the same year that devastated as much as 900 square miles of first central Mozambique, southern Malawi, and eastern Zimbabwe, and then northern Mozambique, affected several million Africans, caused hundreds of deaths, and destroyed crops and dwellings in great number. Cholera came in its wake, and measles followed.

Half of the sub-continent is often short of water, an outcome of climate change. Between 1980 and 2013, the number of record-setting dry months increased by 50 percent in sub-Saharan Africa. In the future, higher temperatures will dry the soil and the air, reducing crop yields and pasture for goats, sheep, and cattle. The great glaciers on Mounts Kilimanjaro and Kenya have shrunk considerably and may soon be gone. Lake Chad is shrinking. The formidable Sahara desert in the north is expanding southward. The deserts of the Horn of Africa and far southwestern Africa are also spreading. The ability of Africans to exist in their accustomed resilient manner is thus compromised in this century by unpredictable shifts in the natural forces controlling the planet's macro-weather as well as its detailed expression at the level of individual countries and peoples. Food security is endangered more and more by climatic shifts, the drying up of the atmosphere, and population increases.

Twenty-First-Century Africa

Today's Africa contains a mélange of fifty-four nation-states of greatly varying populations and geographical sizes: a handful of tiny island states with fewer than 1 million people, mainland polities almost as small containing a few million inhabitants, a number of medium-sized states with 10 to 50 million people, several of 100 million or more, and three among the world's ten most populous nations, soon to hold more than 200 million people each.[2]

That these innumerable peoples still speak their own languages at home (Zambia has seventy languages in use, over which four key indigenous languages and English are superimposed; Nigeria claims about five hundred languages) testifies to the diversity of sub-Saharan Africa—of our inability as observers and scholars ever to speak of one "Africa" or to define "Africa" as having a singular culture or a singular political or social expression.

Leaving aside the Arabic-speaking entities along the northern coast, a very disparate collection of forty-nine nation-states comprises Africa south of the Sahara, from Mauritania in the west, Mali and Niger in the center, and Ethiopia and Sudan in the east southward across the Tropic of Cancer toward the Equator and, ultimately, across the Tropic of Capricorn to South Africa. These many nations and very mixed geographical expressions contain roughly 2,500 disparate peoples speaking as many languages at home, but employing English, French, and Portuguese as governmental and business lingua francas, together with major indigenous trading languages such as Fulani, Hausa, and Mandinka in the west, KiSwahili in the east, and Lingala in the vast Congo. Northern Sudanese speak Arabic; Ethiopians use Amharic and Oromo; Kenyans converse in Kikuyu and Luo, together with Swahili. Nigerians may talk to their contemporaries in Yoruba, Igbo, Hausa, Kanuri, and Fulani, but use English to bridge ethnic differences. Alongside Kikongo, Lingala, and Swahili, the Congolese speak to each other in 215 languages such as Tshiluba, Chilunda, and Chokwe. Zambians employ CiBemba or SiLozi, and the Malawians CiCewa or CiTumbuka. In South Africa millions of urban and rural citizens speak isiZulu and isiXhosa alongside Sesotho and several other indigenous tongues, Afrikaans, and English. Just as there is no identifiable Africa, nor sub-Saharan Africa, so there is no indigenous language that dares to span all of the peoples and cultures of the continent.

It is true, however, that the peoples of sub-Saharan Africa roughly from eastern Nigeria and Uganda south to South Africa share languages that belong to the Bantu linguistic family and have a limited collection of key root words (such as "people" and "meat") in common. But the many Bantu languages bear little similarity to the dominant language families of West

Africa, to the Nilotic languages that spread southward from the Sudan into Uganda, Kenya, and Tanzania, nor to the languages of traditionally pastoral people like the Turkana and Samburu of Kenya and the Maasai of Kenya and Tanzania. In northeastern Africa, the Geez-derived languages such as Amharic, Tigray, and Oromo, and the several Somali languages, again bear no resemblance to the Bantu languages that they often abut. Likewise, the "click" languages of the earliest inhabitants of southern Africa, including the Khoisan, and of the Hadza of Tanzania, predate the arrival of Bantu-speakers and demonstrate the continuation of early forms of political and social organization amid modernity and the growth and spread of more universally understood tongues.

The Faiths

Africa south of the Sahara is more than 62 percent Christian and 31 percent Muslim, with 3 percent or so of the residents of the subregion professing adherence to traditional forms of belief. Less than 1 percent of the remaining sub-Saharan Africans are Hindu, Buddhists, Jews, or other. The Muslims, nearly all of whom are of the Sunni persuasion, are 1 percent more fertile than Christians; by 2050 that will mean a sub-Saharan African total population that will comprise about 1.4 billion Christians and nearly 850 million Muslims.

Arab traders and clerics brought Islam across the Sahara desert to West Africa primarily in the tenth and eleventh centuries of our common era, but Islam spread more widely in the west during the period of the great jihadist upsurge in the eighteenth and nineteenth centuries; Senegal and northern Nigeria experienced powerful fundamentalist revolutions that swept away many earlier Muslim rulers and religious practices. In eastern Africa, Islam arrived largely by sea as Omani and other sailors and traders came on the southwestern-flowing monsoon winds. Omanis ruled much of coastal East Africa from Zanzibar during the first two-thirds of the nineteenth century.

Now Islam is more powerful and dominant in North Africa and north of the Equator and close to the Sahara than it is in the south. As in Morocco, Algeria, Tunisia, Libya, and Egypt, countries such as Mauritania and Senegal in the northwest and the Sudan in the northeast are overwhelmingly Muslim, as are the Sahel states such as Burkina Faso, Mali, and Niger, and the four Somali entities. But Christians and Muslims jostle for hegemony in Ethiopia and Eritrea and to a lesser extent in countries such as Kenya and Tanzania. Nigeria is split almost equally north and south, with more Christians in the

Middle Belt of that country, facing competition from Muslim Fulani. There are influential Muslim communities in Mozambique and Malawi, and even in a city such as Cape Town. Overall, adherence to Islam may gradually both be spreading into new areas and intensifying in older ones, but many of the Christian denominations are also growing in followers, especially in cities.

In this century, Africa will become the global center of Christianity. By 2060, six of the globe's ten largest centers of Christian worship will be in Africa: in Nigeria, the Democratic Republic of Congo, Tanzania, Uganda, Kenya, and Ethiopia, in that order. According to the Pew Research Center, Nigeria will be the third largest of the world's Christian countries, following the United States and Brazil and displacing Russia, Germany, and China. Mexico and the Philippines are also on the new list, sandwiched between the Congo and Tanzania. In 2015, only three African countries were among the top ten.

The majority of Christians are Protestants (57 percent), Roman Catholic (34 percent), Orthodox Catholic (8 percent), and other (1 percent). Protestant denominations include Anglicans (Episcopalians), Lutherans, Methodists, Baptists, fundamentalist churches such as the Plymouth Brethren and the Pilgrim Holiness Mission, and a range of African independent churches, the largest of which is the Apostolic Church of Zion. But the fastest growing and wealthiest, and possibly most influential, of the movements in modern African Protestantism is Pentecostalism, with gospel of wealth congregations in many of Nigeria's cities (such as the Deeper Life Bible Church), in South Africa, and even in Coptic Orthodox Ethiopia. Possibly 12 percent of all sub-Saharan Africans belong to one of the proliferating Pentecostal churches.

In opinion polls, both Muslim and Christian Africans tell inquirers that religious belief is very important to them. The percentage of persons surveyed who said so varied upwards from 69 percent in Botswana to more than 98 percent in Senegal, much higher numbers than in contemporary Europe and North and South America. At the same time, and maybe for the same reasons, in Tanzania, Mali, Senegal, and South Africa (Muslim and Christian countries all) respondents affirmed that "sacrifices to spirits or ancestors can protect them from bad things happening."[3]

African Anglicans have opposed the Church of England's openness to homosexuality; Roman Catholics have dissented from the Church of Rome's willingness to modernize liturgy and practice. Religion is taken very seriously everywhere in Africa, not only among Islamists and followers of independent charismatic Christian preachers. It is central to the very being of Africa.

Kings and Kleptocrats

Some early African peoples had kings and functioned as monarchies. Others were what the anthropologists referred to as acephalous (headless); their traditional forms of governance were more decentralized than autocratic. Whatever our optic, whether of today's century or of earlier ones, Africans inhabiting the sub-continent used many contrasting forms of political organization to govern themselves, and just as many different forms of national expression. Today, African nations are ruled by several kings, but only one actually governs; by a clutch of autocrats and kleptocrats, some of whom are truly despotic; by elected authoritarians; by quasi democrats; and by genuine, full-fledged democrats. In other words, there is no single or dominant political expression that is demonstrably African. Nor can Africans claim to have forged any unique political forms of their own. Their kleptocrats may steal more outrageously than others, perhaps, or some of their dictators may be unusually cruel or their democratic leaders unusually tolerant and respectful, but their homegrown varieties of governance mimic what transpires in Latin America, Asia, and Europe.

Agriculturalists live, not always peacefully, alongside pastoralists, Muslims alongside animists, lighter-skinned persons adjacent to those of darker hues, very tall inhabitants together with much shorter subjects and rivals. Africans inhabit towns and cities; about 65 percent of all Africans are urban and in twenty years that figure will rise to at least 75 percent. Gabon is already 80 percent urbanized. Village Africa is rapidly disappearing.

Much of this proliferating humanity was homogenized by colonial rule—by the expedients introduced for administrative reasons by the several foreign bureaucratized powers. Thus, some traditional cultures and practices were submerged. Others that had never been dominant became so because of colonial patronage and support. In any event, the cultural and economic, as well as the political, maps of Africa were altered, compressed, and centralized. Many cultures and languages lost out. Others, never prominent before, became important because of the predilections and preferences of the interlopers. Old trading patterns were distorted by the new ties to Europe; Africa was forcibly redirected and reoriented. Until recently, intra-African trade was scarce.

The creativity and adaptability of Africans were not lost as the modern overlay of new organizing principles catapulted first North Africa and later much of sub-Saharan Africa into the heart of the global village. Now that 65 percent of all sub-Saharan Africans depend for their reliable information and communication, and their monetary transactions, on mobile telephones, their knowledge of, and participation within, the global village is that much more intense and all-encompassing than ever before. In this century, Africa has become much more fully connected to, almost integrated into, the global economy and global society.

Identity, Ethnicity, and the Modern State

Even though they are now part of the global village, most Africans are quick to define their primary identity as their own "people," their tribe or clan, their ethnic group. Although Africans in Paris or London may be perfectly content to describe themselves as Nigeriens or Beninois, Kenyans or Malawians, and even marry across ethnic or national lines, they "belong" to a home group—even to numerically small, out of the way, ethnicities. Even as they migrate in their millions to Africa's cities, and merge into an urban mass that tries to obliterate primordial loyalties, most Africans still feel most comfortable when they are among their kith and kin, and can express themselves in their home languages. Thus, most sub-Saharan Africans possess multiple identities, and articulate them according to the contexts in which they find themselves in their villages, in cities, as migrants, and overseas.

Being a constituent of a modern African state is but one manifestation of identity; the most successful and best-governed African political jurisdictions now foster such national loyalties, having given their disparate inhabitants a sense of belonging and pride that is still rare in sub-Saharan Africa. Botswana, Cape Verde, Mauritius, and South Africa (for additional historical reasons) have emerged in that sense as full-fledged polities with political cultures that transcend the various ethnicities and village loyalties that previously prevailed. In most of the rest of sub-Saharan Africa, especially those largely pre-institutional places such as Cameroon, Chad, Mozambique, the Republic of Congo, and Uganda—where autocrats still rule—nationalized identities are weak and transient. Those nations and many others are not yet completely realized as the main foci of identity.

This lack of fully formed attachments to the nation qua nation in part reflects the artificiality of many of the post-colonial administrative areas that are now polities. This phenomenon is best noticed in the Francophone states that sweep southward from Mauritania, mostly in West and Central Africa. Originally African real estate that had been arbitrarily allocated to France's West African or Central African federations, these administrative entities were let loose in 1960 or so, and rapidly embraced as African-ruled independent nations. Some, like Senegal and Gabon, made more sense from an indigenous perspective than others; whatever their clouded origins, each of these hitherto French-run polities overnight became a nation-state run by the leading contemporary African politicians on the ground (many of whom had also gained legislative experience in Paris).

British, Belgian, Portuguese, and Italian ex-colonies and trust territories also became proto-nations, often with as little preparation, and with no attention to rectifying arbitrary borders or reconnecting ethnic groups that had been separated by colonial administrative decisions. Nigeria exists as Nigeria because Captain (later Lord) Frederick Lugard thought that the very different halves of the region would be better and more cheaply administered as one. Zambia came into being because there was a protectorate of Northern Rhodesia that had been created out of two previous colonial administrative regions. Malawi, another so-called protectorate, retained its inconvenient shape and borders when it, too, achieved independence from Britain. In other words, although there has never been any primordial logic to the cutting up of sub-Saharan Africa into forty-nine sovereign pieces, that logic was accepted when the founding indigenous fathers (and they were fathers) of modern Africa fought and campaigned for freedom from colonial rule within administrative lines that had previously been demarcated mostly by happenstance, by geographical realities such as rivers or deserts, and by bargains between European foreign ministers. (Note the Namibian pedicle, an unnecessary extrusion that exists solely because a British prime minister wanted to placate his German counterpart.)

Modern Africa thus celebrates diversity. Only a few polities such as the Eswatini kingdom of the Swazi people or little Lesotho (surrounded by South Africa) are homogenous, existing as the homeland of a single ethnicity. Even Botswana is more than the home of the Tswana-speaking peoples. Burundi and Rwanda harbor both Tutsi and Hutu. Mauritius boasts a mélange of Creoles, ex-slaves, Hindi-speaking descendants of immigrants, Mandarin-writing former immigrants from Taiwan and China, and whites originally from France. Ghana has at least a dozen major ethnic groups, and rivalries between persons from the coastal region, Ashanti and others from the center, and groups like the Wa in the north. Some of the new nations were dominated from their independence beginnings by an ethnic group that just happened by accident to reside near new capital cities or railway depots; others were sufficiently strong or influential at the time of independence to insert themselves deeply into initial governing structures.

President Kwame Nkrumah of Ghana, who led the Gold Coast (as it was called) to independence in 1958, attempted to unify sub-Saharan Africa into a single political expression that would have privileged continental-wide integration over separate expressions of sub-national particularity. But none of those who had fought for, or inherited, independence and the right to rule former administrative conveniences as new nations was inclined to put himself or his people under a distant ruler like Nkrumah. Diversity, responding perfectly to pre-colonial and colonial distinctions, thus triumphed and Africa became a collection of small, medium, and large states. (Only the splitting off of South Sudan from the Sudan in 2011 and the joining of what is now Somaliland to Somalia in 1960, are exceptions to African Union rules against meddling with inherited borders.)

Today sub-Saharan Africa's diverse makeup faithfully represents its 2,500 or so ethnicities and languages as well as the decisions (largely) of absent European overlords.

Africans have become accustomed to the national and other lines that separate them from their own kind. They have also grasped opportunities to develop their own countries as opposed to larger, Nkrumah-like, combinations. The African Union (AU), which followed the Organization of African Unity as the regional governing institution for the countries of the continent, collectively expresses the will of all fifty-four members, and is weak because it must respond to all fifty-four, and also because many of its members cannot pay the required annual dues. Housed in Addis Ababa, the capital of Ethiopia, the AU reaches out from a part of Africa that bears little resemblance in terms of geographical or human resources to much of the remainder of its geographical and human domain. Yet that is the effective reality of modern Africa.

Statistical Outcomes

The diversity of Africa shows itself in its outcomes, as well. From measures of health and well-being to measures of income or measures of educational persistence, there are innumerable Africas, especially south of the Sahara. Some countries possess modern roads; some specialize in potholes rather than arteries of commerce. Although mobile telephones are ubiquitous, some polities can count on more reliable service, and easier connections. Likewise in Africa there are many different qualities of governance and leadership; a few countries are minimally corrupt, several are ranked as rampantly corrupt. Rule of law exists robustly in a few of the same places; its absence is lamented in dozens of other nation-states. Similarly, some countries seem perpetually at war with themselves, fighting off insurgents in their midst. The majority of sub-Saharan nations, however, are secure and have not yet been plunged into internecine conflict.

African wealth per capita, one formal measure of how well an individual government delivers services and outcomes to its citizens, varies wildly from the per capita GDP of its smallish oil producers, such as Equatorial Guinea and Gabon, or diamond-wealthy Botswana, downward to bankrupt but potentially mineral-rich Zimbabwe with a GDP per capita in 2019 of about $1,250, or Niger, in a war zone, with a GDP per capita of $1,016. Countries in the middle of the wealth distribution list, like Rwanda ($2,018), Ghana ($4,641) and Kenya ($3,286), do much better, with substantial average per capita GDPs in 2017. Nigeria and South Africa should be very wealthy, but they only report per capita GDPs of $5,860 and $13,498. Overall, as we shall see in Chapter IV, sub-Saharan Africa's economic and fiscal profile is Janus-like, always facing in two directions and rarely fulfilling its potential.

Whatever prosperity there is derives most often from the export of primary resources—petroleum and natural gas; from the mining of precious minerals such as diamonds, gold, coltan, coal, copper, ferrochrome, iron ore, tin, and zinc; from timber; in a limited way from farming; and from charcoal, hides, and skins. Africa exports few manufactured items (except shoes from Ethiopia, beer from Tanzania, and cement from Nigeria), but for many decades sub-Saharan Africa has supplied the world with unprocessed cocoa, shade-grown coffee, fresh flowers, and some tea. Beneficiation of raw materials has heretofore been limited, but more attention is being paid today to such improvements in economic output for export. Tourism is profitable in several countries, mostly where big game still roam. Hydroelectricity is another economic growth area, especially with the coming completion of Ethiopia's Grand Renaissance Dam across the Blue Nile River and ongoing planning for the third phase of the even larger Inga Dam athwart the Congo River west of Kinshasa. But even with both dams eventually on-stream, Africa will still have access to far less electric power than any other continent. Some places, even major economic powerhouses like Nigeria, will for decades be able to count upon less electrical generating capacity than a smallish American city.

Africa as a whole is much better educated than it was a mere thirty years ago, reflecting rising incomes, and an awareness of how important the education of girls is to fertility reduction and national economic growth. Thirty percent of girls now finish secondary school, double the percentage ten years ago. Boys also persist in the same manner, but tertiary education—university schooling—is available only for a tiny proportion of secondary school graduates. And then there is the disappointing statistic that half or more (even in South Africa) of those students who attend secondary school never complete their schooling with an appropriate certificate. So many sub-Saharan Africans are thrown onto the job market with limited skills that formal unemployment rates measure those who cannot find appropriate jobs together with those who do not have the qualifications necessary even to compete for modern paying positions.

One of the saddest stories of contemporary Africa is the failure of most countries to create jobs sufficient to match population growth. And it will soon get worse. If a country's population is growing at a modest 5 percent (and some country populations are doubling yearly) then jobs need to multiply by the same amount to keep pace. But even though much of Africa is growing at rapid rates (Ethiopia at more than 9 percent per annum), economic growth rates still do not accelerate sufficiently to provide the necessary number of new jobs. Especially Nigeria has that difficulty, and so does South Africa.

Unemployment in sub-Saharan Africa has always been higher than in the developed world. Most measures are of formal unemployment, where even an advanced country such as South Africa officially acknowledges about 27 percent formal unemployment. Unofficially, that number doubles, according to informed estimates of the true figure. Many sub-Saharan African countries report 50 percent or more formal unemployment; formal unemployment in Zimbabwe is believed to be more than 90 percent.

These figures do not account for "employment" in the informal sector, where many if not most sub-Saharan Africans make money by selling fruit or gimcracks along the sides of roads or at markets, where teenagers find parking places for drivers in high-rise garages, where men and women offer to wipe windscreens at motor junctions or in traffic jams. Then there is crime, which is always high in the cities of sub-Saharan Africa and in a significant segment of the informal employment sector, especially in countries that are poorly managed and insufficiently well-governed.

According to the Index of African Governance, which measures the delivery of essential political goods such as security, rule of law, prosperity, education, and health, about a dozen African countries are well-governed, another dozen or so countries are improving in their quality of governance, and the remaining twenty-five or so have traditionally been badly governed. That harsh fact means that the citizens of the bottom twenty-five African nations—Chad, Zimbabwe, Nigeria, and the like —receive many fewer services, and distinctively poorer quality services, than the better governed countries such as Mauritius, the Seychelles, Cape Verde, Botswana, South Africa, and Namibia.

Central Africans, Chadians, and similar polities, for example, may have fewer school chances, lower life expectancies and rougher medical care, inadequate roads, reduced access to mobile telephone coverage and broadband width, limited rules of law, less effective agricultural extension services, reduced GDPs per capita, and much more corruption. Their distinct lack of good governance may also have plunged these bottom-ranking countries into round after round of civil conflict. (These issues are discussed at greater length in Chapter III.)

Migrants to Europe, legitimate and illegitimate, often come disproportionally from the ranks of the discontented in those places with demonstrably bad governance. Migrancy also reflects an overwhelming lack of economic opportunity in the home village, the home region, and/or the home country.

Many migrants flee the web of poverty. A 2019 Afrobarometer survey shows that nearly 75 percent of those planning to migrate do so to find a job and escape being poor. Fully 36 percent of all African migrants hope to move to another better-off African country, preferably in their own region. Only 27 percent try to go to Europe, and only a fifth of those actually do go. North America attracts 22 percent of those preparing to migrate.

The majority of sub-Saharan Africans earn no more than and subsist on about $1.90 a day, according to the World Bank. Others earn less of course, and on a continent where wealth disparities are common, inequality is rife, and Gini coefficients are very skewed, there are large and growing gaps between those who get by and those who have plenty. Gini coefficients measure how much income (as a percentage of the whole) the top 20 percent of a population earns versus the lowest 20 percent. On that dimension, South Africa is traditionally among the most unequal, Mauritius and Botswana among the more equal.

The Rise of the Middle Class

Countries in Africa for the first time consist of more than subsistence farmers and lowly paid civil servants. There is a middle class in most polities that the World Bank says approximates a third of the population in one country after another. This emergence of a middle class is new, and a testament to the maturing and the growth of much of Africa. Very small, impoverished, or fragile sub-Saharan nations may lack a significantly sized middle class. But the experience of such places as Senegal, Ethiopia, Kenya, Cameroon, Gabon, and Nigeria demonstrates that Africa is on the move and that a relatively prosperous bourgeoisie is in its vanguard.

By global standards, the World Bank's criteria for "middle class" may be low, but in Africa it does now include those who have overcome the constraints of poverty and embraced Western lifestyles and aspirations. It is a class that has or will soon have the power to determine the future of all but the most extremely despotic African countries. As the population numbers of Africa explode exponentially, so those who are middle class by virtue of their jobs, incomes, their motor vehicles, their fancy houses, and their abilities to travel, will have abundant opportunity to determine the political futures of their nations—to demand more honest, more transparent, more public-interested leaders and political results. As populations surge and middle classes become larger, so the middle class will exert preponderant political power.

The African Development Bank defines middle class persons in Africa as those with yearly incomes exceeding $3,900, or per capita expenditures between $2 and $20 daily. The World Bank's cutoff is somewhat different: It classifies as middle class those African who earn $12 to $15 on a daily basis, on average.

An American data-consulting firm with African connections offers yet another method of classifying Africa's "consumer," not middle, class based on asset ownership and educational attainments.[4] Assets here include mobile telephones, computers, television sets, refrigerators, and automobiles. Employing the consulting firm's definition still brings Africa's consumer or middle class to about one-third of the continent's total population, with ample room for growth. Moreover, using the consumer definition gives us a better sense of the distribution of this new class of Africans: Egypt, Nigeria, South Africa, Algeria, and Morocco claim two-thirds of the one-third of all Africans who consume in a middle class manner. Another approximately 100 million African middle class persons are scattered across the not-necessarily wealthier countries of the continent; poor Ethiopia has more than 10 million middle class consumers, Angola nearly that many, Kenya almost 9 million, and Ghana and Tanzania more than 8 million. Everywhere across the continent, middle class numbers (by whatever criteria) are growing exponentially. As a class they promise to become progressively more influential.

That influence will mostly be exerted in urban surrounds. As Africa's population doubles and triples, so its cities will expand even faster. Twenty-one of the planet's thirty fastest growing cities are African; at least two will be among the five largest globally. They will house many millions of very poor persons, living on the margin. But the middle or consumer class will live there as well, and take charge of their urban as well as national destinies. They will purchase goods like refrigerators, and all of the common electronic tools that signify "middle class" throughout the world.

Already in the cities Africans are enthusiastic patrons of the gig economy, of Uber and similar transportation innovations. But they also put an African spin on the gig economy. Do you want a live goat or a live pig slaughtered for an urban party? Do you need charcoal for the fire? Dial up one of the new gig enterprises in Luanda, Lusaka, or Port Elizabeth and the edible beast will soon be delivered by bicycle, scooter, or motorcycle.

Corruption Swallows Gains

The middle class suffers proportionally more from corruption, however, than other classes in most African societies. Arguably, Africa is the most corrupt continent, with more nation-states than in Asia and Latin America falling into the rampantly corrupt sections of such instruments as the well-respected Corruption Perceptions Index (CPI) and the World Bank Control of Corruption Indicator.

The Nordic countries, New Zealand, Singapore, Canada, and several European countries such as Luxembourg and Switzerland routinely fill the top spots on both rating lists. The Seychelles and Botswana are the only African countries that rank in the upper deciles of the Index and on the Indicator. A few other African countries can be considered only partially corrupted, given their rankings after Botswana. Cape Verde, Rwanda, Namibia, and Mauritius all rank comparatively well, with São Tomé and Príncipe, Senegal, and South Africa trailing. (Chapter V has the details.)

Most other African countries, including some of the larger and more dynamic ones, are regarded by both measuring devices as hopelessly corrupt. For example, the bottom thirty countries on the CPI include twenty-eight African nation-states, with Somalia and South Sudan occupying the very lowest (and most corrupt) places globally as well as in Africa. Just above those two corrupt and unconsolidated nation-states are the thoroughly corrupt polities of Sudan, Guinea-Bissau, Equatorial Guinea, Angola, Chad, the Republic of Congo (Brazzaville), the Democratic Republic of Congo, Zimbabwe, Burundi, and the Central African Republic, reading backward from 180th place to 158th place.

This picture of African peculation and graft taken to extremes illustrates some of the ways in which African leaders have abused their elected offices, become kleptocrats, laundered money overseas and, in short, stolen from their peoples. But corruption is as much a distortion of national political and economic priorities as it is sheer theft. Corruption turns almost every regime away from regarding the public interest as supreme. Bettering themselves and their families becomes a priority for rulers, elected or self-appointed, and the needs of the nation or of its peoples become subordinated to escalating levels of graft that serve an often criminalized set of national leaders. (Leadership is the subject of the next chapter.)

Narcotics trafficking frequently fuels corrupt actions. It also depends on corrupting all levels of officialdom to pursue its illicit activities. Drug-, people-, and arms-smuggling are also tied to escalating spurts of conflict, as terrorist groups and other outlaw elements increasingly battle constituted governments and rival insurgents to control such lucrative commercial opportunities. Profits from several of the existing trading routes across the Sahara to Libya and Europe; from Guinea-Bissau, Ghana, and Nigeria to Europe; from Timbuktu northward across the desert; and from Somalia to Turkey and Europe all support the terroristic predations of Boko Haram, al-Shabaab, al-Qaeda in the Maghreb, ISIS, and other local antagonists. Increasingly, too, these and other attacking groups prey on innocent, even disengaged, citizens and specialize almost entirely in moneymaking activities, sudden raids on civilian targets, and attacks on constituted authorities. Increasingly, they disregard the ideological founding notions of their rebellious Islamist sects and focus on ways of outwitting governments and militaries.

Possibly as many as 15 million to 20 million African civilians, combatants, and soldiers have been killed since 1990 in the continuing civil wars of the continent, fueled as they are by terror, by narcotics and other profiteering, by attempts to overcome the resource curse of precious metals, by petroleum discoveries and exploitation, and by fierce competition for the best farming and grazing lands. (See Chapter VII.) These large numbers dwarf casualties in comparable time periods from Asia or Latin America and include wars between Sudan and South Sudan, and within South Sudan (where cruelties abound and fatalities come from collateral damage and disease as much as from actual combat). The vast fatality numbers also encompass al-Shabaab's depredations in Somalia; Boko Haram's mayhem and Nigerian and Cameroonian military counterattacks; the wild west conflicts between warlord-led vigilantes in the eastern Congo, on and across the Ugandan border, and against the official military elsewhere in the giant Congo. Then there are the Central African Republic's simmering rivalries between Muslims and Christians; the bitter battles within Nigeria between pastoralists and farmers, and between petroleum exporters and local militias; the newish guerrilla struggles between English-speaking insurgents and the French-speaking autocracy that rules Cameroon; rebels who lay waste to parts of northern Mozambique; and the havoc that spills out of the Algerian and Libyan Sahara to embroil Mali, Niger, and Burkina Faso.

French and American troops are there to contain small but potent revolutionary contingents belonging to al-Qaeda in the Maghreb (AQIM) and the Islamic State (ISIS). In Egypt, President Abdel Fattah el-Sisi's autocratic regime engages in a running conflict against remnants of ISIS, especially in the Sinai; neighboring Libya remains divided, with warring factions in the eastern and western coastal cities and ISIS in the deep south. Only Tunisia, coastal Algeria, and Morocco are comparatively free of civil war despite suicide bombings in Tunis and the continued existence and potent harassment by AQIM insurgents.

That great swathes of Africa remain immured in war, and that homicide and other crime rates in its cities, especially across sub-Saharan Africa, remain high (if below soaring Central American levels), means that the nations and peoples of the continent cannot simply settle down and go about the arduous business of development. Indeed, insecurity and conflict inhibit foreign and domestic investment, drive rural dwellers to abandon their farms for equally precarious lives in cities, erode local food production and legitimate trade, and greatly accelerate internal and transnational migration flows.

Africa's overall economic growth potential is curtailed by the inability of many of the continent's political and military leaders to create the kinds of peace and stability that countries such as Botswana and Malawi have long enjoyed. Underground and undersea riches have brought prosperity to some favored countries; so has good leadership in some resource-limited places. But an equal number of Africa's countries, especially south of the Sahara, await the kinds of improved governance and leadership that could usher in sensible economic growth and an era of sturdy security and safety.

The continent's population explosion, now underway, will make the realization of many of these worthy goals difficult, if not nearly impossible. If Africa can contrive a demographic dividend similar to the one that propelled Southeast Asia's cataclysmic economic resurgence in the 1970s and after, then all will be well. But if a demographic dividend remains out of reach, then Africa's much celebrated modern renaissance—its vaunted drive to claim an equal place among the peoples of other continents, to be fully a part of the global village—will stutter and struggle mightily to overcome the vast weight of its unexpected and surprising new people numbers.

The Bursting Cocoon, with Young People Everywhere

Comparatively sparsely settled until now, with Rwanda the outstanding exception, Africa, especially sub-Saharan Africa, has always thrived or at least subsisted well because of its peoples—their resilience, their energy, their craftiness, their endurance, their industry—all in the face of debilitating and fractious obstacles such as disease, limited schooling, poor soils, shortages of potable water and rainfall for crops, and human mismanagement. Although much of Africa has been poor until a rise in wealth in this century—Africans in the 1960s fell behind their compatriots in Asia and Latin America in terms of growth rates and GDP levels per capita—they began to catch up a little since 2005. But that rise in African prospects, following better leadership and governance, an opening up of macro-economies, and Chinese demand for Africa's raw materials, now risks being swallowed up by a population explosion the likes of which has never occurred on such a scale anywhere. How Africa responds before 2025 to this overriding existential threat to its economic, social, and political future will influence whether the world (and Africa) prospers and remains relatively stable, with positive human outcomes.

According to annually updated estimates from professional demographers of the UN's authoritative Division of Population, half of all of the babies born on the planet between now and 2050 will be delivered in sub-Saharan Africa. Africa is growing much faster than any other continent, and the sub-Saharan African sub-continent is experiencing the most rapid population increases anywhere, ever. By the end of our current century, those accelerated developments mean that sub-Saharan Africa will shoot up from 1 billion to 3.6 billion in people numbers, only a little less than the 4.6 billions who will inhabit Asia (mostly from the projected 1.6 billion Indians and 900 million Chinese, plus almost 300 million Indonesians and another 250 million Pakistanis). Europe will be peopled by only 700 millions, the same figure as that predicted for Latin America and the Caribbean, combined. A mere 100 million of us will reside in Oceania and Australasia.[5]

Whereas Africa in 1975 had half the population of Europe, in 2004 it was larger (despite the migration of many Africans to Britain, France, and Germany). In 2020, Africa will have more than doubled Europe's people numbers; by 2050, it is expected to triple Europe's size.

Africa, first by 2050, and then through the end of the century, will expand exponentially in terms of its numbers of people and simply overwhelm both its own previous relatively paltry population counts and expectations and create problems of scale, crowding, and resources that its leaders (and its peoples) never anticipated and still attempt to ignore.

This bonanza of bodies will be unevenly distributed as well, occurring as it will exclusively in sub-Saharan Africa (as opposed to the Maghreb countries), within sub-Saharan Africa mostly in the poorer and least well educated nations, and proportionally more across the tropics than in the far south. Nations that have never been presumed to be central to sub-Saharan Africa's destiny will move to the front of the line in terms of their demographical results and prospects. A few polities will remain relatively unaffected by burgeoning new population problems. But for sub-Saharan Africa overall, and for its internal politics—its economic growth successes (or failures), its straining infrastructures, especially within its cities, its inability to provide sufficient jobs for new adults, and its Malthusian anxieties—no crisis, no war, no drought or cyclone will have prepared sub-Saharan Africans for today's alarming crisis of numbers.

The sub-continent's biggest country, Nigeria, is poised to grow by 2050 from today's 201 million to about 390 million, and then to continue proliferating until in 2100 it encompasses a full 730 million people. It will then be the third largest entity on the planet, after India and China, and bigger than the 420 million people who are expected to reside within the United States. Nigeria's immense population will also account for a fifth of all of sub-Saharan Africa's people. Together, 420 Nigerians will cram on average into every square kilometer of its territory; now about 173 fit into each square kilometer. In 2019, sub-Saharan Africa's second most populous country is Ethiopia, with 112 million Oromo, Amhara, Somali, Tigrinya, and a host of other individual ethnicities. In 2030, the UN estimates Ethiopia's population to be 119 million, by 2050, 145 million. Then its growth slows, for it is anticipated to reach only 150 million by 2100.

By 2050, Ethiopian numbers will be exceeded by the surprising growth trajectory of woefully poor Tanzania, now 65 million. It will shoot up to 82 million in 2030, to 138 million in 2050, and to 316 million in 2100. That vast number of inhabitants will make Tanzania—hardly predictably in 2000 but very likely now—the fifth largest global nation, after the United States and before Indonesia (300 million), and Pakistan (250 million). Following in demographic line will come, also unexpectedly, the Democratic Republic of Congo (DRC), the most expansive piece of sub-Saharan real estate. It grows according to UN estimates from 86 million today to 105 million in 2050 to 220 million in 2100. It will include more people than Brazil, in 2018 already counting 210 million.

Other sub-Saharan African countries will grow as rapidly, most doubling in size over comparable decades. But none will break so boldly into the ranks of the ten most populous nations on the globe. Malawi, resource-limited and therefore a poor nation-state, will double from 14 to 28 million people during the rest of the century. Zambia will shoot up from 17 million to 140 million. Mozambique will more than double, from 30 million to 77 million over the period. Compact Uganda, in contrast, rises from 44 million to 94 million by 2050 and to a startlingly crowded 171 million in 2100. Next door, Kenya, with only one-third of its land arable, and a country that once boasted the fastest fertility growth rate in all of Africa, will increase from

52 million today to 97 million in 2050 and to 160 million in 2100. Rwanda, already Africa's most densely populated entity (five times more congested than Japan), more than doubles from 12 to 26 million between now and 2050 and continues growing to reach an estimated 42 million inhabitants in 2100. (Each square kilometer of that country, on average, will then host 937 persons, compared to 403 now.) The Sudan, sub-Saharan Africa's geographically second largest country, will increase from 45 to 120 million over the century.

In West and Equatorial Africa there will be similar doublings and triplings of estimated population increases. Niger, with uranium deposits rapidly being depleted and al-Qaeda and ISIS remaining massive threats in the near term, will move stridently from 23 million now to 55 million in 2050 and to 139 million in 2100. Mali, with a great divide between its northern residents of the near desert and its agricultural southerners, will expand from today's 19 million to 42 million at the half century and 81 million in 2100. Ghana grows from 30 to 67 million over the course of the century. Chad, which is mostly desert, reflects its poverty and limited educational opportunities by growing rapidly from 15 million to 44 million over that time period. Senegal's rise is about the same. These striking estimated national population totals for Africa and the world are displayed in Table 1.1.

As these representative examples show, nearly all of Africa is exploding. High fertility numbers doom the fast-increasing nations or sections of nations to the demographic realities that inform the UN's Population Division predictions. In sub-Saharan Africa as a whole, women are now having 4.7

TABLE 1.1 Most Populous Countries in the World, including Africa, 2050 (est.)

Global Countries by Population in 2050 (est.)

Country	Population
India	1.6 billion
China	0.95 billion
Nigeria	0.74 billion
USA	0.45 billion
Tanzania	0.32 billion
Indonesia	0.30 billion
Pakistan	0.25 billion
Democratic Rep. Congo	0.22 billion
Brazil	0.21 billion

babies each, on average. Indeed, fertility rates and differences (and schooling or its absence, plus a paucity of family planning and access to contraceptives) largely explain sub-Saharan Africa's explosive growth in people numbers. Southern African women only give birth to 2.5 children, a little above the replacement rate. Better educated, less fertile nation states such as South Africa, Botswana, and Namibia are increasing marginally, at a less upsetting pace. They will grow slowly, according to the UN estimates, because of already low rates at or below the replacement level of 2.1 per woman.

As we move farther north in middle Africa, however, that critical figure rises to somewhere between 5.5 and 5.8 births per mother in western and central Africa. These high numbers reflect the fact that Africans have their first babies, on average, at 22 years old, whereas the global average is 26. Teenage pregnancies are much more common in Africa than elsewhere in the world. Furthermore, the early onset of childbearing leads to shorter intergenerational gaps – the age difference between mothers and daughters. Shorter gaps help to compound population growth rates – the story of Tanzania and the Congo's astounding increases in this century.

In places like Tanzania and the Congo, because mothers, daughters, and prospective granddaughters already exhibit such high fertility numbers, and promise to continue to do so far into the century, official estimates propel those nation-states (and others) to the forefront of African population growth. Nigeria swells as swiftly and inexorably as it does, too, because women in its Muslim north are still giving birth to 7.2 children over their lifetimes, while in its Christian south the fertility rate is only about 2.2 per mother. Everywhere, also, wild population increases reflect the fact that girls are less educated in, say, Nigeria's northern reaches than in its southern states. (In the north, 90 percent of women do not use contraceptives.)

When girls go to school they become pregnant later and want, or end up having, fewer offspring of their own. When potable water is readily available, too, girls do not spend their days on chores, like fetching water from distant wells, or helping their mothers in the fields. So they can go to school and stay in school long enough to obtain at least a lower secondary education, if not the full equivalent of high school. When they do so, fertility rates drop and national populations (as in Botswana or Namibia) stay stable.

For its estimates, with their frightening projections, the UN Population Division assumes that fertility rates in Nigeria and other rising sections of Africa will decline only very gradually over the rest of the century, dipping below 4+ babies on average only after 2035 and remaining at about 2.5 per woman until slipping down to the replacement rate of 2.1 children per woman only after 2045.

Contraceptive use is spreading in sub-Saharan Africa at only a glacial pace. However, demographers are aware, in making their worrying predictions, that infant, child, and maternal mortality rates will continue to fall progressively during upcoming decades, that the HIV/AIDs epidemic is receding, and that many of the other diseases that produce mortality are gradually becoming less of a threat to African survival. But these welcome improvements will not greatly alter the pace of African population rises. Very little now, in other words, can halt or drastically retard the anticipated crescendo of demographical increases in sub-Saharan Africa. Mothers are producing daughters who will produce more daughters, and so on, and those daughters will only very slowly reduce the number of their own lifetime babies.

The UN Population Division's demographic estimates for Africa are regarded as the gold standard. Nevertheless, informed skeptics suggest that the Division may critically be underestimating how quickly fertility will begin to fall in Africa because so many villagers will become urban dwellers (where lots of children are not as much of an asset as they are in rural Africa, and where they are expensive to educate and feed). Women in Africa's cities already have fewer children than their village counterparts. Furthermore, children in cities and towns go to school more easily and more regularly than they do in rural areas. Even partially educated teenagers and young women have fewer children than their peers who are unschooled. More schooling of more young people, especially girls, is likely to lead to lower rates of overall fertility. In Ethiopia, women with secondary schooling produced 2.0 children while their less-educated cousins gave birth to 6.2 young ones. In Kenya, the rural rate of fertility is 4.5; the urban one is 3.1. A non-UN model predicts as many as 1.5 billion fewer Africans than the UN model by the end of the century. Even so, there will be an insufficiency of jobs, just a less drastic absence of employment possibilities. Either way, sub-Saharan Africa, where the big bulge is occurring, has critical problems with which its leaders must cope and consequences its peoples must endure and somehow overcome.

The Youth Bulge

When there are so many births the median age of a society or a continent slopes downward. In contrast to the rest of the world, sub-Saharan Africa is and will continue to be impressively youthful, with a median age in the near term of 18 or 19, at mid-century a still-feisty 25, and, long term over the course of much of the rest of the century a still young 28 years. As Asia, Europe, and the Americas age, so Africa will remain young. And being youthful could theoretically presage a massive demographic dividend, with the sub-continent's youth bulge producing startling rates of economic advance and simultaneously supporting an aging minority.

In 2010, there were 300 million sub-Saharan Africans under 34—a third of the population. In 2030, there will be an estimated 500 million Africans under 34, of a total population of about 1.3 billion. By 2034, Africa will have a larger potential working-age population than China or India. That bulge will continue to grow through 2050, when Africa's unprecedented expansion will begin to steady and slow. By then, sub-Saharan Africa's governments, territories, and cities, even those living in domains where increases will be less than explosive, will have had to react for good or ill to the consequent massive reorientation of the sub-continent's demographic composition, to an implacable search for jobs and existential quests for meaning, and to Malthusian anxieties about possible food shortages and famines.

Although too few African political leaders in 2020 are aroused about coming population surges, the future extreme youthfulness of their constituents, or the possible impact of exploded numbers on party politics, social services, and the fulfillment of personal goals, the trends are inescapable. When and how political leaders respond, possible failures to react in a timely manner, and refusals to appreciate the need to fold these new youth numbers deftly into the body of the nation, are all considerations that affect whether or not the youth bulge will pay or forfeit demographic dividends.

Everyone, even well beyond Africa, will be unsettled by the population surge and especially by its youthful expression. Politically, within their various states, they will obviously represent a constituency that cannot be neglected. But socially, their importance may even be more telling. If the nations in which they reside prove capable and willing to educate them, and to provide sufficient health care, and if state and private businesses create new formal employment opportunities sufficient to satisfy the many new job seekers, then the sharp impact of Africa's youth bulge will be blunted, albeit not eliminated. Much will depend on strengthening its skill set, on harnessing the entrepreneurial talents of these new youth, and on attempting to satisfy their aspirations material and spiritual.

If not, if the half of many national populations that are young feels let down and less than fully engaged—if disillusionment and rejection take root—then one after another sub-Saharan country will find itself deeply stressed, and possibly under siege, because of an inability to satisfy the expectations and needs of its newly matured majorities. Tanzania, as an extreme but critical example, will soon have to cope with a population fully half of which will be in school or looking for jobs. Unless there are major upgrades in the coming decade, the national economy will barely function. It will be unable to offer employment to successive cohorts of 20-year olds. Unless it succeeds in educating girls and, hence, begins to reduce their fertility and their impoverishment, the lack of employment opportunities, together with more and more mouths to feed, could lead (given the unpredictable effects of global warming) to nutritional shortages as well as societal despair, intensified civil conflict, and serious social unrest. High levels of crime—some of it fueled by narcotics trafficking—could become the norm. Political leaders are not as yet anticipating or planning how to avert such possible disruptions. Will they act responsibly over the next few years to channel the ambitions and energies of their legions of young people into constructive, productive pursuits?

The Swelling of Cities

The young people who will constitute half or more of sub-Saharan Africa's countries will congregate in its towns and cities, all of which will swell to accommodate the births that are occurring and will occur in both urban surroundings and larger rural villages (which will soon morph into towns). As a result of continued high birth rates and an undiminished movement of rural dwellers into larger agglomerations, by 2030, if not years before, half of all sub-Saharan Africans will be urban. Rural Africa will gradually but inexorably become underpopulated. Zambia is already there, with about 65 percent of its citizens living in cities and large towns. Other sub-Saharan African countries are following its lead. The citizens of even sparsely settled nation-states such as Chad or Gabon are crowding into those country's largest metropolitan areas.

Whereas in 2010, sub-Saharan Africa held a few substantially sized urban areas, especially Lagos, Kinshasa, Luanda, Johannesburg, and such like, in 2025 sub-Saharan Africa will host one hundred or more 1-million-person-sized cities; Nigeria will lead the way with at least seventy-five new cities of that size. Originally much less populous urban centers, such as Ouagadougou in Burkina Faso, are expanding so quickly (from 893,000 in 2010 to 3 million in 2030) that local services cannot possibly keep pace. Modest crossroads villages in fragile places such as Malawi are likewise becoming urban hubs; Balaka, for example, a once-quiet rural district center, is attracting displaced farmers and descendants of farmers in unprecedented numbers. It will expand to 500,000 or so from its current 20,000 size. Kumasi, the Ashanti capital on the other side of the sub-continent, will increase in the same period from 1,462,000 to an anticipated 4 million. Overall, the towns and cities of sub-Saharan Africa are doubling and tripling in size from now until 2050, albeit growing more slowly thereafter.

In 2019, massive Cairo, population 20 million, the capital of Egypt, was surpassed in size in Africa by Lagos, already bursting with 23 million people. Kinshasa, now 13 million, will also grow larger than Cairo by 2050, probably to 25 million; Luanda, already inhabited by 6.5 million persons; Mogadishu, 6.0 million; Abidjan, 4.7 million; Greater Johannesburg, 4.4 million; Dar es Salaam, 4.36 million; Accra, 4.1 million; and Nairobi at 3.5 million—all will double (some will triple) in population size by 2050. The youth bulge and the wave of migrants from rural areas will coincide to push sub-Saharan African cities to a bursting point. Estimated sizes of cities in Africa are shown in Table 1.2.

Already, in 2019, the cities of the continent (even South African cities) cannot fully serve the anxious and sometimes angry masses within their formal and informal borders. Jobs are scarce and will remain so. That sad fact means that urban residents must constantly scramble to make ends meet.

TABLE 1.2 Africa's Largest Cities, 2019

Rank	City	Estimated Metro Population
1	Lagos, Nigeria	23.0 million
2	Cairo, Egypt	20.4 million
3	Kinshasa, Democratic Republic of the Congo	13.3 million
4	Luanda, Angola	6.5 million
5	Nairobi, Kenya	6.5 million
6	Mogadishu, Somalia	6.0 million
7	Abidjan, Côte d'Ivoire	4.7 million
8	Alexandria, Egypt	4.7 million
9	Addis Ababa, Ethiopia	4.6 million
10	Johannesburg, South Africa	4.4 million
11	Dar es Salaam, Tanzania	4.4 million
12	Casablanca, Morocco	4.3 million
13	Accra, Ghana	4.1 million
14	Durban, South Africa	3.4 million
15	Kano, Nigeria	2.8 million

Criminal activity has become more common. So have panhandling and unlicensed trading; no matter how assiduously authorities attempt to curb vendors by vigorous police action, roadside sellers (and buyers) always return to participate in the commercial needs of their cities.

Urban centers in the West and the North exist in part to provide essential services such as sewage and potable water for their dwellers. They also exist to provide safety and security for residents. But in the newly enlarged African conurbations hardly any such services exist. Sanitary provisions are often inadequate. Clean water is as often supplied by private wells, by tanker truck delivery of water, or by expensive bottled water rather than by a municipal system. Fully 60 percent of Kenyans living in Nairobi, their capital city of 6.5 million people, have no regular daily access to reliable water supplies. Harare, Zimbabwe's 2-million-sized capital, in 2018 suffered cholera and typhoid epidemics because the city had no funds with which to chlorinate its drinking water or to repair rusted pipes. The situation worsened into catastrophe in late 2019, when officials in Harare, lacking $2.7 million a month to import chemicals to treat water coming from reservoirs, entirely shut the city's only water treatment plant. Meanwhile, in the main reservoir "shallow water was green and emitted a choking foul smell."[6]

Sub-Saharan Africa's cities also lack reliable forms of transport across and within their borders. There are few subways or tramways aside from a brand-new underground system in Addis Ababa. Although South Africa brings commuters into the center of Johannesburg by rail, most movement into or across sub-Saharan Africa's urban landscapes is by minivan or taxi. Africans often live distant from their work, and travel across spread-out urbanities is often difficult, lengthy, and expensive. It can take a good hour, for example, to commute from one side of Lusaka, Zambia's capital, to the other.

City life is not for the faint-hearted. Yet, calculating their opportunity costs, Africans are content to abandon villages for congested urban settings. They do so even though they are aware of the dangers and weaknesses of municipal living. They crowd into dismal slums, like Kibera in Nairobi, Chilenje in Lusaka, or Kyalitsha near Cape Town, to better themselves and to enter what they believe to be the mainstream of national life. Whatever their reasons, and their misplaced confidence, migrants are still flowing in unending streams into towns and cities; their movements off the land threaten to denude villages and curtail village life, sucking the commercial air (at least) out of the countryside.

Even when the incomers know, rationally, that the slums for which they are heading are fetid and troubled, they keep going. They know that urban infrastructures are weak, no longer catering responsibly even for wealthy city-folk; they know that jobs will be hard to procure. But to those attracted by the bright lights of the city, essential services are at least theoretically available. There is the chance of drinkable water and electric light. Television is easier to watch than in rural villages.

Although those who move to the city do so with little guarantee of employment, or even of food supplies, their personal or family cost-benefit analysis suggests—not necessarily correctly—that they and the dependents whom they support will be or could be better off in the squalid cities than back home on the farm, where net positive revenues are hard to achieve, and where there are no (urban) amenities. A cocoa farmer or a coffee grower who stays on his shamba or plot of land can do well enough despite fluctuating world prices. But the subsistence grower of maize or sorghum, or even of yams or teff, finds it much more onerous to make a decent living from subsistence crops when rainfall is becoming less predictable and fertilizer more expensive.

Sub-Saharan African countries and peoples are experiencing a massive gravitational shift into cities and towns. Within them, especially within the tarpaper, tin, and scrap lumber shacks that occupy many square miles of land around, and even within, major urban wastelands, there is vitality, self-sufficiency, many daily challenges to survival, and a consciousness that village Africa is worth abandoning for the promise of a central city or a market town.

Authorities struggle to provide housing, schooling, and health care for the millions now affected by those urban choices. They also struggle to satisfy indigenous claims for services—for better governance, steady employment, freedom from crime, and the possibility of an improved future. The inhabitants of the ghettos in turn demand greater accountability and transparency from their local and national leaders. Ultimately, these urban residents insist upon meaningful political participation for peoples like themselves. With that participation they can demand, many believe, a redistribution of national resources in their favor and a greater attention to the economic and fiscal needs of their community and communities like their own.

Yet politicians, especially the ones in power, cannot necessarily satisfy the genuine and perceived needs of the urban millions. There are too many unanswered needs, too many amenities that are lacking. Given how many people are piling into urban Africa, and how many already live there and will be born there over the next thirty years and beyond, Africa and Africans cannot rest easy. Cities are the battleground of today's Africa. Do the leaders of today know what that means, in its fullest sense?

Feeding the Huddled Urbanites

The expanding millions of new Africans will want to eat. Long ago, however, many of the countries of sub-Saharan Africa lost the ability to feed themselves. Nigeria and Ghana once grew enough yams and rice to meet their peoples' needs. But then petroleum discoveries, in the case of Nigeria, transformed farmers into laborers and turned governmental support away from agriculture. A succession of military dictators paid close attention to rent-seeking rather than supporting farmers. By the 1980s, Nigeria imported the major portion of its comestibles, and so did other nation-states with new wealth. Other sub-Saharan nations, in the same era, unwittingly drove their own farmers off the land by subsidizing urban consumers and paying less than world prices for maize and other staple grains grown within their borders. Zimbabwe, an extreme case, even destroyed what had been southern Africa's breadbasket by forcing white farmers and their African workers to flee, thus becoming a polity dependent on World Food Program and U.S. PL480 handouts of maize, year in and year out. More than 4 million Zimbabweans were being fed in this manner in 2019. The United Nation's rapporteur on the right to food said late in the year that Zimbabwe was "on the brink of man-made starvation" with at least 7 million people (almost half of the country's population) requiring assistance.[7]

Foreign aid has also supplied foodstuffs routinely in the arid regions of the Sahel. Mauritania, Mali, Niger, Chad, the Sudan, and Somalia are all in part desiccated, and are prone to severe drought, sometimes famine, especially when the expected rains fail to arrive. In 2012–2013, as many as 20 million residents of those Sahelian nations were severely short of edible food, while millions more were malnourished. In recent years, climate change or global warming has produced severe drought conditions even in usually abundant grain-producing areas such as South Africa. The combination of rapid urbanization and incessant climate change, plus political interference—the taking of land from productive farmers—will hardly foster food surpluses.

Sub-Saharan Africa as a whole can no longer feed itself even if here and there a few countries, such as Malawi, have good yielding years thanks to appropriately abundant rains at the right time. Massive Nigeria, for example, spends $22 billion a year to import rice, wheat, fish, and sugar to supply its millions of people since local farmers are hampered by shortages of credit, lack of land tenure, limited mechanization, and a paucity of extension advice and training. Moreover, these several problems—common to farmers throughout the continent—are compounded by the impact of climate change and climate irregularities. Thus this inability to provide for themselves—especially for the urban masses who may lack plots on which to grow a few maize or cassava plants—will become even more acute as population numbers rise and keep rising. Civil conflicts will also inhibit agricultural and pastoral pursuits. Fortunately, Brazil and the United States probably can produce sufficient grain to feed the Africans who cannot grow their own supplies or purchase it locally. But most bouts of hunger result from shortages of cash; food is usually available if consumers can pay. (In 2019, there were unanticipated severe hunger crises in Zimbabwe because of too little rain in the west and too much rain in the east. Kenya also experienced severe food shortages in some sections of the country, while other areas had surpluses; complicated regulations hindering the shifting of produce across provincial boundaries, inaccurate data, and transport bottlenecks prevented maize from flowing from the zones with abundance inside Kenya to those without.) How sub-Saharan Africans are going to afford vast quantities of imported staples, customarily hitherto grown on house plots or purchased locally in urban markets from kinsmen, is a puzzle.

As the populations of other developing nations expanded rapidly in the last century, especially in Southeast Asia, their incomes rose and thus they had the wherewithal to afford abundant food grown by local farmers. Or the Southeast Asians, wealthy from industry or profitable cash crops, purchased rice and other foodstuffs from landholders in neighboring countries. But the farmers of sub-Saharan Africa are a beleaguered lot, deprived by governmental policies or by mismanagement of affordable supplies of fertilizer and seeds, cut off from urban markets by poor or nonexistent roads, and subject to regulations and price restraints that make it difficult to earn a decent living off the land. Furthermore, when Africans are finding it difficult to feed even themselves off their usually small plots, they will have little surplus, and at present too little incentive, to try to supply the closest urban settlements.

As the peoples of the developed world urbanized in earlier centuries, and farmers fled their rural holdings to crowd industrializing cities, so the persons remaining on the land became more productive. Just over 1 percent of all Americans now till the soil, nevertheless feeding more than 300 million of their fellows and much of the outside world. Africans may demonstrate the same successes as do Americans on their twenty-first-century farms. But African soils are nitrogen-poor, and friable. Without proper tenure, Africans have little security for any investments that they may choose to make in their farming ventures. Very few African farmers have access to irrigation and thus must depend on increasingly erratic rains. And indigenous political leaders and their policies are not providing positive incentives sufficient to persuade Africans to continue to live away from towns and to try to prosper by growing cash crops for their fellow countrymen. Malthus was wrong about eighteenth and nineteenth-century Europe, but his pessimistic predictions may prove relevant for and in contemporary Africa.

Leadership and a Demographic Dividend

Africa's cascading people numbers will not go away. There is no demonstrably easy escape from the demographic avalanche that has already begun to slide over much of sub-Saharan Africa and that is predicted to obstruct economic growth uplift well into the middle of this century. Only then will a fertility decline begin, and only then can Africa plausibly expect to benefit from a demographic dividend similar to the dividend that helped in the last century to transform Southeast Asian nations into developmental tigers.

Although the presence in nearly all of sub-Saharan Africa of a substantial youth bulge—of teenage and 20-years-old-and-older median ages well into mid-century—may somehow give key countries advantages in their battle to grow export-profitable, industrial, agriculture, and mining ventures, real demographic dividends depend less on large numbers of young people in relation to very young and elderly residents than they do on major falls in fertility.

A demographic dividend occurs when a nation-state's birth rate declines and leads to favorable alterations in the age structure of its population. Death rates may also fall, which could complicate the calculation, but the essential point is that the possibility of accelerated economic growth comes most often when the dependent proportion of a population (the very young and the very old) is supported by the laboring cohort that constitutes the working-age group (ages 15–64). First there is a demographic transition, then a chance for a dividend.

With increasingly fewer people to support, countries have windows of opportunity to grow if—and it can be a major contingent "if" in sub-Saharan Africa—their leaders craft progressive economic and social policies that are timely and strategic, and if those policies attract internal and foreign investment. The last is what happened in Malaysia, South Korea, Thailand, and Singapore in the 1970s and 1980s. To some extent it occurred in China as well, after Deng Xiaoping's revolution of the 1980s, plus the one-child edict.

Thailand's transition began with voluntary family planning that increased contraceptive use from 15 percent in 1970 to 70 percent in 1987. That rise in contraception led to a decrease in births per woman from 5.5 to 2.2, dramatically shifting the age structure of Thailand and enabling a demographic dividend.

Rwanda, of the many countries of sub-Saharan Africa that could benefit economically and socially from such a transition and resultant dividend, in 2019 was heading in that direction, encouraged by fairly insistent governmental encouragement and backing. Modern contraceptive use has increased by a factor of four since 2008; Rwandan women now have only 4.6 children per mother, down from 7 and 8. If continued contraceptive use and continued support from the country's political leadership persists, Rwanda is likely to reduce births per woman to 2.2 by 2050, and thus to provide the basis for a demographic dividend in sub-Saharan Africa's most congested country.

Other sub-Saharan African national leaderships either oppose family planning—as President John Magufuli of Tanzania has decreed—have refused or been unable to make contraceptives widely available, or are doing nothing to assist mothers to reduce birth numbers. U.S. opposition to family planning in Africa hardly helps, as well, and thus this lack of financial assistance and antagonism to solving the population problems of the continent propels much of the poorer and least well educated portions of sub-Saharan Africa to continue to rise in people numbers, but not in prosperity or equality. For all of these indigenous and exogenous reasons, large parts of sub-Saharan Africa may miss the demographic dividend that they so desperately need.

Political leaders everywhere in the sub-continent can guide their peoples toward a demographic dividend. Unfortunately, as the next chapter will explain, too many of the political leaders of sub-Saharan Africa are transactional rather than transformational. Too many have short-term horizons; too many are devoted to personal and party advancement rather than the public interest. If sub-Saharan African nations are going first to cope effectively with rising numbers and youth bulges and second, to create something approximating a demographic dividend and bursts of economic and social uplift, then today's heads of state and heads of government need to begin to understand what happened in Asia and how similar solutions may be introduced into and adopted by Africa, or at least by its most progressive countries.

II | The Varieties of
African Leadership

THE POLITICAL LEADERS of Africa come in all sizes, shapes, and persuasions. There are liberal democratic heads of state and heads of government, presidents, and prime ministers; elected democratic leaders who become wily autocrats; strong authoritarians who brook no opposition and respect few freedoms; military men ruling because their followers are well-armed; kleptocrats who govern so that they can steal from the state and its citizens; a few who profess strong support for the public interest; and many who serve clan, family, and narrow conceptions of national "interest." There are few women. Ideology plays little part in the very different styles and mechanisms of governance that these political leaders display. But nearly all of them are transactional; hardly anyone today is transformational in the manner of several of Africa's founding fathers, although Paul Kagame of Rwanda and Abiy Ahmed of Ethiopia are exceptions. Cyril Ramaphosa may be able to join them if he and his party grow from strength to strength in South Africa in 2020.

The talents of those men, and of any women who in future join the ceremonial president of Ethiopia and the influential senior ranks of former presidents and prime ministers, are all much more critical as wielders of power in and for Africa than they are or would be on other continents. Because the political institutions of many of the countries of sub-Saharan Africa are not yet fully formed and many of their states are still not fully nations, political leaders in Africa have much more influence and power, comparatively, than they have in more-developed political jurisdictions where political institutions are endurably established. Political leaders in most of sub-Saharan Africa still have a primary role in shaping their emerging national political cultures, or value systems.

Politically, institutionally, and in other important ways, the conflict-ridden, rampantly corrupted, poorly governed (see the next chapter), and fragile states of sub-Saharan Africa are still embryonic as political entities. They are still finding their way, and their rulers thus have much more authority and opportunity to shape daily and future events than rulers have in Asia, the Americas, and Europe. That is why I refer to many African countries as "pre-institutional" or "proto-institutional."

The Core Competencies

It follows that imaginative and responsible political leadership has the capacity anywhere, but especially in sub-Saharan Africa, to emphasize a ruling design that operates in the public, not private interest, that guides peoples, societies, and states toward destinies that are more advanced, even more enlightened, than they know or have previously experienced.

Leadership is the employment largely of informal means to guide constituents and would-be constituents to embrace the designs and objectives of a political leader and, working in tandem with him or her (and influencing those decisions), to achieve mutually acceptable results. Better leaders avoid coercing citizens to do what they are reluctant to do. Better leaders show constituents the way forward and persuade them to follow. They cajole them. Best of all, they help followers to maximize their own self-interests in pursuit of those mutually agreed-upon goals. Effective leaders mobilize collective endeavors.

Gifted political leaders offer a vision of betterment, mobilize their followers behind that vision, and themselves act with integrity and transparency in order to support and forward that vision. They are inclusive. They enhance the legitimacy that comes with their election to higher office, demonstrate both courage (making tough or revolutionary decisions—such as ending the war with Eritrea) and prudence (disciplined reason in the face of temptations and the attractions of easy populism), show self-mastery as opposed to vanity, and, in Africa, refuse any tendencies to exhibit ostentation (as in lengthy motorcades, elaborate protocols, and lavish pomp and circumstance).

Effective and responsible leaders are also intellectually honest—"with enough wisdom to know [what] we did not know, and enough candor to admit it."[1] Strong, effective, capable leaders want to know and be told what is verifiably real, not to wallow in the fantasies of their acolytes. They strive to understand why proposed economic policies and panaceas will likely work; and they are the first, as President Nelson Mandela was, to reject proposals that perpetuate shibboleths instead advancing progress.

Legitimated, responsive political leaders with high degrees of emotional intelligence (beware the leader "who lacks emotional intelligence. In its absence all else may turn to ash"[2]) and an understanding of their own and their peoples' intrinsic limitations, as well as the solidity or weakness of their particular existential national situations, are capable, even in unusually taxing times, of seeking out the potential choices that will bring the most benefit to their citizens, with the least cost. On that basis, and if they are leaders with vision and skill, they can continue to build trust between ruler and ruled by dedicating themselves to their already enunciated and articulated vision; by continuing to build trust with their constituents by acting consultatively, democratically, and ethically; by behaving in a disinterested and self-sacrificing manner (rare in Africa); by remaining "authentic"; and, again, by concerning themselves in a demonstrative manner with the needs of all of their peoples, not some narrow subset. Building trust is critical, and can rapidly be lost.

Most of all, what consummate, wise, leaders do—what differentiates the Mandelas and George Washingtons from many of their latter-day heirs— is to give their followers and citizens a transcendent feeling of belonging directly and intimately to an enlarged enterprise. That is what Presidents Franklin D. Roosevelt and Kennedy accomplished, what Prime Minister Lee Kuan Yew did in Singapore, what President Sir Seretse Khama did in Botswana, and what Premier Kemal Atatürk did in Turkey. As Kennedy enunciated: "Ask not what your country can do for you—ask what you can do for your country." He continued, "My fellow citizens of the world: ask not what America will do for you, but what together we can do for the freedom of man."[3]

Mandela at and after declaring the reclaimed republic in 1994, Khama and Lee in the 1960s and 1970s, and Kagame now, enrolled their protean citizens in something lofty and potentially ennobling. They gave their followers a real stake in their country, their region, and their continent. They each enabled their followers to feel that they were or had become an integral part of a larger and all-encompassing global village.

The best leaders transmit values that knit their societies together. They forge a common enterprise and unite followers for higher ends. The national enterprise prospers best when leaders construct a mutuality of responsibility, and citizens come to believe in the motives and integrity of their leaders. If rulers can transmit that sense of larger purpose and accordingly give new meaning to the lives of their peoples, then in sub-Saharan Africa as elsewhere their states will prosper and become full nations rather than congeries of different, contesting, ethnic, and interest groups.

Transformers and Transactors

Political leaders in Africa and beyond who exhibit and act on these core competencies, especially the first (developing and expressing a vision for their followers and their nation), are transformational. But most political leaders everywhere, especially in Africa, are transactional. For sub-Saharan African countries fully to join their destinies with the progressive polities of the global village, they need more dedicated transformational heads of state and heads of government. They need leaders who at least lean a little in a transformational direction; transactionalism, by contrast, responds to short-run problems and crises and easily becomes the vehicle for the subordination of the public interest to parochial, clan, lineage, or family/personal interest.

Transactionalism is incrementalism. It is business as usual. Transactional leaders seek to perpetuate themselves and their political parties in office, not necessarily or often to innovate or to be disruptive of existing arrangements that favor ruling elites and parties accustomed to wielding power. Transactional leaders exchange mutual self-regard and mutual interest with their followers; they lead less than they cut deals with voters, with legislators, with corporations, with neighbors and competitors. Transactional leaders govern, sometimes well, but with their own needs rather than the nation's future needs prominent.

In Africa, it is rare to be successfully transformational. President Kwame Nkrumah of the young Ghana articulated a comprehensive vision for sub-Saharan Africa, but could mobilize hardly anyone behind it, over-reached, compromised his own personal and his regime's integrity, and rapidly forfeited legitimacy and leadership. President Jomo Kenyatta of Kenya squandered his vast rational and electoral legitimacy and expressed leadership favoritisms sufficient to deny his transformational capabilities. President Julius Nyerere of Tanzania had a largely unarticulated vision for his country, but never fully developed it and failed to translate it into the kinds of radical policies that would have transformed his inchoate and poor country.

Being transformational in Africa means translating visions into programs of meaningful action. It means awakening peoples to new possibilities; it means replacing inertia with energy. Highly skilled transformational leadership persuades citizens to embrace national rather than parochial self-interested goals; it enunciates high-value core outcomes to which all citizens can devote at least a part of their daily activities. Transformational leaders uplift the spirits and loyalties of their followers and citizens; they offer hope and a sturdy belief in betterment. Such leaders are open to new ideas, promote collaboration, listen thoroughly and consult widely, take measurable risks, and stimulate and encourage high expectations.

The nation-states of sub-Saharan Africa are not going to welcome a brace of transformational leaders anytime soon. Most jurisdictions will instead be governed by transactionalists until new types of leaders arise out of the emergent middle class or until ruling political parties appreciate that mere transactionalists will accomplish little, except for themselves, and that Africa will stagnate until newly trained, more broad-minded, younger leaders emerge with managerial knowledge and visionary ideas.

Leaders Matter

In modern sub-Saharan Africa, leaders more than parties, inherited structures, contingencies, adverse colonial influences, or global power politics (the Cold War, etc.) have determined the decisions of and the directions taken by individual states—often without appropriate inputs from followers and constituencies. Acemoglu and Robinson argue that European colonialism "created an opening for unscrupulous leaders to take over and intensify the extraction" of their pernicious and exploitative predecessors.[4] Having inherited the administrative authoritarianism of colonial authorities, "a legion of ambitious and canny leaders . . . subverted the representative legacy" that had been prescribed and theoretically delivered to them. They proceeded to decree single-party states, agree to military rule, and regard democracy as outdated and antagonistic to economic development.[5]

Only a few of the founding fathers of newly independent Africa rejected this tendency to favor autocracy and espoused participatory methods, preferred to listen and consult, and sought to govern carefully and well. They were the ones, especially in Botswana, who very early trod a different post-independence path—a path that led to prosperity and stability rather than to poverty, civil conflict, and bouts of wild corruption.

Festus Mogae, the third president of Botswana, laments that many of the continent's early leadership cadre had done well for a decade or more, and then "something happen[ed]."[6] Even in the twenty-first century, a plethora of heads of state who had come into office to popular acclaim after ousting earlier autocrats or high-handed soldiers shifted from early consensual and largely democratic modes of behavior to become authoritarians, and to overturn constitutional provisions prohibiting third or fourth terms in office. Joseph Kabila (DRC), Paul Kagame (Rwanda), Yoweri Museveni (Uganda), Denis Sassou Nguesso (Congo-Brazzaville), and Pierre Nkurunziza (Burundi) all did so "for the good of the country," and despite widespread internal and overseas opposition.

In each but the second case, the local opposition became militant, with protests, unrest, and repression following. Riots broke out in Guinea in late 2019 when President Alpha Condé indicated that he, too, would seek to breach term limits and run again for his country's headship.

President Robert Mugabe (Zimbabwe) remained in office by foul means and fair from 1980 to 2017 before being ousted by his cabinet officials and soldiers. Questionable elections had long confirmed Mugabe's hold on power, just as they have kept authoritarian Paul Biya in Cameroon's presidency from 1982 to the present and anointed the familial takeovers of Ali Bongo Ondimba in Gabon and Faure Gnassingbé in Togo from their respective founding fathers. Equatorial Guinea's Teodoro Obiang Nguema family has controlled that small, oil-rich kleptocracy since 1979.

In all of these, and in several other key cases such as the twenty-seven-year rule of the self-professed humanist Kenneth Kaunda in Zambia, arbitrary, single-party domination resulted in political imprisonments, limitations to free speech and assembly, human rights violations, underdevelopment, and widespread impoverishment. That last outcome occurred for most citizens even where abundant wealth from oil or copper fed the avaricious ambitions of ruling elites, as in Equatorial Guinea and Angola, in Zambia, and in military-led Nigeria. Mugabe and his cronies plundered Zimbabwe's tobacco and then its diamond wealth. The Democratic Republic of Congo, with abundant mineral riches, remained poor per capita while its rulers from Mobutu Sese Seko through Laurent Kabila and on to Joseph Kabila extracted—in the case of Mobutu—many billions of dollars in illicit proceeds.

New analyses of these and analogous governing apparatuses in Southeast Asia, Central Asia, and Central America suggest that many of these governments were and are effectively criminalized, or fully criminal enterprises. The men in charge govern not to deliver better official services (like educational opportunity or health care) to their citizens, but to steal from the state and thus to reward themselves, their families, and their close associates. They deny the public interest and ignore the life outcomes of their followers. To that end, they rigged and still rig elections to remain in power, enable a chosen few to join them in selling profitable opportunities to favored contractors and concession seekers, and generally preside over the monopolization (as elected or appointed officials) of any and all exploitable resources. They feed themselves at the expense of their hungry publics.

From these unsavory experiences it is easy to conclude that who leads matters. Inherited predilections and particular structures did not mandate such results. In every case, legacy institutions that were transmitted from the colonial period were simply tossed aside. In Sierra Leone, President Siaka Stevens sought to gather in the wealth that derived from alluvial diamond discoveries; to get at those riches he had to dissolve inherited institutional safeguards and turn himself into a despot. Existing and not yet fully formed political institutions were insufficient to constrain him, or even to caution well-motivated presidents such as Kaunda or Nyerere; the colonial inherited institutions had been insufficiently implanted and were thus relatively easy to discard.

Instilling Political Cultures

Leaders then and now in sub-Saharan Africa have abundant power because the national political cultures are still embryonic, and are thus subject to the vagaries of leadership. The key syllogism remains: leaders create institutions and build nations by establishing acceptable political cultures. By shaping a national political culture, and only by doing so consciously, can institutions emerge out of a newly introduced value system—a political culture. The best leaders breathe life into inherited or dormant political institutions. Or they establish political institutions from scratch. Leaders, either at independence from colonial rule, at independence after apartheid, after a disruptive civil war, at the conclusion of a dictatorship, or after similar sharp breaks with past dispositions, have the capacity in pre-institutionalized jurisdictions (like most of the sub-Saharan African countries at some point in time) to shape their country's political future. They can lead in ways that the founding fathers of the United States did in the eighteenth and nineteenth centuries, as Europe experienced after World War II, and as Singapore and Malaysia advanced to tiger status in the 1960s and 1970s.

As we will see a little later in this chapter, Khama and Mandela provided that variety of positive leadership in the twentieth century, and formed and then nurtured their emerging national political cultures. Mauritius, under the early leadership of Sir Seewoosagur Ramgoolam (1969–1982) and Cape Verde under Pedro Pires (1975–1991 and 2001–2011), also shaped the democratic political cultures of their island states. President Ellen Johnson Sirleaf, Africa's only woman head of state and leader of government (2006–2018), did much the same in battered and very wasted Liberia. Benin became democratic in 1991 after many military coups and two decades of Marxist dictatorship, and, under a succession of elected consensual leaders, remained a West African beacon of good governance until a manipulated election in 2019. President John Kufuor (2001–2009) accomplished a similar reconfiguration of political culture in Ghana after the authoritarian rule of Flight Lieutenant Jerry John Rawlings (1993–2001). Roch Marc Christian Kaboré did much the same in Burkina Faso after popular protests forced its long time autocratic President Blaise Compaoré to flee in 2014 after being the nation's boss since 1987. Senegal embraced similar advances when Macky Sall ousted the compromised presidency of Abdoulaye Wade and introduced inclusive governance in 2012, and was reelected in 2019. But it is only very recently (from 2018) that Nobel laureate Abiy in Ethiopia has attempted to disrupt the arbitrary rule legacies of Meles Zenawi and Hailemariam Desalegn, his predecessors, and to seek to reconfigure the political culture and, in time, the institutional setting of his country.

This is a task for the future for many countries in Africa: Certainly Eritrea's time will come, after Isaias Afwerki's dictatorship is ended. The next-door authoritarian and International Criminal Court–defying leadership of the Sudan's President Omar al-Bashir gave way to more participatory governance in 2019, after five months of concerted protests and the agreement of the army and air force. (In late 2019, a special Sudanese court sentenced Bashir to two year's of confinement in a "social reform" facility.) Street protests also ended the lingering incumbency of President Abdelaziz Bouteflika in 2019. The long-established arbitrary rules in Burundi, Cameroon, Chad, the Comoros, Gabon, Niger, the Republic of Congo (Brazzaville), and even the monarchical pretensions of Eswatini (Swaziland) may conceivably suffer similar fates. Leadership clearly makes a difference for ill, as well as for good (as we will shortly demonstrate). Indeed, astute researchers have concluded sadly that "poor countries are poor because those who have power make choices that create poverty."[7]

An Absence of Women

In 2019, aside from the new ceremonial head of state in Ethiopia, there were no governmental female chief executives in Africa and only twenty female heads of state or government worldwide, a mere 5.6 percent of the possible total. According to Johnson Sirleaf, who stepped down in early 2018 from her Liberian presidency, "Women in Africa face three obstacles. First, they are political outsiders. They represent change, and that can be construed as a threat to incumbent leaders, and to the status quo. Second, party structures are hierarchical and based on patronage; often they are not open to new ideas. Finally, there are barriers arising from a lack of information; access promotes a woman's awareness of her rights—to an education, to equal treatment, and to freedom from violence. Those barriers are reinforced by inadequate campaign-finance laws, which disproportionally hinder women from taking on leadership roles in political discourse."[8]

Informed women are more likely to be engaged in the political process and to hold their governments accountable. Studies show that when women comprise a sizable minority in parliaments and ministries, much more attention than before is paid to social matters, especially health concerns. Budgets, for medicine and hospitals, for example, have increased in states where women are numerous and influential.

Rwanda and now Ethiopia have both vigorously recruited women into their ministerial and legislative ranks. Female Liberians also became prominent during Johnson Sirleaf's presidency, but women in 2019 occupied only a modest fraction of African political positions at the senior national and provincial levels. In parliaments, Rwanda led the way, with more than 61 percent of its seats being held by women. Female legislators occupied more than 40 percent of the places in the Namibian, South African, and Senegalese parliaments. Nine other sub-Saharan African parliaments, including Ethiopia's, counted women at the 30 percent level. But, sliding down on the list, women filled only 5 percent of the national legislative places in Nigeria; 7 percent in Benin; 9 percent in the Central African Republic, Mali, and the Democratic Republic of Congo; 10 percent in Botswana; 12 percent in Mauritius; 17 percent in Malawi; and 22 percent in Kenya and Guinea. Patriarchy continued to rule, as it has in Africa from the onset of independence.

Johnson Sirleaf cogently explained why women have thus far played a less prominent leadership role in African political life. But only implicitly does she demonstrate by her own accomplishments in office that women make a difference to African political discourse, to the transformational potential of African political leadership, and to increasing political attention to the public interest, not the personal interests of the ruling elite. Women can continue to make a becoming difference in African political life, and therefore in the uplifting of Africa more fully, when they are both more numerous in the executive and key ministerial ranks, in parliament, and more sustainably influential across the board. Theirs is another work in progress.

Typologies and Distinctions

Although structure and contingency are important influences on leadership trajectories and decisions in the modern era, the importance of individual agency (personal leadership) is amply demonstrated by past and current examples. In the dark past of sub-Saharan Africa there are the brutal men who rose to run their countries despotically, with little adherence to any norms other than unbridled attacks on their own divided peoples. The notorious exploits of the Idi Amins (Uganda) and Jean-Bédel Bokassas (Central African Empire) in the twentieth century were echoed by the equally cruel military men who presided over Nigeria in the 1980s and 1990s, and robbed it blind. In this century, presidents like Eduardo dos Santos (Angola), Frederick Chiluba (Zambia), and Idriss Déby (Chad) were and are less addicted to arbitrary mayhem than their predecessors, but their subordination of the public interest was and is just as profound, and equally damaging to personal outcomes within their states.

It made a major difference (as will be discussed) that Mandela knitted South Africa together as its first post-apartheid leader, and not Govan Mbeki, Walter Sisulu, or Oliver Tambo—all fine men but less gifted leaders. South Africa arguably has suffered poorer governance and greater corruption than anticipated because Thabo Mbeki (Govan's son) succeeded Mandela instead of Cyril Ramaphosa, now that country's president.

Elsewhere, we can at least wonder what would have happened to Botswana, the African continent's outstanding developmental success story, if ambitious left-leaning revolutionaries backed by Nkrumah had become its founders instead of Seretse Khama, who set a remarkably anti-corrupt, tolerant, democratic course that determined the exemplary post-independent voyage of his desperately poor one-time protectorate. Almost unthinkable in terms of leadership, too, is a Rwanda without Kagame's post-genocidal, very tough and highly controlling vision and execution. Or a Mozambique absent the steady early leadership hand of Joaquim Chissano, compared to the less consultative presidents that have followed, and who have forfeited the relative prosperity, equitable results, and stability that his regime provided. Many other comparisons are possible, including the striking stylistic and methodological contrasts in Tanzania between the largely productive presidencies of Benjamin Mkapa and Jakaya Kikwete and the capricious and heavy-handed actions of John Magufuli, now president.

Of the forty-nine countries of sub-Saharan Africa, in 2020 a dozen or so are full-fledged democracies with clear-minded leaders who, whether transformationally or transactionally motivated, are conscious of how they can best deliver good human outcomes to their citizens. Some of these better leaders may fall short in terms of economic and social results, and some are personally corrupt, but most know that they hold office primarily to serve their peoples, not their families or cronies.

A second set of countries, possibly twenty-five, are both less well led and run (as we shall see in the next chapter). In terms of the Freedom House annual judgments, these places are "partly free," corrupt without being excessively kleptocratic, and nominally elected democracies only. That is, they hold elections, but usually in conditions that favor incumbent rulers. These political jurisdictions are stable because they are tightly controlled, with pressures to conform, and penalties for outspoken dissent. Some of the polities included in this category in 2019 include Cameroon, Chad, Eswatini, Gabon, Kenya, Rwanda, Tanzania, Uganda, Zambia, and Zimbabwe.

A third category of sub-Saharan state includes the many that are war-torn, heavily corrupt, very poorly governed, and—in several cases—in severe danger of failing. Those are the countries without consolidated leadership or, in two cases, not much leadership at all. The Central African Republic, the Democratic Republic of Congo, Mali, Nigeria, Somalia, and South Sudan are all examples of places where consummate leadership is lacking and is heavily challenged.

Overall, too many of today's transactionally focused sub-Saharan leaders project no vision, exude little integrity in their personal lives or in the manner in which they organize their regimes, and sometimes endanger the very life chances of their constituents. They distribute patronage, however, to keep themselves in power. They try to play one internal ethnic group against another, balancing interests, and seek to take advantage of Chinese, Russian, and other foreign offers to help their countries in exchange for resources and influence. A number of the rulers of such countries are hostile to free expression, mistrust open macro economies, and abuse such political institutions (legislatures and judiciaries) that may exist. They favor executive control, only now and then sharing some power with legislators or with officers and soldiers but never with the people.

Positive Leadership Models

In the search for enduring positive African leadership models on which reformers, civil societies, and prospective prime ministers and presidents could build, and against which well-intended new leaders could test their achievements, we examine five contrasting but gifted experiences: those of Khama, Mandela, Kagame, Johnson Sirleaf, and Abiy. .

KHAMA

Employing what he had learned as the heir-apparent to the throne of the Tswana people of Botswana, as a schoolboy and university student in neighboring South Africa, and as a postgraduate student at the University of Oxford and in London's Inns of Temple, Khama led his country and its disparate ethnic groups to independence from Britain in 1966, a few years after a number of other British African colonies and protectorates had been let free. But his was a unique accession of responsibility; able because of his inherited traditional legitimacy as a paramount chief to rule authoritatively and without too much indigenous input over what had been a very underdeveloped and out-of-the-way British protectorate, Khama chose to eschew the heavy-handed approach favored by Nkrumah, Kenyatta, Nyerere, and Kaunda—the then-dominant English-speaking architects of African governance. Within Botswana, he could have abridged or limited democracy, almost without fear of internal rebuke. Intellectually honest in a way that few of his peers were, however, he distrusted easy answers, rejected what he called the "histrionics" of some of his fellow African presidents, and knew either instinctively or because of his education in South Africa and Britain that taking shortcuts to prosperity and to ethnic harmony would not work. Alone among his contemporaries, he decided to govern strictly democratically and without distributing patronage (which encouraged corruption and distorted priorities). He refused to follow those of his peers who espoused the rather wooly tenets of Afro-Socialism, who preferred one-party states so that they could minimize competition, and who professed belief in various forms of autocracy.

Khama espoused unfashionable notions about the need for substantial measures of political participation, respect for human rights, and probity—all imperatives that were rarely championed in state houses on the continent in the 1960s and 1970s. He favored the independence of judges, regulated capitalism rather than state-centered and state-directed enterprises, free speech and free assembly, freedom of worship, and respect for individuals as well as for groups—ideological preferences that were in practice anathema to most of his ruling contemporaries (and to a number who came later). Consciously, too, he pioneered a political culture for the peoples of Botswana that responded to their immediate and long-term needs and that nurtured new democratic political institutions and institutional frameworks that have endured to this day.

As a result of the careful, incremental, foundations that Khama laid and his immediate successors (Sir Ketumile Masire and Festus Mogae) elaborated upon, Botswana now enjoys a strong rule-based democracy, solid independent political institutions, an absence of internal strife, well-crafted instruments of governance, and—critically—a deep sense of pride for the nation among all its inhabitants, whatever their original loyalties to separate ethnic groupings. Khama constructed a nation of the disparate constituents of his patrimony. A number of other sub-Saharan polities, some intrinsically better human- and physical-resourced than the young Botswana, are still awaiting their own nation-builder.

NATION-BUILDER

Khama believed that he was obligated, as a leader, to establish a nation, not a patrimonial edifice constructed of patrons and clients. Hence he assumed the role of tutor as well as president. His vision was to create an informed public, to institute deliberative democracy (even though Khama never knew that construct as such) in an embryonic nation that was still dirt poor (its only export resource was beef from cattle), very uneducated (in terms of secondary- and university-level degrees), poorly provided for in terms of health clinics, and still without the underground diamonds that were discovered only later.

Khama said that his main goal was to "do good." To him that meant refusing to countenance autocracy of any kind. (He traveled to China and North Korea and to some of his African neighbors, such as Malawi, and was appalled at what he saw and experienced.) "Dictatorships and tyrannical systems of government are hatched in the minds of men," he declared, "who appoint themselves philosophers, kings, and possessors of absolute truth."[9] He informed Botswana's parliament that such attempts to rationalize personal rule rather than people rule would hinder Botswana's attempt to raise itself and all of its peoples to a higher economic plane. He specifically decided that Botswana would be a country governed by ideals, not narrow ethnic criteria or individual greed.

Khama was a democrat "through and through."[10] That is what his close associate and successor as president called him, with affection and respect. Khama was also explicit about what he was attempting as a leader to do: to propagate a positive ethos—a comprehensive political culture—that could provide the medium on which the infant Botswana could gradually grow modern, democratic, political institutions. A key factor in furthering such a "positive ethos" was an executive (himself and his successors) who acted fairly, never arbitrarily, listened, could be seen and heard to be consultative, behaved modestly and chastely, and kept his hands out of the public till. All around Botswana the leaders of larger and more powerful African countries were (in Khama's mind) mistreating their own peoples, running roughshod over the protests of opponents and critics, and making a mockery of their democratic pretensions. He expressed contempt, for example, for Malawi president Hastings Banda's interminable motorcades, pomposity, and his appalling human rights record. Other African would-be potentates who "cheated their people" also aroused his ire.

Khama demonstrated to his own people, and eventually to an array of skeptics in Africa, that the even-handed Botswanan approach could produce significant economic growth, social harmony, and political stability. Khama embedded a strongly buttressed rule of law regime, rare in Africa at that time, and insisted upon the independence of judges. He stressed inclusivity and accountability across his government. He eschewed the pomp that was so common in Malawi and most of the other new, tightly-ruled, nation-states of the sub-continent. He made his ministers and officials fly economy (not first class) to other African and global destinations. He doubled down on integrity, an attribute that so many of his contemporaries then and since in Africa have ignored or obscured. Khama well understood that even he, the possessor of abundant rational as well as electoral legitimacy, could forfeit that critical leadership foundation if the peoples of Botswana began to question his personal and political honesty.

Personally and presidentially, Khama was determined to implant universal good governance values that would, in his mind, place his peoples and his country on a beneficial, straight, upward course. By so doing, Botswana could become a beacon of insightful brilliance in and for Africa, and a counterpoint to what he considered the profligate and misleading (if not deceitful) political posturing of his fellow heads of state and heads of government. Leadership, for him, was guardianship, a possibly paternal but responsible stance. He believed that he was anointed president in order to offer a strong moral and practical compass for his peoples. That meant creating an open society, a tolerant society, and a democratic society.

Khama demonstrated his qualities as a leader by fostering three crucial policy initiatives:

1) Within six years of taking office, he ended his country's reliance on British budgetary support, by controlling expenditures and improving revenue flows. To him and to his citizens, such a rare (for Africa) accomplishment exemplified his disdain for living off handouts from abroad. But most of all such an action declared that Botswana would not live off rents—that its officials were not skimming assistance from abroad to line their own pockets.

2) Ten years after independence, Botswana ended its use of the South Africa rand and created its own currency, the pula, in order to cease importing its white-run neighbor's inflation and deflation, but also in order to give its peoples one more unifying symbol with which to identify and be proud.

3) When rich gem diamond pipes were discovered beneath the sands of Botswana and their exploitation fully realized by the mid-1970s, Khama resisted the rent-seeking resource curse that had corrupted Nigeria, Angola, and other African petroleum producers, beguiled and misled countries like Zambia and Zaire (now the Democratic Republic of Congo) to borrow against copper and other mineral wealth, and later shifted many other African raw material producers away from macroeconomic fundamentals to booming and busting with no attention to economic fundamentals and administrative discipline.

Khama could have followed the common African pattern and nationalized the diamond mines, or simply tried to aggrandize to increase the fortunes of the ruling Botswana Democratic Party or his own family. Instead, he cut a very favorable deal with South Africa's De Beers Mining Corporation to share management and profits, but under Botswana's ultimate control and to its great benefit.

Such explosions of new, relatively easily acquired, national wealth led many other developing nations to corruption, distorted priorities, and appreciated currencies. Not so in Botswana. Khama knew from the very start of his government that his colleagues and other public servants would as easily be tempted by inducements as their counterparts in other African countries. Conscious of this danger, Khama (very much like Lee Kuan Yew in Singapore) appreciated that his young, untried, government could easily fail and fall if corruption took root. So throughout his ethos-setting time as president, Khama preached against taking advantage of public positions for private gain. He punished close colleagues who succumbed to temptation; he demanded that his ministers and officials pay their debts quickly and obtain no bank loans. He and Masire prosecuted members of the political elite who were suspected of cheating and peculation. No one was spared.

If leadership is judged by results, then Khama accomplished two outstanding outcomes:

1) The political culture and value system that he inaugurated and bolstered during his fourteen years in office proved sufficiently strong and effective to be sustained and strengthened by his millions of constituents, and by his now four successor presidents. Pre-institutional under Khama, Botswana now has robust political institutions and a vibrant democratic political culture that is the envy of most of Africa.

2) The political culture that he introduced led to responsible governance in the public interest, to careful and austere management, to frugality, to the husbanding of mineral wealth, and to a record of economic growth (thanks, of course, to diamonds, but mostly to well-managed diamond riches) over decades that is unparalleled on mainland Africa, and that has resulted in well-distributed (not unequal) wealth throughout what is now a mature and emergent Botswanan economy and society. (Beef exports and high-end tourism have also contributed to Botswana's very high regional annual GDP per capita totals.)

Over several decades in the last century, and for much of the present century, Botswana's per capita GDPs grew 7 percent or so a year. Now it continues to grow, but more slowly. Khama's leadership constructed a platform for prosperity on which his successors and his nation could build. Botswana consistently ranks among the best governed and least corrupt African countries. Its people take pride in their country and more and more think of themselves as citizens of Botswana, no longer primarily as Bamangwato, Bakgatla, Bakwena, or Bakalanga, component ethnic fractions of the whole. As Khama would have hoped, too, Botswana pulls much more than its intrinsically tiny weight on the African and global scenes. Khama set high and largely uncompromising standards that his successors have followed, and to which the citizens of his country now adhere as a matter of course. Khama was truly transformative, and his peoples benefited.

Mandela's enormous contribution to South Africa, Africa, and the world was less as a decision maker—less as an exponent of advanced methods of governance—than it was as an ethical setter of example, as an unblemished guide to the promised land of partnership, comity, equity, and reconciliation. But Mandela also knew, experienced, and understood what effective leadership consisted of: "Listen to me," he told a fired-up mob of antagonists a year before South Africa's independence, when the townships around Johannesburg were alight with mayhem and violence. "I am your leader. I am going to give you leadership. . . . As long as I am your leader, I will tell you, always, when you are wrong."[11]

From his early days of African National Congress (ANC) prominence, during his several trials in apartheid-era courts, during his long imprisonment on Robben Island, and after emerging from incarceration and becoming the ANC's above-ground dominating personality, Mandela espoused a clear vision; he consciously mobilized first his followers and then a nation and finally a continent behind it; he always demonstrated an acute emotional intelligence; effortlessly, he exuded intellectual honesty, self-mastery, and prudence; he emphasized integrity in his being and his actions; and from a reluctant followership and from the top echelon of the ANC demanded and insisted upon inclusivity—on himself becoming much more than a party chief, or even a partisan chief of a ruling faction. Most of all, exercising his great gifts of gesture, symbol, and authenticity, Mandela gave to the peoples of South Africa (and then the world) what all peoples crave—a feeling of being an integral and worthy part of a glorious enterprise the likes of which were innovative for South Africa and for Africa (although Nkrumah had tried his flawed best).

From the moment that Mandela arrived in Johannesburg from the rural Transkei and from his undergraduate college, he became a political leader in training and then a young political leader of the ANC's Youth League and its Transvaal provincial executive. His vast empathic gifts commended him to potential followers. By the early 1950s, by which time Afrikaans-speaking nationalists had established themselves in power in South Africa and had begun to tighten the screws of apartheid, Mandela had emerged as a natural leader capable of commanding others. Jailed under the broad wording of the new Suppression of Communism Act, he gained greater legitimacy as a tactician and leader. From about 1953, his vision and inspiration were fundamental to the ANC's resistance to apartheid. By the time of the Sharpeville massacre in 1960, the banning of the ANC, and the clear sharp-edged confrontation between African resisters and the security forces of apartheid, Mandela was not the sole leader of the ANC but one of several top strategists and articulators of an elaborate and evolving spiral of militant opposition.

Mandela advanced his and the ANC's cause in a famous speech from the dock at the end of the Rivonia trial. Mandela declared that he had been fighting against white domination, that he cherished the ideal of a democratic and free society "in which all people live together in harmony with equal opportunities." It was an ideal, he declared, "which I hope to live for and achieve. But if needs be, it is an ideal for which I am prepared to die."[12]

Twenty-seven long years of imprisonment followed. Mandela broke stones and sewed mailbags, but he also burnished his leadership credentials inside the cells of Robben Island by persuading hostile fellow prisoners, some of whom were younger, were from other political movements, or were common criminals, to accept his nondespairing approach to the long-term struggle against apartheid, and to be guided by him in their collective attitudes toward hard labor, the utility (or not) of hunger strikes, prison food, their jailers, the possibilities of escape, and—in time—whether or not he should accept an early release from Robben Island. Mandela knew that establishing and then maintaining his legitimacy was critical, especially in the aftermath of the Soweto uprising of 1976, which brought a large cohort of young persons into prison who were suspicious of Mandela and of the relatively moderate methods of the ANC.

By the mid-1980s, the National Party government that ruled South Africa finally understood that there could be no peace, no forward movement, no cessation of the guerrilla struggle against apartheid without Mandela's cooperation and approval. When he walked out of prison in 1990, finally free, he was seventy-one and ready for Africa's supreme test of political leadership. He had to win over those who had been resisting apartheid from within the country by sabotage and militant protest together with those who had been waging a largely desultory war from outside. His approach to them and to the supreme and complex problem of transferring lasting power to a new ANC-controlled national administration was profound. He advanced a vision that was at once militant but pragmatic, flexible, and adaptive to changing and newly revealed circumstance. Being intellectually honest and transparent helped, especially when he realized that long-held ideological imperatives were no longer sensible.

Mandela refused to take on airs. He remained the warm, decent, polite man that he always had been. That manner, his stature and legitimacy, and his convincing ability to advance a clear vision of a post-apartheid future, enabled Mandela to cast aside the competition over primacy that would have undermined his leadership and the ANC just at the moment when its triumph over apartheid and the National Party was becoming more certain. Absent Mandela and his unwillingness to accept anything other than a peaceful transfer of power and a meaningful accommodation of defeated and soon to be marginalized whites, the violent struggle between white and black might well have resumed and South Africa's destruction been assured. Instead, facing that Armageddon, Mandela (assisted by the negotiating skills of Ramaphosa and the calculated sensibilities of President Frederik W. de Klerk) forged an independence for Africans that respected Afrikaner and white human needs, brought contending Africans into the larger whole and persuaded opponents to lay down their arms, and convincingly promised a final dispensation that all dissident factions could embrace. Mandela became the great consolidator, largely by the force of his vision and the integrity that he had established in prison and immediately thereafter.

As the first president of an independent South Africa, Mandela attempted to deliver a substantial peace dividend. He espoused a program of economic modernization, an opening of schooling to Africans who had long been deprived of such opportunity, and a democratizing of what had been an almost exclusively white-run corporate endeavor. Mandela refused to stigmatize previous enemies or ways of life. He was under pressure from within the ANC to establish an authoritarian state. Instead, Mandela emphasized the importance of a strict adherence to the rule of law; he welcomed the writing of a very liberal and rights-respecting new constitution; he insisted that all manner of governmental appointments be made on merit. In these several ways, Mandela created a democratic political culture for the reborn South Africa. That was Mandela's most significant leadership contribution to the evolution of South Africa.

Mandela soon made it clear that reconciliation with the defeated enemy was more important to him than almost anything else. In order to avoid any possibility of renewed strife, the various strands of the rainbow nation that he had called into being from the wreckage of apartheid had to be woven together by his hands and efforts. No one else could so deftly knit the nation together across the color chasm. No one else could demonstrate that inclusionism was more than just a slogan. Mandela wanted all South Africans of whatever persuasion, belief, bias, and color to come to believe that they were one people. Doing so, he believed, would uplift all of them spiritually even if he could not begin immediately to provide commensurate material benefits for all.

Forgiveness established Mandela's moral supremacy. Gestures of concil-
iation were acts of courage that resonated far beyond South Africa. He visited the chief architects of apartheid and dined with several in his home. He
opened his residence to the former commander of the Robben Island prison
and to the outgoing head of the country's national intelligence service. He
lunched with the man who had prosecuted him for sabotage. He visited the
widow of one of the principal architects of apartheid. More so, he united the
new nation by donning the colors and uniform of South Africa's victorious
(mostly white) rugby team after its world championship victory over New
Zealand.

Thereafter, in his remaining years as president and his post-presidential
years as world peacemaker, leadership icon, and global sage, it mattered less
how he governed (Thabo Mbeki took most day-to-day decisions), than how
he positioned the ANC and his immediate political followers. For him there
could be no abridgement of fundamental liberties or human rights. For him,
all four of the freedoms were untouchable. When he handed the reins of
power to Mbeki, and later when he assumed the role of elder statesman,
Mandela (just as Khama had done) deplored arbitrary actions, impure
motives, shortcuts that were rationalizations, and almost anything that deprived peoples of the accountability and ethical behavior that they deserved
from their regimes and their politicians. Mandela's behavior and actions, like
Khama's, epitomized the essence of good leadership.

KAGAME

Unlike Khama and Mandela, the president of Rwanda can hardly claim to
be a thoroughgoing democrat, or even a consensus-building quasi-democrat.
Kagame is a naked authoritarian, with substantial legitimacy as a genuine
modernizer. But what truly distinguishes him and his long reign as the
headman of Rwanda is his close attention to improving the public good and
the daily lives and outcomes of his 13 million densely packed constituents.

As a Ugandan-based military commander who had undergone training in
the United States and had been the sometime intelligence chief of Uganda's
army, Kagame responded to the 1994 genocide in Rwanda by invading
Rwanda at the head of a Tutsi army to save as many remaining Tutsi lives as
possible and to restore order in his country. Initially that meant imprisoning
Hutu perpetrators of genocide or pursuing them and their ethnic compatriots
into the nearby forests of the Congo. Subsequently, after Kagame had become prime minister (under a titular but powerless president), he focused on
rebuilding, stabilizing, and pacifying the desperate land that had lost at least

800,000 Tutsi and had seen 200,000 Hutu flee into the Congo, Burundi, Tanzania, Uganda, and overseas.

Kagame was no mere military leader with rudimentary ideas about organizing a reborn state and a responsible government. By 2000, when Kagame acceded to the nation's presidency, he had articulated a vision for the emergence of war-damaged Rwanda as the Singapore of Africa. Even though Rwanda lacked most of Singapore's advantages (its perfectly positioned harbor, its geographical location at the crossroads of a good third of the globe's commerce, its well-educated and advanced-skilled population, and its very high wealth per capita), Kagame nevertheless became determined at least by 2005 (if not before) to transform a very poor state with natural resources no more promising than shade-grown coffee (subject as it is to fluctuating world prices) into a well-functioning, promising, potentially middle-income jurisdiction in the heart of equatorial Africa. Kagame has been called a "developmental patrimonialist."

What Kagame presumably admired most about Singapore, the city-state that had been willed into modern existence by Prime Minister Lee Kuan Yew from 1965, was the careful and conciliatory manner in which Lee had transformed a pirate-infested, gang-influenced, wildly corrupt, unruly port city into a thriving metropolis obedient to and willing to be conformed by the vision of Lee and the centralized way in which he and his government made decisions. They took those policy initiatives in the public interest, as defined by Lee, but were punctilious about not stealing from the people. Most of all, in Singapore, innovations such as shifting the Malay- and Chinese-speaking populace to English as a common tongue, the compulsory mixing of ethnic groups in high-rise housing estates (to prohibit ghettos and ensure comity), and the introduction of air conditioning throughout the city, had a modernizing purpose. Lee's government delivered progress (as enunciated from above) but also gave the city-state the stability, the rule of law, an emphasis on education, attention to medical services, and the prosperity that attracted international investment and soon increased the per capita GDP of its citizens many times over. In 1994, Rwanda's GDP per capita was $205. It rose to $698 in 2014, to $765 in 2017, and to $819 in 2019. The country's GDP per capita has been growing at 8 percent in recent years.

Kagame's goal, since about 2005, has been to bring first world educational opportunities to Rwanda, along with major improvements in life expectancies and other medical outcomes. Following a Brazilian model, Kagame pioneered cash transfers to the poorest persons in the country. He also promoted major infrastructural improvements. Non-Rwandans have been assisted in their efforts to upgrade health care in rural areas. Such innovative technological initiatives as drone deliveries of blood plasma to rural clinics are now routine. From 2005 to 2019, Rwanda has experienced falling rates of maternal and infant mortality, and mildly rising life expectancy rates. Educationally, primary school persistence rates have climbed from low levels to 57 percent in 2017. Life expectancy rose from 2000 to 2019 from 48 to 67.

Kagame has thus performed as a leader on those dimensions. But he has also echoed Lee (and Khama) by greatly lowering crime rates in Kigali, Rwanda's capital city of 921,000. Newly professionalized police (after 2004) even pursued litterers, making Kigali a compulsorily pristine locale (certainly by the standards of African cities). Kagame and his city officials outlawed street vending and imprisoned persistent offenders, a unique curtailing of the informal sector that is otherwise little known in Africa. Pascal Nyamulinda, the mayor of Kigali and a Kagame appointee, asserts that Kagame's laws "must be respected." Moreover, the decision to stamp out informal "hawking" once and for all was essential. In what could stand as a central motif for Kagame's regime, the mayor said: "If you have to choose between a mess and discipline, I will choose discipline."[13]

Kagame simply refused as a leader to countenance crime, thus delivering levels of safety and security that are unknown in most other cities in Africa. The president tellingly also virtually eliminated what had been a casual epidemic of corruption throughout the country. His method copied Lee: to preach against the evils of corruption (there were billboards throughout Kigali warning of its evils and forbidding such behavior: "He Who Practices Corruption Destroys His Country"); mercilessly to prosecute alleged offenders; to remove from office any elected or appointed public officials, even associates of the president; and—most of all—to remain untainted himself by accusations of improper enrichment. Rwanda is still perceived as more corrupt in Africa than Botswana, the Seychelles, and Cape Verde (and less corrupt than Namibia, Mauritius, South Africa, and all of the other sub-Saharan African states), but its rating by the Corruption Perceptions Index increased from eighty-third place in 2005 to fifty-first place in 2019—a remarkable jump in perceived probity and one unprecedented in Africa.

When Kagame's great reform program had begun to accelerate after 2005, he copied President Mikheil Saakashvili in Georgia and significantly downsized the civil service, finding ghost workers and existing bureaucrats who were inefficient or deemed superfluous. Competitive tests were introduced for the first time to improve competency and make merit appointments. Rwanda has also raised civil service salaries consistently.

In order to improve Rwanda's ratings by the World Bank's *Doing Business* reports, Kagame reduced bureaucratic controls and the number of permits required to open commercial concerns. His government minimized regulatory burdens and red tape of most kinds. His aim was to produce a more investor-friendly (and Singapore-like) corporate environment, but also to make it at least conceivable that isolated and remote Rwanda could boast some of the advantages that accrued to Singapore.

As a result of all of these and many other innovations and initiatives, not least the careful subordination of Rwanda's peoples to the clear-minded edicts of its president, the country's governance ratings have risen, its civil service is better motivated than others in its African neighborhood, its peoples are relatively prosperous compared to past decades, and Kagame can assert that he has brought stability and improved living standards to his disciplined polity.

But there is no question about who is in charge. Free speech, media, assembly, and association are restricted, and Kagame has imprisoned or brutally assassinated a number of his vocal opponents. In late 2018, the government banned "humiliating" cartoons of politicians and officials. Rwanda is tightly regimented, but Kagame would argue that his leadership abilities have produced more and better personal and national outcomes for his peoples than those supposed deficiencies would imply. Kagame also says that his decision to rewrite constitutional prohibitions against becoming a virtual president for life were essential if Rwanda were to keep moving ahead on its developmental trajectory, and continue to provide good returns to its citizens. These are high-flown rationalizations, of course, but Kagame has nevertheless remained popular among his people. Like Lee, he has produced the returns that he said that he would produce.

As an uncompromising (if profoundly paranoid) leader, Kagame's tenure demonstrates the importance of an ambitious vision, the virtue of mobilizing behind such a vision, the importance of intellectual honesty and self-mastery in pursuing visionary objectives, the relevance of legitimacy and the personal integrity that supports legitimacy, and the attributes that flow from the construction of a national edifice (and a nation) of which its citizens can be proud.

JOHNSON SIRLEAF

Her skills honed at Harvard's Kennedy School, at the United Nations Development Program, and in Liberia itself, where she was a cabinet minister, Johnson Sirleaf used a matriarchal talent for conflict resolution and an experienced understanding of macroeconomic realities to reestablish a robust Liberian nation in the years after 2006 to her term-limited and term-respecting retirement in 2018. Johnson Sirleaf inherited a state as war-torn as post-genocidal Rwanda. In Liberia's case, the tyrannical warlord Charles Taylor and his followers had laid waste to much of the country and parts of Sierra Leone between 1990 and 2003, with reconstruction delayed for another three years until Johnson Sirleaf could be elected president.

Liberia had been ravaged, its spirit and its infrastructure greatly damaged, its poverty palpable. Electric power was mostly unavailable. The country's iron ore mines and rubber plantations no longer functioned. Its battered citizens wanted to escape. Johnson Sirleaf understood that her supreme task was to revive a sense of wholeness and oneness among the various ethnic groups and rural and urban conglomerations that comprised her country. She needed to unite those who were descended from American slaves and those up-country people who had for too long been discriminated against; she also needed to bring together those who had supported Taylor and his ilk and those who had fought and won the ferocious war against him.

These were daunting tasks, initially assisted by a large UN peacekeeping force and by a large cadre of American advisors and returned Liberians who had been living in the diaspora. By personal example (which became somewhat contested), and by stressing her own accountability and transparency, Johnson Sirleaf gradually restored the nation's macro-economy and its exports of iron ore and timber. China purchased most of these and other raw materials; Liberia's foreign exchange earnings grew and the national income rose. But Johnson Sirleaf only with difficulty managed to turn the lights back on in Monrovia and other cities; shortages of skilled workers and budget shortfalls made achieving the key components of Liberia's revival difficult and time-consuming. And then the Ebola epidemic hit.

To her credit, however, Johnson Sirleaf adhered carefully to a democratic agenda and ensured the holding of free and fair elections. To enhance ministerial accountability, reduce corruption, and eliminate obfuscating bureaucrats, she sacked thousands of civil servants and investigated allegations of graft and peculation within their ranks. She introduced a tough code of conduct for all public employees, gave new authority to a General Auditing Commission, opened the country's economy and reformed the public financial management system, joined the Extractive Industries Transparency Initiative to protect the country's major manufacturers and mining projects from corruption, declared her own financial assets and mandated that cabinet officials do so as well, and strengthened the capacity of the Public Procurement Commission to erect new barriers to kickbacks. She also employed American and other contacts and support to build capacity within the public service and to emphasize the need for new standards of honesty.

Johnson Sirleaf can justifiably claim that her presidential campaign against pervasive corruption paid off. Liberia improved its scores on the Corruption Perceptions Index from 8 to 37 (on a 100 point scale) from 2004 to 2015, though falling to 32 in 2018. The World Bank's Control of Corruption Indicator showed similar major upward shifts in its numbers.

Manifest personal will was the key to these positive results and to the improvements in managerial efficiency that marked Johnson Sirleaf's twelve years in the Liberian presidency. Imposing Kagame-like strictures on Liberians would not have worked, especially after the Taylor despotism. But Johnson Sirleaf was otherwise inclined anyway, preferring democratic methods and such leadership virtues as transparency. Although challenged by rivals and possibly compromised by the questionable activities of her sons, Johnson Sirleaf's integrity remained largely intact during her presidential years. She also attempted, with mixed success, to disrupt the corrupt preferences and activities of her associates and governmental subordinates.

The proof of Johnson Sirleaf's leadership accomplishment is less the shared Nobel Peace Prize that she won in 2011 or the Africa Leadership Prize that she won in 2018, after stepping down from her presidency, than it is the uplift in Liberia's political, economic, and social results that she can rightly claim to have engineered. Politically, Liberia held a free and fair election in late 2017, with voters peacefully choosing George Weah, whom she had defeated in 2005, as her successor. Economically, Liberia's destroyed infrastructure has been revived, and the lights largely stay on in Monrovia, the capital. GDP per capita rose from $240 in 2003 to $703 in 2019. Liberia also grew economically over that period at more than 8 percent per year. The country's scores on the Index of African Governance increased from 40 in 2007 to 52 in 2018. There is potable water, better sanitation, and improved trash collection in the cities. Life expectancy rates have risen from 56 to 64 (2006 to 2018), despite the Ebola toll. Infant mortality numbers have fallen from 78 per 1,000 in 2006 to 52 in 2017. Johnson Sirleaf led a battered country back from the precipice of physical collapse and spiritual despair. She mostly succeeded in giving Liberians reasons to be proud of and invest in the future of their country

ABIY AHMED ALI

Not as yet fully tested and a young forty-three, Abiy became prime minister and head of government in Ethiopia only in 2018 (the head of state is ceremonial). But he immediately demonstrated that, as Ethiopia's third top leader since the despotic Marxist Derg was overthrown by Tigrayan-led insurgents of the Ethiopian People's Revolutionary Democratic Liberation Front in 1991, he possessed a transformative vision for his country and its disparate peoples. Soon after taking office, Abiy showed his preference for inclusivity—for knitting the major human components of the Ethiopian confederation together without favoring one or another of the major ethnic groups (as his predecessors had done). He also issued a number of edicts to democratize the political operation of his nation, and to reassure the country's far-flung constituents that they would be heard, almost for the first time since the Derg was ousted. He quickly appointed a woman as Ethiopia's head of state and brought a number of women into his slimmed-down cabinet. He released more than 13,200 political prisoners, including a number of journalists. He welcomed home the heads of armed opposition groups and legalized the Oromo Liberation Front, the Ogaden National Liberation Front, and the exiled opposition movement "Ginbot 7," all previously considered terrorist operations. He asked one of the opposition leaders to chair the national electoral board. He appointed a noted human rights lawyer to the supreme court. He mollified protestors who had attacked the government of his immediate predecessor.

But Abiy's intensely popular, strikingly successful, and most disruptive initiative was an unexpected decision to resume diplomatic relations with neighboring Eritrea, an official enemy since the abortive two-year war between both countries ended in 2000. He even ceded contested mountainous territory back to Eritrea. Those initiatives led to quick and symbolically significant visits by Abiy to Asmara, Eritrea's capital, and to the rapid reopening of telephonic communications, and air and rail traffic, between the previously estranged countries. Families were soon visiting relatives that they had not talked to or seen for almost twenty years. Landlocked Ethiopia, which had only in 2018 established a brand-new rail line to Djibouti, on the Red Sea, could now once again send rail traffic along the old line to Massawa, Eritrea's closer Red Sea port. The line had been shut since 1998.

As a further important peace making initiative, Abiy acted early to abate hostilities in Ethiopia's Ogaden region, where restive Somali separatists had long been at odds with distant rule from Addis Ababa. But it is not yet evident in 2020 that Abiy's boost of people power will dampen the intense ethnic competition that his predecessors had unleashed and then attempted to bottle up. Abiy, despite being little known nationally or internationally prior to being anointed prime minister by the ruling Revolutionary Democratic Front, had abundant credibility within that party as a longtime revolutionary military officer and as someone who had earned respect in combat against the Derg. Additionally, and very critically for today's Ethiopia, he is a member of the Oromo ethnic group, the largest of the country's eighty or so major ethnicities. Emperor Haile Selassie, who ruled Ethiopia as regent and then as absolute monarch from 1916 to 1974 (including the era from 1936 to 1941 when Italy invaded and controlled the country), was an Amhara, the traditionally dominant ethnic group and the one aligned for centuries with the Ethiopian Orthodox (Coptic) Church. Mengistu Haile Mariam, the despotic head of the Derg, was also an Amhara, Ethiopia's second most numerous ethnicity. Meles Zenawi, however, who led the army that ousted Mengistu and his allies, was from Tigray, a less populous (6 percent of the total) ethnic area nestled up against the Eritrean border. Hailemariam Desalegn, who became prime minister after Meles's sudden death in 2012, was from Amhara. Thus, before Abiy was appointed by the Revolutionary Democratic Front, the Oromo had long felt marginalized. They had protested Desalegn's rule, and their own exclusion from power, in 2018 and before. Abiy's accession was essential to mute those anti-regime complaints, and to set the 112 million Ethiopians on a political course that (under Abiy) will presumably be much more progressive than when Meles jailed opponents, curtailed the press, limited free speech, reduced freedom of assembly, and altered the 2005 election results to favor him and his followers.

Abiy's relative youth sets him apart from many other political leaders in sub-Saharan Africa, and in the Horn of Africa. That he comes from a new generation with very different ideas about how parties and politicians should wield their power is welcome in Ethiopia and refreshing in Africa more widely. But Abiy, from an ethnic group that includes Muslims as well as Coptic Christians, also is a member of the newest and among the largest religious dispensations in sub-Saharan Africa. Abiy is both a liberationist belonging to a tightly run national political movement that, under Meles, brooked no dissent, and an adherent of Protestant Pentecostalism, one of Africa and Ethiopia's newest and most popular religious sects. Like comparable church movements in Nigeria and South Africa, Pentecostalism in Ethiopia preaches salvation through prosperity, through doing well for oneself and one's family. Abiy has been a member of one of Ethiopia's largest Pentecostal congregations for a decade.

It is much too soon to assume that Abiy's attitudinal, stylistic, and politically attuned approach to Ethiopia will continue to be deft and well received, or to believe that his seemingly effective emotional intelligence will carry him and his administration to leadership heights that are rare in Africa. Those are imponderables. But Abiy's approach to the premiership has given him and his constituents great hope that Ethiopia's peoples have at last turned a corner toward democracy and essential freedoms for all. Abiy favors increasing educational opportunity and medical services. He has uttered the right words against corruption. Economic advances, assisted by the country's alliance with China but prey to high inflation rates, should build upon the era of good governance that Abiy appears to have inaugurated and that may soon be validated statistically.

Abiy accepted the Nobel Peace prize in 2019 for his brokering of the accord with Eritrea, and for his many other symbolic and precedent-shattering political innovations in Ethiopia. Unifying the nation and subordinating the regional and ethnic identities that were promoted by Meles, is his dominant theme. (He created a new political party to accomplish this task.) But there are powerful rivals and opponents, even within the Oromo ethnic group. Those dissidents, and many others, want to use separatist claims to gain autonomy and agency within the Ethiopian nine-state federation. That could be Abiy's undoing, and a consuming distraction. Already even Oromo rivals have protested violently in the streets and the Sidama, a people in southern Ethiopia who constitute 4 percent of the country's total population, in late 2019 voted to create a new autonomous region of their own, possibly the tenth state.

Modern Leadership and the Rise of the Middle Class

Abiy may prove a harbinger of leadership attainment for sub-Saharan Africa. Just as Khama's model of austere leadership deportment was for the most part disregarded outside his own country for much of the twentieth century while the despotic, autocratic model exemplified by Afewerki, Amin, Bashir, Bokassa, Bongo, Mengistu, Mugabe, several Nigerian generals, Obiang Nguema, and many others prevailed, so Abiy's manner may join with the equally impressive leadership examples of Ramaphosa and Sall to establish progressive, democratic, ethical guideposts for the rest of sub-Saharan Africa.

If so, despite the very different national contexts in which each of these modern leaders operates, each will also be responding to sub-Saharan Africa's twenty-first-century demographic realities, to its new aspirations within a more closely knit globe, and to the challenges of modernity and nationalism that were left unresolved by their predecessors.

Sub-Saharan Africa is more and more the home to a middle class with bourgeois sentiments and aspirations that hardly existed thirty and twenty years ago. The World Bank, using a low threshold, suggests that a full third of sub-Saharan adults are middle class in terms of their incomes of \$3 a day. (See Chapter I.) Whatever the estimated income level, there is no question but that most of the nations of sub-Saharan Africa do host a middle class that is growing in size, in voting power, in cultural and economic influence, and in aspiration. Pew Research Center opinion polls show that middle class attitudes prevail in the growing metropolises of sub-Saharan Africa, and even extend into its rural agricultural fastnesses. This emergent middle class aspires to the material and spiritual benefits that its counterparts in Asia, Latin America, and Europe enjoy. Its members have often attended universities or worked overseas; social media gives them an intimate connection to the rest of the world. Africa is no longer apart, or cut off.

These kinds of considerations drive Abiy and his transformational-leaning peers. Creating more public benefit makes essential political sense. Indeed, the new leaders are more aware and more concerned to deliver high-quality political goods to their constituents than previous ruling generations. Although it would be premature to conclude that the days of evil klepto-cratic strong men are over, certainly their numbers will shrink when and where voters, especially middle class voters, can gain hegemony over their various national political destinies.

As sub-Saharan African countries begin to experience the proliferation of peoples that promises to overwhelm the sub-continent and a number of its key nations and cities by mid-century, so the most thoughtful and forward-looking of the new leaders may appreciate that mere transactionalism will provide too few answers or good outcomes, and that plotting bold new courses—developing innovative responses—is imperative if the polities of the sub-continent are going to improve the daily lives and outcomes of their national families and peoples. These are high orders of need; without exemplary, visionary leaders of utmost integrity, courage, and ability, Africans may stumble, and be unable to take their rightful places in the new world order.

III | Governance, Politics, Democracy

HIGH-QUALITY LEADERSHIP EVERYWHERE, but especially in Africa, creates good governance. In turn, good governance enables positive outcomes for citizens: enhanced security and safety, economic growth, solid infrastructures, access to speedy broadband, educational opportunities, the availability of clean water, advanced public health treatments and capable care, elevated standards of living, freedoms of speech and assembly, respect for human rights, and a variety of other political and social attainments that are only possible when the governed benefit from accomplished and responsive government.

Governance is performance, the delivery of quantities and qualities of essential services by a constituted authority that controls territory, whether at the municipal, the provincial, or the national level. Centuries ago governments—constituted bodies of authority—replaced sovereigns. Citizens subsequently expected, sometimes demanded, that their new governing bodies provide ever better and broader kinds of services. Constituents at various points refused merely to be organized by, dictated to, and taxed from above, by a governing authority. Their expectations grew as taxation became more of a transaction and less of an imposition. Ultimately, a sense of social contract took hold: the modern state could govern only if it won the consent of the governed and, in return, if it met the needs and desires of the inhabitants within its governmental orbit.

Governments hence exist in theory and in practice to serve their citizens. Otherwise, they act illegitimately. In the real world, of course, the results of most governing experiments—the modern nation-state—are mixed, with some proportion of a citizenry wanting more governmental services provided for them and another proportion wanting less, including fewer restrictions and lower taxes. Thus, there is a constant tension between the powerful and demanding state and the smaller and less responsive state.

An overriding consideration, however, is that all citizens of all countries want to be served well. That is what citizens seek from and expect of the nation-states in which they live. It follows that nation-states in the modern world, and in Africa, are responsible for the provision of what we label "political goods" to their citizens. Deep down, that is the primary legitimating justification for states and governments. Political leaders and ruling elites may in some circumstances, however, and certainly in Africa, utilize states for narrower purposes—to elevate an ethnic group over other ethnic groups; to gain privilege and power for a minority, a region, or sets of particular believers; or simply to shift national resources and rents from public to private hands.

Another characteristic of contemporary African politics is its zero-sum mentality. Sharing the rewards of rule is expected in Mauritius, Cape Verde, Botswana, Namibia, Ghana, Nigeria, and a few other African polities. But it is anathema to political elites in such places as the Sudan, Cameroon, Chad, both Congos, Uganda, Rwanda, Burundi, and a number of other nation-states. To rulers and ruling elites go the spoils—once.

Serving the public interest motivates a number of contemporary African heads of state and heads of government. But they constitute a minority. Many other leaders prefer to equate the interest of their political party, their lineage, their family, or their ethnic group with the general public interest. If they come from majority or dominant ethnic or language groups, they may argue that what is good for the largest constituent group within a country qualifies as the satisfaction of the public interest. Only the more responsible and responsive heads of state and heads of government promote broad, Mandela-like, conceptions of the public interest.

Democracy and Freedom

"Democracy" is less helpful than "governance" in differentiating among the nation-states of Africa. "Democracy" tells us whether a political entity holds free and fair elections, more or less, whether the regime in power tolerates dissent and opposition, whether rules of law are real, and whether the separation of power doctrine means anything on the ground. It might tell us whether the executive is constrained or not by the provisions of the country's constitution, such as term limits. But whether a nation is designated democratic or quasi-democratic tells us too little about whether or not citizens are making progress in achieving their life goals. Some democracies, even elected democracies, may adhere to democratic forms without paying more than lip service to the needs and preferences of their citizens. Moreover, even some nominal democracies are authoritarian and kleptocratic in their operations. Transactional leaders want to be reelected, but not necessarily in order to advance the best interests of their constituents.

Democracy is an imperfect optic through which to assess African attainments in the twenty-first century. Some researchers contend that there is now more of that attribute than ever before in the continent's history of independent, post-colonial, nations. They contrast the current era to earlier decades when there were more military takeovers, more madcap dictatorships, and more autocracies being propped up by Cold War rivalries and support. There has been but one successful military coup in this century. Nevertheless, as we shall see later in this chapter, many African states are still being ruled without much regard for most customary democratic practices. Public opinion, civil society discourse, and even the reasoned critiques of opposition parliamentarians make little difference to the modalities of rule for many of Africa's heads of state and heads of government.

In 2019, by at least one authoritative count, there were as many "defective democracies" (15) as there were "hard-line" autocracies (16).[1] What is more, between 2015 and 2019, much of Africa fell backward away from democracy toward more autocracy, or at least less democracy. By at least one measure, Uganda and Mozambique, once solidly democratic, became only "moderately" democratic. By another metric, more political leaders managed to evade constitutional term and age limits by abolishing both. *The Economist* reported in 2019 that twenty of Africa's fifty-four states were ruled by authoritarians.

The Freedom Scale

When Africans campaigned in the 1950s and 1960s to oust colonial overlords, they sought their freedom. Translated into KiSwahili, CiCewa, CiBemba, isiZulu, isiXhosa, Mande, Hausa, Sango, or the other languages of sub-Saharan Africa, or into French, English, or Portuguese, that was the cry of the masses mobilized behind the nationalist politicians. That every ex-colonial possession in Africa eventually gained its freedom and its independence as a nation-state hardly guaranteed the establishment of democracies. The attainment of freedom instead sometimes led to illiberal, albeit independent, governments, and to early regimes of founding fathers intent on shutting the doors behind them. This liberating generation for the most part demanded unity rather than pluralism, a neo-patrimonial grasp of spoils rather than any sharing, and an aggregation of rents and other resources to benefit dominant political parties, dominant politicians, and dominant ethnic and religious groups.

Freedom has since become an approximate synonym for democratic practice in an independent manner, with particular emphasis on the four traditional freedoms of religion, expression, assembly, and from want. (Freedom from fear was an original essential freedom, too.) The index prepared by the well-respected Freedom House, an international NGO, uses these manifestations of what it calls "freedom" and what others might call "democratic practice" to distinguish among the states of Africa. Through an elaborate annual variety of specialized opinion polls of experts, it evaluates whether a country is free, partly free, or not free. For example, in 2018 Freedom House judged Angola not free, with an overall score of 26 (of 100). Benin, Botswana, Cape Verde, and South Africa were judged free, with scores of 82, 96, 90, and 78 respectively. Burkina Faso, Côte d'Ivoire, and Nigeria were called partly free, with scores of 60, 53, and 50 respectively; Kenya scored 48, and was termed partly free. Burundi was not free, with a score of 18. The Central African Republic, Chad, Djibouti, Egypt, Equatorial Guinea, and Eritrea were termed not free, with scores of 9, 18, 26, 26, 7, and 3 respectively. Both Congos were judged not free, with scores of 17 and 21. And so on.

Freedom House's ratings depend on how well a country, as judged by panels of experts, provides political rights such as a proper electoral process, whether it permits political pluralism and encourages full participation, and how thoroughly its government functions. Answers to questions about a country's protection of civil rights and liberties depend on the extent of a country's freedom of expression, protection of individual rights, and how much respect there is for the rule of law. Freedom House's electoral process category rates countries as electoral or liberal democracies, with the latter implying a "more robust observance of democratic ideals and a wider array of civil liberties." Most of the "free" countries are liberal democracies; some of the partly free countries might qualify "as electoral, but not liberal, democracies."[2]

These ratings, helpful as they are, tell us too little about what a government is doing for its citizens. We can easily distinguish between crude autocracy and a true electoral democracy, but the differences between various kinds of electoral democracies, all judged "partly free," are hard to calibrate without a more elaborate and more fine-grained methodology. That is what "governance" provides. It also avoids the parsing of varieties of electoral conduct or the scrutinizing of a country to see if it is, in fact, a liberal democracy. (The definitions of a liberal democracy are contested.) Such adjudications prompt too many questions that depend on subjective more than objective readings of observable data. "Governance" more precisely defines whether citizens are benefiting, and how, from their incorporation into this administrative regime and not that other one.

In Africa there are democratic and nondemocratic states, and lots of in-between gradients of state. There are polities run by despotic kleptocrats, polities run tightly by unsmiling strict authoritarians, polities run by mild-mannered democrats who share power with legislators and tolerate opposition, and several additional takes on all three typologies. But in order to understand why only some of the peoples of Africa are advancing economically, politically, and socially, and why others are not, and why some are even regressing in their human results, we need to examine forms of governance, not democracy, to learn why it is that the more informative tripartite division is between the well-performing, the less-well-performing, and the underperforming states of the continent (in terms of governance).

Political Systems and Parties

Those varieties of governance work within and despite political systems that vary much more in what they produce by way of laws and governance than in their intrinsic structures and frameworks. We might, nevertheless, expect that the formal construct of each system would or could influence how governance is deployed, and how the peoples of individual states prosper and advance. We might suppose that the rule of kings, the rule of presidents within and without accompanying parliaments, and the rule of prime ministers within more traditional parliamentary systems would each differentially influence the democratic or governance attainments of their national regimes. We might further suppose that it would matter in terms of governance outcomes whether a state elected its representatives of the people by the first-past-the-post method, by proportional representation, or by some complicated combination of those two prominent governmental choice options. In terms of scores on the Index of African Governance, or on a number of other useful indexes that bear on governance, however, those distinctions of form appear to be far less important than the quality of a state's leadership and the extent to which leaders have already socialized their peoples within a political culture that is markedly democratic in ethos and intent. Leaders drive governance outcomes.

Africa has three kings, one in the north in Morocco and two in the south—in Eswatini (formerly Swaziland) and Lesotho. Each has prime ministers nominally responsible to elected parliaments, but only in Lesotho is the prime minister truly a head of government, with his monarch being largely ceremonial. In the other cases the prime ministers are less heads of government than they are chiefs of staff to the monarch. In Morocco more than Eswatini, the prime minister genuinely attempts to take the concerns of the people and the legislators to the king who, not infrequently, gives the prime minister and the legislature opportunities to enact laws on behalf of his subjects and the future of all of Morocco. Eswatini's prime minister is more of a deputy to the capricious king, and represents the monarch to parliament and voters.

A number of Africa's elected presidents together with their parliaments behave as if they were in fact monarchs, responsible to no one, except conceivably in a few cases to the officers of the national army. Those presidents dictate the direction that parliamentary representatives and the nation pursue, make decisions about fuel and grain subsidies, permit or curtail amounts and kinds of dissent, decide what and who appears in the media, determine educational curricula and offerings, erect public health facilities, expand the provision of electric power, oversee diplomatic relations, and much more. Often they decide how elections will be held, who will stand, and whether or not they will produce near unanimous or less overdetermined results. These are the electoral-authoritarian governments. Cronies of the leader actively aggrandize commercial or industrial opportunities and exert oligopolistic control of important sectors of the economy. These very tightly controlled places house political prisoners, have no free media or other easy methods of expressing opposition, rig elections (or stuff ballot boxes), and tend to establish ruling family or party dynasties. Algeria, Angola, Burundi, Cameroon, Chad, the Comoros, Djibouti, Egypt, Equatorial Guinea, Eritrea, Gabon, Mauritania, Niger, the Republic of Congo, Rwanda, Togo, and Uganda fit this description.

A third kind of political system in Africa boasts heads of states elected separately from their legislative compatriots. In those mixed parliamentary-presidential systems the executive has predominant power although the legislature can refuse to sanction pet executive projects or policies, and passes budgets and approves expenditures. This is an American-like political system despite the fact that the legislatures are all styled as parliaments, with elected speakers and committee responsibilities similar to those found in parliaments or legislatures around the English- or French-speaking world. Botswana, Burkina Faso, the Central African Republic, Côte d'Ivoire, Ghana, Liberia, Malawi, Mali, Mozambique, Namibia, Sierra Leone, Zambia, and the island states of Cape Verde, São Tomé and Príncipe, and the Seychelles are examples. Nigeria, despite its complex thirty-six-state federal arrangement, with executive and legislative authority shared between the states and the national government, is another nation-state where presidents are powerful (as are governors), but where executive authority is also shared with parliament.

The pure parliamentary model offers a fourth way of governing an African state. In keeping with that globally common approach, elected parliamentarians in turn select the leader of the majority or the largest political party to be prime minister. South Africa's parliament appoints the head of the majority party to be president, but she or he is more responsive to the dominant political party than to parliament. In the other cases, she or he serves at the pleasure of parliament, can be brought down by a no-confidence motion, and is styled head of government, not head of state. These few African states, namely Ethiopia, Mauritius, and Tunisia, also have ceremonial presidents with even less power than their European counterparts. In 2018, Ethiopia selected a woman to be its nonexecutive head of state, a first.

Somalia has a legislative assembly that elects a president who functions as head of state. But Somalia is still an undefined and little-governed political space that shares effective governance with the al-Shabaab insurgency and with local warlords. Somaliland, to its north, actually delivers services within its globally unrecognized but well-functioning jurisdiction. Freedom House labels Somaliland partly free. Somaliland uses the mixed parliamentary-presidential political mechanism to organize itself and its institutions. Libya has a UN-authorized prime minister and parliament, but they try to exert authority only in and around Tripoli, in the country's western section. Libya's eastern region, known decades ago as Cyrenaica, is led in parts by warlords, in Benghazi and its surround by an autocratic general receiving funding from Egypt and the United Arab Emirates. The self-named Sahrawi Republic of Western Sahara exists in exile in camps in western Algeria while Morocco occupies what the African Union considers a separate African territory of Western Sahara.

South Africa, alone of the democratic jurisdictions of Africa, employs an Israeli-like unvarnished proportional representational system to elect its members of parliament. At independence in 1994, the African National Congress (ANC), which Nelson Mandela was soon to lead to victory in the country's first full franchise poll, adopted proportional representation as the most expedient basis on which to hold a rapid election. That approach avoided the need to create constituencies. It also had the perhaps unanticipated effect of giving the ANC and its top leaders total control over its elected parliamentarians. They were and are beholden to the party, not to the electorate, for their seats and their incumbencies. Where party discipline in first-past-the-post parliaments is difficult to maintain except through patronage and promotions, proportional representation leaves an elected representative's votes completely at the command of the ruling party. (Subsequently, because South Africans had correspondingly little influence on their elected representatives, the latter were assigned newly delimited constituencies. They serve those constituencies but are still elected every five years according to their ranked places on the official party list.)

The more common African method of electing parliamentarians is by the first-past-the-post method (as employed in Britain, Canada, and the non-parliamentary United States). Under this arrangement, representatives are more responsible to their constituencies and often are superseded in subsequent elections by persons viewed as more loyal to new or overlooked interest groups within those constituencies. (Multiple member constituencies suffer far less from such shifting constituency loyalty tests.) In order to avoid too much independence on the part of representatives under single-member constituency systems, some African political parties insist that persons vying for parliament obtain prior approval from the party and its head office.

Clearly, parties everywhere want to exert as much control as possible over their nominal followers and candidates. In Africa, they do so mostly by fiat, and by controlling the allocation of party financial support for candidacies. In Nigeria, a special and complicated case, candidates for parliament have to purchase their candidacies with very large cash payments to their respective parties.

Overall, large sections of Africa lack representative political participation and representative democracy. Despite the undeniable fact that Africa is more democratic than it was in the 1990s—that is, now there are more nominally democratic regimes than there were then—and that the rising middle class has more influence now than it has ever had, far more relative power adheres to executives than elsewhere in the world. Party leaders still exert a vast amount of control over party members. Presidents and prime ministers either rule peremptorily or with great authority; ordinary parliamentarians have less autonomy than they would have in established (developed world) parliamentary systems. Whereas voters in mature constituency systems might be able to sway the voting tendencies of their representatives, doing so in

Africa is much more difficult, even in the purer and fuller democracies such as Botswana and Mauritius. Parties and their ruling elites still command high levels of obedience.

Elections

More freer and fairer elections are being held in Africa in recent years than ever before. Even so, holding elections need not indicate anything more democratic than adherence to outward forms and image management to appease international opinion. Ostensibly well-conducted polls tell us hardly anything about how open and inclusive a state might be, or how comfortable a ruling party administering the election might be to adverse outcomes. Nevertheless, the sheer exercise of asking voters to make choices has occasionally produced unexpected and salutary results, as in the Gambia in 2016 and Tunisia in 2014. The electoral exercise has the potential, certainly, to strengthen democratic impulses even though there are still many elections in Africa that are used simply to entrench and provide cover for existing nondemocratic or quasi-democratic regimes, as in Algeria in 2019, Cameroon in 2018, Rwanda in 2017, and Egypt in 2014.

In late 2018 and throughout 2019, Africa held several decisive elections, one after a four-year delay, two others on schedule and as open as contests with bitter rivalries and lots of covert expenditures can be expected to be. The Democratic Republic of Congo balloting was flagrantly manipulated to produce a supposedly compliant successor to eighteen-year president Joseph Kabila, who became a member of the nation's senate with the continuing power to dominate both politics and graft. But Madagascar, Namibia, and Senegal produced reasonably well regarded results and Nigeria, after a week's delay orchestrated by President Muhammadu Buhari, the incumbent, finally voted for him overwhelmingly despite fierce opposition from former vice-president Atiku Abubakr's backers and despite many allegations of vote-purchasing, missing ballots, security failures, and the like. Only 35 percent of the eligible 80 million Nigerians cast ballots, however, establishing some kind of negative African record.

All of these polling examples demonstrate that even if actual ballot stuffing is no longer what it was and even if the biased counting of results from polling stations is harder to accomplish because of mobile telephone reporting, social media news chains, and international observers, incumbents can still use their control over the airwaves and television, and also the press, to ensure that fuller pre-poll coverage goes to a ruling party. Governments still in office can and do obstruct opposition parties, especially in rural voting districts. Regimes in charge have been known to gerrymander constituencies so that urban voters presumably favorable to an opposition are underrepresented in the distribution of parliamentary seats. Or they can provide proportionally fewer actual polling places for urban citizens. That unfair distortion results in long lines of persons waiting to cast ballots; some become discouraged and go home before they can actually vote.

Even as Zimbabwe's election results in 2018 were much less compromised than they had been during the Mugabe era from 2000 to 2013, the winning Zimbabwe African National Union-Patriotic Front (ZANU-PF) still used intimidation in the overweighted rural areas, control over all media outlets, draconian legislation to obstruct freedom of assembly, an outdated voters' roll, and a refusal to revise the delimitation of constituencies to prevail over the opposition Movement for Democratic Change.

These methods are all manipulative, and sometimes difficult to detect and deflect, as in Zimbabwe's 2015 and 2013 distorted returns. But some heavy-handed incumbent governments use tougher tactics: they find excuses, as in Senegal and Benin, to bar certain candidates from running for presidential office. Or they lock up candidates, Russian style, on the eve of electoral exercises. This infamously occurred in Rwanda, although a panel of judges subsequently (long after it mattered) tossed out the charges and freed the sometime candidate.

Straightforward, fair elections do occur routinely in Botswana, Cape Verde, Mauritius, Namibia, South Africa, Ghana, and Senegal, but many other voting exercises are at least to some degree tainted by what governments do in the run-up to the actual poll, and because of their often more substantial purses. Even in places such as Nigeria, where the competition is heavy and cutthroat, the national government in power and the various state governments attempt to disrupt any level electoral playing fields that are nominally in place. In South Africa, the 2019 election was marked by skullduggery at many local levels. Too much was at stake then, and is at stake in open elections generally in Africa, for such contests to become simple, transparent, fairly administered attempts to discover the true will of the people. Indeed, Malawi's Constitutional Court went so far as to annul that country's 2019 presidential election, calling for a total re-run in 2020. The Court determined—in a first for Africa—that so many irregularities had occurred that the 2019 poll results simply could not be allowed to stand.

Governance Makes a Difference

Assessing levels of democracy and freedom are important in understanding how Africans are governed. So is an appreciation of the validity of the electoral process that ratifies democratic achievements and sometimes alters the persons and parties in charge of Africa's realization of its full economic, political, and social potential. But, in terms of a fuller sense of whether the peoples of Africa are obtaining the quantities and qualities of the political goods that they need to advance and catch up to the gains on other continents, we need to examine governance in some detail.

In order to improve outcomes for Africans, in order to provide a careful and thorough analysis of the extent to which the expectations of African citizens are being met, we measure the qualities and quantities of "governance" that Africans receive. Only by distinguishing in that manner between the more successful countries and the less successful ones is it possible to discover how those nation-states at the back of the governance queue can move forward. That is, what do the poorer performing polities need to do to provide more "governance"—more services—to their inhabitants? On which categories and sub-categories of the governance agenda should these underperforming countries concentrate so that their citizens can rise up at least to the African mean, or even up to an arbitrary global standard for service attainment?

Governance as a public good may be divided into five components or major categories. These are the political goods that people expect (sometimes only hope) that their governments will provide:

1) Security and Safety
2) The Rule of Law and Transparency (Freedom from Corruption)
3) Political Participation and Respect for Human Rights
4) Sustainable Economic Opportunity
5) Human Development: Education and Medical Services

Within each of these categories are a number sub-categories, to finely tune measurement. Fifty-seven sub-categories examine specific political goods; aggregated, they provide quantifiable results for the five categories of political good.

Security and Safety

Of these five categories of political good, the paramount one is security. Unless a country and its peoples are secure—free from invasion, free from internal conflict, free from attacks by rivals for land (as in Nigeria), free from suicide bombings by rebels—the attainment of fundamental human needs such as economic growth, personal prosperity, social advances, and the enjoyment of basic freedoms and liberties is difficult, if not impossible. That is why being secure, and having a sense of security from invasion and warfare as a resident and citizen, is such a central and overarching political good. Societies cannot easily function without the assurance of being free from attack—a reality that is lacking across large swathes of Nigeria, the Democratic Republic of the Congo, the Sudan, South Sudan, Somalia, parts of northeastern Kenya, northern Mozambique, northwestern and far northern Cameroon, southern Chad, much of the Central African Republic, parts of western Uganda, most of northern Mali, northern Niger, and northern and some of southern Burkina Faso, and eastern Mauritania. The status of the citizen is severely compromised in all of those places and regions; insecurity lurks around many a corner. Countries in Africa that harbor these major pockets of insecurity clearly are delivering governance less well than their neighbors and peers who can claim an absence of conflict either within their borders or at their borders.

A country either suffers from internal civil wars and other serious conflicts, or does not. And the seriousness of those conflicts can be ascertained by looking at the number of combat deaths recorded within a state in a year. (The internal wars of Africa are discussed in Chapter VII.) The eastern Congo, like South Sudan, is beset with several calamitous internal conflagrations: Confronting the generally under-resourced national army and UN peacekeeping forces in both jurisdictions are marauding rural desperadoes, vigilante groups, rogue armies, and a variety of non-state actors. In the North and South Kivu districts of the eastern Congo, for example, few civilians are secure from pillage, rape, and murder.

Safety within a state is a second necessary component of good governance. Being ensured of personal safety within a country means being kept safe from personal harm by government, in Africa invariably by a national government. Its task is to maintain a tight lid on crime—on robbery and burglary, for sure, but primarily on assaults and murder. Ideally, states try hard to make the streets of their cities and their far-flung rural villages safe—a daunting goal for under-resourced police forces, especially in the poorer nations.

Safety is a question of crime rates; the number of homicide deaths per hundred thousand is the usual measure, with the United States showing about 5 per 100,000, Canada 2 per 100,000, and Denmark 1 per 100,000. El Salvador in 2019 reported more homicides than any other country, with 83 per 100,000. The World Bank figure for Honduras is 57 per 100,000 and for Venezuela, 56. Jamaica's number is 47 per 100,000. Lesotho follows with a rate of 41 per 100,000. In South Africa, there are 34 homicides per 100,000 per year. The Central African Republic reports 20 per 100,000, and Mexico and Puerto Rico, 19. Homicide numbers per 100,000 in the Democratic Republic of the Congo are 13; Botswana, 10; Ethiopia 8; and Zambia, 6, all possibly underestimates.[3]

If an African state controls no more of its territory than the capital city, if it cannot project kinetic or much soft power to its peripheral borderlands, if it lacks a monopoly of force within any section (or more) of its domain, and if it fails to repress potential secessionists, then the state is insecure, unsafe, and probably on the verge of failure. Governance measures how weak, and how nearly failed, an African country may be. Declining scores can also indicate which states are in danger of slipping into the kinds of conflicts that stem from inabilities to provide much in the way of services like paved roads, schooling, and functioning health clinics. Citizens, especially from purposely disadvantaged ethnic groups, sometimes give up on their states, and defect toward a non-state actor, a warlord, or Christian or Islamist insurgent bodies.

The Rule of Law and Transparency

Once it is secure, especially, and comparatively safe, an African nation may begin to satisfy other expectations of its people. Foremost should be a mechanism to adjudicate disputes while simultaneously strengthening the norms and folkways of the nation's peoples. If this establishment or acceptance of codes and procedures to regulate the operations of the state and the interface between the state and its citizens becomes a robust and enforceable rule of law, if the state has the ability to enforce contracts and other legal agreements through the law and via appeals to its court system, then—and only then— are citizens able to resolve differences with fellow citizens or against the state without recourse to arms. When such a rule-of-law regime exists mostly in the breach, however, foreign investors, industry, and tourists stay away. Indeed, absent a formalized body of law—whether the English Common Law or the French Napoleonic Code—that is regularly and fairly applied by prosecutors and judges, and obeyed by the executive and the legislature, societal bonds can loosen, disputes become settled primarily by aggressive means, and commercial dealings become risky. Most of all, when the application of a nation's rule-of-law regime is limited or weak, and judiciaries are seen as rubber stamps for the executive, insurgencies arise and states fail.

Determining how much or how little rule of law a country provides to its citizens (the second political good) can best be approximated by the World Justice Project's Rule of Law Index, based on both hard and soft numbers for judicial independence and the like. Transparency is easily quantified by using the scores supplied annually by Transparency International's Corruption Perceptions Index, the World Bank Institute's Control of Corruption Indicator, and the national ratings of the Index of Public Integrity. (We discuss corruption and these measuring schemes at greater length in Chapter V.) Overall, corruption is weighted as highly as security and safety because it affects every other form of governance service delivery.

Political Participation and Respect for Human Rights

The third political good registers how freely and robustly citizens in a country participate in the national political process. Do they truly possess "voice"—do they have agency? Essential freedoms are intimately involved in this political good: Do citizens in practical terms engage without hindrance in elections? May they compete freely for elected office? Do national party and executive officials respect a country's presumably democratic institutions (the legislature and the courts)? Do they respect civil society and provide political space within which democracy is permitted to function? Does the political elite tolerate dissent? Are the press and the media completely or partially independent? Are the essential freedoms of religion, assembly, media, and the press, including the freedom to investigate the actions of the executive and the members of parliament, respected?

Political participation is determined by the holding of free and fair elections. Respect for human rights can be evaluated yearly by an index prepared by academic researchers who derive most of their results from official U.S. and other governmental reports.[4]

The very last two freedom categories (media and speech) are exceptionally important because a fearless, uncensored media presence is essential to the entire process of positive governance. States with media capable of investigating, interrogating, and possibly criticizing their own governments without being sanctioned or boycotted by the executive, and without fearing recrimination, safeguard citizens against official attempts to crush criticism and dissent.

Few breakdowns of civil order, few state failures, have ever occurred in polities with an open (not state-controlled or state-influenced) media. This result contrasts to the many nations that either own the main television and radio outlets outright (as in Zimbabwe) or through friendly intermediaries (as in South Africa). It further separates those few African states where the press is privately owned and critical of unwise governmental actions from the many regimes in which the media either self-censor or slavishly take the side of government without serious investigation.

Absent an independent and unthreatened media presence, accountability is harder to achieve. Politicians can more easily hide from their constituents and make decisions without much scrutiny. They can let contracts or cut other kinds of deals that only benefit insiders. Without a free media, too, the checks and balances that are meant to undergird democratic practices atrophy; lives for citizens can easily become more brutish and cruel.

Sustainable Economic Opportunity

Enjoying and benefiting from rising GDPs per capita are among the goals of most Africans. This fourth political good measures how well governments are providing those kinds of officially offered services. In addition to GDP per capita figures, we can gain helpful information from Gini-coefficient measures of inequality and from annual levels of inflation. The Gini-coefficient figures tell us what percentages of the population receive the top 1 percent and 5 percent of incomes and how little the bottom 10 and 20 percent of the people earn. That is a standard measure of inequality; most African countries, with South Africa in the lead, are among the more unequal in the world.

When states support policies directed at economic growth and fiscal probity, when they attempt to nurture a macroeconomic and fiscal environment conducive to individual and national growth, and when they make it easier to open businesses, obtain electric power, or employ labor, they are contributing to the satisfaction of this fourth political good. (No African states today reject the fundamentals of capitalism even though some still believe in the utility of state-owned or military-owned state corporations controlling critical sections of their economies, as in Algeria and Egypt.)

The responsibilities of a government under this fourth political good include such fundamentals as prudently operated national money and banking systems guided by a well-functioning Central Bank. An efficiently managed national currency is also important; using the American dollar or some other international currency in place of a national currency works as well so long as supplies of that local dollar or pound are not artificially manipulated by a government intent on arbitraging to benefit its ruling elite. The relative integrity of a country's commercial banking system is revealed by an instrument called "Contract Intensive Money"; it tells us whether citizens trust their nation's banks. Government deficits as a percentage of GDP are also relevant. Finally, data in the World Bank's annual *Doing Business* report provide a reasonable proxy for the overall corporate environment.

Furthermore, to achieve satisfactory governance scores for this fourth political good, an administration needs to construct and maintain robust arteries of commerce such as railways, roads, harbors, and airports. Otherwise, the costs of imports will soar and exports will be expensive to ship and insure. Good paved roads are critical for all-weather connections between farmers and city dwellers; Africa has the fewest paved roads per capita of any continent; more of its people than those on any other continent live more than 2 kilometers from a paved road.

Africa also has the least available electricity on any continent. This fourth good thus measures each country's electrical generating capacity. Diagnostically, it becomes immediately apparent that even the largest and most advanced African countries have paltry supplies of power. Certainly they have too little energy to support existing and future industrial developments. Even South African manufacturing enterprises and those in many other sub-Saharan African countries are subject to frequent load shedding and blackouts. Unless rural Africans turn to new small solar-powered devices, they are forced to rely for light at night on expensive kerosene lanterns or wood-burning fires. Spain alone has generating capacity sufficient to power all of sub-Saharan Africa. A small American city can power all of Nigeria. (We discuss power supplies in the next chapter.)

Given the nature of the modern economy, governance under this fourth rubric must also grow the number of people with access to broadband services. Without increased access to broadband and to modern mobile telephone networks, citizens cannot fully participate in the global economy or even attempt to sustain themselves economically. In 2019, only 11 percent of sub-Saharan Africans had regular access to broadband Internet from computers. Others accessed the Internet from their mobile telephones.

Mobile telephone usage is much higher in countries like Kenya and Uganda than it is in Madagascar or Chad. The differences in usage levels in West Africa also vary strikingly. Overall, 65 percent of sub-Saharan Africans use a mobile telephone daily and, in most countries, there is about 90 percent coverage. The weak link is the availability and power of cell towers; densely populated countries can afford an array. In more sparsely populated nations towers may end up being erected only near the main population centers. Fortunately, because diesel powered cell towers have been subject to theft of fuel and disruption because of poor roads or combat, many cell towers are now powered by the rays of the sun and solar panels. (This subject is discussed at greater length in Chapter X.)

Human Development: Education and Medical Services

After security and safety, what Africans (and most other peoples) demand of their governments are greater and greater access to educational opportunity and public health services. States have everywhere usually been the providers of such forms of political good. Although African children do sometimes attend private schools and obtain medical care at private clinics, the African state is the customary provider of these political goods for the majority of its people. Enhanced educational opportunity for Africans thus includes the provision of sufficient places in appropriate school facilities at the primary and secondary levels for citizens of each state. In the educational arena they include primary and secondary school persistence rates (rather than literacy accomplishments) for girls and boys. Those numbers allow us to decide whether a country's educational systems are strengthening outputs (more students finishing upper levels of schooling)—a general proxy for overall achievement. Accurate information on the quality of teachers (a major issue) in most countries is unavailable despite the fact that it is a crucial variable in determining educational results. Nor are there good data on textbook provisions or the physical condition of school buildings. Nowadays, access to university is required as well. The governance index can use the proxy measure of persistence to ascertain the percentage of a country's students in all three levels of education; it is a better output measure than functional literacy. But it may not do more than hint at difficulties in countries where the local educational systems are plagued by corruption, a paucity of textbooks, cramped physical spaces, and a frequent absence of teachers. Some wealthy school systems may be able to afford computers for their students, but electricity is not always available in rural areas and its delivery may be very spotty in urban schools. (For more on Africa's educational challenges, see Chapter VIII.)

On the public health side of the fifth political good, life expectancy data provide an easy way of differentiating between African states and whether health outcomes are improving or not. Since life expectancy is a major but general proxy for the health of a country, we can employ data on infant mortality and maternal mortality rates to learn in a more detailed manner whether some of the key aspects of life expectancy are improving or not. Good governance includes doing what a nation-state can do to raise the first figure and lower the second two.

Additional aspects of the public health component of this last political good offer more data on how well a country is improving the medical outcomes of its peoples. They include fundamentals such as the availability of clean water (only 50 percent of Africans now have it); modern water-borne sanitation systems (only available to 30 percent of Africans, almost none in rural areas); and easy access to medical professionals (there are more African trained midwives, nurses, and physicians in Europe and the United States than in Africa, where they gained their early expertise). Advanced technical equipment, such as X-ray machines, is scarce. Sometimes, too, as in Zimbabwe during the soaring inflationary era before 2009, basic supplies such as sutures and bandages are unavailable, thus crippling essential services and crippling governance outcomes. (For more on health advances, see Chapter IX.)

Diagnosing Weak and Strong Governance

Employing such data, specifying exactly what governance entails and analyzing outcomes under the above five categories of analysis, African governments (and civil societies, international lending institutions, and bilateral donors) can hold themselves fully accountable. And they can examine how each performs compared to the results for their peers and neighbors. The ultimate purpose of such careful measurement is diagnosis: to discover in what areas governments are performing well, and in what areas they could improve their delivery of essential services. It is also possible at a very fine-grained level to decide, using these data, on which functions of government and administration should those who govern Africa and those who assist it direct their energies. On which subcategories should executives focus political will, for the good of a nation and its peoples?

This elaborate attempt to measure governmental performance or service delivery for the peoples and nations of Africa has been embodied in the Index of African Governance, created in 2006 after a decade of experimentation, and now carried forward in a slightly less rigorous manner and issued semi-annually by the Ibrahim Foundation. In its original form, the Index was intended to rely as much as possible on objective data rather than the subjective opinions of experts or panels of experts (which provide the results for many other indexes that reflect aspects of governance and related matters).

Some of those objective data naturally have to be proxies; life expectations, country by country, offer a proxy way of ascertaining health outcomes. From the start, the Index of African Governance also measured outputs, not inputs. That is, it measured what a health budget produced (lowered maternal mortalities, say) not how much was spent by a government on health improvements (monies which might or might not have been put to good use).

The data with which to measure governance are drawn from the best available international and many national sources. The World Bank, the International Monetary Fund, the World Health Organization, the UN Development Program (UNDP), the UN International Children's Fund (UNICEF), and many other similar international bodies assemble and prepare valuable data sets on one or more aspects of governance. However, because the numbers in most of these international data banks are compiled from national African statistical offices that vary in quality and resources, the reliability of the numbers for some countries can be compromised. That is why early versions of the Index of African Governance cross-checked the international against a sampling of locally obtained data on critical components of governance.

The overall results of the measurement efforts now embodied in current versions of the Index of African Governance allow African heads of state and African villagers alike to compare their own national governance results with those of neighboring countries, but purposely not against any arbitrary global standards. The end product is a full governance portrait of each African country, now more than a dozen years old. Thus, current data are joined by very telling longitudinal assessments; it is now possible to see exactly how Africa governs itself, and how it now governs itself overall much more effectively than at the beginning of the century. Country by country, too, political leaders, civil society advocates, and corporate heads can determine what they must now do, subcategory across subcategory, to strengthen their provision and the betterment of essential services. This strengthening will be essential as Africa's people numbers explode, and as some of sub-Sahara's most impacted polities face wholly new challenges.

The Governance Results

After a dozen years of analyzing national governance in Africa, it is clear that, of Africa's fifty-four countries, ten are high-performing. Out of 100, their total scores across the subcategories of governance range from 80 to 63. Below that first group is a second, larger group of moderate performers with scores clustered from 59 to 40. A bottom group of twelve damaged and mostly failed states exhibit scores ranging from 39 to 12. The scores come from summing the subcategory scores within each category, and then adding the total category scores. Every subcategory is weighted equally within the larger category, but because some categories contain fewer subcategories, the ultimate weighting of subcategories differs even when the categories themselves are equally weighted.

The states that received the highest governance scores in 2018 were mostly African countries that consistently have been ranked since 2006 as among the top ten continent-wide. In a rank order that has included the same top five countries, and the same six out of the first ten countries, since 2006, they are: Mauritius, the Seychelles, Cape Verde, Namibia, Botswana, Ghana, South Africa, Rwanda, Tunisia, and Senegal. Kenya and São Tomé and Príncipe scored 59, just under the cut off level. All of these states are secure, although Kenya suffers incursions by al-Shabaab from neighboring Somalia. All of the high-performing states are also regarded as safe, except for South Africa, with its very high homicide levels. The first five countries have comparatively low levels of perceived corruption. All are comparatively wealthy, in the African context. Additionally, these top ten nations mostly have better roads, better health outcomes, better educational results, and reasonably free judiciaries, as compared to the rest of Africa.

A careful analysis of the performance of the African states in this first group shows that it is possible in the twenty-first century for Africans to govern themselves well. South Africa was a nation even before it became independent, free, and African-ruled under Mandela and his associates. (Arguably, that good governance could not have been achieved without Mandela's leadership.) But the others on the high-performing list had to make the transition from colony to nation by giving their peoples a new sense of identity. This was relatively easy in the more compact, less populous, places, and somewhat more difficult in the medium-sized examples, such as Ghana and Senegal. In each case, however, leaders provided the vision to bring their peoples together behind a common purpose, and to show them what good governance could deliver in terms of human outcomes.

The key ingredient in each of these well-governed states has been visionary, largely responsible, leadership. That leadership introduced a democratic political culture that enabled strong political institutions to be established and nurtured, and now to flourish. As a result, most of these top ten governance nation-states can boast strong rule-of-law regimes, thriving political institutions, respect for human rights, lower levels of corruption than average, solid security, sustainable economic prospects, relatively robust infrastructures, and educational and health outcomes that are more advanced than those of African countries lower down on the Index of Governance list. These top states attract foreign investors and donors, further build their already hefty per capita GDPs, and construct nations, not just states.

Rwanda entered this charmed circle only in 2018, a testament to President Kagame's leadership skills and his determination to build a nation out of the post-genocidal debris that his government inherited. Despite his autocratic predilections and his preference for delivering governance more then democracy, he has improved the lives of his people. Rwanda demonstrates that African states are able greatly to strengthen their services and their service deliveries. With visionary, and in this case uncompromising leadership, the lives of citizens can be uplifted. However, Kagame's undertaking provides only a partial model. Botswana's long history of development success with full democracy shows that the Khama model may be followed to benefit whole nations.

Other states, even those at the higher end of the Index of African Governance, may be able to emulate Rwanda, Ghana, and Senegal in improving their governance scores and showing that determined leadership can bring good results even to growing African populations. The following two collections of ten African states include several countries that could easily be candidates for rapid governance growth and improvement.

Moderate Performers

Those growing in their governance scores and potential attainments include Benin (58.7), which showed severe slippage in 2019, Burkina Faso (57.1), and the recently liberated Gambia (54.9). But the list of moderate performers on the governance index also includes Tanzania (where President John Magufuli appears to have defaulted from high promise into despotism), monarchical Morocco, Lesotho, Zambia (where President Edgar Lungu prefers to exercise power arbitrarily, and plans to seek a third presidential term), Malawi, Uganda, and Côte d'Ivoire. The English-speaking nations in this group are either tiny (the Gambia and Lesotho), or medium-sized. Two of the group are autocratically led, two are fledgling democracies recovering from dictatorships that were overthrown by popular action and a contested election. Several of the individual nations in the group have at one point or another since 2006 been ranked more highly than they are now, largely because of executive failures and electoral participation problems.

The next ten or so African countries in rank order are Liberia, twenty-third; and Niger (both economically poor and with substantial educational and health challenges); Mozambique (still containing two ongoing civil conflicts, and suffering from creeping authoritarianism); Sierra Leone (with major health deficiencies); Algeria (an enduring single-party autocracy); Mali, twenty-eighth (with its ongoing strife and battles against al-Qaeda in the Maghreb and ISIS); Egypt, twenty-ninth (a dictatorship imprisoning its people and fighting against ISIS); authoritarian Togo; corrupt and politically fractured, and now Russian-influenced Madagascar; Eswatini (a monarchy ruled idiosyncratically); Nigeria, thirty-third (despite President Buhari's well-voiced views about good governance), the autocratically-run Comoros; Ethiopia thirty-fifth (whose low standing cannot reflect the leadership improvements since 2018); and Cameroon, ranking thirty-sixth, which has both a long-in-office ruler and an ongoing internal war that may also be too recent to be reflected in the 2018 Index scores.[5]

The Bottom Dozen

The remaining African states, from rank-order place 37 (Guinea), and numbers 38, 39, and 40 (Djibouti, Zimbabwe, and Mauritania), are all troubled and tightly led, with poor human rights records and diminished educational and health results despite the resource riches of Guinea and Zimbabwe and the accumulated cash-producing foreign bases in Djibouti. Wealthy Gabon is forty-first with a score of 42 and Guinea-Bissau is forty-second despite its reputation as sub-Saharan Africa's primary narco-state.

The final list of African states, ranked from 43 down to 54 (Somalia) all harbor either ongoing civil wars, escalating episodes of terror, or persistent civil strife. They are all poor, by African standards, and customarily led badly. They include: Burundi, where torture of political prisoners was documented in 2018; the oil-producing but kleptocratic Republic of Congo and the possibly post-kleptocratic oil state of Angola; Chad; the Democratic Republic of Congo; Equatorial Guinea; the Sudan; and the Central African Republic, all with internal conflicts and heavy-handed, corrupt leaders. Dictatorial Eritrea, fractured and hardly functional South Sudan, and the collapsed state of Somalia bring up the rear. Except for Angola, all of the states at the end of this list are at war. All export oil except for the Central African Republic and Burundi. But Burundi has its cattle and the Central African Republic exports gold, diamonds, and timber.

Given long-running internal hostilities, given massive amounts of corruption, it is no surprise that these last dozen African states rank so low on the governance scale. Except now in Angola since the rise of the regime of President João Lourenço, they are led for the most part indifferently or autocratically. As a group of states, and individually, they provide almost no services to their citizens. Nearly all of the states harbor ongoing, violent, civil insurgencies. As nations, they deliver little to their inhabitants but strife. In some cases, their levels of corruption, with the distorted priorities that accompany large-scale graft, lead first to the criminalization and capture of their regimes, if not their states, and then to diminished human outcomes and the loss of citizens' trust in government.

Regional Governance

For a short period in the 1960s and 1970s, the nations of East Africa attempted to fashion a Nkrumah-like dream of a united Africa for themselves. But the East African Community, as it was called, collapsed because of Tanzania's envy of Kenya's economic and political dominance. Today there is a much more promising East African Community that has a legislative assembly, a central court to try transnational cases, an embryonic regional common market, and a customs union. There is talk of an East African constitution and political federation.

This experiment in regional government also includes more states than the original Community: Burundi, Rwanda, Uganda, Kenya, South Sudan, and Tanzania. But Burundi has been feuding with Rwanda and Rwanda and Uganda are not getting along. Furthermore, Kenya and Tanzania have revived their 1960s-era trade war, with Tanzania (despite the common market) imposing duties on Kenyan candies and Kenya putting retaliatory imposts on Tanzanian flour. Real integration is still distant.

Other African subregional organizations such as the Economic Community of West African States (ECOWAS) and the Southern African Development Community (SADC), which includes Mozambique and the Democratic Republic of Congo as well as all of the English-speaking countries south of the Congo, have not as yet progressed toward the establishment of real subregional governments and common markets, but they share electrical grids, legislate together, hold summits, and sometimes act forcefully in concerted manners against the makers of military coups within their specific subregions.

There is potential for the sharing of common services and for reducing tariff walls, as well as for coming to the aid of members of subregional blocs when natural disasters occur. But there is as yet little appetite to interfere as a subregion in the anti-democratic maneuvers of subregional members. (South Africa systematically refused to rein in dictatorial behavior in Zimbabwe.)

At the regional level, the African Union has long been hindered in its ability to act as a governmental instrument by its prevalent financial weakness, by the unwieldy nature of having to respond to and act on behalf of the diverse needs and preferences of the contradictorily voiced assembly of fifty-four competitors, and by the mostly authoritarian impulses of its most powerful constituents.

The newly ratified African Continental Free Trade Area may soon permit Africans to boost their trade within Africa and across countries that now purchase few goods from their neighbors. But regional governance differences may prevent its smooth implementation and full use. (This matter is further discussed in the next chapter, as are economic antagonisms between, for example, Ethiopia and Egypt and others.)

Governance and Democracy: The Future

Creating good governance and sustainable democratic political cultures throughout the large sections of Africa that are edging in those directions or are as yet still resistant to such disruptions of existing autocratic ways of rule will depend on the emergence of a new generation of self-aware and forward-looking leaders (as Seretse Khama was in the 1960s), a deepening of the influence of middle class voters and opinion makers, and, thanks to both of those trends, the building and strengthening of political institutions (like the rule of law) capable of curtailing the neo-patrimonial executives who have so far been influential in retarding Africa's economic, social, and political growth.

Such evolutionary changes will result in executives controlling less of government and less of national politics than they now do. Opposition parties will be more able than now to compete on level playing fields. More elections will be fully fair. Minorities and disadvantaged ethnic groups will have as many rights as majorities and favored ethnicities, lineages, and clans. Democratic norms and procedures of all kinds in many nations will embrace such globally-favored practices as plural democracy, which enhances the performance of good governance. Mandela's emphasis on inclusivity will become more of a common expectation and insistence.

When many of these alterations in the fabric of governance take place, Africa will have made a healthy transition from autocracy and incomplete governance to the consolidation of democracy. The trend is in that direction, and will accelerate as the middle class grows larger and bourgeois values predominate more completely than in the past.

IV | African Economies and Their Challenges

POPULATION NUMBERS THROUGHOUT most of Africa will continue to increase severely in most parts of Africa for the next thirty years. Unless women in sub-Saharan Africa suddenly cease having more than two and sometimes as many as seven children, the gross labor force, unskilled and skilled, in almost every country will continue to grow despite existing, alarming, formal unemployment rates of 40 percent or more. To meet the minimum income needs of their citizens, to create a more robust consumer society, to grow the tax base on which governments fund their provisions of services and welfare, and to attract more and more external investment, sub-Saharan nation-states hence need to create jobs—the smarter, the more enduring, and the more capable of contributing a beneficial multiplying boost the better. New jobs are the key to sub-Saharan Africa's future—to its increased prosperity, to its fuller integration into world trading systems, and to winning its several internal battles against fundamentalist insurgents and other ostensible revolutionaries.

Nothing can contribute more to sub-Saharan Africa's peaceful and successful modernization than the creation of new employment opportunities in numbers sufficient to match inevitable rises in population numbers and the size of national youth bulges. If those job increases can be engineered through the establishment of export processing zones, new manufacturing industries, beneficiation of mineral resources, attention to agriculture, the growth of tourism, and the origin and marketing of new kinds of services, Africa and its peoples will benefit and their national economies expand.

Getting there, despite the fact that many sub-Saharan African countries are trying to grow rapidly off a low base, will not be easy or simple. Africa is the globe's poorest continent, with a sub-Saharan African average annual GDP per capita in 2018 of $1,574 . A full 65 percent of sub-Saharan Africans earn less than $2 per day. Ninety percent of all 200 million Nigerians are living below the national poverty line of $1.90 a day. So are 60 percent of Congolese (Kinshasa) and 25 percent of Ethiopians and 15 percent of all South Africans. Without new formal jobs, even the steady drift into the informal sector—vending from regulated stalls, roadside selling, urban hawking, auto-parking hustles, and crime—cannot hope to provide most persons aged 18 to 34 (and others) with the kinds of incomes that would enable them to feel wanted and productive, much less able to clothe and feed themselves adequately. Farming is a declining pursuit in many large countries; we cannot begin to hope that the land will absorb all of these (surplus) workers. Nor are there any non-resource bonanzas on the horizon to provide succor for individuals and countries.

National Average GDPs per Capita

Using per capita GDP data, we find that sub-Saharan Africans subsist on incomes as low as $244 a year. Ten nation-states show earnings below $1,000 per year. The people of another thirteen nation-states manage somehow on less than $2,000 per year. The citizens of just five polities earn between $2,000 and $3,000, bringing them to the brink of middle-income status. Nine nations may be considered successfully middle income, with GDPs per capita between $3,000 and $5,000 annually. All of the countries in sub-Saharan Africa with incomes above $5,000—ranging upward to $28,000— are the truly wealthy countries, a total of twelve that include the major petroleum exporters, diamond and precious metal producers, several countries with remunerative tourist industries, and two that are manufacturers. Several belonging to this wealthiest group are among Africa's most sparsely populated; three are islands; one has an advanced infrastructure; another is the continent's most populous. One harbors three ongoing civil conflicts. Not all, but a number of these wealthy nations are, by continental standards, among the best governed and best managed. Most are among the continent's least corrupt entities; two, however, are rampantly corrupt. Thus, given these snappy sketches, there are no easy generalizations to make about either

Africa's wealthiest or its poorest countries. Indeed, even some of the countries with the most abundant natural resources (such as the Democratic Republic of Congo) are still comparatively poor while tiny places like the Seychelles, with no mineral resources, are immensely rich. And wealth per capita also hides unequal distributions of resource rents, as in Angola and Equatorial Guinea. In both of those last countries ruling elites are rich while most inhabitants are poor and deprived of basic services. Ethiopia, although poor, can claim the distinction of being sub-Saharan Africa's most equal economy.

According to World Bank figures (2018), the poorest African jurisdictions are the war-torn South Sudan ($244), Somalia ($499), and the Central African Republic ($725). Slightly wealthier and also conflict-ridden and dictatorial is Burundi ($770), along with Liberia ($826), Eritrea ($844), and the Democratic Republic of Congo ($887), all under $1,000. Those are the poorest of the poor. (The Western Hemisphere's poorest nation is Haiti, with a 2018 GDP per capita of $868.)

Group II, the struggling poor in Africa, from $1,000 to $2,000 average annual GDPs per capita, includes Niger ($1,016), Zimbabwe ($1,080), Malawi ($1,202), Mozambique ($1,247), Sierra Leone ($1,526), Madagascar ($1,555), the Comoros ($1,552), Togo ($1,570), Guinea-Bissau ($1,740), the Gambia ($1,714), Burkina Faso ($1,870), Uganda ($1,864), Ethiopia ($1,891), and Chad ($1,941).

Five countries comprise Group III, the not yet middle-income nations, up to $3,000 in annual average per capita incomes: Rwanda ($2,036), mineral-rich Guinea ($2,194), Benin ($2,266), Senegal ($2,712), and Tanzania ($2,946).

Those African nations with average annual per capita GDPs between $3,000 and $5,000 may be considered fully middle income: labor-providing Lesotho ($3,130), Kenya ($3,285), the islands of São Tomé and Príncipe ($3,351), Cameroon ($3,694), Mauritania ($3,949), cocoa-producing Côte d'Ivoire ($3,953), copper-rich Zambia ($4,050), cocoa-growing and oil-pumping Ghana ($4,641), and the Sudan ($4,903).

Comparative incomes in North Africa are: Egypt ($2,495), Morocco ($3,007), Tunisia ($3,491), Algeria ($4,123), and Libya ($7,798). The last two are petroleum producers; the first depends mostly on agriculture and natural gas exploitation. Libya's GDP per capita does not necessarily reflect worsening violence and petroleum exporting difficulties in 2019.

The wealthiest countries (over $5,000) of sub-Saharan Africa, on an annual per capita basis, are topped by the tiny, sparsely populated, tourist-dependent, Seychelles ($28,963), small, very corrupt, and petroleum-pumping Equatorial Guinea ($24,816), fabric and electronics assembler Mauritius

($22,278), oil-and iron-rich Gabon ($18,183), Botswana, with diamonds and tourism ($17,354), South Africa ($13,497), Namibia ($10,475), with uranium, copper, and diamonds, Eswatini ($8,496), Cape Verde ($6,831), Angola, Africa's second largest oil exporter ($6,388), giant Nigeria, Africa's largest oil producer ($5,860), and the Republic of Congo ($5,359), which also has petroleum resources. Sub-Saharan Africa as whole contains both bit-terly poor countries and comparatively rich ones. Table 4.1 contains the full data, by nations and groups.

Another way of looking at wealth creation is to examine which coun-tries are growing rapidly. Ethiopia, off a low base, grew at 9.2 percent a year in 2019 and 7.7 percent in 2018 as a result of new, Chinese-sponsored, export processing zones and shoe and textile manufacturing activity. Thanks to its oil discoveries, Ghana has been growing at 6 percent. Others experiencing exceptional increases in annual GDPs per capita include Rwanda, Côte d'Ivoire, Senegal, Benin, Kenya, Uganda, Tanzania, and Burkina Faso—all benefiting from rising agricultural and mineral prices. Lesotho, with labor exports to South Africa and some textile shipments to the United States, has been growing at more than 4 percent per annum. South Africa, however, is hardly growing at all, and in recent years has been in recession for several quarters. Nigeria is also growing more slowly than its peers.

As a whole, sub-Saharan Africa's economic growth spurt mostly ended in 2016 and 2017, with the region as a whole rising less than 1 percent in 2017. But 2018 was better and 2019 achieved an overall sub-Saharan African growth rate of 3.8 percent. (Nigeria, South Africa, and Angola were low

TABLE 4.1 Africa's GDPs Per Capita, c. 2019

   I - S. Sudan, $244; Somalia, $499; CAR, $725; Burundi, $770; Liberia, $826; Eritrea, $844; DRC, $887

  II - Niger, $1,016; Zimbabwe, $1,080; Malawi, $1,202; Ethiopia, $1,891; Chad, $1,941

 III - Rwanda, $2,036; Guinea, $2,194; Benin, $2,266; Senegal, $2,712; Tanzania, $2,946

 IV - Lesotho, $3,130; Kenya, $3,285; Morocco, $3,000; Zambia, $4,050; Ghana, $4,641; Sudan, $4,903

  V - Nigeria, $5,860; Angola, $6,300; Cape Verde, $6,831; Namibia, $10,700; S. Africa, $13,400; Botswana, $18,300; Gabon, $18,183; Mauritius, $22,278; Eq. Guinea, $24,816; Seychelles, $28,963

performers but the rest of sub-Saharan Africa grew more than 5 percent in 2019.) Even at that relatively acceptable overall rate, sub-Saharan Africa will not be able to keep pace with the enormous surge in its population numbers. Creating sufficient new jobs thus becomes difficult, if not impossible, when economic advances lag behind population rises.

Inflation detracts both from growth and GDP increases. Incoming investment slows or ceases. A number of African countries, such as the Sudan and South Sudan, in recent years endured annual inflation levels as high as 70 percent. Zimbabwean inflation levels in 2019 reached at least 42 percent; Nigeria's inflation in 2019 was about 25 percent. On average, in 2019, sub-Saharan Africa's annual inflation increases were nearly 15 percent, a subtraction from stability and a break on improved betterment attainments. Furthermore, most of these relatively high inflation values reflected escalating prices of primary foodstuffs, hitting the poorest citizens the hardest. (Food fills the main part of the consumption baskets that most African nations employ to calculate their inflation numbers. It is also important to note that inflation in Africa usually follows food production declines because of rain failures and droughts. Import price hikes can also add to the burden. So can inflation in Africa result from interest rate shifts overseas that cause domestic currencies to depreciate.)Whatever the cause, when the inflation number exceeds about 20 percent it really begins to affect developmental prospects deleteriously.

National improvement prospects throughout most of Africa south of the Sahara are also retarded by shortages of revenue. The fiscal capacity of sub-Saharan African states has long been constrained. Many countries have value added or sales taxes, and these provide welcome revenues. Others rely on customs imposts. Several are more dependent than they would like to be on budgetary and project support from donors.

Hardly any African country has managed to collect income taxes in a meaningful manner. In Europe, the Americas, and Asia, states on average are able to collect 40 percent or so of GDP. In Africa, collecting 20 percent of GDP through taxes is a goal, rarely met. The effective collection levels in many jurisdictions are 12 percent and lower, and more of the total comes from large enterprises, not from formal smaller businesses or many individuals. The informal sector, fully 34 percent or more of the overall economy of Africa as a whole, pays almost no taxes. (North America's informal sector comprises only about 9 percent of its economy.)[1]

This is in part a circular problem. If potential taxpayers were receiving the services that they desired and if they believed that their rulers were transparent about how revenues were expended and were accountable for the results of those expenditures, citizens might prove less reluctant to pay taxes. And without such revenues, the delivery of services, overall performance, and good governance obviously suffers. Moreover, to administer an equitable taxing regime, the government needs funds for civil service salaries.

Africa's better governed states have fewer problems collecting taxes, but even in those dozen or so polities, the people's understanding of the role of taxation is largely absent, and naturally resented. But Africa will modernize only slowly and haphazardly until it can obtain substantially more tax revenue routinely.

Petroleum and Natural Gas

Without petroleum gushing out of (mostly) undersea reservoirs, sub-Saharan Africa's biggest producers would have far fewer compellingly large export prospects. Before global prices collapsed in 2017, Africa was generating immense profits and hefty rents from its oil extraction industry. Much of those generous proceeds found their way into politician-connected pockets. Nigeria and Angola, at 2.2 million and 1.9 million barrels a day, respectively, are by far the major producers. They rank thirteenth and sixteenth, respectively, in terms of global output totals. Two land drillers, Algeria and Egypt, follow in terms of production values, but Egypt and Libya's totals (on good days) are about half of those of Algeria (582,000 and 528,000 versus 1.1 million barrels per day). Africa's sixth largest provider of petroleum is Equatorial Guinea, with a modest total of 317,000 barrels a day, followed by South Sudan at 255,000 barrels per day (on good days, when clashes between warring parties are infrequent), the Republic of Congo at 227,000 barrels per day, and Gabon at 210,000 barrels each day. The remaining dozen African producers of oil supply between 160,000 and 20 barrels a day to the global market. New producers like Ghana, Kenya, and Uganda are expected shortly to join the ranks of serious suppliers of petroleum.

Allegedly, the Democratic Republic of Congo, which now pumps about 25,000 barrels a day from wells along its Atlantic Ocean coast, also holds massive reserves of underground petroleum, some adjacent to continental shelf waters already successfully exploited by Angola. There is even more petroleum, geologists say, in the eastern and central sections of the vast Congo. An absence of pipelines, difficult logistics, and civil war all inhibit proving and then pumping that underground oil. Additionally, corruption in the Congo and in its oil sector is already so intense that controlling officials seem perversely to approve the same deals over and over (rents), without ever granting serious concessions to companies from overseas.

Africa has also become a significant exporter of liquefied natural gas from proven reserves in Algeria, the world's fifth largest producer by value, and from Nigeria, the thirteenth biggest producer by value. Angola, Equatorial Guinea, and Libya are the next most prominent producers, but they rank twenty-eighth, twenty-ninth, and thirtieth globally by value, each with less than 1 percent of total global production in 2017. Nigeria satisfies 2.5 percent of the global demand and Algeria about 6 percent. Serious supplies of natural gas have also been proven in Mozambique and in its coastal waters, and offshore in neighboring Tanzania.

The Other Exports

In addition to the black gold of petroleum and the natural gas that is its sometime by-product, sub-Saharan Africa's soils harbor a vast array of hard minerals, many of which have long been either extracted from underground deep deposits or removed from great open pits reachable from the surface by oversized excavating equipment. It also sells numerous agricultural products that supply niche markets in Europe, China, and the United States. But, in the summary listings that follow, note that sub-Saharan Africa is predominantly a producer of unprocessed raw materials, whether dug from or grown in the ground. Except for South Africa and Ethiopia, and smatterings elsewhere such as textiles in Lesotho, there are no significant manufacturing nodes on the sub-continent. Agriculture remains labor intensive, and so does underground mining, but much of the other mineral deposits are more and more exploited with imported machinery. Sub-Saharan Africa as a whole cannot hope to provide abundant new jobs given its contemporary dependence for foreign exchange earnings on the export of petroleum, natural gas, hard minerals, and farmed crops to wealthy countries in the developed world. Note, too, that only South Africa, Nigeria, and Angola each receive more than $10 billion annually for their total exports.

Except partially for South Africa, petroleum revenues, and then mineral returns, drive export earnings everywhere in Africa. Nigeria's petroleum shipments, now more to China and Europe than to the United States, are worth about $45 billion annually, depending on the world price of crude oil. Included in that yearly export amount are almost insignificant sales of cocoa and oil seeds. Less than 1 percent of the total consists of manufactures and cement. Angola's oil returns amount to $26 billion a year, with diamonds being responsible for 1 percent of the total. China, India, and the United States are Angola's main export partners. Equatorial Guinea, with $4 billion worth of petroleum sales, also survives entirely because of oil. India, China, and South Korea buy most of it.

South Africa still digs out large quantities of gold and smaller carats of diamonds. It also has iron ore deposits, platinum, palladium, manganese, ferrochrome, and much coal. It exports motor vehicles, steel, electrical and mechanical machinery, citrus fruits, a little aluminum, and beer and spirits. Of its $90 billion worth of exports, about 32 percent goes to Asia, 23 percent to Europe, 8 percent to the United States, and the remainder to Africa.

The Democratic Republic of Congo mines diamonds, copper, cobalt, cadmium, gold, coltan (a mixture of columbium and tantalum), tin, and tungsten, all worth more than $8 billion annually in recent years. More than 53 percent by value of those minerals is sent to China, 24 percent to nearby Zambia for processing and shipping (presumably for transfer to Europe). Only 6 percent is exported directly to Belgium.

Zambia is one of the largest producers of copper in the world, with total sales of more than $5 billion a year, along with another $0.5 billion worth of gemstones, tobacco, and maize. Its biggest trading partners are China, India, South Africa, and the United Arab Emirates. Guinea's bauxite exports are now matched by the diggings from a new, rich, iron ore body; China buys both resources, and is directly exploiting the iron deposits. Zimbabwe mines ferrochrome, nickel, gold, and platinum, plus some iron ore and coal, its total exports (half of which are Virginia tobacco) reaching about $2.2 billion in total. Malawi ships flue-cured tobacco to China, sugar and tea to Europe, and dried legumes and some maize to its neighbors—all worth $1.4 billion yearly.

Botswana is the world's largest producer of gem diamonds, exporting yearly more than $5 billion worth, plus some beef and electrical equipment to Asia, Europe, the United States, and South Africa. Namibia vacuums diamonds from coastal sea floor deposits and has one of the largest (now Chinese-owned) open-pit uranium mine properties in the world. It also exports fish, zinc, and copper, the overall total worth $3.5 billion, with more than 40 percent by value going to Europe, another 40 percent to African countries, and the remainder to Asia and the United States.

In West Africa, Sierra Leone's $1 billion worth of commodity sales include crustaceans, iron ore, diamonds, and titanium. China, Belgium, Côte d'Ivoire, and Romania buy those goods. France, Belarus, and China receive the Central African Republic's gold, timber, and cotton, worth $200 million a year. Liberia yearly ships a total of $200 million worth of gold, iron ore, rubber, coffee, and timber to Poland, Switzerland, the Netherlands, the United Arab Emirates, the United States, and China.

From East Africa, Kenya exports $5 billion worth of tea, cut flowers, coffee, legumes, and titanium, mostly to the United States, the Netherlands, Pakistan, Uganda, and the United Kingdom. Uganda's $3 billion worth of exports consist of gold, coffee, tobacco, tea, and cocoa beans; these products go to the United Arab Emirates (presumably for reshipment), and to Uganda's African neighbors: Kenya, Rwanda, and South Sudan. Tanzania is a shipper of $6.4 billion worth of gold, diamonds, tobacco, cashews, coconuts, and dried legumes to India, the United Arab Emirates, Switzerland, South Africa, and China. Rwanda's $1 billion worth of commodities include coffee, gold, tantalum, vanadium, zirconium, and tin. It sends those commodities to the Democratic Republic of Congo, the United Arab Emirates, Kenya, Thailand, and the United States.

After aluminum processed from imported alumina and bauxite (largely because of the availability of inexpensive hydroelectricity), Mozambique's leading export, mostly clandestine, is heroin. Imported from Pakistan via Somalia and Zanzibar, or directly into its own northernmost ports, it has become exceedingly profitable. Mozambique transships heroin either to South Africa, for sale there, or onward by air to Britain and Europe. The Mozambican trade mirrors the heroin shipped to Europe from Kenya and Somalia, and also imported by sea in dhows from Pakistan.

In the Horn of Africa, coffee is the key foreign exchange earner (a total of $3 billion yearly) for Ethiopia, much of it going to the United States, but manufacturing is becoming increasingly important, comprising 10 percent of exports. China and Europe receive those products, mostly shoes and textiles. Gold is still significant. From its farms, Ethiopia ships cut flowers to Europe, along with sesame, and qat, which it exports locally. Saudi Arabia, Germany, and Switzerland are other major recipients of shipments from Ethiopia. Newly befriended Eritrea produces gold, animal products, and hides and skins for sale mostly to its Red Sea neighbors. Crude oil shipments comprise nearly all the $1.5 billion exports from both the Sudan and South Sudan. Nearly all of their crude oil goes to China and Malaysia.

Overall Trade

Sub-Saharan Africa's total annual exports are valued at about $122 billion, with imports averaging about $161 billion, resulting in a substantial trade deficit often met through borrowing and foreign assistance. Raw materials comprise more than a third of all exports, intermediate goods another third, consumer goods about a fifth. As a percentage of total regional GDP, exports amount to 27 percent and imports to 31 percent. (See also the discussion of China's trade with Africa in Chapter VI.)

As already noted, the five key sub-Saharan African exports are petroleum and natural gas ($85 billion), gold ($14 billion), diamonds ($8 billion), bituminous coal ($4 billion), and ferrochrome ($3 billion). The key imports are raw and refined petroleum ($19 billion), pharmaceuticals ($3 billion), uncut diamonds ($2 billion), and electrical and electronic equipment ($2 billion). Table 4.2 details these amounts.

The region's major purchasers of commodities are China (8 percent of the total), India (6 percent), the United States (6 percent), South Africa (from other African states, 5 percent), and Germany (5 percent). The main providers of imports are China (18 percent), South Africa (8 percent), Germany (7 percent), India (6 percent), and the United States (6 percent). Because Africa does not belong to one of the globe's big trading blocks, it is handicapped. It also lacks any trading center of gravity.

There are few surprises: In recent years China has eclipsed the United States to become the main provider of imports and buyer of exports after the nations of the European Union. As a supplier of imports, China has managed to be more efficient than many in-country African industries and, as a consequence, has driven many locally based African firms (including textile manufacturers in northern Nigeria) to suspend operations. African consumers

TABLE 4.2 Africa's Trade: Main Exports and Imports, 2018

• Total Exports	$122 billion
– Petroleum and Gas	$85 billion
– Gold	$14 billion
– Diamonds	$8 billion
– Ferrochrome	$3 billion
• Total Imports	$161 billion
– Refined petroleum	$19 billion
– Pharmaceuticals	$3 billion
– Uncut diamonds	$2 billion
– Electronics	$2 billion

have benefited through lower prices, but the growth of indigenous industry has often been crippled.

In terms of African incomes, without China's purchases Africa would be less wealthy than it now is, and far less well poised to cope with its on-rush of new people. Africa's prosperity and its ability to meet the needs of its many millions of future people hence depend primarily on the health of China's domestic economy. So long as China requires Africa's petroleum, copper, ferrochrome, tobacco, and more, so African countries will have the possibility of prospering (or at least maintaining the economic status quo) through the sale of their abundant primary resources. Were China to reduce its purchases, or shift exclusively to Australasia, the peoples of Africa would suffer. Western nations, India, and Japan are now and would in the future be unable to take up the slack. Moreover, China is the global pricing leader for so many of the primary resources that Africa sells; without China's de-mand, African mineral supplies would find few buyers and whole national economies would falter. Delivery of satisfactory services would be difficult. Without Chinese purchases now and for the next three decades, Africa has no way of attempting to satisfy the service needs and consumer expectations of its burgeoning populations.

Industry and Manufacturing

Clearly, most of the countries of sub-Saharan Africa are positioned precar-iously between a population juggernaut that is barreling down on them at relentless speed and a decidedly languid ability to produce the jobs, incomes, and social benefits that could—in theory—provide a welcome way of buffering onrushing demographic numbers. Sub-Saharan Africa will shortly host the largest unemployed and underemployed labor pool in the world. In Southeast Asia, in the late twentieth century, population increases were absorbed by new industrial opportunities, mostly in and for the telecom-munications sector. Can sub-Saharan Africa, with a vast potential mass of underserved consumers, produce similar kinds of outcomes? How might the region as a whole or, more likely, a number of countries within the region, conjure such a beneficent result?

In sub-Saharan Africa only 10 percent (and falling) of the region's cur-rent GDP comes from manufacturing. Investment in this economic area from private and public, domestic and international, sources is low, and not increasing appreciably. British and American legislation gives preferential access to a variety of goods manufactured in sub-Saharan Africa, but only a handful of African countries attempt to take advantage of such tariff-reducing possibilities.

Only a few African examples can be considered positive precursors. Mauritius de-emphasized the cultivation of sugarcane, its colonial staple and major foreign exchange earner, when it achieved independence. Under far-seeing leaders, Mauritius created export processing zones for textile manufacturing and then moved upstream to wool fabric processing (Mauritius has few sheep) and, finally, to telecommunications and electronics assembling. It attracted Taiwanese and Indian investments, prospered, and now is the second most wealthy non-oil earner per capita in the African Union. Today, its $3 billion worth of exports include processed fish, textiles, electronic equipment, raw sugar, molasses, cut-flowers, non-knit men's shirts, knit t-shirts, and diamonds (the last presumably in transit). France, the United States, the United Kingdom, South Africa, and Italy are the main destinations of Mauritius' products.

Ethiopia has much more recently established export-processing zones. The successes of its industries, especially the manufacturing of shoes from locally tanned leather and the knitting of fabrics in those zones, has contributed to Ethiopia's recent rapid economic growth experiences. A Chinese-owned concern produces pharmaceuticals outside of Addis Ababa. Industry is new to Ethiopia, but with official support and Chinese entrepreneurial training, Ethiopia is managing to reduce its high levels of unemployment. That has meant attracting labor away from less productive agricultural pursuits, a model that other large sections of sub-Saharan Africa could presumably pursue if the overseas markets were available and the costs of labor were competitive.

There are successful manufacturing examples elsewhere in Africa, too. In Nigeria, Chinese-owned factories smelt steel and make ceramic tiles and cardboard boxes. In Lesotho, Chinese and Taiwanese companies make various kinds of clothing, including jeans and athletic wear, for American and European chain stores. There are Chinese-sponsored Free Trade Zones in Benin, Djibouti, Ethiopia, Nigeria, and Zambia, and an Indian-backed Free Trade Zone in Mauritius.

Uganda and Zambia are also advancing in manufacturing, in both cases growing this sector by 5 percent a year (from a low base). Zambia is fabricating its own copper into exportable products (also called beneficiation). Uganda processes its own coffee and tea, has a new gold refinery, and produces steel, cement, and fertilizer. Nigeria is Africa's largest producer and exporter of cement.

But, even in Ethiopia and in long-industrialized South Africa, the real costs of labor in Africa are higher than in comparable situations in Asia. Among the major obstacles to Africa becoming the next assembly outpost for American and European telecommunications equipment, or even a stitcher of first or second resort in the chain of clothing production (as in Bangladesh, Cambodia, Laos, Nepal, Sri Lanka, and Vietnam), are real labor costs.

Comparing nearly six thousand enterprises in twenty-nine countries, researchers at the Center for Global Development in Washington, DC, concluded that factories in Africa were 39 to 50 percent more expensive to open and run (depending on size, with larger firms more costly) than similar operations in Asia and South America. Even establishments in an experienced African industrialized state such as South Africa were more costly than they were elsewhere. Labor charges are very high there despite massive unemployment; restrictive laws regulate how workers work. Relatively high minimum wages curtail South Africa (and Africa's) ability to compete on cost grounds against (particularly) Asian factories. South Africa and Africa also lose out because of educational deficits and shortages of skills in the labor force. Then there are infrastructural impediments such as contorted and high cost transportation networks and, even in South Africa, unstable electric power supplies. The prevalence of red tape and corruption (discussed below) also hurts.

South Africa has the advantage of long years of industrial activity and well-functioning ports on established waterways of commerce. Kenya, Tanzania, Ghana, and Senegal also have harbors on major shipping lanes and the last two states are relatively close to Europe. But even those latter four states, with several potential commercial advantages over, for example, Africa's sixteen landlocked countries and those that suffer from poor governance or civil conflict (or both), are less robust growth candidates than they might appear. Their labor is too expensive: combining all factors of production (high minimum wages, power charges and availability, ease of transport, restrictive regulations, etc.) the real labor cost of a Kenyan worker is more than $2,000 a day; in Bangladesh the cost per worker (on the same basis) is under $1,000 a day. Likewise, the capital cost of a Kenyan industrial employee is estimated to be $10,000 versus $1,100 in Bangladesh. Kenya's GDP per capita income is marginally higher than Bangladesh's, but Senegal, with a GDP per capita number under Bangladesh's, still has labor and capital costs per worker that are double those of Bangladesh. Only Ethiopia, where European fashion brands are beginning to produce goods, can claim labor costs roughly at the Bangladeshi level.[2]

Several African countries have tried to gain competitive edge by reducing the costs of doing business, as measured by the World Bank's annual *Doing Business* report. In Ethiopia, Kenya, Malawi, Rwanda, Tanzania, and Uganda it is now easier to open an enterprise (more often a service than an industrial entity) than it was in the past. But, as a World Economic Forum study concluded, most African countries perform poorly in terms of such criteria as political stability, governance effectiveness, regulatory quality, and—critically—the rule of law.

Another measure of the African business environment is exemplified by the novel Global Markets Complexity Index, first issued in 2019 to cover eighty-three countries across thirty-one components such as market, regulatory, and operational complexity. Singapore, the Nordics, Australia, and the United States rank in the top of eight categories ("most valuable") while Zimbabwe, Nigeria, Mali, Togo, Pakistan, and Bangladesh are in the bottom group ("only the brave"). Mauritius rates highly, in the second ("utility players") designation, and Botswana, Namibia, Morocco, and Tunisia are in the fifth cohort ("upstream paddlers"). The other African countries listed are in the sixth and seventh (of eight) designations.

As a collective, moreover, Africa lacks a sizable regional, integrated market, essential for industrialization. Intra-African trade amounts to only 16 percent of all trade, as compared to 51 percent in Asia and 72 percent in Europe, and only a small portion of that intra-regional trade is locally sourced (as opposed to coming from Asia and Europe). There have been recent attempts to create such a sizable African trading bloc beyond the existing East African, southern African, and West African internal customs arrangements, but until 2019 too little came of those efforts, and of the trade synergies that a commercially united Africa would create.

In midyear, however, the Gambia became the twenty-second state to sign the African Union's African Continental Free Trade Area agreement. Nigeria joined a few weeks later, giving heft and promise to Africans hoping to reduce tariff barriers across the continent. (Of all fifty-four states, only Eritrea refused to sign.) Both the Gambia's ratification and Nigeria's accession set in motion potentially the world's largest common market, with 1.3 billion people now, and many more to come. The area's combined GDP is $2.6 trillion and its annual consumer spending about $1.4 trillion.[3] Africans hope that the new free trade zone will lead to massively reduced tariffs, generate new employment possibilities, mesh the operations of existing subregional trade zones, and increase intra-African trade by as much as 52 percent. All of these cited realities, plus much of sub-Saharan Africa's historic dependence on the exploitation of its primary resources and its resulting lack of manufacturing experience, will inhibit the region's shift from digging and harvesting to a reliance for jobs and incomes on factory outputs.

Tourism

Tourism is already a large earner of foreign exchange for several African nations even though experts in the field assert that the annual number of visitors is much lower than a continent with rich historic and natural resources deserves. More than 63 million tourists came to Africa in 2017, an increase of 9 percent over 2016.

Expansion of this sector is conceivable, again depending on labor costs, improved infrastructures, and strengthened governance.

In 2017, Africa's biggest tourism earners were South Africa ($8.8 billion), Egypt ($7.7 billion), Morocco ($7.42 billion), Nigeria ($2.5 billion), Tanzania ($2.3 billion), Mauritius ($1.7 billion), Tunisia ($1.3 billion), the Sudan ($1 billion), Kenya ($0.93 billion), Uganda ($ 0.92 billion), Ghana ($ 0.85 billion), and Botswana ($ 0.7 billion)—a total of about $30 billion. For comparison, U.S. tourism receipts for the same period were $210 billion, Spain $68 billion, and Thailand $57 billion.

In terms of the World Economic Forum's Tourism and Travel Competiveness Index for 2017, Africa's leading countries were South Africa, Mauritius, Kenya, Namibia, Cape Verde, Botswana, Tanzania, and Rwanda, in that descending order. The Forum rates performance in this realm according to a state's business environment, safety and security, health and hygiene, human resource and labor market, and ICT readiness. Chad, Burundi, the Democratic Republic of Congo, and Mauritania were the African countries least ready to welcome tourists.

One of the key missing ingredients in the African tourism picture is the failure of most African countries to open their skies to competitive and increased airline connectivity. Too much depends on the lengthy negotiating of bilateral agreements between countries within or outside of Africa. Air travel charges are comparatively higher than they are in Asia and South America, and much higher than in Europe. A number of African airports and immigration authorities are not yet receptive to tourists. Furthermore, too many sub-Saharan countries apply ticket taxes and airport charges above the world average, inhibiting large-scale tourism.

Sometimes it is easier and less expensive to fly from one African destination to another via Europe since cross-African travel by air is at best difficult, despite Ethiopian Airways' various attempts to knit west and east, and north and south Africa, much more effectively than ever before. Ethiopia's Addis Ababa airport is seeking to become a bigger arrival hub (in terms of visitors) than Johannesburg, in South Africa. The World Economic Forum believes that air transport and the air infrastructure are the biggest challenges for travel and tourism development in Africa.

Second, members of Africa's middle class are not yet touring their own continent. The large amounts of cash that intraregional tourists spend so well in Asia and Europe are absent in Africa. As the middle class in Africa grows in number and in purchasing power, a potentially large consumer demand may be stimulated. Only in South Africa, and from South Africa to neighboring countries, does it already exist. For the time being Africa thus will be compelled to continue to rely for sizable boosts to its tourism industry on Americans and Europeans crossing the seas, and on Chinese visitors, mostly arriving in large groups.

Third, Africa is not husbanding its natural resources and natural beauty as well as it could. About 7 percent of sub-Saharan Africa's limited forest cover disappears annually in key states. South Africa lost critical habitat and many varieties of animals between 2000 and 2018. Poaching big game is also helping to denude several countries of the fauna that tourists come to see. (See Chapter XI.)

The most slippage in terms of overall touristic progress between 2015 and 2018 occurred in two otherwise advanced and high-ranking countries: South Africa and Namibia. In the first, overall safety declined, thus scaring tourists and reducing their total number. In the second, sustainability diminished over the same period because of losses of forest cover and deteriorated water quality. The World Economic Forum also criticized Namibia's failure to exploit its cultural resources and noted its evident shortages of trained personnel. It indicated, too, that Tanzania had a vast untapped potential for historical and cultural tourism, with many little-visited sites that it could promote.

Overcoming a number of these reported problems in the scaling up of Africa's tourist industry would boost arrivals and expenditures. But, given the hesitancy with which so many African nations welcome tourists and, outside of South Africa, Mauritius, Kenya, and Botswana, the lack of preparation of their national responses, it is not likely that sub-Saharan Africa's jobs crisis will be resolved in the near term appreciably by the tourist sector.

Agriculture

As many as half of all sub-Saharan Africans today depend on agriculture for their sustenance and their livelihoods. No other continent has such a large proportion of its inhabitants engaged in tilling the soil and guarding and following herds of sheep, goats, camels, and cattle. But even if possibly half a billion people are today tied in that manner to the land and livestock, they are only in some limited instances producing cash crops for domestic or overseas sale. Agriculture in the region contributes about 12 percent of total GDP but as much as 64 percent of labor force occupation. In theory, again, that last number could swell to absorb large portions of, and give meaningful wage employment to, this century's population bulge. Africa's abundance of unemployed persons of working age could gain meaningful jobs if agricultural pursuits could (as in Asia and Brazil) become increasingly profitable and provide growing opportunities for large-scale wage employment. Only 10 percent of the available soil south of the Sahara is today being tilled, and another 10 percent grazed, so there is no intrinsic shortage of land. But there are other formidable obstacles that deter massive transfers of job seekers from urban to rural domains and pursuits.

Farming and animal husbandry have not hitherto been particularly profitable pursuits for the peoples of Africa. Nearly all farming operates outside of, or on the fringes of, the cash economy. Most white maize and cassava (manioc) is grown to feed immediate families; only occasional surpluses are available for sale. Likewise, true yams are grown for local consumption in West Africa. Ethiopians produce grains like wheat, teff, millet, barley, and sorghum. Subsistence agriculture is the predominant mode except for those who grow cocoa on small holdings in Ghana and Côte d'Ivoire; coffee on shaded terraces in Ethiopia, Rwanda, Kenya, and Uganda; tea in Kenya, Tanzania, Uganda, and Malawi; Virginia tobacco in Zimbabwe and flue-cured tobacco in Malawi; citrus crops in South Africa; cut flowers in Kenya and Ethiopia; and oil seeds of several types and cashew nuts in Tanzania and Mozambique. South Africa, Kenya, and Tanzania are growing avocados for export. Sugar, produced on plantations in South Africa, Zimbabwe, Zambia, Malawi, and Kenya, could be grown more intensively if world prices were responsive. Likewise, beef shipments to Europe and elsewhere from Botswana could increase if Europe and China wanted more than they now receive.

But providing jobs on the land attractive enough to draw persons aged 18 to 34 out of the cities (or to prevent them from leaving villages for urban centers) has in recent years appeared Sisyphean, at best. It has thus far proved difficult to overcome Africa's inherent obstacles: Most of the sub-continent's agricultural and pastoral production depends on rainfall during roughly six months of each year. Thanks to climate shifts, that rainfall (as explained earlier) is now unpredictable and erratic. Often it is more than ample; too frequently it is sparse. In the last decade absolute annual millimeters of rain have decreased by 20 percent. And the high heat of the tropics has accelerated evaporation. Farming as an occupation is therefore becoming more, rather than less, precarious. Large-scale commercial agriculture, employing sizable numbers of people, is similarly becoming less and less profitable because, across the sub-continent, so little terrain is irrigated (only 3 percent) and water is becoming more expensive and harder to locate.

To add to the woes of Africa, many of its agricultural lands are situated in the equatorial tropics between Cancer and Capricorn. Because of that geographical truth, the soils of most of the sub-continent's countries are nutritionally poor. Sub-Saharan Africa lacks the rich loams and deep black earths of the American Midwest and Western Europe. Instead, the soils that most Africans till are thin, friable, and poor in nitrogen. They often consist of unworkable heavy clay. Unlike the terrain of most of Asia, Europe, and Latin America, plowing on sub-Saharan Africa's terrain is hard and much of the soil preparation is still done by back-breaking hand labor, or—at best—by oxen. In Africa, only two tractors plow each 100 square kilometers of arable land; the global average is two hundred tractors on the same hectarage. In theory, once again, more labor could easily be employed on Africa's farms—but not if their toil is only profitable at the margin.

To make the realization of rising incomes off the land even more difficult, compared to Asia, Europe, and America—or even Brazil—African soils are assaulted by heavy downpours. Soils thus mineralize rapidly in a destructive manner that is prevented in temperate climes by frost. Those periodic drenchings also wash out what few nutrients the African soils may still possess. Organic compounds leach out of the soil because of high tropical temperatures, as well. Even commercial fertilizer, where it is available and not too costly, cannot retard such persistent mineral losses. Moreover, when the lands of Africa are worked over, year after year, they lose what little nutrient values that they once possessed. Pastoralists also face the same general problem when their goats and sheep repeatedly graze grasslands that are much less productive than they once were.

Generations ago, Africans learned to let their lands lie fallow for years at a time. This shifting cultivation pattern and pastoral reliance on such transhumance practices (moving crops from used fields to new ones) forestalled or even prevented declining soil productivity and exhaustion. But those were practices suitable to sparsely settled populations, not to increasingly urbanized and increasingly fertilizer-dependent peoples.

Indeed, even where shifting cultivation practices are successfully employed, soil degradation remains a constant hazard because of the modern planting of nutrient-leaching cash crops such as coffee or demanding grain crops such as maize or teff. Goats and sheep trample thin soils and strip anything that grows. Trampling also sometimes leads after heavy rains to destructive erosion.

Even under the most favorable circumstances, the tropical lands of Africa are far less productive than their temperate counterparts in South Africa, Asia, Europe, or North America. Crop yields are far below average yields elsewhere in the world, possibly (but not only) because African farmers on average use 9 kilograms of fertilizer per hectare, well below the 100 kilograms per hectare that is the global norm. They also employ fewer pesticides than the global average. Moreover, the continued exploitation of marginal lands intensifies desertification. As soil fertilities decrease, so the loss of vegetation to hungry herds and desperate farmers permits once productive districts to be absorbed ecologically by the Sahel, and the drier lands north of the Sahel to be annexed by the Saharan desert. When the harsh Harmattan wind sweeps across and south of the Sahara, too, it blows sand and fine dust southward toward the villages and cities of Nigeria, Cameroon, and other tropical jurisdictions. Along the way it destroys vegetation for thousands of miles, year after year.

African agriculture, moreover, is a collection of monocultures, none of which is good for the underlying firmament. Maize, manioc, yams, and the rest all suffer, too, from various plant diseases and pests that flourish in and because of the sheer fact of being in the tropics. Those diseases and pests would be eradicated by frost in temperate regions. Leaf borers chump away at maize crops and fungus despoils manioc. Sheep and goats, the movable bank accounts of poor pastoralists, and cattle, die frequently from epizootic diseases such as rinderpest and East Coast fever. Elephants may trample crops ready to be harvested. Baboons pillage fruit and maize cobs.

Farming and grazing is not for the faint-hearted anywhere. It is certainly a much tougher and less lucrative pursuit in Africa than in temperate climes except where good management, irrigation, and modern husbandry produce sleek herds of well-fed cattle and rows of well-tended oranges, quinces, lychees, apples, coffee, tea, sugar, wheat, cut flowers, and the rest. Even if so much of Africa's agriculture is hardscrabble, there are immensely successful and well-regarded commercial farming enterprises in several countries.

The key question from now until 2030 or so, and thereafter, is how to overcome the many obstacles to Africa's agricultural renaissance. In addition to the complications of geographical location, fundamental endowment, and massive climate change, there are also shortages of finance for small-scale (and even larger) farming enterprises, an almost complete absence of tenure and title (against which farmers can borrow), a paucity of technical assistance such as that once provided by colonial-era extension workers, seed and fertilizer shortages and high costs, and trade barriers within and across Africa and between Africa and Europe and America. As we shall see later in this chapter, too, African farmers are poorly served by access to paved roads and therefore by the ease of marketing their crops, by the availability of electric power (solar is slowly replacing even more expensive kerosene lamps), and by the kinds of lifestyle improvements that might keep educated sons and daughters on their family farms. African universities spend little time and effort on the problems and future of agriculture, and on how it could be enhanced. Very little attention is being paid to fostering agricultural innovation through research and training (on the model of American land-grant universities) and many contemporary Chinese institutions.

Attracting ambitious Africans into the farming sector was always going to be difficult at the best of times. Now, with so many Africans leaving the land for the bright lights of the overcrowded cities, only entrepreneurs with vision and great persistence will try valiantly in future years, as a few have done already, to overcome the many ineluctable traditional and contemporary obstacles to making agriculture the engine of the African renaissance. If a few succeed as others have already done, and if that movement persists profitably, then and only then can African leaders hope to provide jobs and opportunities for their many new citizens. Responsible leaders and governments can lower the barrier and at least make such a return to the land plausible, even desirable.

Electric Power

Agricultural processing ventures, industrial developments of all kinds, tourism, educational advances, and progress in delivering positive medical outcomes all depend to a significant extent on the availability of reliable supplies of electrical power. Africa, especially the nation-states of sub-Saharan Africa, has, however, always been short of such readily accessible energy. As an entire region of about 1.3 billion people, it generates no more electrical power than a country like Spain, with 46 million people. Nigeria alone, with a population of more than 200 million, generates only 1 percent of the power available to 360 million Americans; a small American city's electrical generating facility could meet most, if not all, of Nigeria's current needs. Even South Africa's total current electricity capacity (5,000 MW) is puny compared to that of the least populated American states such as Delaware or Alaska. Hence the widespread employment by industries and merchants, and wealthy residents, of backup generators; to utilize, they cost at least three times as much to operate as does receiving power from national grids. (Nigeria, where 80 million people lack access to the national grid, is the globe's largest purchaser of generators.) But at least owning diesel-powered generators avoids the blackouts and load shedding frequencies that are still so much a part of the daily African experience. African demand for power has simply far outstretched available supply.

In 2019, only 35 percent of sub-Saharan Africans had regular access to electricity from a national grid. Beyond those who can afford generators, nearly all of the rest of the peoples of the region rely on solid biomass energy sources for cooking and heating, and sometimes for lighting. Taking account of Africa's population explosion, according to the World Bank, by 2050 only another 5 or 10 percent of Africa's residents will have gained access to steady increments of power off the grid. (More than 80 percent of South Americans receive such power today.)

On a per capita basis, sub-Saharan Africans receive less than a third of the power resources available to Southeast Asians and a tenth of that consumed by South Americans, those African numbers and results having declined from absolute and relative levels prevailing in the last century. African governments (most electricity providers are state-owned) have invested far less in the renewal of their mostly fossil fuel generating plants and transmission facilities than Southeast Asian, South American, or even Central Asian nations.

High-income developed countries consume electrical power at about 11,000 kwh per capita annually. The average consumer across the countries of the developing world uses just over 1,000 kwh a year. In sub-Saharan Africa, that figure reaches only about 500 kwh per year. If South Africa's per capita usage is subtracted, the per capita yearly consumption of electricity by sub-Saharan Africans is only about 150 kwh a year. Another statistical measure shows that sub-Saharan Africa constitutes 18 percent of the world's land mass and 20 percent of its people (now swelling enormously), but produces less than 3 percent of the globe's electricity (soon to increase thanks to new hydroelectrical facilities).

The World Bank indicates that national electrical generating capacities should grow ideally at the same ratio as national population increases, so as to meet demand. But even without the population surge that is now ongoing, most of sub-Saharan Africa trails anticipated population rises by 2 percent a year, thus compounding a desperate problem that shows little sign of receding immediately. Mauritius is a rare exception to this generalization, and Rwanda is catching up faster than its neighbors.

Even within sub-Saharan Africa itself, the disparities are stark. South Africa's electricity grid connects 90 percent of its people, albeit sporadically. (In the southern summer of 2019-2020 South Africa could not keep its lights on and its factories running.) But for Nigeria that same figure is about 50 percent. Thanks to the output of its massive new dam, Ethiopia's generation of power should before too long be sufficient to supply all of its people. But less fortunate countries, such as Kenya and Mozambique, will only very gradually improve their capacity to enable more than 20 percent of inhabitants to join their respective national grids. The Democratic Republic of Congo, the physical size of Western Europe, has a vast hydroelectrical potential but today, thanks to underinvestment and lackadaisical governance, offers electricity to a mere 6 percent of its 87 million citizens, most of whom live in cities and even there scramble for reliable access. Zimbabwe, a long-troubled nation-state of 15 million people with a historically strong but recently crippled infrastructure, can only reach 38 percent of its presumed customer base. Its installed electrical generating capacity was rated at 1,940 MW, but, as recently as 2019, was producing only 845 MW. In 2018, those figures were 1,400 MW of capacity but only 1,045 of production. According to its own officials, to meet current needs Zimbabwe requires 1,600 MW and to modernize its industries and run them efficiently it needs to produce 9,000 MW a year.[4]

Elsewhere energy needs are as great, but power grids reach only 5 to 10 percent of potential customers, as in Rwanda, a country that seriously seeks to become the Singapore of Africa—but on an installed capacity of only 218 MW yearly. That limited ready access to electricity, as is the case in most of sub-Saharan Africa, greatly slows Rwanda's expansion and its delivery of social as well as economic services. Little by way of agro-processing can prosper with—at best—intermittent energy supplies. Nor can Rwanda easily realize its ambitions to become an inland transport hub and to modernize across several dimensions. As in much of Africa, too, the power that is readily available is also very expensive at $0.18 per kwh—seventeen times the price of power in Alaska. Even now, therefore, nighttime flights over Rwanda (and most of Africa) show only Kigali and a few other towns lit up. The rest of the country is dark, a major contrast to any flight over a small European country such as Belgium, where streetlights are so bright and show up so much from space that they have to be dimmed or turned off.

Renewable Energy Resources

Despite petroleum deposits and wells in some of the major producing states, and new reserves of natural gas, especially in eastern Africa, much of the sub-continent's electricity is still produced by coal-fired thermal plants. South Africa, especially, has abundant supplies of low-quality coal and fuels 80 percent of its grid's output (10 percent or so is from nuclear-generated power) from coal. Elsewhere in Africa a third (soon to increase) of all available electricity comes from hydroelectrically generated power, most of the rest from thermal. But because combusting coal and natural gas provides so much of sub-Saharan Africa's electricity, its wholesale cost is double average U.S. charges ($74 mwh versus $35 mwh)—thus further inhibiting industrial and consumer growth. At the retail level, some African charges have been as high as $0.50 per kwh, although the average is much less. Several researchers argue that at typical low levels of household consumption (and high prices) it hardly pays state-owned and other firms to supply power to individual dwellings. Privately financed thermal power plants in Nigeria have proven unprofitable because of the difficulty of collecting payments for delivered electricity. At the industrial level, some countries have long subsidized their main industrial nodes of employment, such as the Zambian copper mines and Mozambique's massive aluminum fabricating plant—thus compelling consumers to pay even more of the shared total cost.

The obvious answer to both escalating power charges and crippling power shortages is for Africa to begin to generate even more of its electricity from solar, wind, innovative geothermal, hydro, and even nuclear sources. (Kenya already leads Africa by producing 70 percent of its power from renewable resources.) Since the sun shines on much of Africa for 300 or so days a year, and since the average cost of solar supplied electricity is now—on average—competitive with hydro- and certainly thermal-produced power, large-scale as well as household solar installations should give Africa an easy fix and much more available electricity. Whereas Africa now has fewer than 1 percent of the world's solar panels, it harbors 40 percent of the globe's solar energy potential.[5]

Unfortunately, except for new wind powered plants in South Africa and a proposed scheme to install 365 turbines in the Lake Turkana region of Kenya, the rest of Africa is not pursuing renewable energy possibilities very energetically. In and around Africa's cities one can see rooftops and municipal buildings with solar panels. But only South Africa has implanted vast arrays of sola capturing panels across parts of its terrain.

Converting sun rays to electricity—solar power—is still in its infancy as a conclusive answer to Africa's energy requirements. But more and more projects are coming on stream. A Dutch firm is planning to provide off-grid, pay-as-you go solar power to 1 million Nigerian households by 2025. Smaller solar generating projects have been installed in Rwanda, the Gambia, and Sierra Leone. Zambia also has many local experiments. Several countries—Chad and the Sudan, in particular—have established solar-powered hydroelectric pumping stations. Many more smallish installations are being added to the sub-continent's generating capacity and some are already connected to the grid. Parts of Zambia, Malawi, and Kenya are successfully using solar cells embedded in simple plastic strips to power endless separate light-emitting diodes or mobile telephones. Purchased inexpensively, these strips may have a key role in lighting Africa and recharging batteries. An innovative company created by two Eritrean brothers operating out of Uganda has sold and installed solar-powered lanterns, small kits for lights and battery charging, solar water pumps, solar street lights, and solar panels for large buildings (such as medical schools, hospitals, and teacher training colleges) across seven countries, even in such desperate and business-unfriendly places as South Sudan, the Central African Republic, and the Democratic Republic of Congo.

Nuclear-generated power is only available now in South Africa. But, in 2019, a dozen countries from Egypt and Algeria through to Kenya, Uganda, and Zambia were contemplating embarking on the inevitably long road to generate electricity in this manner. Russia, China, and South Korea are potential builders of the necessary plant and suppliers of the fuel and equipment. The high costs of purchasing facilities from one of these vendors, or even from France or the United States, are often set against nuclear power's great energy density, which means—once constructed—that nuclear installations are inexpensive to run and produce reliable and inexpensive power for forty to sixty years. They do so in theory, of course, and if the incurred debt payments are not impossibly onerous for the nations concerned. (Under former President Jacob Zuma, South Africa tried to arrange with Russia to build new nuclear-generating plants, but that scheme turned out to be mostly a magnet for corrupt rent-seeking, and the project was halted by his successor.)

One of the key reasons for the tardiness of Africa in turning to solar (and wind) as the solution to its energy crisis is the absence of high voltage transmission lines from those locales where solar and wind are or will be installed. (This deficiency also inhibits the easy movement of hydro power from its new supply points to the urban areas and industrial conglomerations that need it so desperately.) In addition to transmission line bottlenecks, Africa's grids do not interconnect.

Sub-Saharan Africa has four independent electricity power pools. They spread the provisioning and the costs of power beyond national borders. The Southern African Power Pool, established in 1995, links twelve countries from the Democratic Republic of Congo to South Africa. It shifts Congolese, Mozambican, and South African surpluses, when available, to the smaller and less energy-efficient jurisdictions of the subregion.

The West African Power Pool, created in 2000, does the same for the fourteen members of the Economic Community of West African States (ECOWAS). Much of its power is generated by natural gas and hydroelectric flows. The West African Pool has two quasi-independent sectors: one encompasses Senegal, the Gambia, Mali, Sierra Leone, and Liberia; the other includes Nigeria, Niger, Benin, Togo, Ghana, and Côte d'Ivoire. The Central African Power Pool, organized in 2003, serves eleven nations from Chad to Congo (Brazzaville). It suffers as a grid from small and very isolated national systems that, only with difficulty, interconnect with others.

The East African Power Pool was only put together in 2005. It runs all the way from Egypt to Tanzania and includes polities that belong to both the East African Community and the Nile Basin Initiative. The surplus output from the Grand Renaissance and other dams in Ethiopia and the Sudan should by rights feed into this grid and thus make power available in the south when it is abundant in the north, and vice versa. But many of the intermediate transmission lines between different parts of this pool are yet to be built, as in West Africa. One of Africa's little recognized and little pursued tasks is the full creation of what could be a very effective continental-spanning electricity supply system.

Thus far, the distribution of electric power to all corners of Africa, especially to places of high population and too little generating capacity, is one more work very much in progress. A physical shortage of transmission lines, an absence of the connecting circuits that would securely tie different systems to each other, the theft of critical equipment and long sections of one or more savannah-spanning wires, poor reserve margins in national systems, persistent underinvestment in necessary facilities and electronics, and inadequate legal and dispute resolution arrangements have thus often kept one or more of the pools from expanding to cushion unexpected cross-border power surges or unforeseen breakdowns. As yet, too, there is no easy way to mix and match needs and availabilities across the different pools, or even across much of West Africa's two sub-pools.

But there is progress in the alternative energy realm. Rwanda is now extracting methane from Lake Kivu and burning it to fuel a part of its electrical needs. Kenya is exploiting geothermal hot spots along the Great Rift valley and deep within the sulfurous heart of the Menengai volcano for the same purpose. Despite the environmentally unfriendly extraction of methane, more of both energy sources will be exploited in the years ahead to add to the total supply of nonthermally generated electric power.

Hydro Power

In terms of the energy needs of Africa, hydrogeneration is being greatly expanded, with much more potential available. This is the case despite the rainfall shortages that greatly reduced the promised power that was designed to be generated along the White and Black Volta Rivers in Ghana and along the White Nile in Uganda and that may in future lower generating output from some of the newer installations across Africa.

Fortunately, flows of water from the Blue Nile River in southwestern Ethiopia (where mountain elevations soar to 14,000 feet) and from the Congo River, after it drains much of the middle of Africa, are anticipated to be abundant and largely uninterrupted. That is where the continent's new dams are being completed and contemplated. In the first instance, Ethiopia's Grand Renaissance Dam, the tallest in Africa, is scheduled to be finished in 2022 with a generating capacity of 6,450 MW per year, more than double the output of Egypt's Aswan Dam. [The location of the dam is marked on the map at the front of this book with "GR."] It will be the seventh largest dam in the world and the largest in Africa, will flood 1,700 square kilometers of forest along Ethiopia's border with the Sudan and create a reservoir holding 74 billion cubic meters of water, twice the capacity of nearby Lake Tana. It is intended to multiply Ethiopia's existing capacity for power by a factor of five and to supply all of the country's current needs and more. It is designed, further, to provide power to other parts of energy-short Africa and thus to earn Ethiopia significant amounts of foreign exchange. (Egypt has threatened to bomb the dam if it dries up the Nile River downstream, thus reducing the Nile's traditional agricultural renewal flooding in lower Egypt. (Demanding that Ethiopia fill the lake behind the dam much more slowly than planned and guarantee 40 billion cubic meters a year for Egypt's Nile River flow, Egypt is naturally trying to protect the water lifeline and access that it has had for millennia. Many bouts of mediation are in store.) Again, however, the absence of transmission lines and facilities, and Ethiopia's lack of connections to regional grids, will inhibit the sale of Ethiopian electricity and the alacrity with which Grand Renaissance power can relieve people in sub-Saharan Africa of their electricity shortages.

There have long been plans to build a third dam at Inga on the Congo River. If constructed, it could conceivably supply even more power than the Grand Renaissance Dam, a projected 39,000 MW, costing $100 billion or more. If that addition to the two existing, more modest, dams at Inga is ever realized, most of the now unfilled power needs of southern Africa could be met, with room for expansion. (The third Inga dam would produce three times the power that is now generated by the Three Gorges Dam on the Yangtze River in China.) But, given the vicissitudes of the Congo's current government in Kinshasa, and its poor local and international standing, it would be unwise to expect a new facility to be brought on-stream in the present decade.

In addition to supplies from the Grand Renaissance Dam, much of Africa's hydroelectricity generation will continue to come from its other major installations. They include environmentally insensitive dams across the Omo and Neshi Rivers in southern Ethiopia, old and new dams on the Nile River north of Khartoum that have submerged critical archaeological ruins and displaced communities of Nubians but give the Sudan electrical self-sufficiency, dams in Uganda athwart the Victoria Nile, the 2,500 MW Cahora Bassa Dam across the Zambezi River in Mozambique, the 705 MW Kariba Dam (also across the Zambezi and oft-generating less than its capacity), the new and older dams on Zambia's Kafue River, proposed and existing installations along the Kunene River on the Angolan/Namibian border, a dam across the headwaters of the Orange River in Lesotho to supply power and water to Johannesburg and South Africa, and new dams in Ghana and Gabon, where the terrain is less rugged and water moves sluggishly.

In addition to these major projects for the generation of electricity, smaller and local hydroelectric projects will continue to be important in supplying power and irrigation water. Already 150 projects with a capacity of 10 MW or less are in place, with many more coming. Rwanda, with thirty-six micro dams constructed or contemplated, is among the leaders in this arena. Kenya, Ethiopia, and South Africa have numerous micro projects underway, as well. There could come a time in the near future when a large proportion of Africa's growing electricity needs are met from these kinds of local, less environmentally disruptive installations. Malawi, Zambia, Mozambique, and Uganda all have surveyed possible projects on this model, a few of which are installations decommissioned in the aftermath of the colonial era.

Producing power in the amounts that Africa so desperately requires to industrialize, to grow economically in several dimensions, and to provide jobs for its new potential wage earners is a major task of coming days, and a challenge to consummate political leadership. Africans are going to have to draw upon more and more solar, some wind, expanding hydro resources, and the strengthening and rapid integration of transmission grids to accomplish the task. China, already the contractor for so many of Africa's existing dams, will doubtless continue to help, but whether it can do so at a cost that Africa can afford to pay going forward is a fundamental question for African political leaders and African taxpayers.

Arteries of Commerce

A robust infrastructure contributes significantly to both industrial and agricultural productivity. Europe, South America, North America, and then Southeast Asia and East Asia all grew economically on the back of entrepreneurial initiative, capital availability, and good governance. But the construction of roads, railways, canals, and harbors greatly facilitated the rise of industry by easing shipping and other carrying charges and by lowering the frictional costs of both transportation and communication. New roads and rails helped also to enlarge domestic markets and tie regional ones together. Vastly larger consumer aggregations could be served more effectively than before thanks to modernized arteries of commerce that link cities and towns, cities and the countryside, and span larger and larger geographical spaces.

Yet, with only a few exceptions, Africa lacks extensive road, rail, and air facilities of the kind that efficiently tie rural villagers to capital cities, towns, and mid-sized cities to political and commercial capitals, and one African country to another. Its existing and refurbished road and rail networks are inadequate for the potential bursts of manufacturing and agro-processing growth on which its various national futures depend. Moreover, existing harbors are shallow and crowded, forcing ships to wait days before they can dock and unload. (In 2018, tiny Togo's Lomé port overtook Lagos, Nigeria's main harbor, as the West African destination of choice for containers, thanks to persistent delays and congestion in Lagos.) International airports are comparatively few and airline connections—especially within and across Africa itself—sparse. Only 5 percent of global air traffic lands or takes off from a sub-Saharan African airport, in part a result of unnecessary protectionism by receiving countries.[6] The failure of a number of African national airlines is also a contributing factor.

At the down-to-earth level, however, sub-Saharan Africa's most basic commercial artery deficiencies begin with a road system that is still rudimentary (considering population and commercial increases) and largely interconnected only occasionally. Compared to North Africa, sub-Saharan Africa sorely lacks well-maintained paved roads. This is a failing that Africans of most backgrounds and classes complain about, loudly. They demand better transportation facilities from their politicians and governments and, almost in every country, equate improved governance with improved access to all-weather roads. Only 40 percent of the inhabitants of rural sub-Saharan Africa live within 2 kilometers of an all-season road—by far the lowest reported level of accessibility in the developing world.

Combining main and secondary roads, not all of which are paved, sub-Saharan Africa in 2018 had a road network roughly 1.5 million kilometers long. Another 0.5 million kilometers may be considered passable earth tracks. In the cities there are 200,000 kilometers of paved roads. These numbers translate overall into 109 kilometers of classified and 149 kilometers of unclassified roads per 1,000 square kilometers of territory, meaning that sub-Saharan Africa's road density per square kilometer is only 30 percent of Asia's and 6 percent of North America's. Or to express some of these contrasts across other illuminating numbers, in South Asia half of all roads are paved, in North America two-thirds of all roads are paved. But in sub-Saharan Africa only 10 percent of the existing roads are paved. The paved road network totals in sub-Saharan Africa translate into 0.79 kilometers of roadway per thousand people—one fifth of the world average. Moreover, that tiny figure is cut in half when Botswana and South Africa's paved roads are subtracted from sub-Saharan Africa's total lengths.[7]

Of the forty-nine sub-Saharan African political jurisdictions, only the compact island state of Mauritius claims a road density statistic that is adequate by international standards—933 kilometers per 1,000 square kilometers. Rwanda, a very densely peopled country, shows 110 paved kilometers per 1,000 square kilometers, Uganda 80, and South Africa only 50. At the other end of the scale, Angola's paved roads per square kilometer figure is only 0.62, the Central African Republic's 0.11, and the Democratic Republic of Congo's 0.10. Most of the mainland nations of Africa show paved roadway length numbers of under 10 kilometers per 1,000 square kilometers.

The Democratic Republic of Congo, the region's largest nation, in the decades since its independence in 1960 has steadily lost (not gained) paved road total kilometers. Its entire network is today smaller than the one it inherited at independence from Belgium in 1960. In 2011, that extensive country could count only 1,800 kilometers of paved roads. In 2018, that number had risen only to 2,250 kilometers. It comprised only 1 percent of the giant Congo's entire, badly maintained, mostly earth and gravel road network. At one time Kinshasa, the Congo capital, was tied by road (as well as river in some cases) to the inland cities of Kisangani, Lubumbashi, Goma, and Bukavu; now these routes are poorly maintained and difficult to traverse. Even river transport capabilities have regressed. Air travel is much too expensive for popular use as a connecting medium, and domestic air services have questionable safety records. Chad, Ethiopia, the Sudan, the Central African Republic, Tanzania, and Nigeria are also road-poor, but not so desperately as the massive Congo.

The wealthier, better-governed, more industrially modern states in sub-Saharan Africa benefit from tighter and stronger roads and road links. South Africa, Namibia, Botswana, Zambia, Uganda, and Ghana in part grow economically because their extensive advanced paved road networks give them commercial advantages over their poorer and fractured neighbors. South Africa boasts an excellent paved road network fully 58,000 kilometers long; its roads are among the best on the continent even though its per capita and per square kilometers ratings are lower than some of its neighbors. Its harbors are among the best managed in Africa, as are its several international and domestic airports.

Botswana, mostly desert and poor at independence in 1966, could then count only 12 kilometers of paved roadways. Now, next door to South Africa, it has a well-maintained paved road network of about 9,000 kilometers, plus a colonial built railway that connects the country to South Africa's ports, and also provides a rail conduit south for Zimbabwe, Zambia, and the Katanga Province of the Congo. Landlocked Botswana's road system is now so extensive that it is possible to cross the immense distances of the Kalahari Desert to enter Namibia and to carry on across Namibia to the Atlantic Ocean coast.

In stark contrast, Nigeria, Africa's most populous country, has long been served only weakly by its paved and unpaved roads, by creaky railways, by badly run and inherently dangerous domestic air services and airports, and by overcrowded and unsafe harbors. Chinese contractors in recent years have attempted to upgrade its main rail connections, like the lines between Lagos and Kano and Lagos and Calabar, and worked intensively on many of the key roads. These efforts have lowered the percentage of roads in Nigeria that are frequently termed "impassable," thus making it more feasible to transport agricultural produce to markets. But numerous areas in the northern half of the country (where Boko Haram attacks) still lack good roads and good connections between rural areas and state capital cities.

Ghana, on the West African shores of the Atlantic Ocean, has fewer per capita kilometers of paved roads, a total length of 16,560 kilometers, two major ports, and a rail network similar in length to that of Botswana.[8] Kenya has constructed a major new standard gauge rail line with Chinese help.

These vast disparities of paved roads per person and per area suggest the many thousands of kilometers of paved roads, paved and unpaved, that Africa still needs to construct to support its existing and coming populations and their commercial and, possibly, their industrial aspirations. These challenges, many addressed by political leaders in key countries with critical construction and financial assistance from China, should enable several forward-looking nations to prepare stronger foundations for potential economic growth spurts. Others, just as needy, will doubtless follow the road and rail-building examples of the pioneers.

The creation of a "pothole" index would correlate well with improving economic prospects; countries with better maintained roads, and more of them, can move produce from farm to market more easily than other places with less extensive road lengths. Better roads permit fertilizers to reach the farmers less expensively, and also to move harvested crops (and mineral discoveries) to market with fewer losses.

One more condition strengthens the need for improved and better maintained roads in Africa. The World Health Organization labels the roads of Africa among the most dangerous on earth. In Kenya, South Africa, Eritrea, and Nigeria automobile fatalities are among the globe's most numerous annually. In South Africa, an average of 43 persons a day or 16,000 a year lose their lives in traffic incidents, six times Britain's road accident totals.[9] Furthermore, according to the South African Medical Research Council, 60 percent of those killed on the highways had blood alcohol levels well over legal limits.

Better road and rail links, and upgraded harbors and airports, will enhance Africa's ability to absorb new population numbers and meet the developmental challenges that accompany those increases. Some countries, such as Kenya, with Chinese help, are revamping their long-distance infrastructure to make it more likely that more people can travel widely and take the entrepreneurial ideas of the cities to villagers and other rural dwellers. Job creation everywhere will be eased by strengthened arteries of commerce, by dredged and widened ports, and by a host of other infra-structural betterments that could be the fruit of enhanced leadership and upgraded governance. Africa's growing middle class and its aspirations to join the global village need a transportation network worthy of the mid-twenty-first century.

The Other Arteries

Equally important to the development of profitable commerce, industry, and agriculture in Africa are the new arteries of commerce that typify the con-temporary digital age. Having a robust and intensifying mobile telephone network accessible to nearly all of an African nation's inhabitants is essential in the contemporary era. Cost moderation and service reliability are key, for consumers as well as factory owners. So are the regular additions of telephone towers powered by solar panels (to avoid diesel refueling needs and theft). Wide and fast broadband is also critical. But these issues, mobile telephonic capabilities, the role of social media generally, and technological advances and their profound rule in the ongoing development of Africa are discussed at length in Chapter X, "Technology Advances Africa."

Going Forward

Every issue raised in this chapter emphasizes how Africa might meet the real human needs of its existing and soon-to-swell labor force. Expanded service industries, new manufacturing possibilities, stronger tourism capabilities, and innovative attention to agricultural upgrades could all provide opportunities and the creation of numerous new jobs. Furthermore, since African agriculture is not as yet as productive as farming elsewhere in the world, manufacturing is still embryonic, and mining is increasingly capital intensive and employs relatively little labor, renewed attention should be paid to smaller-scale, more labor-employing enterprises, many of them in or on the edge of Africa's large informal economic sector. A good example is the Otigba computer village near Lagos. Generally, the informal or close-to-informal arena is less trou-bled by the unfriendly environments for commerce and growth that typify the formal sector. Those less conducive to growth concerns include high unit costs, bureaucratic obstacles, and corruption, all of which need to be over-come – as they have been in countries such as Rwanda.

A research report in 2019 suggests that middle class African consumerism is growing so rapidly that it could be a welcome engine of growth for the continent. There is more discretionary spending power than ever before. About 130 million families from Algeria, Egypt, and Morocco to Nigeria and South Africa now have disposable incomes that total $680 billion or more—a bonanza for Africa.[10] But this chapter has also sketched the obstacles that will have to be overcome if Africa is going to transcend its current economic challenges, forge a series of renaissances across critical sectors of enterprise, and produce the quantity and quality of livelihoods that Africa now needs.

v | Corruption Retards Progress

THE NATIONAL ECONOMIES of Africa would all grow much faster, and deliver uplifting benefits to their citizens, if they had improved roads, faster broadband, better airports and flight connections, more electricity, easier access to capital, and—above all—increased doses of good governance. Among the key components of strong governance, as we have seen, are such critical components as a robust rule of law and an enhanced sense of transparency. Both go together, and that latter attribute strongly reduces the practice of both grand and petty corruption by politicians and officials and, simultaneously, upgrades national per capita GDPs.

Corruption is an insidious cancer of national bodies politic. Corrupt practices harshly cut across classes and castes, cripple institutions, unsettle communities, and infect the very structure of people's lives. Corruption destroys nations and saps their moral fiber. Moreover, corruption is invasive and unforgiving. It degrades governance, distorts and criminalizes national priorities, and privileges skimming natural resource wealth, patrimonial theft, and personal and family gains over concern for the commonweal.

Much of the globe is infected with corruption, sapping 3 percent of annual per capita GDP across large swathes of Africa (and similarly in Asia and Latin America). The World Bank says that $1 trillion or more is lost each year to corruption, globally. About one third of that total may be forfeited annually in Africa.

Conquering corruption, or at least moderating political or corporate corrupt behavior, can enable the planet's least well-off peoples to prosper and to begin to experience substantially better human outcomes. Combating corruption is among the important initiatives to strengthen overall human outcomes everywhere, but especially and very urgently in Africa.

An African Scourge

In Africa and elsewhere, corruption is mostly devoid of conceptual mystery. It is the conversion of a societal good—a communal good—into personal gain. It is the obtaining of "influence" through underhand payments or promises of reciprocal rewards. Usually corruption is denominated monetarily: how much has a corrupt politician or official stolen from the people? In many African countries, notably the Democratic Republic of Congo, cash-filled brown envelopes frequently change hands. Over-invoicing, construction projects that are paid for but never completed, and the hiring of nonexistent employees are but a few of the ways that such outright theft is accomplished. But persons of power can also corruptly favor syndicates or corporations—or even foreign political entities—by proffering them influence that is against the public interest, and without explicit transfers of cash.

"Getting things done" is a frequent rationalization of corruption. But underlying corrupt attempts to gain advantage over others, or to gain preferment of some kind, is something very basic to the human species, or even to all primates—greed. Another motive is "getting what others get," or not losing advantage to others. No one likes to be disadvantaged or to be thought of "as a fool" for not benefiting from easily available perquisites, or from at least the benefits that similarly placed persons are gaining licitly or illicitly. A police person on the beat in, say, Uganda, looks to see what his colleagues are doing. If others are "getting away" with sleaze, she or he usually wants to do the same.

Greed, in other words, is hardwired into the human condition. Corrupt acts therefore flow from a natural, even rational, urge to improve one's status and earnings. Both the giver and the taker of exchanges that are fundamentally corrupt seek to improve their places in the universe, their rents and wages, their standing in the queue of benefits, and even their access to positions and persons of power.

Corruption is deeply based on reciprocity, on the cultivation of exchanges of favors, on gift-giving and taking, and on something more tangible than a mere handshake or verbal promise. Corruption contains acknowledgments of power, acknowledgments of primacy, and acknowledgments of what well-placed individuals can do and how they can assist less fortunate, less well-placed individuals.

It is also true that the processes of corruption lubricate whatever wheels permit the vehicles of life and the wheels of the governmental-citizen engine to roll faster, roll in a preferred direction, roll more surely, and roll at all. In these last senses, corruption is a method of allocating scarce or purposely scarce resources to the highest bidders (not the most deserving). Corruption can minimize disadvantages based on status, class, color, or religion, and partially overcome discriminatory behavior visited upon, say, a minority or an ethnicity. An ethnic Indian businessperson in Tanzania or a Chinese entrepreneur in Gabon could remedy any roadblocks to success by paying substantially for permits or licenses otherwise only available to indigenous persons, but the unequal system would still remain in place.

The standard definition of corruption is "the abuse of public office for private gain." Transparency International and others expand that all-purpose definition by explaining that abuses of "the public trust," not just abuses of public office, are corrupt. Thus, when officials of FIFA undermined the level fields of bidding for the World Cup and other contests, such as the Africa Cup, these were abuses of the public trust even though no FIFA board member or official had been elected to "public" office.

Given abuses of either public office (narrowly or broadly construed) or the public trust, it is obvious that corrupt acts include asking for or receiving bribes (whether those which are employed to gain a good or service, those which are intended to accelerate service delivery, or those intended to deprive others of benefits or property), extortion (coerced bribes or payments in kind), kickbacks (a form of extortion in which contracts are over-invoiced so that there is room for contractual profits and payments to those who decide who will win the fake bids), embezzlement (blatant theft from the public purse), nepotism (giving a rewarding position or contract to a relative rather than allowing a meritorious or competitive exercise to take place), padding salary rolls with "ghost" workers, graft (awarding public contracts without honest competition), paying hush money or blackmail, and arbitrarily appropriating public resources for private use. Each of these and many other corrupt acts involve deceit. Each evades accountability and transparency.

Many far-ranging academic investigations have confirmed that there are no societies that condone corruption; those traditional cultures that accept gift exchanges still expect them to be transparent. Every African country, and the African Union, condemns the practicing of corruption, extortion, and nepotism. Each has strong laws intended to curb anything that might be designed to influence the performance of official duties, to interfere in the bidding process for construction and other contracts, or to defeat justice.

Nevertheless, few nation-states in Africa, north or south, escape participating deeply and unforgivingly in corruption; few therefore escape major losses to their citizens on the order of 2 to 3 percent per annum directly on account of the costs of grand and petty corruption. That drain on personal, corporate, and national finance is telling, wasteful, sometimes criminal, and frequently the proximate cause of a state's descent into civil conflict. In several near-bankrupt states, such as Zimbabwe from 2000 to 2009, corrupt elites from the president on down plundered so much that their country could not pay its bills or purchase petrol (gas) for its consumers.

The existence of corruption in a regime or administration greatly distorts priorities: road or rail links might be built, or built in the wrong place, not because they are needed or located appropriately but because leaders profit from such construction, and the kickbacks that ensue. Big infrastructural efforts provide opportunities for big transfers of wealth into well-placed private pockets.

Least and Most Corrupt

On the basis of three standard, global, measures, Africa is mired deeply in corruption. Although a few African countries rise above their peers and neighbors to earn rankings on the higher, less-corrupt end of these international scales, many crowd the bottom, where the globe's most corrupt, most kleptocratic, and often most troubled polities are to be found. These are the states of the world where grand corruption prevails, where a number of the globe's more unsavory authoritarians rule, where citizens receive little from their governments, and where poverty, deprivation, and discrimination are difficult to avoid.

For more than two decades, we have relied for our measurements of comparative corruption on two very similar subjective indexes of corruption with global reach. Now there are additional indexes with comparable methodologies and many more that focus on subsets of corrupt behavior.

They all use the perceptions of expert observers to rank countries in the world (and in Africa) according to how corrupt they are as compared to their peers and regional neighbors. Despite legitimate questions about whether external perceptions, no matter how scientifically gathered, approximate actual experience, the existing indexes constitute the gold standard. They offer the best methods devised so far comparatively to measure corrupt activity across the globe and across Africa.

The best known and most widely used measures of corruption are Transparency International's Corruption Perceptions Index (CPI) and the World Bank Institute's Control of Corruption Indicator (WCCI). (Transparency International, a well-regarded NGO based in Berlin, has battled corruption since 1993. The World Bank Institute is a part of the World Bank in Washington, DC.) The first was issued originally in 1995, the second in 1996. In 2019, the first rated 180 countries, the second 215. A third, newer, rating system is the Index of Public Integrity, also created in Berlin, in 2016. It ranks 120 countries, but proportionally fewer in Africa. Of those that it does score, South Africa is rated as least corrupt (#42 from the top), with Namibia second (#45). At the bottom, along with Venezuela and Yemen, are Burundi, Cameroon, Congo (Kinshasa), and Chad, in that descending order.

The Nordic nations and New Zealand are always at the apex of all three lists, sometimes with Finland in the lead, sometimes Denmark, and occasionally, New Zealand. The top ten least corrupt countries additionally include Iceland, Singapore, and Canada. Sometimes Germany, the United Kingdom, the Netherlands, or Luxembourg, and occasionally Switzerland join the elite dozen or so. The United States is always in the next decile or so, along with France. Uruguay ranks best in South America, the Seychelles and Botswana in Africa. At the very bottom of both listings are such paragons of virtue as North Korea, Venezuela, Iraq, Afghanistan, and three dozen African nations.

In 2019, when the Seychelles displaced Botswana as Africa's best performer, it was twenty-seventh on the CPI list, with a computed score of 66 out of 100 points (first place Denmark scored 87). The next least-corrupt African countries were Botswana, thirty-fourth (score of 61), Cape Verde, forty-first (score 58), Rwanda fifty-first (score 53), Namibia fifty-sixth (score 52), and Mauritius, also fifty-sixth (score 52). São Tomé and Príncipe was sixty-fourth (46), Senegal sixty-sixth (45), South Africa seventieth (44), Tunisia seventy-fourth (43); and Morocco and Ghana, both eightieth (41), ahead of India and tied with China. Rwanda jumped almost forty places between 2006 and 2018, falling back slightly in 2019.

The Thoroughly Corrupt

From this point on the CPI list (with comparable scores on the WCCI indicator), African countries fill up a majority of the ranking spots. Zambia is

113th, followed by Sierra Leone, Niger, and Gabon. Malawi is 123rd. Below those mostly but not wholly corrupt entities, the CPI places the Comoros, Kenya, Mauritania, and Nigeria (146th), the Central African Republic and Cameroon (153rd), Madagascar, Mozambique, and Zimbabwe (158th). All of the remaining countries of Africa fall below this arbitrary cutoff, in descending order: the two Congos, Eritrea, Angola, Chad, Equatorial Guinea, Guinea-Bissau, [North Korea,] Libya and Burundi, [Afghanistan,] the Sudan, [North Korea and Yemen,] South Sudan (179th), and Somalia (180th).

The preceding list should indicate, at a minimum, that corruption has captured nearly all of Africa. Indeed, not one country, not even top performers the Seychelles and Botswana, can (unlike Singapore or Finland) truly say that they have completely extirpated the scourge of corruption. Nor can well-performing Mauritius and Senegal, which rank below the first two on the scale. South Africa fell one place from 2017 to 2019 because of major corruption scandals involving its president and many key members of the ruling African National Congress (ANC). Thus, even states with relatively reasonable scores should not be considered free or more than partly free from the incubus of corruption.

Even more definitively is that conclusion correct for those many African states lower down on the list than South Africa. Those bottom polities are steeped in corruption. In some cases they are thoroughgoing kleptocracies, even criminalized states where the main purpose of holding office is to loot—illicitly to employ the absolute authority of executive office to transfer the coffers of the state into private and family hands (as in Angola during the long reign of President Eduardo dos Santos; the even longer reign of Mobutu Sese Seko in Zaire/Congo; the rule of Zimbabwe's Robert Mugabe, his second wife, and their cronies—from 1980 to 2017; and the continuing presidencies of Yoweri Museveni in Uganda and Teodoro Obiang Nguema in Equatorial Guinea).

The above ranks and numbers inform us of the relative impact of corrupt dealings in Africa now, and over time (the rough order of places has changed little over the years). But it still cannot convey the elaborate composition of the corrupt acts that roil the supposedly tranquil waters of Africa, provide great riches to the big men who capture many whole states, or enable their smaller cousins to extort tidy sums from clients and customers of bureaucracies. In many African states, being in a position of authority means being in a position to fleece supplicants (petty corruption) and, if very fortunate, being in a position to distribute contracts for large-scale projects—to decide which firm or foreign nation wins bidding procurement wars (grand corruption).

In a subsequent section we discuss how and why Botswana, the Seychelles, Cape Verde, and Mauritius largely have avoided becoming as corrupt and corrupted as their neighbors. We also show how the Zambians et al.—but not Burundi, Cameroon, Chad, and the like—attempted to defeat corruption, and failed.

Petty versus Grand Corruption

In virtually all of Africa's nation-states, possibly excepting the top half-dozen or so, petty corruption persists. It is rampant in those jurisdictions ranking below South Africa on the CPI.

Petty corruption daily affects millions of Africans, intruding corrosively on their work, their errands, and their leisure pursuits. Grand corruption is less visible, less obvious to most Africans as they make their daily rounds. But it is far more destructive and insidious, and the impact of grand corruption harms them and the lifeblood of their countries more than they often easily grasp.

Petty corruption is the handing over of relatively small sums (as much as the equivalent of $15 every day for Kenyans) for governmental acts that should by right be available freely to all citizens. It is often a form of extortion: the official behind the grille never refuses outright to provide a birth certificate, a marriage license, or a driving permit. He or she simply makes it clear in perfect bureaucratese that he or she is much too busy to search for or stamp any documents until he or she is appropriately induced (rewarded), possibly with "tea money." Queues are interminable; if the petitioner wants to jump the queue or receive timely attention to his registration or other necessities a "gift" to the official behind the grille becomes appropriate. Facilitation payments are the norm almost anywhere in the developing world where there are still regulations that can be interpreted by an official, or where the delivery of a service—no matter how routine—can be exploited for personal gain. That is why petty corruption is often labeled "lubricating" or "speedy" corruption.

Physicians or nurses in hospitals throughout much of Africa are accustomed to receiving envelopes stuffed with cash. Otherwise, attention in government, even private, hospitals may be delayed or diverted. Teachers in many nations are accustomed to receiving gifts of cash at the beginning and end of terms, and before holidays. Places in schools and good grades are often dependent on such gifts. Parents would not want their children to be neglected or held back.

Roadblocks, set up by traffic policemen or vigilantes, are an expedient method of extorting payments from motorists attempting to proceed normally down highways or busy city streets in many African countries. At a roadblock, drivers frequently are falsely accused of having a broken headlight, a cracked mirror, or otherwise of breaching opaque rules. A small payment, especially if it is dark and the police or pseudo-police are menacing, allows an automobile or a passenger bus to proceed. I had my own experience with a Constable Moyo in Zimbabwe that was contrived, petty, annoying, and costly ($20, equivalent to a week's pay for a laboring Zimbabwean).

In Kinshasa, the capital of the Democratic Republic of Congo, traffic cops receive 80 percent of their income from what are euphemistically called "informal tolls." Every driver must pay a protection fee to the police. "This is done by sticking a [driver's] fist out of the [car] window at certain junctions . . . and dropping a note worth [30 US cents] into a waiting policeman's hand."[1] Drivers who try to avoid this particular "squeeze" find themselves subject to very large fines for (imaginary) offenses, which the police can invent at will. Part of the cop's take goes to his superiors. There are daily quotas.

In Sierra Leone, offenders on trial routinely negotiate lighter sentences by paying fees to clerks and magistrates. In Sierra Leone's hospitals, even during the Ebola epidemic, nurses' handbags became illicit pharmacies from which drugs were sold to patients. No cash, no medicine.

At Nigeria's international airport, hustlers working in cahoots with security personnel slow down queues so that they can sell access to the fast-track lanes for $10. Since Nigeria is a very large country where its 200 million citizens are accustomed to escalating levels of petty corruption, nearly everyone is compelled daily to endure the system or to use it for her/his own gain.

As long ago as the 1990s, a Tanzanian Supreme Court justice reported that corruption at all levels of government was widespread. It harmed the delivery of police enforcement services, impinged dangerously on judicial independence, deterred honest efforts to collect taxes and all kinds of official revenues, and distorted the distribution of agricultural and commercial land. Civil servants were being appointed in violation of proper procedures. Massive personal tax evasion was facilitated by high-level bureaucrats in exchange for appropriate remuneration. Commodities and fuels were being traded on the black market thanks to special favors and kickbacks. Numerous contracts were let falsely.

In neighboring Kenya, a decade later, 80 percent of police recruits paid bribes in exchange for their jobs. The notion of corruption had seeped so thoroughly into the pores of the rural labor force that village men began saving large sums as early as possible to procure those opportunities, and many others. There was a price for everything, and everyone knew the price.

In 2013, Transparency International's Global Corruption Barometer survey revealed that 53 percent of Kenyans had bribed policemen and 30 percent had bribed judges. Another survey reported that persons supposedly providing state services for free demanded bribes 65 percent of the time. Fifteen percent asked for it a second time, 10 percent a third, and 4 percent a fourth time. These survey answers are not at all surprising, and replicable up and down the continent.

At the petty level, Malawian bureaucrats, no less skilled than their Nigerian or Ivoirean counterparts, changed rules and norms in order to inveigle bribes from befuddled compatriots; every transaction had to be accompanied by official stamps, many signatures, and much documentation—some of it invented on the spot by the public servant in charge. They slowed down the delivery of permits and licenses, the better to extort healthy payments.

These are the ordeals experienced daily across much of Africa. Small sums are exchanged to avoid being hassled, to get to work on time, to complete an errand, to obtain that vital permit, to gain a necessarily slight advantage over someone also waiting interminably in a queue or seeking attention in a hospital. Although less developmentally destructive and somewhat less wasteful in aggregate terms than the effects of grand corruption, petty corruption is still a massive waste of time and cash and damaging economically wherever it is common. Petty corruption also eats away at the social structure of nations and undermines trust and governance. Routinized petty corruption is pernicious, unrelenting, and enervating.

Grand Corruption

Grand corruption hardly interferes with the day-to-day routine activities of citizens. They go about their business, lubricating and providing speed payments whenever necessary, but without necessarily being aware of exactly how their political or other officials are enriching themselves at their expense. Grand corruption, by contrast, is the large-scale theft of state privileges and opportunities for private gain. The UN Office on Drugs and Crime calls grand corruption the kind that "pervades the highest level of national government, leading to a broad erosion of confidence in good governance, the rule of law, and economic stability."[2] Grand corrupters are often called kleptocrats since kleptocracy is the widespread shifting of a state's patrimony into private hands.

Vice-President Nguema Obiang Mangue, son of the notorious klepto-cratic dictator-president of oil-rich Equatorial Guinea and a seasoned klep-tocrat on his own, flew to Brazil on a private plane in late 2018, supposedly for medical treatment; from him Brazilian police and customs officials confiscated large amounts of cash (more than $1.5 million) and handfuls of monogrammed watches worth $15 million. Earlier he had forfeited cash, automobiles, Michael Jackson memorabilia, and a $30 million mansion in Malibu, California, to escape imprisonment in a U.S. Department of Justice action under its "Kleptocracy Initiative." A French court also convicted Nguema Obiang of embezzlement and seized almost $100 million worth of assets (apartments, cars, and high-end art). Twenty-five supercars owned by Nguema Obiang were auctioned in Geneva in late 2019 for more than $13 million.

President Denis Sassou Nguesso has been president of the Republic of Congo (Brazzaville) since 1997. French authorities have identified more than $70 million worth of properties and luxury goods that his family owns in and near Paris. Global Witness in 2019 discovered that the president's daughter, through a Cypriot straw company, purchased an 1800 square foot condo-minium in Manhattan's Trump Tower in 2014 for $7 million in cash. The condo's monthly maintenance fees are tens of thousands of dollars. Some or all of the purchase price derived from a Congolese contract with a Brazilian company that transmitted payments into the Cypriot account. That account also received at least $20 million in 2014 directly from the Republic of Congo – taxpayer funds ultimately.

Global Witness also tracked the activities of President Sassou Nguesso's son, also named Denis, and nicknamed "Kiki." Kiki purloined about $50 mil-lion worth of government funds and trafficked them through six European countries, the British Virgin Islands, and the U.S. state of Delaware. Oil revenues and kickbacks from a fake Brazilian company provided much of the $50 million. This vast money laundering exercise gave Kiki access to ready income abroad; it was used for fancy cars, houses, and the usual playthings of the children of kleptocrats.

Grand corruption breeds inequality. Grand corruption therefore is even more directly antagonistic to a nation's economic, social, and political prog-ress than is petty corruption. And the sums sometimes are often huge. Grand corruption misdirects national policy, substituting projects that benefit in-dividual leaders or small groups of associates for those squarely in the public interest. Much of the proceeds from Zimbabwe's diamond mines, for instance, went to President Robert Mugabe, his wife Grace, army chiefs, and Emmerson Mnangagwa, his presidential successor.

Instances of grand corruption are common in nearly all developing countries. But an indictment of Zambia in late 2018 by the *Economist* could stand for comments on nearly all fragile states where grand corruption rules: The real reason Zambia had run up debts equal to 59 percent of GDP from 2005 to 2018 was not because of the fall in the price of copper, Zambia's main export commodity, but because the nation-state was "run by an inept and venal elite who used easy credit to line their own pockets. Much of the money Zambia borrowed was squandered or stolen. Bigwigs skimmed from worthy-sounding contracts. When the country brought bright new fire engines their price somehow ballooned by 70 percent, to more than $1 million each. Its new roads mysteriously cost twice as much per kilometer as its neighbours'. Its airport terminal was designed to accommodate an improbable ten-fold jump in traffic. A slide into authoritarianism made corruption harder to check."[3]

When Frederick Chiluba, an evangelical Christian, became president of Zambia in 1991, he sought systematically to loot state resources. He discovered a secret bank account kept in London to facilitate national security purchases. Soon, the only person in the ministry of finance authorized to disburse funds from that account was shifting monies from the special account into Chiluba's personal one. He purchased fancy suits in Switzerland and property in Belgium and South Africa, rewarded the ministry official, and proceeded to obstruct an anti-corruption investigating commission. Eventually, for these and many other offenses, a British court convicted Chiluba of stealing $58 million. His wife took $300,000 worth of goods from the furnishings of state house and was also convicted.

Less conspicuous siphoning of state funds took place in Zimbabwe in 2001 when President Robert Mugabe awarded the nation's largest contract to his nephew for the construction of a modern international airport. In South Africa, frigates and aircraft were purchased from France and Sweden so that leaders of the ruling African National Congress (ANC), particularly then–defense minister Zuma, could take a healthy cut via the kickback route. More recently, a South African corporate executive, admitted giving cash bribes (called "monopoly money") to high-ranking members of the ANC executive and stuffed $22,000 into a fancy handbag for Zuma. An ANC cabinet minister, he testified, liked receiving an annual Christmas basket that contained four cases of fancy whisky, forty cases of beer, and eight cut-up lambs.[4] "Corruption is now deeply embedded in the ANC at all levels," a researcher concluded. "In parts of the country it more closely resembles a criminal enterprise than a political party. Tender corruption, the rampant plundering of state assets, and kickbacks have become the new normal."[5]

Burundi, one of the globe's poorest polities, was pillaged by a president who demanded cash for all cabinet and bureaucratic appointments and benefited personally from every official construction contract. Tanzanian cabinet ministers found a way in 2014 and 2015 to take large amounts of cash out of the national electricity monopoly's reserve fund and deposit the proceeds in private accounts overseas.

The "Cashgate" scandal of 2013 revealed that at least twenty-five Malawian cabinet ministers and their staffs had systematically over-invoiced their departments for expenses and falsified payrolls—all to the tune of at least $54 million. The managers of local banks and the country's accountant general were in on the scheme, as was the national budget director. He was killed to keep him from exposing the vast fraud.

Another Malawian scam occurred when the government-controlled Strategic Grain Reserve purposely sold most of its supply (donated from abroad during a food emergency) instead of keeping it to alleviate the shortages that followed. At that point, with maize scarce, the Grain Reserve had to buy new supplies in South Africa, thus costing the country and consumers. And whatever pre-crisis maize still remained in storage was sold quietly to favored government ministers and traders, who then profited enormously from rising prices. The manager of the Reserve used his gains to purchase a five-star hotel, and much else. Later, benefiting from impunity, he became minister of finance.

The Need to "Eat"

The resource curse is also fundamental to grand corruption. Where there is oil and gas, and sometimes diamonds or even copper, cobalt, and iron ore, politicians at the apex of their societies can allocate concessions and permits to favored producers, and reap the proceeds personally (rather than the state). In Africa this has happened in Angola, Chad, the Republic of Congo, the Democratic Republic of Congo, Equatorial Guinea, Gabon, Nigeria, South Sudan, the Sudan, and Zimbabwe.

As a member of Zambia's cabinet admitted rather proudly: "There is nobody who is not using my philosophy of [the] politics of benefits. There is nobody who goes into Parliament because of allowances. There is no more patriotism. Patriotism was only there when we were fighting colonialists. . . .

I know people will say Munkombwe has gone into government because he wants to eat but who does not want to eat?"[6] In Africa French speakers refer to *bouffer*—"to gobble." KiSwahili speakers talk of about having or getting *mchuzi*—"sauce."

Nigerians have long perfected the art of getting "chop." The twentieth-century decades of extreme military-dominated greed, serial chicanery, and the repeated looting of the national treasury culminated in the unstoppable thefts of General and President Sani Abacha and his fellow officers. Petroleum revenues rolled in, so one regime after another inventively conceived ways to turn those ample rewards into personal gain.

Fake public contracts for phantom projects was one approach. A $7 billion mill never rolled any steel, a $3 billion smelter produced no aluminum. Another $5 billion was just lifted from the national treasury and carried to Switzerland, where Abacha had 120 bank accounts that held at least $670 million when he died in 1998. But his overall wealth probably amounted to $4.3 billion. Earlier, General Ibrahim Babangida had run off with $12 billion. Those amounts probably do not even approximate the total amounts that Mobutu Sese Seko stashed abroad when he ran Zaire. Nor do they equal what Eduardo dos Santos and his family took from Angola's oil riches. We also do not know how enormously much the Obiang dictatorship in tiny Equatorial Guinea has purloined, again from oil, and from his people.

When civilian rule returned to Nigeria in this century, the looting continued, but at a somewhat diminished scale. The first head of Nigeria's innovative Economic and Financial Crimes Commission prosecuted a federal police inspector general on 149 counts of money laundering for embezzling about $50 million of police funds. He charged the governor of an oil-pumping state who, it turned out, had properties all over the world. The governor was caught in Britain carrying about $1.6 million in cash. Later he forfeited $7.9 million and was impeached by his state legislature.

Much more recently, Nigerian President Goodluck Jonathan's chief security advisor awarded fictitious and phantom contracts for the purchase of jet fighter aircraft, helicopters, bombs, and ammunition—all presumably intended to strengthen the nation's air force as it battled Boko Haram, the Movement for the Emancipation of the Niger Delta, desperadoes in the Middle Belt, and pirates in the Gulf of Guinea. But the equipment was never ordered despite vast sums being transferred to nonexistent external companies in order to benefit the advisor and his cronies.

At a slightly less elevated level, as late as 2019, federal politicians and high state and federal public servants were still trafficking in ill-gotten earnings and abusing elected office for private gain. The army's war against Boko Haram was continuing to fail because officers sold the rations meant for their soldiers or took bribes to let questionable miscreants slip through cordons. They were also in cahoots with oil thieves in the Gulf of Guinea. In Nigeria, it was said, "you're more likely to get into trouble with the police authorities if you don't pay a bribe than if you do."[7]

In late 2019, the mayor of Nairobi, Kenya's capital city, was arrested for awarding construction contracts to close aides and gaining big kickbacks, misappropriating (stealing) government funds, forging documents, and money laundering. Tens of millions of dollars were involved, as well as the gold jewelry and clothing that he wore for a decade.

Abundant opportunities exist in every developing and even some developed countries for those who are politically or bureaucratically powerful to abuse their public positions for vast private gain. Avarice never stops at the edge of a presidential palace or a prime ministerial residence.It is the indulgences of those at the top of a governing pyramid that sanction the grasping of others lower down the greased totem pole of corruption. Whole nations consequently make corruption a way of life. That process saps the nation's resources, diverts tax and royalty payments from national to private purses, and once again robs ordinary citizens of deserved political goods such as school textbooks and safe cities.

Recounting all of the ways in which leaders of Africa and their henchmen make money off the public, illicitly but frequently without any punishment or recourse, could easily fill an entire chapter of this book. The scams are inventive, their audacity memorable, and whether grand or petty corruption is involved, every example cheats fellow citizens and cheapens life—and sometimes endangers health and security—for whole African populations. Corruption is insidious, as these examples have shown, and malicious. It shifts wealth from hard-striving citizens to politicians and, admittedly, sometimes poorly paid functionaries. But it does not enlarge the productive capacity of a state. Nor does it provide new sources of domestic investment; the big hauls of grand corruption are usually secreted overseas. As these examples have shown, there is absolutely nothing developmentally positive about grand corruption.

Winning the Anticorruption Battle

Encouragingly, even though much of Africa has been captured by corruption and despite the fact that many of its leaders are kleptocrats, intent on amassing their own fortunes rather than enhancing the welfare of their constituents, the anti-corruption impulse in Africa is alive and well, and often vigorous. Botswana has remained essentially noncorrupt since its independent inception in 1966. Mauritius, Cape Verde, the Seychelles, and Rwanda are additional outliers, each having rejected corruption as a way of politics and of leadership. Senegal and Ghana have more recently moved away from condoning corrupt practices.

For other African nation-states to follow these front-runners—to embrace the exemplary Botswanan model—will take time, major governance and leadership reforms, and a host of political and social improvements. Nonetheless, becoming a bastion of noncorruption is eminently possible. That is the stark lesson of Rwanda, recalling the swift conversion of Hong Kong and Singapore from rampantly corrupt developing world city-states into noncorrupt, rapidly rising, modern territorial successes. It is also the enduring contribution of visionary, inclusive leadership in Botswana, as discussed shortly. Determinations by national political leaders to attack corruption at its source are essential to successful, sustainable, anticorruption efforts.

Assaults on the fortress of corruption demand wholesale attention to a number of other societal reforms, plus the shoring up of vital national institutions. Fundamentally, in order to oust corruption from an African nation and to remove the acceptance of corruption as a way of life from its dominant political culture, the state needs laws sufficiently strong to comprise a deterrent. Nearly all African states have such legislation on their books. Some also have investigatory commissions mandated, as in Hong Kong, Singapore, Mauritius, Botswana, and dozens of other African nations, to pursue allegedly corrupt politicians and officials without fear or favor. Uganda established a special Health Monitoring Unit specifically to reduce extortion in that sector. Within five years to 2015, it reduced bribery in the national health service from 50 percent of all patient interactions to 25 percent. But corrupt dealings have since resumed.

As a part of its drive against corrupt practices, Rwanda in late 2018 legally expanded the definition of corruption to include making decisions on the basis of favoritism, friendship, or hatred as well as the usual bribery, influence peddling, illicit enrichment, abuse of power, and demanding "excessive" money. The new law also provided incentives for whistleblowers to inform on corrupt miscreants. Moreover, new special anti-corruption courts were established to help to prosecute offenders; the country's ombudsperson was tasked with orchestrating Rwanda's renewed assault on corrupt practices. This upgraded anti-corruption machinery strengthened Rwanda's already notable determination to extirpate all manner of chicanery, in line with the dictates of President Kagame.

But having good laws and skillful investigators and prosecutors may not alone erase impunity; an independent judiciary composed of judges whose verdicts cannot be swayed with cash or promises of promotion is fundamental. Too many African countries have politicized their supposed anticorruption commissions and given effective impunity to highly placed offenders. Moreover, in only a handful of African nations can the judges be considered strictly free of executive control.

Critical, as well, in overturning corrupt practices is the strengthening of accountability and transparency by supporting and welcoming a vigilant, observant media capable of uncovering and detailing abuses by politicians, officials, and other corrupt leaders. Auditors-general with forensic experience and ombudspersons to receive and investigate citizen concerns and complaints are also intrinsic to the anticorruption battle. Forty-six African countries have ombuds offices. South Africa's ombudsperson (titled the public protector) performed decisively in that country's identification of corrupt dealings and in taking President Zuma to court. There is a role, too, in this difficult combat, for large-scale outside audits of whole countries, such as the massive examination of Malawi's official books in 2015. In that same year, Kenya's own auditor-general reported that only 26 percent of the government's financial statements were "true and fair." A full 16 percent were "misleading." Essentially, the Kenyan government could not account for the largest proportion of its then $16 billion budget.

A Free Media

As Nelson Mandela said, "I cannot overemphasize the value we place on a free, independent and outspoken press. . . . Such a free press will temper the appetite of any government to amass power at the expense of the citizen."[8] A free press and a free media are critically essential if citizens hope to contain, or at least to combat, corruption. Absent the searching spotlights of journalists and crusading editors, much that goes on behind closed government doors, or in corporate corridors, will remain dark, hidden from a public, and, indeed, even from inquiring minds within an administrative machine.

Kleptocrats, often autocrats, usually try to curb the activities of the media within, and sometimes outside their countries. Too much scrutiny will reveal corruption or other illicit abuses of public office and, conceivably, arouse cynical and suspicious citizens. Or, in some situations, political leaders with lots to hide persuade wealthy "friends" to purchase and thus rein in overly inquisitive journalistic enterprises. That has happened in a number of African nation-states, and in a one-time bastion of press freedom such as South Africa.

Even easier, in some ways, governments that fear sunshine impose direct state control on broadcast media such as television and radio, or even own newspapers directly. In Zimbabwe, corrupt for decades, the state directly publishes the largest two daily newspapers, owns the only television service, and controls the primary radio outlet. (Most Africans obtain their news from the radio.) It even, as in so many other countries, permits mobile telephones and SIM payment cards to be used only by registered persons. It has not managed directly to censor or otherwise restrict broadband or other Internet services, as other more technically proficient regimes have done. But that could come.

In Tanzania, President John Magufuli has banned radio stations and newspapers. He also ended the live coverage of Parliamentary proceedings. A freelance journalist disappeared under suspicious circumstances. A Cybercrimes Act prohibits "insulting" Magufuli. Other kinds of communications and social media blogs have to be officially registered, for a fee.

The official Press Freedom Index prepared by Reporters without Borders rates 180 countries and puts Eritrea, North Korea, and the Sudan at the bottom of the list. Finland, the Netherlands, and Norway stand out at the top.

Media freedom is heavily compromised in North Africa and sub-Saharan Africa. Botswana, Cape Verde, Kenya, Malawi, Mauritius, Namibia, and South Africa are largely tolerant of media inquiries, but in African countries such as Angola, Burundi, the Democratic Republic of Congo, both Sudans, Tanzania, and Togo the media are heavily controlled and journalists find ferreting out information about questionable behavior perilous as well as difficult. In 2019, in previously mostly tolerant Nigeria, President Buhari and his legions abruptly entered an Abuja courtroom to grab a prominent American-based Nigerian journalist whom the court had earlier released from jail. Furthermore, a bill being debated late in the year in Nigeria's National Assembly would make "hate speech" a capital offence. In the likes of Equatorial Guinea and Eritrea there are no unshackled media; free expression is heavily curtailed. Performing a watchdog role and attempting to pinpoint losses of integrity (so that citizens can judge for themselves) is difficult and positively dangerous in much of Africa.

A Swazi editor was fired for exposing the prime minister's shady land deals. In South Sudan, a newspaper was shut after it suggested that the president's daughter was unpatriotic for marrying an Ethiopian. In Zimbabwe, two print journalists were detained and tortured by the security forces when they asked questions about financial shenanigans. Under a since-deposed Gambian dictator, death threats and middle-of-the-night arrests were visited upon reporters who refused to sing the regime's praises. (In 2019, a special commission was uncovering horrendous abuses.) In Zambia, its president forced the nation's main independent newspaper, which campaigned against graft, to shut down.

Where the media is interfered with there is always much more corruption. The more draconian the restrictions imposed by anxious rulers, the more corrupt behavior there is to expose. Under those conditions, the work of uncompromised newspapers and television and radio outlets is essential if civil society has any hope of holding corrupt political leaders and other public servants accountable. Transparency depends in part on publicizing the results of anti-corruption activities as widely as possible. Shining a luminous light is the first step in exposing nefarious activities. That brightness also makes it difficult for public servants to steal, take kickbacks, favor friends, and more.

One of the great triumphs of modern investigative journalism, comparable to the battle against graft and theft in Boss Tweed's New York at the turn of the twentieth century, occurred in Ghana in 2015. An enterprising reporter working for a local media company captured nearly five hundred hours of video that showed judges on the state's highest courts asking for bribes, extorting cash from litigants in exchange for favorable verdicts, and negotiating the release of prisoners for stiff fees. Thirty-four judges and 150 other court personnel were ultimately removed from their august positions. But their sackings did not necessarily mean that citizens in that country or in similar ones could count on the media to help them keep track of and expose corrupt practices in all of their mendacious variety.

Additional simple expedients, such as what the Americans call "Freedom of Information" laws and methods for employing court orders to extract government-held information, do not exist in an effective manner everywhere. Where they do, and where such orders are obeyed, actions can be initiated against corrupt entities and individuals. Usually, however, there are no easily available or even findable documents capable of suggesting avenues of inquiry to journalists. Incriminating evidence must therefore be found in a suspect's new wealth, extensive foreign trips, or association with suspicious criminalized elements. Sometimes, however, good sleuthing turns up actionable information about how public servants falsified accounts, did the shady bidding of superiors, or made decisions clearly against the public interest. Thorough investigatory journalism can also discover when presidents fail to pay taxes or evade taxes by clever maneuvers. Transparency in these kinds of instances depends on good gumshoe work by journalists and civil society, and on mistakes made by corrupt perpetrators.

That is effectively how the extent to which the Gupta clan, from India, joined President Zuma to "capture" South Africa for corrupt purposes, was finally exposed. The Guptas essentially enrolled Zuma's family members and his closest African National Congress colleagues in a vast scheme of kickbacks and bribery; the Guptas and senior politicians gained great wealth. Finally, in 2017, the public protector and the media's sleuthing exposed what had constituted the capture of the state by Zuma and the Guptas. Zuma and his co-conspirators were ousted, and the Gupta-Zuma empire shut down. The U.S. Treasury's Office of Foreign Assets Control sanctioned the Guptas in 2019 and blocked all transactions between financial institutions and members of that family. In 2020, a newly recruited head of the cleaned-up National Prosecuting Authority vowed to clean out the stables by pursuing literally hundreds of complex cases of corruption among Zuma's implicated cadres.

Occasionally in the developing world, citizen, corporate, or donor interests encourage transparency. The media may then be allowed to examine governmental actions to see that such activity is in the public interest, as occasionally in Uganda. In democracies, budgetary and official expenditure information is readily available. But in kleptocracies, those kinds of data are too often hidden or falsified. Revealing suspicions or showing partisanship may even prove life-limiting.

The U.S. Foreign Corrupt Practices Act, and similar legislation in the United Kingdom and Canada, is increasingly being employed to ferret out, prosecute, and then deter corruption in Africa. For example, in late 2018, the recent finance minister of Mozambique was nabbed in Johannesburg as he was about to board a flight to Dubai (after arriving from Maputo). A Lebanese businessman was simultaneously arrested in New York and three Swiss bankers in London. As revealed by the U.S. Federal Bureau of Investigation and the International Monetary Fund, the former finance minister had accepted $200 million (on behalf of the then president of Mozambique, the defense minister [subsequently the president], and others) in exchange for favoring an Abu Dhabi logistical concern that wanted to be the prime recipient of contracts associated with building out the country's nascent natural gas industry. As one of the co-conspirators explained, "In democratic governments like ours people come and go, and everyone involved will want to have his share of the deal while in office, because once out of the office it will be difficult."[9]

Other Innovations

All innovations that improve transparency are valuable. That is why the removal of rules for the sake of rules, or rules for the sake of bureaucratic convenience, are best eliminated. It helps to remove anything that allows agents of the state to be tempted to abuse their authority. The less discretion available to such intermediaries between the administration and the public, the fewer the opportunities there are to extort payments for services—to lubricate transactions. Similarly the fewer the permits that must be obtained, the fewer the customs categories, the fewer the barriers that citizens have to hurdle to complete their daily errands, and the fewer the everyday interactions with police personnel, the fewer the chances are that someone with power will attempt to wield it against civilians.

Much of traditional petty corruption vanishes when polities put all or most of their transactions with citizens online. Digitizing the permit application process eliminates nearly all of those interventions that would hitherto have constituted perfect opportunities for graft.

Each of these progressive reforms or innovations is important in all attempts to battle corrupt operations to a standstill. Each is necessary. But none, on its own, can curb corruption completely. Strengthening political institutions (or reforming them so that they can operate responsibly) is another relevant and necessary objective. But doing so is only a part of the package of change that must occur if societies are to shift from corrupt to noncorrupt sides of the ledger. Whole societies, not just sections of the whole, need to be transformed if societies long mired in chicanery and sleaze are to embrace ethical universalism and begin the long walk back to good governance and a robust rule of law.

Fortunately, although assaults on corrupt practices across Africa are hardly universal and not widespread, there is a brighter light increasingly being shone on corruption everywhere. The influence of social media across cultures and countries and the almost universal use of mobile telephones and the information that they transmit to disparate peoples mean that the evils of corruption are now well disseminated. The citizens of African polities long accustomed to the pall of corruption now know that they need not endure it at home—that they can hope to emulate those several countries that have broken the golden corset of corruption, or at least lessened its domestic yoke around their lives.

Increasingly, the ills of corruption are being illuminated within Africa; corruption no longer lurks in the shadows, unspoken and unacknowledged, but is ever present, exposed, and ever destructive of national priorities. The disease that was little discussed before the 1990s in much of Africa is now named as one of the two or three central odious conditions of our times. We fortunately know what the remedies are; given sufficient political will those remedies can be administered within the more corrupt jurisdictions of Africa to the immense benefit of its long-suffering peoples.

Energetic and emboldened civil societies are significant as well. They can act as the vanguard of citizen-wide concerns and, using social media and other new technological methods, refuse to accept fraud and graft by rulers and ruling elites. Social media notifications were used to enlarge and hasten the scale of Oromo demonstrations against Ethiopian corruption, to strengthen the public protector's position in exposing Zuma in South Africa, to energize protests against Ugandan plundering, to help to oust presidents in Algeria and the Sudan, and to bring the concerns of large numbers of Nigerians to the attention of state and federal regimes there.

Leadership Essential

Little of what is suggested above by way of advances, and little of the overall attitudinal societal shift away from corruption, happens absent political leaders committed to erasing corruption as a customary way of life and rule. Leaders send signals to their colleagues, officials, and functionaries. Without affirming moves away from business as usual—as President Sir Seretse Khama did in Botswana and Prime Minister Lee Kuan Yew accomplished in Singapore— and without imposing a new sense of integrity on themselves and on their close associates, transitioning away from the expectation of profiteering at the public's expense is difficult and unlikely. In order to reorient grasping grand corrupters and their petty imitators, the commitment of the new or reforming leader must be credible and her or his personal deportment visibly chaste. Leaders who are compromised personally, such as Kabila, Museveni, Sisi, Zuma, and President Bakili Muluzi of Malawi, and therefore illegitimate in the eyes of their publics, doom any anticorruption efforts to early failure.

No winning campaign against corruption succeeds without leaders who articulate a vision of noncorruption, who mobilize their immediate and distant followers behind that vision, who are themselves accountable and transparent, and who are able over time to socialize whole societies to accept the benefits and responsibilities of eschewing influence seeking through contract fraud, speed payments, and similar queue-jumping mechanisms. Those kinds of African leaders do more than just set out the goals of a just society: they educate, they instruct, and they assemble enduring administrative edifices of anticorruption.

Few anticorruption crusades have succeeded that have not been leader-conceived and leader-driven. That said, since responsible political leadership clearly makes a material difference in these kinds and other kinds of political circumstances, especially in the poor and pre-institutionalized states that are common in Africa, how do we nurture those kinds of willing reformers? The lessons derived from anticorruption efforts in twentieth-century Asia and Africa emphasize leadership that emerges when publics are better educated, more middle class, more bourgeois, more aware of their participation in the global village, and much more demanding of their elected or appointed rulers. With Africa's maturing and enlarged middle class, that time is near.

Sometimes, too, as in contemporary Rwanda, rulers can impose values on constituents and rapidly transform a corrupt society into one with little corruption and little crime. Always, leadership of some determined, appealing kind there must be. Indeed, citizenries on their own cannot cleanse whole societies of the scourge of corruption; from among their ranks, and from the ranks of those they elect, they must find leaders appropriate for the massive task of constructing a noncorrupt enterprise.

Political cultures are greatly determined by leadership signals, leadership approaches and postures, and leadership sins of both commission and omission. Reforms, therefore, can only happen when new political leaders arrive who are insistent upon positive change. They do so at the beginning of their incumbencies, or at some later stage in their political ascendancy when a striking break with the past seems appropriate. President Kagame did so ten years into his uncompromising paramountcy in Rwanda.

Those leader-initiated disruptions of prevailing attitudes toward and pursuits of graft may be implemented legislatively, with the imposition of new kinds of legal constraints (and exemplary prosecutions and trials). Or they can follow the exposure of peculation and chicanery by an aroused media, by conscientious auditors, by independent investigatory bodies, and by the actions of whistleblowers. But none of these many methods of unveiling corruption and encouraging citizen protest has by itself led to significant reductions in domestic levels of corruption. To succeed in a truly transformational manner, these initiatives need to be embraced and then championed by political leaders who can proclaim a new vision and sell that vision of a corrupt-free society to their followers.

Botswana as Forerunner

The experiences since the 1960s of Botswana and Mauritius showcase the upside of positive leadership. The first polity has consistently been the least corrupt country in Africa, recently joined by the Seychelles, as well as a rapid economic grower. Thanks to honest management, a strong rule of law, tolerant democratic good governance, and an unwavering commitment to integrity at the highest levels of political and governmental life, Botswana performed well without compromising democratic values, without limiting free expression or freedom of assembly. Mauritius, similarly, under Sir Seewoosagur Ramgoolam, its initial prime minister, refused to condone corrupt practices. Despite investments from Asia, and despite varied approaches to the nation's development, Ramgoolam and his successors inculcated a political culture of inclusiveness, democracy, fairness, and noncorruption that has enabled the island nation to become one of Africa's wealthiest, with far less sleaze than most of its off-shore and mainland compatriots.

Botswana early showcased the great standard-of-living benefits of a noncorrupt national ethos and approach. Khama decided, upon achieving independence for Botswana in 1966 (formerly the British-run Protectorate of Bechuanaland) as its first president, that corruption was the ruin of the still young other recently decolonized states of Africa. Understandably, knowing his neighbors, he feared that the contagion of graft would spread into his thinly populated, resource-poor outpost of freedom. He knew that sub-Saharan Africa's other early leaders, like Presidents Kwame Nkrumah in Ghana and Sékou Touré in Guinea, were greedy; the retreat of colonial oversight aroused avarice among the newly empowered. Khama wanted to avoid such results in his country. Like Prime Minister Lee Kuan Yew in Singapore a few years earlier, he reckoned that to permit corrupt behavior in a fragile new state like Botswana would coarsen its people and weaken their potential for growth and betterment, and make progress much more difficult to manage.

Khama consciously instructed his close associates, public servants, and citizens never to view their national emancipation as an invitation to personal enrichment. He made it a rule that cabinet ministers and other high officials should avoid being indebted and should quickly cover any bank overdrafts. Khama, boldly as a nation-builder, said that "doing good" was his "real religion."[10] Eschewing anything that smacked of corruption was thus essential to his vision. He knew, furthermore, that demonstrating personal integrity and regime integrity was fundamental to such a campaign against corruption. Central to such a vision was a decision to shun the trappings of autocracy despite his other persona as a paramount chief of Botswana's largest ethnic group. For him, unlike so many contemporary African heads of states, being a "big man" was not necessary. He abandoned the patrimonial pretensions of his peers.

Khama lived modestly. He himself traveled by road, but without the long motorcades that typify many other African presidencies. He insisted that his vice president and other senior leaders of the government travel by air in economy class, unlike the first-class travel common in other African countries. Khama understood that legitimacy and integrity were core competencies of effective and transformational leadership. He also appreciated that he could not simply instruct his followers to avoid anything that could be or appear unethical. More sustainably, he sought to construct a lasting edifice of noncorruption that would outlast his relatively short reign, and it has. Four subsequent presidents have built powerfully on his foundations, making the landlocked country's high per capita incomes, extensive roads and effective tourism infrastructure, its schools and university, its attention to the public health needs of its citizens despite high HIV/AIDS rates, and additional praiseworthy accomplishments a testament to Khama's early eschewing of the expected pay-for-play that so damaged Botswana's African competitors.

Khama's enduring achievements, and his unblemished integrity and legitimacy, are all worth aspiring to by today's African leadership cadres, and the sub-continent's civil societies. Beating back corruption and thus delivering economic development, improved governance, and a sustainable belief in the overarching national enterprise are goals available to any of Africa's ruling regimes when they are ready to renounce kleptocratic and rent-seeking ambitions. To satisfy the continent's protesting (and other) widespread citizen demands they need but begin to emulate Khama's example, and take a few (certainly not all) lessons from Kagame.

VI | The China Factor

SOLVING AFRICA'S CENTRAL concerns of the mid-twenty-first century—
how to grow economically as its population surges and how to create more
and more jobs for its burgeoning labor force—depends on China. Likewise,
enabling Africa to improve its human security and human welfare in most
of its component nations depends on China. Third, strengthening Africa's
infrastructural architecture depends mostly on China. Without steady domestic Chinese economic growth and the behemoth's consequent continued
need for primary resources derived from Africa, however, prospects for many
of the latter continent's nation-states are, at best, problematic. Chinese demand drives African prosperity, raises world prices for primary products, and
has made it possible for a number of the polities of Africa to accumulate
wealth, to uplift their peoples, and to begin to play larger roles on the world's
stage. In this decade, and later, Africa and China are bound together syner-
gistically in ways that cannot readily be replaced by trade, aid, or attention
from the United States, India, Russia, Brazil, or Europe.

In 2019, China's domestic economic engine was weakening. Its world-
supplying factories were also reducing production. In part reflecting an
intensifying trade war with the United States and the pressure of American
tariffs and growing tensions and uncertainties caused by Sino-American sabre
rattling, in part a result of Beijing's attempt to restrict credit, in part a consequence of effective higher wages in China than in Vietnam and Bangladesh,
and in part a result of the increasingly heavy-handed state control of both the
Chinese macro- and micro-economies, China's economic juggernaut appeared

to be seizing up. Imports of iron ore and coal were reduced; some Chinese thermal power plants were shut. (The coronavirus epidemic in 2020 added perilously to China's—and Africa's—insecurity.) Depending on whether this pause in the relentless growth of the globe's most populous power is a pause, or a significant readjustment, its short- as well as long-term impact will reverberate throughout the African continent. Who else will buy Africa's primary commodities? Who will purchase its (limited) manufactured and agricultural goods? Who will lend generously so that Africa can construct its dams, pipelines, railways, and roads?

Terms of Trade

China from 2005 to 2019 has been the major purchaser of Africa's petroleum, natural gas, iron ore, coal, cobalt, coltan, copper, ferrochrome, vanadium, cadmium, platinum, titanium, palladium, manganese, uranium, zinc, and lead. China buys Africa's diamonds and gold. It imports vast amounts of timber. African and transplanted Chinese farmers produce maize, soybeans, sugar, and tobacco for the Chinese market, as Saudis do in the Sudan. A few consumer goods additionally are manufactured in Africa for export to China. Ivory, rhinoceros horn, and pangolin scales are illicit transfers from Africa to China. Incoming tourists from China, comparatively numerous in South Africa and Kenya, are another profitable export earner.

There are only a few other large-scale purchasers to which Africa could sell its primary commodities. The United States once purchased large quantities of Nigerian, Angolan, and Equatorial Guinean petroleum, but its own new domestic shale-released supply has reduced its thirst for foreign oil and gas. (Nigeria's petroleum exports in 2016, worth $27 billion, went to India, the United States, Spain, France, and South Africa, in that order.) The United States still purchases the ferrochrome, platinum, and palladium that it cannot buy elsewhere, but, alongside China, European countries are the chief consumers of African minerals. Only cobalt and coltan, valuable for the manufacture of mobile telephones, aircraft, and military equipment, are sought from the Democratic Republic of Congo and Zambia equally by the United States, Europe, and China. India is in the market, too, for African minerals, but on a scale dwarfed by the other major industrial countries. Some coal mined in Mozambique finds its way to Brazil. In short, Africa's continued prosperity primarily depends on the health and vigor of China. So does Africa's exciting attempt to give its peoples full citizenship in the global village.

China has long sought to ensure its immediate and long-term energy security. To that end it has proffered loans and debt relief in exchange for guaranteed supplies of petroleum from Angola, helped build in order partially to control the pipeline and pumping facilities that send South Sudanese petroleum to Port Sudan on the Red Sea, is upgrading Nigeria's entire oil industry, and is active directly through Chinese state-owned producing and serving concerns in sixteen other African countries with substantial petroleum reserves. Algeria, Angola, Cameroon, the Central African Republic, Chad, Egypt, Gabon, Ghana, Kenya, Libya, Mauritania, Niger, Nigeria, the Republic of Congo, the Sudan, South Sudan, and Tunisia all have on-going arrangements with Chinese petroleum extracting and servicing companies.

China receives at least 22 percent of its imported oil, 1.4 million barrels a day, from Africa. In 2017, China purchased $20 billion worth of petroleum from Angola (12.2 percent of its total oil imports). The Republic of Congo supplied $3.4 billion worth (2.1 percent of the total). (Russia and Saudi Arabia were the dominant exporters of petroleum to China, sending 15 percent and 13 percent of China's total purchases, respectively. Angola was next.) The imports from Congo represented a 61 percent increase over 2016; the amount from Angola rose by 43 percent over 2016. Countries in the rest of Africa supplied less than 1 percent each of China's petroleum needs in 2017, but that trickle of oil into China nevertheless represented substantial incomes for the smaller-producing countries of Africa.

Because China is one of the key industrial economies of the world, it also buys base metals and other minerals from Africa. Its own reserves are insufficient to satisfy normal domestic demand, and most of its own ores are low grade and costly to mine. Therefore it turned to Africa as long ago as 2000 and steadily, until and despite the 2019 downturn, relied more and more on imports from Africa to feed its own unquenchable requirements for the components of steel-making, a very broad range of consumer products, electricity generation, and more. In 2018, more than $40 billion worth of iron ore, copper, manganese, bauxite, ferrochrome, zinc, cobalt, and uranium were obtained from Africa. Liberia and Sierra Leone supplied the iron ore. The Democratic Republic of Congo and Zambia shipped the copper and cobalt; manganese arrived from South Africa, Gabon, and Ghana; bauxite came from Guinea and Ghana; ferrochrome from South Africa (supplying a full 72 percent of China's needs) and Zimbabwe; and zinc was sourced from Zambia and South Africa. Uranium is now available to China from Niger and from a large Chinese-owned open cast mine in Namibia.

In 2017, South Africa alone exported $19 billion worth of metals and minerals to China, $10 billion to the United Kingdom, $7.5 billion to the United States, $6.2 billion to Germany, and $6 billion to India. South Africa's major sales to all of these countries (and others) were primarily gold, diamonds, platinum, motor cars, coal, and petroleum, in that order. South African diamonds in the same period were shipped to the United States, India, Hong Kong, Belgium, the United Arab Emirates, China (receiving 7 percent of the total in dollar value), and Israel, in that descending order.

Timber, mostly African teak, is another valuable African commodity that Liberia, the Republic of Congo, the Central African Republic, Gabon, and Zambia sell to China. Cash comes in, of course, but large swathes of what remains of Africa's rapidly shrinking forest cover disappears. Indeed, in 2019 international investigative NGOs asserted that Chinese firms were stripping forests in Gabon and the Congo (Brazzaville) and causing immense environmental damage. Payoffs to both governments facilitated this continued devastation.

China and Indonesia are among the last global nations where smokers are in the majority. China has therefore become not only the best, but one of the last markets for Virginia tobacco from Zimbabwe and flue-cured tobacco from Malawi, where tobacco accounts for 96 percent of export revenues. Côte d'Ivoire and Ghana send cocoa to China, too, but their big markets are still European. South Africa ships wine, wool, sugar, and fishmeal to China.

Africa buys far less from China than it sells. Most of Africa's imports from that source are of consumer goods, textiles, electronic goods and equipment, machinery, motorcycles, t-shirts, clothing, mattresses, sheets and pillowcases, footwear, kitchen utensils, and some processed food. In 2019, Chinese textile manufacturers reported a surge in orders from Africa, especially from Ethiopia and Nigeria. Côte d'Ivoire is the globe's largest importer of rice from China. South Africa even buys sausage casings from China.

Total trade between Africa and China amounted to $122 billion annually in 2018, less than the European Union's $154 billion total, but far more than India's $63 billion (up from $7 billion in 2001), the United States' $36 billion, the United Arab Emirates' $20 billion, and the Japanese, Swiss, and Saudi Arabian $14 billion annual trade totals. Japan's total trade with Africa amounts to $9 billion a year.

From 2006 to 2018, China's total trade with Africa soared by 226 percent. India's total trade has grown faster, at 292 percent over the same years. The European Union increased its trade with Africa by 41 percent. But trade between the United States and Africa fell in the same period by 41 percent, Brazil's by 38 percent.

Without Chinese purchases of their raw materials, a number of African countries would suffer acute balance of payments problems. And Kenya, where trade with China has grown eightfold since 2008, now is so dependent on an incoming cascade of imported Chinese manufactured goods that— almost alone of the larger countries of Africa—it yearly pays out more to China than it receives. That trade imbalance is worsening, and making it very much harder than ever before to raise foreign currency from other, non-Chinese, sources with which to repay China. Being enmeshed with China thus has its constraints and downsides along with its many advantages.

Investment, Construction

Not only is China the predominant purchaser of African primary commodities. It is also a heavy investor in many sectors, and the builder of first resort when an African nation-state seeks to construct a major dam, pipeline, railway, or road. Much of Africa has come to rely on Chinese expertise, Chinese cash (even if it comes with eventual heavy interest costs), and Chinese ingenuity to realize its compelling infrastructural objectives. This mutual interdependence has injected China and Chinese methods, operations, personnel, and avarice deeply into the heart of Africa; almost no African country has managed to pry itself loose from China's enticing and all-enveloping tentacles.

Approximately 75 percent of all Chinese investment and activity is focused on constructing or reconstructing Africa's physical underpinnings. And of that 75 percent, worth more than $60 billion in 2019, a very large proportion is devoted to building dams and hydroelectrical facilities. China's promised fund for African infrastructural improvements is positive for African growth and, additionally, boosts Chinese construction profits.

China has recently erected or is now completing more than three hundred dams, including a handful of major structures in Ethiopia and the nearby Sudan, in Gabon, in Uganda, and in Zambia. It has built thermal power facilities in Botswana, Ghana, Kenya, Nigeria, Tanzania, Zambia, and Zimbabwe; a major new standard-gauge 472-kilometer (but loss-making and expensively financed) railway linking Mombasa to Nairobi and western Kenya and southern Uganda (where there are oil deposits ready to be exploited); a pipeline in the same direction; a vital new $3.4 million, 756-kilometer electric rail line between landlocked Addis Ababa and Djibouti, on the Red Sea; a coastal railway in Nigeria along with its refurbishment of the Lagos to Kano rail line and its double tracking of the same line as far as Ibadan; the refurbished Tazara rail link between Tanzania and Zambia and the similarly upgraded Takoradi to Kumasi rail line in Ghana; the skyscraper headquarters of the African Union in Addis Ababa; and dozens of airports, hospitals, party headquarters, bridges, telecommunications facilities, presidential mansions, stadia, sport arenas, a fish pier, and many other essential edifices in a plethora of African countries.

The new ring road around Nairobi was constructed by China. So were many newly paved roads in Malawi and a long highway toward the Sudan in Ethiopia. Almost every African country now boasts an important lengthy road or roads built or paved by Chinese contractors. China erected a military intelligence headquarters in Zimbabwe. In the Sudan, with which nation China has a particularly close relationship, China constructed a new international airport in Khartoum and built an oil refinery. China erected a much-needed oil refinery in Nigeria. It added a sparkling glass wing to Zambia's international airport. China sent orbiting satellites into space to improve communications within Nigeria. But, possibly China's most unusual or most innovative addition to Africa's arsenal of improvements and new facilities is the wrestling stadium that President Xi Jinping of China handed over to President Macky Sall of Senegal in 2018. Elsewhere in Senegal, China is paying for commuter rail links, a highway from Dakar to Touba, and an industrial park. In Egypt, in 2019, China was even fabricating an entirely new city.

These important projects have helped to modernize much of Africa and restore other, existing road and rail links to their one-time glory. Hydroelectricity-generating dams have begun to power cities and homes across the continent, and have enabled factories and other essential enterprises to function more effectively. Yet, many of these important projects have been completed and paid for with funds borrowed on not so generous terms from China. As in the Chinese-constructed major port in Sri Lanka, leased back to China for ninety-nine years, and an aborted, partially-built railway in Malaysia, becoming indebted to China has its serious downside. Angola took Chinese collateralized aid for its oil industry and has now lost control of 80 percent of its oil revenues for twenty-five years as a way of reimbursing China. A few years ago, Ghana exchanged 13,000 barrels a day of petroleum for a $3 billion loan, still unpaid. Kenya collateralized its Port of Mombasa to guarantee payment for a very costly Chinese Export Import Bank loan that paid for the construction of its standard gauge railway from Mombasa to Nairobi. Payment is due soon. In 2018, Zambia pledged its national electricity transmission system to obtain Chinese financial backing for a hydroelectric project on the Kafue River to which the International Monetary Fund refused to contribute. (Zambia's external debt to GDP ratio reached 60 percent in 2019, or 28 percent of national expenditures.) In late 2018, Sierra Leone canceled a $400 million loan from China that was meant to pay for the construction of its new international airport, fearing indebtedness. But then President Julius Maada Bio said that he was instead seeking China's help to build a critical $1 billion bridge, and might possibly renegotiate the price of the airport and its financing. The Republic of Congo is another African nation that owes China substantial sums.

The International Monetary Fund estimated in late 2018 that 40 percent of the nation-states of Africa were approaching dangerous levels of debt to China. (Johns Hopkins University's China African Research Initiative estimates that Africa between 2000 and 2017 accumulated as much as $143 billion in still to be repaid loans from China.) Already, in 2019, interest payments to China from Ghana, Angola, Zambia, and Nigeria absorbed a worrying more than 20 percent of government revenues. Little Djibouti, autocratically run, has major French, American, Japanese, and Chinese military bases from which it derives rents and other economic benefits. But it has also borrowed heavily from China's Export Import Bank, and may soon be unable to pay what it owes. About 80 percent of Djibouti's staggering total foreign debt is promised to China for port improvements, a water pipeline, and an International Free Trade Zone. China periodically hints that it will forgive some of its loans to some particularly poor African nations. But it never indicates which countries and regimes will be so favored. And very few borrowings have thus far been retired.

Export processing zones sponsored by the Chinese state in Africa have, however, proven an unqualified success. They are intended to foster growth in the host country, and greatly to reduce operational costs, thus making it easier for Chinese companies to set up shop, and profit. Zambia's zone focuses on copper products, shoe manufacturing, and mushroom growing and packing. Ethiopia's zone focuses on shoe and pharmaceutical manufacturing. Nigeria's zone produces oil-based commodities. Rwanda's zone concentrates on light manufacturing. The newish Chinese-constructed trade zone in Djibouti is meant to facilitate fabrication of components brought from Asia, for onward sale to Europe. (Singapore sponsors a similar zone in Gabon. Turkey has a zone in Djibouti competing with China's. Mauritius's own Indian-backed zone processes seafood for export, produces clothing, and assembles a range of technological and other light manufactured products, plus innovations in the cyber-realm.)

In terms of foreign direct investing, firms from the United States, the United Kingdom, and France still pump more cash into Africa, but Chinese private and public direct investments grew from $16 to $40 billion from 2006 to 2018, slightly less than France's $49 billion total.

Aid of Several Kinds

China's goals in Africa are not wholly mercantile. It has successfully out-maneuvered Taiwan in Africa; only Eswatini still recognizes Taiwan's sovereignty. It has successfully bolstered its support in the United Nations, in a succession of other international forums, and extended its Belt and Road Initiative to the northeastern corner of Africa. China also anchors BRICS, the economic development organization of Brazil, Russia, India, China, and South Africa. China knows that influence and "friendship" are relatively easy to purchase and its leaders, President and Premier Hu Jintao and Wen Jiabao initially, and now Xi Jinping and Wang Qishang, his deputy, tour Africa annually, host periodic summits, and lavish attention even on the smaller African polities. Since 2009, top Chinese leaders have made eighty trips to forty-three African countries, a veritable tsunami of attention. (Turkey's president Recep Tayyip Erdoğan has ventured to Africa thirty times; France's president Emmanuel Macron has set foot in Africa nine times from 2017 to 2019; Prime Minister Narendra Modi of India has visited eight countries.)

No criticism of Africa emanates from China. The principle of "no interference" has long guided China's involvement with Africa and meant, then and now, that even the most outrageous human rights violators are welcomed in Beijing and extolled in their home countries. Dictatorship and despotism in Africa obviously cannot concern China, which exhibits many of the same arbitrary tendencies, especially under Xi Jinping. Nor does oppression in an African entity (for example, the Sudan), or conflict in, say, South Sudan, much concern China if petroleum or other resources continue to find their way without interruption toward Shanghai and Chengdu.

Chinese assistance to Africa comes in many forms. It differs from Western and World Bank foreign aid, most of which is project-specific, socially inclined, and well rationalized. China instead gives and mostly lends to support commodity purchasing by its own operatives, or to secure concessions, again for Chinese state-owned and sometimes quasi-public entities. Its grants and most of its lending ultimately goes to support Chinese private or state-controlled concerns that have bid on or been allocated choice contracts. In turn, the winning Chinese firms mostly rely on imported Chinese labor to fulfill their contractual obligations. In 2019, about 200,000 mainland Chinese workers were toiling away on construction and other projects in Africa.[1]

Many Chinese firms assert that to accomplish their allotted tasks satisfactorily they need Chinese workers, both for ease of communication and also—primarily—because of the reliability (docility?) and the in-born work ethic of Chinese nationals. Those characteristics translate into a well-nourished ability to take orders and not complain. (A major Chinese corporation's bid to build a key refinery in Uganda specified that 60 percent of the labor force would be supplied from China.)

China remains largely indifferent to the short- or long-term results overseas, no matter how adverse, of the Chinese effort. Nor does it concern itself, even at the Olympian level, with the internal political results of its assistance. If local leaders strengthen their personal grip over a party or a nation because of Chinese backing, or if presidents, prime ministers, and cabinet ministers enrich themselves from Chinese aid funds and only devote a small portion of China's largesse to the needs of citizens, that is of little concern. China wants to be seen by whichever regimes are in power as a reliable partner—as a key interlocutor that will support local political functionaries, refrain from criticism, and accomplish whatever missions are assigned to it by a host government.

Everything China does is in furtherance of such a cynical, self-serving objective. Even its decision to supply medical corpsmen and other military peacekeeping personnel to the UN for deployment in South Sudan and Mali should be viewed in this light. Its base in Djibouti, however, is more likely situated there to keep a close eye on the United States' assertive efforts in the Horn of Africa (and elsewhere) and to provide an embryonic forward base when China seeks to be a presence in the Indian Ocean and its surround. China's Djibouti base can also guard the Belt and Road extensions to Africa and, along with its managerial control of Djibouti's container terminal, keep an eye on the nearby choke-point entrance to the Red Sea and the Suez Canal.

Assisting African Development

Since the affairs of Africa in this century have been of sustained concern not only to the ministry of foreign affairs and, recently, China's military command, but also to its ruling hierarchy, it is no surprise that every transactional relationship between even ostensibly private Chinese enterprises and Africans, especially African states, exists within the orbit of state control. The Chinese ministry of commerce and its Bureau of International Economic Cooperation initiate, coordinate, and approve most of what happens between China and Africa. The Bureau supervises the firms that are dispatched from Beijing or Shanghai to realize various kinds of official and unofficial projects in one after another African country. Farming and fishing endeavors (and most, but not all, of China's influence in and assistance to rural Africa), are organized by the Chinese ministry of agriculture. China and Nigeria have together produced hybrid rice seeds, for example, and Nigeria thereafter imported a large number of Chinese-produced rice mills for distribution to the nation's thirty-six states. Medical aid, which is a little noticed but important contribution of China to Africa, is arranged by its ministry of health; Africans have traveled to China to study public health and, particularly, to learn how China responds to its own public health emergencies (of which there are no shortage).

China's educational ministry sends teachers—a kind of peace corps—to more than thirty African nations. Some have ended up in African universities; many others serve in secondary schools. China also provides educational scholarships for more than 20,000 African students a year to study at Chinese universities and technical institutes, plus many student exchanges. In 2018, President Xi Jinping promised Africa 50,000 new university scholarships and 50,000 training opportunities for seminars and workshops. There is a special Chinese training course for journalists from Africa. (More Africans pursue higher educational opportunities in China each year than in the United States and the United Kingdom.) The Chinese clearly use access to educational opportunity for political ends. They say that providing scholarships and workshops for Africans (and for many other foreigners) helps people to understand China's political system and to eschew bias against things Chinese.

A limited amount of what Americans would consider humanitarian assistance comes from several Chinese ministries, not least foreign affairs and commerce. Beijing also established a Center for International Poverty Alleviation in Beijing; it trains African officials (and others) by introducing them to effective poverty relief projects in various Chinese provinces.

The true total of all of this assistance is difficult to calculate, and contested. China's persistent lack of transparency makes whatever number exists rather questionable. So is the hidden quality of China's motives. Nonetheless, grants qualify as developmental assistance, and some (but not all) concessional borrowings also should be classified in that way. But regular loans should be excluded. The most perceptive American researchers thus conclude that only a puny proportion of the myriad economic transactions between China and Africa (and the rest of the developing world) should fully be considered as foreign aid in Western terms. The West and Japan tout their relatively high levels of aid to Africa over many decades, but China does less in the same mode. Thus, the majority of all initiatives and endeavors, no matter what the Chinese say, are for the overall purpose of facilitating China's mercantile and influence-strengthening objectives. In 2018, Chinese aid to Africa, properly accounted for, probably amounted to about half of the value of individual

European, Japanese, and American assistance efforts. One research team concluded that from 2000 to 2014, 40 percent of $122 billion, or $49 billion, of Chinese financing in and for Africa could be considered philanthropic (according to OECD definitions). In that same period the United States gave aid worth $107 billion to Africa.[2]

The inverse of whatever we might conclude are effective Chinese eleemosynary efforts in Africa is its systematic support of some of Africa's least savory military operations and operatives. China has not hesitated to cozy up to autocratic despotisms and military regimes motivated by plunder. However, China has not characteristically armed African security forces to enhance its own sphere of military influence or to engage in cold war campaigns against the West. Instead, China's willingness to supply weapons, training, uniforms, and intelligence to a number of African nation-states is intended to secure its own enduring access to petroleum and minerals.

For ideological reasons, Communist China backed several of Africa's early liberation movements, and supplied them with arms and training mostly to oppose Soviet-backed rival insurgencies, but also because the movements in question were thoroughly anti-colonial. As a result, Zimbabwe's current ruling elite has ties to China that go back to the 1960s. And, in much more recent times, China has delivered military hardware to Zimbabwe, to the Sudan (from which it has long purchased petroleum), to Angola (because of oil), and to insurgent groupings in what has since become South Sudan. China constructed arms factories in the Sudan and Uganda earlier in this century. Its equipment also fueled both sides of the Ethiopian-Eritrean War of 1998–2000. In the same era, China notoriously swapped ample deliveries of heavy guns for eight tons of Zimbabwean ivory. In 2003 and after, its supply of jet aircraft and ammunition played a part in the massacres of Darfuri civilians by the Sudan and its vigilante proxies. Those Chinese-provided weapons were also used against the Beja in the eastern Sudan and against the southern Sudanese in the war that led to South Sudan's independence.

Nowadays, China may supply as much as 27 percent of the weapons and military hardware that flows licitly into sub-Saharan Africa; China is the largest provider of small and medium arms to Africa. Chinese versions of the AK-47 assault rifle and much other materiel of war is transferred regularly to at least seventeen African countries. (China is the fifth largest provider of small arms to the developing world.) But China's fullest bilateral military linkages have been with Angola, Ghana (jet fighter deliveries), Nigeria (more jets and patrol boats), South Africa, the Sudan (those jets, transport vehicles, and much more), Zambia (aircraft and medical personnel), and Zimbabwe (jets, uniforms, intelligence training, and the staff college). China has conducted joint military exercises in Cameroon, Gabon, Ghana, and Nigeria. (India has done the same in Kenya, Tanzania, and South Africa.)

Russia, competing with China, is among Africa's largest suppliers of arms. It sells Algeria 80 percent of its lethal imports and lesser amounts to Tunisia, Egypt (which bought fighter jets), and a host of sub-Saharan nations. Burkina Faso bought Russian helicopters and air-launched missiles. Greatly overshadowed in Africa by China in terms of non-lethal kinds of trade, in 2020 Russia nevertheless is a major platinum producer in Zimbabwe and a digger of diamonds in Angola. Russia's trade with and investment in Africa increased by 185 percent from 2005 to 2015.[3] It has military advising and hardware supplying roles in the Central African Republic and Madagascar, where it recently interfered in a national election and now has commercial interests in the gold mining sector. It is running major cyber disinformation campaigns in a dozen vulnerable African countries. Russia has signed military cooperation agreements with Burkina Faso, Burundi, and Guinea, and discussed helping Mali. Further, Russia is attempting to sell nuclear plants to several Africa countries.

Germany and the United States are additional key providers of legal arms to Africa. Other shipments of black-market arms flow into Africa's conflict zones (see the next chapter) from old Soviet and Libyan stocks, and from North Korea. More benignly, China trains many of the armies of the forty-nine sub-Saharan African countries. Its 1,200 peacekeeping soldiers are attached to eight UN missions in Africa, from Darfur to South Sudan to Mali and the Republic of Congo.

On the outer fringes of Africa, too, China played a role in combating Somali piracy in the Gulf of Aden and the Indian Ocean. Its frigates were an integral part of the UN/EU patrols. China sought by such means to boost its knowledge of what other powers were doing in and around the Indian Ocean and to help to ensure its continued maritime access to vital African resources.

Soft Power versus Soft Power

The United States has receded from Africa, downgrading its diplomatic presence, posting few senior officials to Africa, paying less attention than before to the challenges of today's Africa, especially sub-Saharan Africa, and issuing degrading utterances from the White House. In contrast, China has redoubled its steady attempt to achieve unquestionable influence in and throughout the continent. Winning and keeping friends has long been a paramount goal, accomplished by steady party-to-party contacts, frequent inter-parliamentary exchanges, a vigorous wooing of political leaders and personnel, and lavish hospitality at home and abroad.

China's embassies are now more numerous in Africa than those of any other country. Its fifty-two embassies exceed the U.S. total of forty-nine, France's forty-seven, Germany's forty-three, Russia's forty, Turkey's thirty-eight (up from a mere twelve), Brazil and the United Kingdom's thirty-six each, and Japan's thirty-five. Additionally, China sends military attachés to forty-five countries. Chinese foreign ministers make tours of African capitals a priority. China staffs and funds Confucius Institutes in fifty African countries to showcase Chinese culture and propagandize on behalf of the current Chinese leadership. It also supports a serious think tank at Stellenbosch University in South Africa.

Confucius Institutes are set up through partnerships between a Chinese university, a host country university, and the Office of Chinese Language Council International (Hanban), an influential language and culture promotion organization under China's ministry of education. Hanban supplies a Chinese director and language and culture instructors to each Institute.

Additionally, in 2020 all Kenyan students from standard 4 (age ten) will be able to study and continue learning Mandarin through secondary school. Uganda has made Mandarin a mandatory course in its secondary schools. In South Africa, thanks to Chinese financing, Mandarin has been available as a learning option in primary and secondary schools since 2014.

Chinese state-controlled media have also managed on a regular basis to seed a range of African newspapers with Chinese-supplied "news" articles, to provide "spots" on innumerable radio programs across the continent, and to do the same for television. The *China Daily* produces an *Africa Weekly* in English to improve its hold on African readers. International news from Chinese television is available on local stations across sub-Saharan Africa on an almost hourly basis. China Radio International gives Mandarin lessons routinely over the air. The Beijing-based StarTimes Group has become one of Africa's most important media companies, increasingly influential in the booming pay-TV market, notably in Nigeria and East Africa.

The Downside

Undeniably, China's massive insertion of itself into Africa has rewarded the continent with innumerable benefits, material and otherwise. But unlike the earlier external occupiers and exploiters of Africa and Africa's peoples, this twenty-first-century imperialist invasion differs from its predecessors because of Chinese management's failure fully to engage Africa's inhabitants in a mutually productive enterprise. It disdains African labor, and rarely builds capacity or transfers advanced technology to its ostensible partners (as its reviled twentieth-century colonial predecessors did with a vengeance). Most damaging to Sino-African relations, however, has been the seeming contempt of the Chinese managerial class at the industrial and construction project level, and also in agriculture and fishing pursuits, for African workers. In elite discourse, Chinese envoys and negotiators are respectful and genial; at the plebian social level, recurring outrages occur across the continent.

The Belgian, British, French, Italian, and Portuguese colonizers of Africa were always few, and determined to transfer skills as rapidly as possible to Africans so that they could accomplish their exploitative and imperial designs more speedily and inexpensively. Even the merchants, missionaries, and white settlers, when they arrived to lord it over Africans, still needed local assistance. These outnumbered outsiders all had to fashion collaboration as best they could and to build capacity among local populations. But contemporary Chinese construction crews, railway restorers, pipeline extenders, bridge builders, and even mining operators try to do as much as they can without advancing Africans into the supervisory ranks, without teaching them how to upgrade their skills, and without giving them much transparent knowledge of how China, on the ground, constructs cost-effective and efficient industrial platforms.

Chinese firms, state-owned or otherwise, always say that they want to "get the job done." So, unfamiliar with and possibly fearful of African workers, they employ as few Africans as they can (even as grunt labor) and often import the equivalent of indentured servants from China. Some of these latter recruits are from or in prison gangs, transferred from home. Clearly Chinese project managers do not want to waste time by training Africans to do more than menial work. And sometimes, on a continent with soaring unemployment rates, they do not even deign to do that. A few African leaders have complained, but for the most part African leaders, removed as they often are from the actual projects, have permitted China to import labor forces from the distant mainland and to let them come and go without leaving anything much behind (except the finished construction) for their supposed African counterparts.

Angolan roads and railways have been built by Chinese companies with Chinese money. They employ Chinese contractors (not African ones), and import a relatively high proportion of the labor force required to uplift the host country's previously weak infrastructure. In one project in Benguela for a new stadium, the Chinese firms involved hired 700 Chinese overseers, engineers, and laborers, and only 250 Angolans. In Harare, the capital of Zimbabwe, a country with unemployment levels as high as 90 percent, Chinese state contractors erecting a military staff college relied on several thousand workers transported from China and housed surreptitiously behind barricaded walls in a posh suburb. Very few Africans were allowed to work, or even to ferry supplies.

Elsewhere in Zimbabwe, where alluvial diamond deposits once yielded rich results, the Chinese-owned mines employed only Chinese labor. Again in Zimbabwe, where Chinese corporations own small plantations growing animal feed for export to China, the farm laborers are Chinese, not African. Even in Zambia, with a long tradition of underground and open cast copper mining, Chinese-owned enterprises have allowed Africans to perform only rudimentary laboring tasks, under Chinese foremen and middle managers.

Clearly, there are or must be mining or construction projects where China has been compelled by shortages of its own imported labor to rely on African workers. And there are innumerable private Chinese-owned startup factories across the continent that sensibly only employ local labor, and even promote local talent into managerial positions. But too many big Chinese-constructed dams, roads, and railways are still being erected with as few Africans being employed as possible.

This obdurate refusal to do what every earlier and even contemporary out-side entrepreneurial force has done—to employ the locals—has been explained away by Chinese diplomats and senior managers as something linguistic or something cultural. Chinese managers and industrialists have doubtless felt more comfortable employing their own kith and kin; they believe that kith and kin will work harder and for longer hours than their African poten-tial replacements. They will not need interpreters. But Chinese industrial supervisors also contend—occasionally even in public—that Africans are lazy or too lackadaisical. They assert the stereotypical descriptions common to those who have had little acquaintance with the "other," in this case echoing Chinese prejudices against Africans.

Chinese employers in Africa sadly believe that their own personnel are more obedient, more efficient, more reliable, and more trustworthy than potential African employees. As alien managers, they also are aware that African employees would report them when they tried to cut corners or be-have in an unconscionable manner. Outrages a few years ago on the Zambian mines illustrate the extent to which Chinese owners and managers attempt to ignore safety regulations, reduce wages, and push their local workers hard—all in attempts to fulfill or over-fulfill quotas for mining output or construction timeliness. Zambian miners preferred to seek comparable work at Swiss, Canadian, South African, or Indian-managed copper mines. They reputedly are safer and their employees better paid; Human Rights Watch rated the Chinese operations sub-par, as they did on the copper mines in nearby Katanga, Congo. The Chinese operations, ironically, were distinctly unfriendly to the local unions and to unionization. Dangerously, too, at one Zambian coal mine Chinese managers fired shotguns at employees protesting safety lapses.

Chinese managers in Africa also keep their social distance from Africans, another source of resentment. Most Chinese middle managers and other employees refrain from mingling with their local workers, reserving social outreach for official engagements with politicians and high-level bureaucrats. This practice has not endeared Chinese in Africa to their local counterparts. The communities that Chinese firms create in Africa around and to support their imported enterprises, dam building projects, power plants, and so on, are therefore socially thin, and isolated. Even, or especially, the imported laboring force are discouraged from associating after work with Africans. Sometimes the Chinese living quarters are even ringed with barbed wire and other barriers to discourage fraternization.

Chinese firms rarely invest socially in their locales and their leaders hardly engage in anything of a communally enriching nature outside of work. Even the executives and managers seldom socialize outside their own co-hort. A transplanted Chinese fishing enterprise and community in Senegal keeps to itself as much as possible. Many Chinese workers and managers, and even Chinese traders and shopkeepers, avoid African company. In general, researchers report that: "social relations between ordinary Africans and Chinese are marked by a tension between mutual admiration and mutual loathing." Certainly, they view each other "with suspicion." They share negative perceptions of each other, perhaps because Africans and Chinese interact only occasionally in intimate ways. Chinese managers tend to be aloof toward their African staff and engage with Africans only hesitantly. But conceivably the most influential determinant of strained relations is that the Mandarin character for Africa translates literally as "negative continent." The result of these flawed social contacts is that Africans in large number believe that their Chinese bosses and coworkers harbor racist attitudes and act accordingly.[4]

In extenuation, Chinese executives and many managers assume that they are in Africa only temporarily, to accomplish a work objective. Unlike their colonial counterparts, they are not in Africa to transmit a so-called civilizing imperative. Nor are they in Africa to become acquainted with a new culture and new ways of life. They can afford, they presumably believe, to ignore everything but their work responsibilities. And so relations across the color, cultural, and continental lines are sometimes very rough, as many Africans and a handful of the political leaders of Africa have asserted. In Zambia at one point a decade ago one politician campaigned boisterously against Chinese influence in his country, and was elected president. Candidate Michael Sata voiced the indignation of his constituents when he called the Chinese exploiters, and accused them of paying slave wages to African workers. "We need investors, not infesters," was one of his better lines.[5] Then he traveled to Beijing, was presumably rewarded in some manner, and never again complained about Chinese incivility, racism, and so on.

Competition and Despoliation

Africans complain with some reason about Chinese insensitivity that borders on, or perhaps crosses over into, racism. Kenya deported a Chinese manager in 2018 who was filmed denigrating Kenyans and making racist remarks. But the angry complaints of traders and petty merchants are more about unfair competition. Sometimes those complaints come from consumers as well as competitors: flip-flops fall apart, unlike African-manufactured but more expensive counterparts. Imported t-shirts are flimsier, but cheaper than those made in the African continent, sometimes ironically by Chinese-, Taiwanese-, or Hong Kong-owned mills. Furniture assembled in China, even possibly with wood originally from Africa, arrives in a market in Nairobi or Dar es Salaam, say, at a less costly price than locally fabricated versions. In Ghana and Togo textile merchants (mostly women) attempted to keep their businesses going despite imports from China; eventually, however, the cost differences were too great, and they abandoned their stalls. Across the subcontinent, long-established secondhand clothing dealers discovered that they could not continue in the face of comparable imports from China. Leather manufacturers in Lesotho and Madagascar had to quit in the face of incoming Chinese products. Even in the famed centuries-old indigo dying pits of Kano, northern Nigeria, Chinese competitors choked off local small businesses.

Ultimately, too, Chinese imports drive out indigenous goods and indigenous wage earners, leaving only the inferior imported product on the market. Unfair, say many Africans, even though the availability of a variety of inexpensive consumer goods from China enables Africans of modest means to possess items that previously were unaffordable. The flooding of African markets by cheap goods from China—radios, televisions, bicycles, mattresses, and even chickens—has its obvious benefit despite the angry expressions of traditional vendors.

In northern Nigeria before the turn of the twenty-first century there were a dozen or so major textile factories, some of which were owned by entrepreneurs based in Hong Kong. None of those mills, and few of the textile manufacturers in Lesotho, many of which were Taiwanese-owned, still exist. Chinese imported fabrics undercut the local goods in terms of price more than quality, and jobs and foreign exchange are lost, to the detriment of African economic and social advances.

There is also the curious, if prosaic, case of the local traders in Lusaka, Zambia, who were incensed to the point of mayhem when imported Chinese chickens could be purchased from Chinese merchants in the nearby slum markets for less than chickens grown and hawked in-country by Africans. The locals, accustomed to selling whole chickens, feathers unplucked, from the backs of their bicycles, were also annoyed when Chinese traders out-hustled them. The Chinese traders rose even before sunrise to reach the markets hours earlier than their local rivals.

More damaging to Africans in out-of-the-way corners of the continent has been a refusal by many Chinese concerns to respect the land, as well as its traditional occupants. Unless an African government has specified contractually that only limited kinds of environmental damage are permitted—and sometimes not even then—Chinese firms pay little attention to such restrictions or seek to minimize ecological collateral damages in a commonsense manner, or even in a manner that fully respects African traditional ways of life. Such adverse impacts occur almost everywhere that Chinese contractors and miners operate. Often local African communities fail to persuade Chinese firms to adopt better practices and to obey regulations that their governments may enforce laxly, or not at all. Chinese concerns, once again, are usually in a rush to finish their assignments and make their quota, to complete a job, and then exit.

This is often the case on large-scale endeavors, where bonuses may be available for timely performance or other set goals. But the rough manner in which individual companies or contractors treat Africans in general and, especially, the African societies through which they pass while road- or rail-making, bridge building, and the like, often turns entire ethnic groups against the neo-colonial antagonists within their midst. For example, a small village along the mainland side of the Mozambique Channel suddenly discovered in 2015 that China coveted its fine beach sand. By that point a Chinese company had wreaked havoc on the dunes of sand on which small villages were poised. Its heavy earth-moving equipment had blocked traditional water channels and caused floods that wiped out those very villages. In total, the Chinese operations despoiled more than 3 million square feet of wetland, all to exploit vast supplies of uhligite, a rare black and tan mineral found in the Mozambican sand dunes and also, globally, elsewhere only at Lake Magadi in Kenya. Uhligite helpfully binds cement, mortar, tile, bricks, various ceramics, and most adhesives. Since China is the planet's largest consumer of cement and concrete, an odd mine found in an isolated village became sufficiently important for Chinese miners (there were no locals employed) to run roughshod over the community and any indigenous environmental concerns.

One of China's largest construction companies also mined huge quantities of sand from the Kenyan coast near Mombasa to construct the new standard gauge rail line to Nairobi, evading environmental regulations in the process. Instead of filing new environmental impact statements as required, the China Road and Bridge Corporation just went ahead in 2016 and excavated an offshore reef. Kenya's National Environmental Tribunal finally put a stop to this despoiling, but long after much of the reef was gone. Even so, digging for sand began in the same area in 2019 to support the construction of a new container terminal in Mombasa. This time a Japanese-funded Dutch dredging operation was involved, again without up-to-date environmental permits.

Gold is obviously more luring than sand, however important the latter's mineral content. In Ghana in 2012, hundreds of miners were arrested for mining gold illegally in the nation's north, after 10,000 or more Chinese hopefuls had crowded onto the newly prospected fields of likely wealth.

Chinese oil-exploration activities in both the Sudan and Gabon are allegedly responsible for environmental messes, new lakes of spilled petroleum, and the like.

Outside of Dar es Salaam, Tanzania, Chinese builders uprooted more than 1,000 families to make way for an international airport that was never erected, for want of funding. Chinese-constructed Ethiopian dams (ones that the World Bank refused to fund for environmental reasons) are shifting thousands of local farmers away from their long-hoed fields.

In other African locales, Chinese contractors have been accused of shoddy workmanship and of purposely cutting corners (and costs) too sharply. In many cases infrastructural improvements completed by Chinese firms had to be junked or redone. A general hospital in Luanda, Angola, opened to great applause. But cracks rapidly appeared in its walls; the Angolan authorities tore it down. In the same country, new macadam roads washed away in the first rains. Waters also destroyed a 130-kilometer road from Lusaka, Zambia, southwards toward Chirundu on the Zimbabwean border. A power plant in Botswana had to be rebuilt from scratch.

Respect for Human Rights

China officially and in practice is indifferent to the quality of governance in the countries in which it operates. As President Xi Jinping reiterated at the 2018 annual Forum on China-Africa Cooperation (FOCAC), China would never impose itself (unlike those earlier colonialists) on its African partners. He extolled China's "win-win" cooperative policies with Africa and promised no interference with the political or developmental pathways of the nation-states of the continent. "China follows the principle of giving more and taking less, giving before taking and giving without asking for return," Xi said. He went on to say, further, that "China-Africa cooperation must give Chinese and African people tangible benefits and successes that can be seen, that can be felt."[6]

In practice, no interference means condoning any kind of despotic or oppressive government that is adopted by African recipients of Chinese assistance. It means turning away from any official Chinese pronouncements that could be construed as judgmental. China coddles dictators and ignores or undermines Western efforts to shame human rights violators. It backs administrations that are condemned and sanctioned by the United Nations. Indeed, as Chinese governments have persistently demonstrated, they will do business with any government that is in office, no matter how it got there and no matter how it uses or misuses funds from China. Even those African rulers who personally pocketed the largesse that was nominally distributed to their governments for canceling official recognitions of Taiwan are still embraced without even an implied grimace.

In that light, China always remained a good friend of former president Omar al-Bashir's despotic regime in the Sudan despite his indictment for war crimes by the International Criminal Court. It awarded honors to, and always welcomed visits from the late President Robert Mugabe of Zimbabwe despite his reputation as a corrupt, malign stealer of elections. For those two, and other gross malefactors such as former President Eduardo dos Santos and his family in Angola, the Mobutu and Kabila regimes in the Democratic Republic of Congo, President Teodoro Obiang of Equatorial Guinea, President Denis Sassou Nguesso of the Republic of Congo, President Abdel Fattah el-Sisi of Egypt, or the Bongo family of Gabon, China is friendly and supportive. Partially, China believes on very contested evidence—and despite official African enunciated views to the contrary—that Western-style democracy and respect for human rights are poorly suited to African conditions. Africa is there to supply China with raw materials and votes in the United Nations. Anything else is of secondary concern, as astute Africans have long suspected.

China has long barred the Security Council from criticism of repressive African regimes. It does business with the most outrageously corrupt African kleptocrats. It does nothing to stop the use of its weapons by nations intent on attacking their own citizen-rebels. China can claim that it is not responsible for policing Africa, that it tolerates human rights excesses more than it approves of their application to minorities or other disadvantaged groups. Moreover, China persecutes its own minorities and forbids even religious expression, so why should it behave any differently abroad? China censors its own population, denying free expression, as do many African regimes (with less skill). Until very recently, it essentially even condoned big and small animal poaching by Chinese nationals, and allowed those criminals to bring their loot back to China.

Africa Still Needs China

Despite the many rough edges to their interpersonal exchanges and the distinct possibility that China is neither altruistic nor un-self-interested in its dealings with Africa, that some its commercial practices are sharper than they need be, and that African nation-states may be falling into a debt trap of Chinese design, sub-Saharan African countries cannot make progress in these middle years of the twenty-first century without continuing, even boosting, their extensive exports to China. If the Chinese economy slows down and the price of petroleum and other primary commodities remains low, Africa cannot but suffer. Many of its resource-endowed entities will have too few other outlets; their export engines have long been geared up to serve China. Few sub-Saharan nations and none in the north have salted away funds from their fat years (when petroleum sold for more than $100 per barrel) to tide them over possible years of lean.

More jobs could be created if and when African countries insisted that all laborers on any kinds of projects would have to be local, not imported. More jobs could also be created if Africa established more export processing zones, like the successful ones in Ethiopia and Rwanda. More skilled positions, now too few, could be filled by indigenous young persons when—possibly with Chinese help—key African countries invest more heavily in skill-based training. Africa could also refuse admission to more than a limited number of Chinese managers and foremen. But all of these possible improvements to the Sino-African partnership, and many other potential economic, educational, medical, and social upgrades for Africans, will depend on the countries of Africa regaining leverage vis-à-vis China. Until now, massive China has engaged with Africa largely bilaterally, putting small and medium-sized African states at a considerable disadvantage. If Africa began systematically to deal with China as united body, or at least from subregional combinations such as SADC—the Southern African Development Community—Africans might be able to insist on better labor and human rights policies, and be ready to monitor the flow of financial funds to elites.

Commercial and political relations between much of Africa and China are here to stay. The question for the future, however, is whether Africa can turn the resulting discourse, commodity sales, import purchases, and other interactions into a true win-win (in Xi's words) for both sides of what has become a deeply enmeshed, valuable, tense, flawed, and essential relationship.

VII | Terror and Civil Conflict

I N 2020, TOO many of Africa's nation-states, both north and south of the Sahara, remain penetrated by combatants, infiltrated by insurgents, and damaged deeply either by the self-inflicted wounds of civil conflict or attacked from within by Islamists supported from without and loyal to externally propagated ideologies.

In their founding years, independent northern and southern Africa harbored conflicts that tore new nations apart. In contemporary times some of those civil wars linger, joined as they have been since the dawning of the new century by newly spawned fundamentalist revolutionaries and by reactionaries who regard constituted authority and modern political instrumentalities as illegitimate, even *haram*—"forbidden."

Although there are fewer civil conflict deaths per year than there were in the 1980s and 1990s, there are many more episodes of terror, (and terror-related fatalities), than there were in those times. And the seemingly intractable nature of some of the internal conflicts and of many of the campaigns against terror give the impression that sections of Africa—Egypt and the Sinai; Algeria, Libya, and the Sahel; the Horn of Africa and Kenya; Nigeria and its northeastern neighbors; and the Democratic Republic of Congo—are today immured in warfare that will not easily end. Weighing in, too, in some of the battlegrounds are African peacekeepers and foreign military detachments taking the side of indigenous defenders and so far thwarting the forces of terror without achieving conclusive victories. Yet, in 2018, Ethiopia and Eritrea unexpectedly resolved their long mutual cold war and Ethiopia peacefully but only for a time reduced the severity of several internal conflicts.

Africans and their outside partners are slowly moving to contain terror and terrorists, but declaring victory against the forces of revolution and insurrection is premature. It is still a massive work for the future. In addition to the swirl of repetitive civil conflict in such disparate African countries as Burundi, Cameroon, the Central African Republic, the Democratic Republic of Congo, South Sudan, and the Sudan, dangerous depredations of Islamist terror continue to convulse Somalia (and Kenya), Nigeria (and Cameroon, Chad, and Niger), and Mali (and Burkina Faso and Niger).

In those last three long-running theaters of Islamist-inspired war about 86,000 civilian lives have been lost since 2008, roughly 23,000 in Somalia, 60,000 in Nigeria, 3,000 in Mali, and more than 1,200 in Burkina Faso and Niger.[1] Despite energetic local and international anti-terror operations, including active American, British, and French intervening forces, victory in these wars on terror is still distant. Similarly, the many existing internal civil conflicts continue without easy chances of peace.

The Terrorists

Each of the four dominant terror movements—al-Shabaab in Somalia, Boko Haram in Nigeria, and al-Qaeda in the Islamic Maghreb (AQIM), recently joined by the Islamic State (ISIS)—is largely homegrown, ostensibly but no longer fervently fundamentalist, and motivated today in significant part by profits from various illicit smuggling operations. In many respects, these four smallish but still greatly dangerous movements of terror resemble marauding bands of criminals more than they still do religiously or ideologically inspired crusaders.

Originally, each of these movements of terror was infused with Salafist and other conservative Islamic doctrines. In Somalia fervent preachers and embryonic leaders certainly sought to provide order and a sense of godly rectitude in a zone convulsed by corrupt warlords in the aftermath of governmental collapse in the 1990s. In Nigeria, Boko Haram was catapulted into action by high levels of governmental corruption, by decades of insufficient schooling, and by a paucity of jobs, but it was also founded by idiosyncratic clerics who, one after another, imagined harms (and insults) that were little grounded in reality.

The origins of war in the Sahel were somewhat more diffuse. The nomadic non-Arab, non-Berber Tuareg of the southern Sahara (and northern Mali) felt and actually were discriminated against by the African-controlled government of Mali (as well as by neighboring African governments), and thus the

Tuareg had objective reasons to protest when leftover Libyan arms became widely available after the fall of dictatorial Muammar al-Qaddafi in 2012 in nearby Libya

The disaffected Tuareg joined up with what became AQIM. That served their interests and the purposes of AQIM. But after France's decisive military intervention in northern Mali in 2013 squelched the Tuareg rebellion and chased AQIM militants back into the Sahara, whatever local motivations may have stimulated the original upsurge were subsumed by a descent into all out war in northern Mali, northern Burkina Faso, and northwestern Niger. AQIM and ISIS (and not the Tuareg) targeted those three national governments and French and American counter-terrorist detachments. The conflict continues today despite the presence of 4,500 French and 1,200 American troops, plus lethal U.S. drones based in Niger. Moreover, Burkina Faso and western Niger in late 2019 replaced Mali as the epicenter of AQIM and ISIS attacks on handy targets such as gold mines and other sources of plunder. The terrorists in this region were more lethal than ever at the end of 2019.

All four terror movements have morphed into mercenary endeavors that employ individual suicide bombers, trucks filled with explosives, raids on refugees and refugee camps, and sorties against convoys and army patrols to protect their trading ambitions and extend their loci of power. The terror movements attack churches, intimidate civilians, bribe border guards and officials, purchase weapons from international purveyors of guns and ammunition (al-Shabaab has acquired small drones), and manage for the most part to thrive despite the anti-terror efforts of American, British, Dutch, and French special forces, the Nigerian army, and AMISOM (the Kenyan-led African Union Mission in Somalia).

What distinguishes all four war operations from their eighteenth-century Muslim jihadi predecessors in the Sudan, in Senegal, and in northern Nigeria is their use, naturally, of modern weapons and tactics, especially their focus on suicide bombings, hit-and-run raids, kidnappings, and (in Boko Haram's case) of an ideological veneer that preaches the rejection of Western forms of education. What is similar, at least rhetorically on the surface, is the eighteenth-century determination to recreate the idealistically "perfect" years of the Islamic first century, a quest that finds some echoes in today's teachings.

In what is now Somaliland (not Somalia) a late nineteenth-century/early twentieth century Islamic movement led by Mohammed Abdullah Hassan, a patriot whom the British called the "Mad Mullah," was more anti-imperialist than Islamist, but he certainly aligned himself and his effective movement with what would now be considered Salafism.

In 2020, the Mullah's collective putative successor, al-Shabaab, is poised to continue bombing Mogadishu, Somalia's beleaguered capital, and surrounding even distant villages; Boko Haram is capable of resisting Nigerian security roundups; and AQIM (sometimes allied to the Islamic State) persistently raids well beyond Timbuktu and Gao, even penetrating Bamako and Ouagadougou, the capitals of Mali and Burkina Faso, from distant bases on the edge of the Sahara. More than 200,000 Malian civilians fled their homes in 2019 to escape AQIM and ISIS attacks; at least 600 lost their lives.

In Niger, AQIM and its offshoots harass northern outposts and even menace Nigerien, American, and French military responders. Egypt still battles the Islamic State in Cairo, Luxor, and the Sinai, and fends off bombings in the Nile Delta. The Islamic State threatens Tunisia, too. Few polities and few peoples are totally immune from the contagion of terror that now engulfs Africa. No easy end to these violent wars is at hand.

Attacking al-Shabaab

The insurrectionists in central Somalia, and periodically in neighboring Kenya, are known as al-Shabaab —"the youngsters." Al-Shabaab emerged out of the defeated shell of Somalia's Organization of Islamic Courts (OIC), an umbrella grouping of a patchwork of local sharia courts that had sprung up, sporadically, in about 2004 in the absence of any national law-enforcing mechanisms. (Siad Barre, Somalia's last dictator, lost his popular mandate in 1991, regional clan-based warlords creating what passed for governance in his stead.) When invading Ethiopian troops (funded in part by the United States) destroyed the vigilante troops of the OIC in 2006, the radicalized militant youth wing of the sharia movement gradually regrouped in southern Somalia. The Ethiopian intervention greatly helped to motivate and radicalize youthful Somali allied to the OIC. As al-Shabaab, they subsequently became a formidable and well-armed instrument of terror. It now has links to, and some financing from, al-Qaeda, but its ambitions and leadership are local. It also contends with a small group of rival combatants financed by and tied to ISIS.

From 2008 to 2011, the youngsters of al-Shabaab terrorized much of central and southern Somalia from their major base in Kismayo, at the mouth of the Juba River. From this hub, they preyed on and exerted a type of quasi-sovereignty over the towns and countryside north from Kismayo to Mogadishu, the nominal country's nominal capital. They imposed strict sharia-type prohibitions on the people and towns that they controlled.

Al-Shabaab feeds its troops and buys arms based on an extensive racket-eering operation, with illicit trade in charcoal to Saudi Arabia and Yemen bringing in an estimated $10 million a year despite a UN ban on such exports that has been in place since 2012. Al-Shabaab also profits from smuggling contraband sugar across the border into Kenya, a commerce that is worth another $10 million or more a year. Since 2015, it is suspected that Kenyan AMISOM forces facilitate much of this cross-border commerce.

Al-Shabaab sells hides and skins from sheep, goats, and camels to Saudi Arabia and Yemen, raids neighboring Kenya, and has kidnapped and held for ransom relatively wealthy Somali and Kenyans (and a few foreigners). Beginning in 2018, al-Shabaab also began taxing travelers at roadblocks and imposing "duties" on farm produce and livestock sales. (Al-Shabaab's roadblocks are said to be less onerous than those set up by Kenyan soldiers.) The UN Monitoring Group on Somalia and Eritrea claimed in 2019 that al-Shabaab was collecting as much as $10 million a year per roadblock, suffi-cient to sustain much mayhem.

Al-Shabaab exerts little influence, however, over the Somali pirates who, until very recently, were ambushing oceangoing shipping in the Indian Ocean and the Gulf of Aden. Most of those miscreants came from the northern reaches of Somalia proper, and from Puntland, a semi-autonomous satrapy that al-Shabaab has only recently infiltrated. (After Siad Barre's fall, greater Somalia broke up into Somaliland [a largely democratic, northern former British colony], Puntland [once Italian-run], and Somalia [also under Italian colonial rule before World War II]).

Al-Shabaab also runs drugs. That means repacking shipments of heroin and raw opium (of various kinds) from Afghanistan, Pakistan, and India for onward transfer to Europe via Kenya, Djibouti, the Sudan, and Egypt. It traffics in methamphetamines or their precursor chemicals for shipment to Nigeria and onward to Mexico and the United States. The profits of these and associated commodities are substantial and a driver of the relentless war-fare that consumes Somalia. Indeed, if al-Shabaab's opponents could cut off the sugar and narcotics trades that it traffics, and the arms that it buys from shady merchants in Djibouti, Dubai, Yemen and, ultimately, China, Russia, and North Korea, the local war could conceivably be won. Instead, the fight against al-Shabaab continues. The brunt of the military effort on the ground consists of an African Union-mandated operational force—AMISOM—led by an Ethiopian general and consisting of troops mostly from Burundi, Djibouti, Ethiopia, Kenya, Sierra Leone, and Uganda. That force assists the still embryonic and weakly directed Somali National Army, the security force of the federal government of Somalia, a largely unelected and somewhat ineffectual body run since early 2019 by President Mohamed Abdullahi Farmaajo.

Al-Shabaab mounts suicide and other bombing attacks on Mogadishu and the government in that city from its moveable bases in central Somalia. Over the last decade, al-Shabaab depredations have displaced as many as 2 million Somali from their homes and caused 500,000 refugees to flee across nearby borders. In 2019, as in earlier years, a handful of al-Shabaab loyalists attacked a bank, hotel, and a flat complex in one of the wealthier sections of Nairobi, Kenya, very far from their home base. Western analysts believe that al-Shabaab's remaining fighters probably number between 5,000 and 7,000 men and women. They may control as much as 20 percent of Somalia. Their advantage is guerrilla stealth. Al-Shabaab also uses its small drones for reconnaissance.

In pursuit of al-Shabaab are AMISOM's 20,000 troops, the Federal Army's 19,000 soldiers, and a very small contingent (500 persons) of the U.S. Joint Special Operations Command and an even smaller battle group of Britons. The U.S. force and the Somali army established a series of outposts across Somalia. There they train and advise the national army, but also engage in kill-or-capture raids of their own. They develop informant networks, engage in electronic surveillance, and try to out-maneuver al-Shabaab. But, because of lackadaisical, and erratic backing from the White House, expert observers from the International Crisis Group, a former U.S. ambassador, and others agreed in 2019 that the battle against al-Shabaab was "on autopilot," without a coherent strategy.[2]

Instead, the United States has bombed incessantly, relying on a fleet of American drones flown from Djibouti. Since 2015, the drones have eliminated several al-Shabaab leaders and generally targeted critical groups of the armed "youngsters." There were at least forty-seven strikes by American drones and other aircraft in 2018. In 2019, the number of air attacks on al-Shabaab bases and personnel greatly increased, with twenty-four occurring in the first three months of the year. Hundreds of combatants, and some civilians, forfeited their lives. But, despite impressive Western firepower and surveillance from the skies, and despite the united stands of Kenya, Ethiopia, and their neighbors against al-Shabaab, the war of terror continues briskly in 2020. It handicaps Somalia's ability to shed its beleaguered insecurities. Good governance cannot exist without the proto-state becoming free from terror.

The Kenyan general then commanding AMISOM reported as long ago as 2017 that the war would not easily be won largely because of the limited cohesiveness of his multinational fighting forces, their equipment deficiencies, morale issues, corruption within their commands, the inefficiency of the federal army, and because of al-Shabaab's shifting tactics. Al-Shabaab has governed its own noncontiguous, central Somali territories firmly and consistently, which residents in at least some of those otherwise harassed communities have come to appreciate.

Battling Boko Haram

Boko Haram began as a backward-looking opponent of Western (i.e., modern) education, and as a nihilistic critic of virtually all other conventional secular practices in the Muslim states of northern Nigeria. At its heyday—roughly 2012 and 2013—Boko Haram controlled much of Borno State, Nigeria's northeastern-most redoubt, encircled Maiduguri, that state's capital, and raided as far west and south as the cities of Kano and Abuja. It reinforced its ranks by kidnapping children as "wives," sex slaves, and combatants. Its youthful brigades specialized in suicide bombing attacks on schools, mosques, and markets.

Although it began as a backward-looking ideological movement to cleanse Muslim Nigeria of "Western" learning, and thus to purify Muslims, by 2013 and now in 2020 Boko Haram is almost entirely a murderous movement of marauders. It includes about 5,000 "soldiers" and few significant slices of Nigerian real estate.

The mystery is why the very large and powerful Nigerian military did not long ago—as President Muhammadu Buhari promised—"wipe out" Boko Haram. Since Boko Haram, on the run from the Nigerian army, several years ago expanded its zone of discontent to include those parts of Cameroon, Chad, and Niger that neighbor Borno, the Nigerian army has also been aided by formidable fighting forces from Chad and security patrols from Cameroon and Niger. It has also had serious assistance from a local militia called the Civilian Joint Task Force. Using its local knowledge, the Task Force has provided vital intelligence, manned security checkpoints, and carried out raids.

American surveillance and intelligence have also helped the Nigerians, as have British reconnaissance missions. But, as the Americans and Britons have often indicated, the Nigerian military effort has periodically been weakened by officers and politicians padding military ranks, by shoddy supplies, and by the theft of funds meant for the war effort. Soldiers complain about long tours of duty that leave them with no days off for months, worn-out equipment, inadequate rations, and pilfering by their commandants. Nigeria's armed forces, hampered by the corrupt practices in their own military officer ranks, have been incapable for the past twelve years of quelling the Boko

Haram insurgency and ending the suicide and other bombings of innocent civilians in all four countries. Its "strategic hamlet" policy failed, because of the army's inability or failure to defend the settlements into which farmers and families had been grouped. Few commanders or soldiers are local and capable of conversing in Kanuri, the language of Borno and Boko Haram. Morale is low. For these reasons, and also because Boko Haram has managed to hide, guerrilla-fashion, in hard-to-penetrate forests, the remnants of the insurgent force remain at large, capable (as also is al-Shabaab) of raiding encampments and sending lone girl suicide bombers to blow themselves up in front of mosques. As of late 2019, about one hundred of the originally three-hundred-plus girls kidnapped in a massive and notorious raid in 2013 on their homes in Chibok in Borno were still held (or were otherwise unaccounted for) by Boko Haram.

In 2019, too, Boko Haram was joined in Borno by the Islamic State West Africa Province, a fighting body that split off from Boko Haram in 2018, possibly with funds supplied by ISIS. (Ansaru, a third secession from Boko Haram, is active to the west of Borno.) ISIS has attacked army bases and ambushed patrolling Nigerian army soldiers, successfully struck the military in Chad, and caused hundreds of military casualties. There are doctrinal differences between Boko Haram and its newish replica. But what drives all three groups in 2020 is resource plundering in order to continue fighting and smuggling.

What makes the rise of the Islamic State (ISIS) in West Africa so worrying in northern Nigeria and Chad is its tactics, largely dictated by distant ISIS funders and managers. It avoids killing Muslims and focuses on attacking Christians and the Nigerian and Chadian armies, lends money to aspiring entrepreneurs to win their backing, and coopts rather than coerces villagers who may have grievances against the state. In short, this local ISIS version cultivates relations with local communities. It has also joined hands with Fulani (Muslim) herders to compete against and attempt to oust Christian agriculturalists from valuable lands across northern Nigeria.

In order to deprive Boko Haram and ISIS of even more dangerous income streams, in 2018 the United States, in close cooperation with Nigerian authorities, China, Russia, Britain, and Norway, decided that a small amount of fissionable high-grade enriched uranium sitting in a research reactor in Kaduna—distant from Boko Haram's main operational area, but of possible interest to them—should be removed to prevent the movement from making a potentially lethal dirty bomb. No one had any idea that Boko Haram knew of the reactor's existence, but the United States and its allies hardly wanted to take chances. So in a remarkably rapid undercover exercise, American forces flew on a Russian aircraft to remove the uranium and to dispatch it on the same plane to China.

Combating al-Qaeda in the Maghreb (AQIM)

AQIM disrupts governments and citizens across the region known as the Sahel—from Mauritania east to Mali, Burkina Faso, and Niger, plus Chad. This is a region where population numbers are increasing even faster than much of the rest of sub-Saharan Africa—from 78 million in 2019 (including Chad) to a projected 200 million in thirty years. But it rains less across the Sahel than it once did, the Sahara desert encroaches, and grazing livings are very much harder to make. Farmers fight against pastoralists. Food insufficiencies are endemic. And the existing governments of this region (except for authoritarian Chad) are fragile.

The AQIM throughout nearly all of this region, plus Boko Haram at its southeastern end, has gained footholds in the Sahara-Sahel borderlands that extend into Algeria and Libya. Islamism is a potent and relatively new force. French legionnaires and paratroopers had to intervene in 2013 when Tuareg and Algerian Islamists, using pilfered Libyan surplus weapons, captured Timbuktu, Gao, Kidal, and other northern Malian cities and towns, declaring a breakaway republic in the sub-Saharan Sahel section of northern Mali. The rout of the Malian army in that year, the jihadists' ability to hold the northern towns for months—until the French arrived —plus a coup that overthrew the national government, showed how weak governments of the Sahel were, and how rapidly stability could deteriorate.

When French forces had pushed back these self-declared revolutionaries, the remaining factions (not those led by Tuareg tribesmen) affiliated themselves with AQIM and subsequently with ISIS. Today AQIM derives at least some of its financial backing and "legitimacy" from central al-Qaeda, and sometimes joins ISIS for tactical reasons, but its inspiration is trans-Saharan and its methods mostly indigenous, hostile to Tunisia and Algeria as well as to the weaker sub-Saharan border nations, and aligned from time to time with various Libyan factions. The United States launches periodic drone strikes against ISIS enclaves in Libya.

Instability in the Sahel has spread from Mali to eastern Mauritania, northern Burkina Faso, and western Niger. (As many as 1 million Burkinabe have been displaced from their homes by hostilities in their country.) There are very local quarrels and localized grievances against central governments, but a prominent feature is each country's weakness. The ruling regimes in each jurisdiction are unable, on their own, to project power from national capitals into the fractured and afflicted parts of their states. Each government relies on outsiders and European and American firepower to oppose the Islamists and maintain a semblance of peace.

In 2017, the French formed a military attack group known as the G5 Sahel. It comprises soldiers from Burkina Faso, Chad, Mali, Mauritania, and Niger. The group operates against all manner of disrupters—the AQIM jihadis, of course, but also drug and people traffickers, local and trans-Saharan criminals, and the like. By curtailing the smuggling of contraband as well as migrants, it tries to reduce the number of Africans transiting the Sahara en route to Europe, as well as to end attacks on the countries of the Sahel.

According to a confident French general, without his forces the Sahel governments "would collapse on themselves." Jihadists in the region were simply not strong enough to mount attacks on national capitals and did not control substantial territories, but "they had been effective in persistently sapping the resources and authority of the national governments."[3]

The United States also remains active in the region. It constructed a large drone aerodrome near Agadez and sends small numbers of Special Forces (despite a partial troop pullout in 2019) to help the Nigeriens strengthen their ability to pursue AQIM operatives. Meanwhile, the French help the Malian army curtail depredations north of Timbuktu and keep close eyes on AQIM facilities in the Algerian Sahara. Ultimately, a conclusive victory in this war of terror, as well as in the others, depends on preventing AQIM from continuing to profit from transporting cocaine (from Peru and Colombia, via Ghana, Nigeria, and Guinea-Bissau) and other smuggled contraband such as cigarettes across the Sahara to Algiers and Tunis, and thence to Europe. AQIM also has made millions of dollars from kidnapping prominent foreigners (including official Canadians) and collecting large ransoms. Only by drying up AQIM's real mercantile reason for existence can this insidious branch of Salafist-inspired mayhem be eliminated. It will also help to prosecute the war against terror in this region if the Americans and the French win the support of local authorities, not just those in the capital cities.

ISIS is an additional threat to peace in the region. Indeed, the U.S. Africa command fears a movement southward by insurgents allied to ISIS that goes beyond Mali and Burkina Faso and is directed against the coastal countries of Benin, Côte d'Ivoire, Ghana, and Togo, and the American military transport and logistics hub near Ghana's main airport.

Winning the War

Because African governments, even Nigeria's, are unable to win the war on terror on their own, and because the efforts of France and the United States are purely military exercises that depend on chases, interceptions, and drone firepower, too little attention is being paid to curtailing these movements' access to global financial markets, to the sources of their illicit supplies, or to preventing narcotics from being trafficked successfully beyond the Sahara to Europe. Instead, the war on terror has become one of sneak attack and suicide bombing, retaliation, regrouping, and maneuvers by enemy and ally.

That description, however, does too little justice to the scale of some attacks still being perpetrated in 2019 by al-Shabaab, Boko Haram, AQIM, and ISIS. Two separate bombings killed 376 and 196 Somali people respectively in Mogadishu; Boko Haram exploded suicide vests outside a mosque and a market, killing 80; AQIM managed to shoot up a hotel in Ouagadougou. ISIS militants attacked a Malian military outpost in late 2019, killing fifty Malian soldiers. A week later, it hit a base of the Nigerien army near the border with Mali, causing seventy fatalities.

In order finally to defeat the terrorists, renewed vigilance, better searches of potential young bombers in Nigeria and Somalia, and redoubled patrols in the vast desert wastes of Mali and its neighbors are essential. So is enhanced drone surveillance by the Americans and an upgrading of the lethal firepower of the drones based near Agadez. Following the money and making insurgency unprofitable and difficult is crucial. Even so, terror will continue to be a way of life for a small subset of miscreants. There is nothing noble or religious in their pursuit of drug profits, or of their criminal enterprises generally.

Civil Wars and Civil Conflicts

Although al-Shabaab, Boko Haram, and AQIM all emerged out of (and today take advantage of) local insecurities, intramural antipathies, and the myopia or incompetence of official governments and their mostly transactional leaders, the non-terroristic civil conflicts within African states are and have almost always reflected majority-minority discrimination or feelings of powerlessness on the part of disfranchised ethnic, religious, or linguistic groups, authoritarianism and kleptocratic tendencies on the part of rulers, a clear failure to share the wealth and the available developmental or infrastructural advances, unfair elections and reelections, anticonstitutional third-term-breaches and opposition to restrictions on fundamental freedoms.

Until a state is secure, a key political good supplied by a functioning political jurisdiction, it cannot govern. Nor can it provide essential services to its people. Without fundamental security it cannot modernize, cannot develop. The inability of a number of African nation-states to keep their citizens safe and secure (as discussed in Chapter III) has meant and still means that significant proportions of various citizenries in a range of affected countries can and do feel themselves oppressed. That feeling of being "done to" by a national administration leads to grievances that can easily be translated into identity (sometimes ethnicity) crises. Belonging to a nation comes to feel wrong. Those "wronged" inhabitants instead embrace ethnic, religious, or some other identity that substitutes for belonging to the state.

People can easily feel threatened, especially when new local leaders powerfully suggest that they are preyed upon solely because of their identity. Once groups begin to believe that the state (or its ruling cabal) is failing in its social contract obligation to protect them, and to afford them the same opportunities and rights available to other groups, hostilities can easily erupt. Offended or marginalized peoples believe, or are induced to believe, that they are receiving less than their due from a central government, as in today's Cameroon.

When these feelings of alienation are compounded by evidence (or construed evidence) that national political leaders are stealing from the people, benefiting themselves and their own kin at the expense of the entire citizenry, flaunting their corruptly acquired wealth, and putting the satisfaction of personal or party greed before the delivery of adequate political goods to their constituents, then the possibility of an aroused public reaction becomes strong, as does bitter civil conflict. This is what happened in the Sudan in 2019, when protestors ousted President Omar al-Bashir because of widespread corruption, recently enacted subsidy reductions, price hikes for bread and fuel, and shortages of food. Much of the same antagonism erupted in Algeria against the long cabalistic rule of generals and industrialists propping up the infirm presidency of President Abdelaziz Bouteflika, leading to his removal. Corruption, greed, discrimination, and the loss of regime legitimacy are at the root of the Ambazonia rising (see below), the long internal wars of South Sudan, several of the civil conflicts within Nigeria, the nominally religious strife in the Central African Republic, and the drivers of the various internal Congolese conflicts.

Wherever in Africa civil wars arise and persist, abusive political leadership is often responsible. We have seen in Chapter II that political leaders in Africa exert a greater influence over events, particularly cataclysmic ones, than they do in other parts of the more fully institutionalized world. The more resource-rich or potentially resource-rich the state, the more leadership avarice and zero-sum political approaches from state house and ruling party headquarters precipitate conflict. The more already fractured the state, the easier this process is. States rarely burst into flames without political elites distancing themselves from their nationals, depriving them in some manner of just rights and just deserts, and without protesters putting up or following self-selected leaders.

Conflict in Africa characteristically follows (not precedes) state weakness. No African polity that can be characterized as strong harbors conflict or the likelihood of conflict. The weakest states do—like Nigeria and the Central African Republic, for instance—and those who are tending toward collapse like South Sudan, the Sudan, Burundi, and the Democratic Republic of Congo—all failed states since at least 1985 in the Congo's case and 2011 in South Sudan—always contain tinder for conflagration. Weak or fragile states disappoint most of their citizens and always lie at the cusp of failure, and conflict. When the state begins to break down, when it loses legitimacy and systematically becomes unable or unwilling to provide meaningful quantities and qualities of political goods to its inhabitants (as explained in Chapter III), then war within the state almost inevitably follows.

Civil wars do not occur primarily because of unresolved colonial legacies, poorly drawn borders that put tribal groups on the wrong side of arbitrary lines, or because of ancient hatreds between peoples who share the same general territory and even, sometimes, the same language, religion, and same history. Nor do ethnic differences themselves often precipitate war, except when unscrupulous politicians lead their followers back into defensive crouches that depend on the embrace of ethnic identities. Sub-Saharan Africa is the home of thousands of linguistically and ethnically differentiated groupings (as discussed in Chapter I), but the sheer number and existence of so many small and large entities hardly proves or implies that conflicts are either primordial or unavoidable. The same ethnic groups that live peacefully in Zambia contend against each other fiercely on the other side of the nearby border with the Democratic Republic of Congo.

Where ethnic groups nowadays attack representatives of other ethnic groups strictly because they are "other," and hence perceived dangerous, those assaults reflect politically inspired hate-mongering and zero-sum competition for scarce resources much more than they are atavistic or xenophobic outbursts. Ethnic conflict, in other words, is as manufactured in Africa as it is in the Balkans, India, Sri Lanka, Myanmar (Burma), and beyond.

Furthermore, outbreaks of civil war are better ascribed to the inadequate political leadership and greed of national regimes and their resulting poor governance. When a government is seen as behaving even-handedly, ethnic strife is rare; when a government is unfair to some segments of its citizenry, perhaps being perceived as privileging one ethnic group over another, the ill favored grow restless and revolt. Groups that feel themselves discriminated against thus strike back against authority when politically participatory channels are blocked, when the out-group fears for its life, and when the state attacks and triggers a corresponding response.

Competition for extractive resources, and the rents that flow from the exploitation of both them and other commodities also motivates much of the conflict within Africa. Who gets the petroleum royalties and revenues has always stimulated conflict—in Nigeria, in the Sudan and South Sudan, in Libya, and elsewhere. The same kinds of antagonisms arise over diamond wealth, years ago in Angola and Sierra Leone, and now in the Demcratic Republic of Congo, but not in well-governed Botswana. The urge to monopolize profits from coltan drives a good part of the conflict in the eastern Congo. Cobalt is another mineral that has greatly appreciated in value and precipitates tussles over its control, especially, again, in the Democratic Republic of Congo. Copper is a third metal produced in the Congo and a source of competitive greed between Kinshasa and its Katanga Province. Gaining ascendancy over natural gas royalties occasions competition and skirmishes in Mozambique. The Central African Republic's Muslim-Christian war is about diamonds, timber, and gold as well as religious differences.

Horrific casualty numbers indicate how costly these internal wars continue to be for much of Africa. From 1990 through 2018, conservative estimates indicate that 12 to 15 million Africans, primarily civilians, lost their lives in the brutal intrastate conflicts of the continent. Those totals include as many as 7 million in the Democratic Republic of Congo, 5 million in the Sudan and South Sudan combined (since they were once one), 1 million or more in Somalia, 500,000 in Burundi, and much smaller but still sizable numbers in Nigeria, the Central African Republic, Mali, Niger, Burkina Faso, Cameroon, and the Comoros, in that rough order. The fatalities occurred both in the crossfire of war and as a result of intense collateral damage, especially starvation and disease inflicted upon innocent populations as civil wars raged all about them.

The collaterally damaged include several million women raped and gang raped in the interethnic combats of the two Sudans and the Congo,[4] and the millions of massively food deprived persons in all three of those countries, especially 10 million or so in the Sudans and 6 million in the Central African

Republic. Then there are internally displaced persons numbering as many as 13 million since 2012, mostly in the two Sudans and the Congo, and 7 million compelled to become refugees (externally displaced persons) from the same places and the Central African Republic in the same period. In part, the internal wars of Africa have also helped to fuel the great waves of migrants who cross the Sahara to the Libyan coastal cities and then try to flee across the Mediterranean Sea to Europe.

Africa's Several Wars

Other long-running wars continue to fester in the Democratic Republic of Congo. In its northeastern reaches, several local militias and warlords are murdering civilians throughout North and South Kivu provinces. A newly embattled frontier has also been opened along the eastern border of Congo with Uganda, where there are but few Muslims, with a group calling itself the Allied Democratic Forces. It receives financial backing from ISIS and has declared itself a new "province" of the Islamic State. Fighting in the Kasai region, a separate conflict, has left more than 3,000 dead, while the mayhem in the country's east claims dozens of lives each month.

These conflicts are mostly fueled by resource-driven avarice; the militias try to control mining wealth derived from coltan, diamonds, and gold. A large UN Peacekeeping Force of 19,000 soldiers under an assertive mandate but weak leadership has largely been ineffective in restoring peace to the region. Although authorized under a UN Chapter VII mandate to intervene actively to stanch conflict, it has been reluctant to engage fully in combat, especially against the shadowy militias that dominate the eastern Congo. Partially as a result, this area was plagued by a major Ebola epidemic in 2018, 2019, and 2020. (see Chapter X).

The Sudan and South Sudan

South Sudan began functioning as an independent state in 2011, after emerging victorious following a long, immensely destructive war against the government of the Sudan. That war in what was then Africa's largest geographical entity had begun in 1983, after the initial discovery of petroleum deposits in what is now South Sudan elicited resource envy among officers from the area serving in the Sudanese army.

Arabs from the northern and central regions of the Sudan had always dominated political life in what was an Anglo-Egyptian Condominium and, effectively, from 1899 to 1956 a British colony with a famed elite civil service. Nilotic-speaking Africans, predominantly Dinka, Nuer, Shilluk, Azande, Bari, and others, were in a minority nationally, but populated the southern region abutting Uganda, Kenya, the Central African Republic, and Ethiopia. The southerners long felt discriminated against by the northerners: they had been less well-educated, were distinctly different in appearance, and followed traditional cultural practices; they herded cattle; they rarely learned Arabic; and they were Christians and animists rather than followers of Islam.

Finding oil gave southerners, led by the Sudan People's Liberation Movement/Army, an impetus first to seek autonomy within the Sudan (and share the potential wealth) and then, after being rebuffed by a succession of regimes, to demand independence. As many as 2 million southerners lost their lives in the intrastate Sudanese conflicts of 1983–2010. Meanwhile, as the Sudanese army attempted to squelch the southern rebellion, so the Sudan fought to contain other incipient revolts in its own Beja region in the southeastern Sudan, in the Nuba Mountains and the Blue Nile provinces just north of what became South Sudan, and—notoriously—in the Sudan's far western province of Darfur, on the Chadian border. Hostilities there from 2003 were sufficiently murderous, with Sudanese aircraft bombing and strafing local non-Arab oppositionists and Sudanese armed Arab militias attacking villagers and resettlement camps from armored cars and on camelback, that Western powers and the UN imposed sanctions. In time, this unleashing of the Sudan state's might against civilians led to the International Criminal Court's indictment of President Omar al-Bashir as a war criminal. Because of his direction of genocides in Darfur, the Nuba Mountains, the Blue Nile District, and in what is now South Sudan, commentators called Bashir "a serial genocidaire."[5]

The north-south war ended in 2010 thanks to an American and Norwegian joint mediation effort, with the Sudan and South Sudan finally agreeing to share and jointly operate a Chinese-constructed pipeline that pumps oil northward from the petroleum fields athwart the new dividing border to a Sudanese port on the Red Sea. Revenues from oil were intended to support the rapid development of the poorly endowed South Sudan, with its 11 million people. But such hopes were quickly shattered when President Salva Kiir, a Dinka (the largest ethnic group in the South Sudan) and Vice President Riek Machar, a Nuer (the second largest grouping), sometime comrades-in-arms, disagreed on power sharing and on the manner in which the pending largesse from oil (and other kinds of well-documented externally-driven corrupt spoils) would be distributed. By 2013, South Sudan was bitterly divided by war, Dinka assaulting Nuer and their allies. The national army quickly became a largely Dinka attack force, directing its considerable kinetic energy against detachments that retreated defensively into Nuer-held areas.

Very soon, and from 2013 through several aborted peace agreements until a recent one in 2018 that was modified in 2019, Dinka and Nuer soldiers fought across much of South Sudan, often embroiling, sometimes enlisting, ethnic group militias that originally were not party to the fray or to its underlying arguments. The horrific atrocities perpetrated by both sides on each other and on innocent inhabitants caught in the crossfire were among the most ruthless in combat anywhere. Gang rape was an instrument of widely employed subjugation, as was wholesale mutilation, the cutting off of food supplies and the resulting starvation of thousands, and the spreading of disease and death. Easily as many as 400,000 South Sudanese quickly lost their lives. Another 2 million fled into exile and 1 million were displaced internally.

UNMISS, a UN peacekeeping force, tried unsuccessfully for several years to separate the warring ethnicities. Despite the size of UNMISS, and its multinational composition and authority, its 17,000-person contingent was largely ignored, overridden, and sometimes attacked physically. It could not save the South Sudanese from themselves, or from their factional fighting. Now, in the aftermath of a supposedly "final" peace treaty and the resumption of a functioning government in South Sudan with a Dinka president and a Nuer vice president, there is a faint chance that a year or so without fratricidal conflict could conceivably lead to peace and fulfilling development.

Nonetheless, South Sudan continues tense, with battles between the national army and smallish indigenous groups that were not signatories to the 2018 peace agreement. That peace pact called for the questionable integration of the two Dinka and Nuer warring units into a new national army, for Machar again to become the lead vice president (among five with that title), and for an interim government under Kiir to establish its legitimacy and demonstrate an ability to cooperate prior to new national elections in 2022. For bitter rivals still seeking rents from oil, this is a tall order. Separately, and together, they may each lack the necessary political will to foreswear short-term gains in order to reap long-term rewards. Neither leader trusts the other. Nor do their followers. The potential spoils from a fully functioning oil extraction process are too great.

Central African Republic

In the oft-neglected Central African Republic (CAR), the simmering martial contest for control of the country between the Muslim Séléka movement and the Christian anti-Balaka group continues, but at lower levels of intensity than in the past. The war began in 2012 when Séléka ("coalition" in Sango, the country's main language), a loose amalgam of Central African northerners, Chadians (probably paid by that neighboring nation's president), and Sudanese mercenaries swept southward across the sparsely populated country toward Bangui, its capital near the Congolese border. Accusing then-president François Bozizé of reneging on peace agreements from earlier years, and of failing to authorize cash transfers to supportive northern fighters, the Séléka movement forcibly deposed him in 2013. More than 5,000 civilians and defenders lost their lives in the ensuing combat and another 1.1 million Central Africans—a fifth of the nation's population—were displaced. Bangui's international airport became a place of temporary shelter and many other tent camps were erected on the outskirts of the city.

Bozizé was succeeded by Michel Djotodia, a Muslim from the north, but his government and Séléka perpetrated a number of outrages against civilians; pillaging, raping, killing; forced displacements were soon the norm. Those depredations were resisted at first by an anomalous variety of southern Christian and animist vigilante groups that styled themselves anti-Balaka, and were determined to take the country back from the Muslims. (Balaka may originate from "balle"—against—an AK gun.) Anti-Balaka was just as vicious in settling scores as Séléka had been. Fortunately for CAR civilians, France (the overlord of what was once the colony of Ubangi-Shari) landed paratroopers to restore order and to work closely with an African Union peacekeeping mission—MISCA—that also sought to pacify the country.

President Faustin-Archange Touadéra took office in 2016, but his administration has been largely dependent on French and UN troops to keep order, prevent atrocities, and establish a minimally successful array of peace processes. His government also wallows in corruption, which limits the extent to which it can operate in any effective manner to rein in the various Séléka and anti-Balaka factions, or even regain official hegemony in the critical diamond-producing sections of the country.

MINUSCA, the UN's peacekeeping force, now has nearly 15,000 personnel in the CAR. Fortunately, its mandate to protect civilians and dismantle militant groups is robust. It has also begun to disarm, demobilize, and reintegrate thousands of combatants, mostly from anti-Balaka factions.

With funds from Canada, the European Union, and the World Bank, the UN is further promoting a number of anti-violence peacemaking efforts at the communal level. But, as standoffs in and around Bangui demonstrate, MINUSCA has been reluctant to intervene forcefully lest volatile situations are made worse. Also, more than sixty UN soldiers have been killed keeping the peace; the CAR reputedly is among the most dangerous arenas in which the UN currently operates, rivaling only the nearby Congo. It is also a territory in which humanitarian NGOs are frequently targeted by one of more of the militias. For such philanthropic endeavors, the CAR has been more dangerous than Afghanistan, Iraq, Syria, or even Somalia.

In late 2019, at least fourteen different Séléka and anti-Balaka militas, plus an inner Bangui warlord, were fighting sporadically for primacy in sections of the Republic, and for what has become effective control over the movable wealth of a country that is still intensely poor, per capita. That wealth principally includes diamonds, from alluvial mining areas in the northeastern and southwestern sections of the CAR, gold panned and collected near Bria in the center, timber cut without permits, uranium produced in the north, and the smuggling of other contraband into Chad and Cameroon. Narcotics and weapons may also pass through the CAR, heading north. Séléka makes money as well by illegally taxing the movement of cattle and trucks in the CAR's north and east.

And there is even more mayhem. In the provinces outside of Bangui and the southwestern sections of the country, "a plethora of armed groups offer 'protection' one day, the next they repress. They raze villages, extract rare minerals, levy tax, loot humanitarian supplies, kidnap people for ransom, set up racket schemes and impose tolls to trucks and people."[6]

Russia entered this combat zone in 2018, and has since assisted with arms and training for the CAR government. It supplies and organizes mercenaries, backs shady Russian entrepreneurs who are gaining control over the local exploitation of diamond and gold deposits, and has introduced an advisor corps that now helps to run the CAR and keep President Touadéra in power.

Peace agreements forged in 2014 and again in 2017 have helped to tamp down conflict. But, because so much of the combat that roils the CAR is local and localized, with armed groups jostling for control over income-producing patches of the whole, it is hard even for UN and French force commanders to know which set of fighters "owns" which area of the disparate land. More than two-thirds of the CAR has been penetrated by hundreds of different militias, only some of which exert control over territory.

The International Criminal Court has indicted individual leaders from both of the main indigenous warring factions, one of whom was captured in France. Throughout, the African Union attempts to mediate between warring parties.

Both Séléka and anti-Balaka, only vaguely centralized as they are, appear to be franchising their operatives and operations so that local strong-men can skim whatever revenue-producing opportunities there may be in their particular locales. In early 2020, the Popular Front for the Rebirth of Central Africa engaged in fierce battles with the Movement of Central African Liberators for Justice for control of the strategic northeastern town of Birao, and had to be repulsed by MINUSCA.

As in so many other African civil wars, ideological differences and struggles for power have been overtaken by combat largely for profiteering purposes. Armed groups thus obtain the means they need to keep fighting, and fighting provides the means. The economic incentives to perpetuate chaos and instability over peace are obvious, and lucrative.

Nigeria Beyond Boko Haram

Boko Haram remains Nigeria's main internal conflict. It convulses much of Borno State in the far northeast. But farther south there are four other destabilizing civil conflicts that continue to shatter the disturbed terrain of Africa's most populous and, in some ways, best educated and most middle-class nation.

In Kaduna State, west of Borno and also heavily Muslim, clashes break out periodically between local Islamic and non-Islamic agricultural peoples and Fulani (Muslim) herdsmen seeking traditional or sometimes new pastures for their cattle, sheep, and goats. Ownership of land is contested, and fought over. But neither the state government nor the federal government has been able to prevent these frequent clashes over access to basic resources.

Similar kinds of disputes break out into violence periodically in Nigeria's central section, called the Middle Belt. There residents of towns and cities attempt forcibly to prevent incomers ("immigrants") from other parts of Nigeria from settling in their residential areas because of competition for jobs and, in some cases, for land on which to pasture animals or grow crops. Internecine hostilities in the Middle Belt, Nigeria's bread basket, have caused a major fall in agricultural production, costing an estimated annual loss of about $14 billion. These conflicts, and the ones farther north between herdsmen and farmers, have also accelerated a massive drift of families off the land and into urban centers.

Near Abuja, the national capital, but also in some of the northern Muslim states such as Kaduna, the federal government and some of the state governments have clashed with Shiite Nigerians (Sunni is by far the dominant Muslim persuasion in Nigeria) who claim to have been persecuted because of their religion. Calling themselves the Islamic Movement of Nigeria and led (now from prison) by a militantly pro-Iranian cleric, the Shiites managed in 2018 and 2019 to attack the Nigerian military in Zaria in Kaduna State as well as in Abuja and its suburbs.

Established in the northern states of Nigeria in the 1980s, the Islamic Movement runs its own schools and hospitals and adheres closely to Iranian government positions. (Boko Haram condemns Shia Nigerians allied to this movement as heretics.) For the most part the movement caused little trouble before its leader was arrested in 2015; most clashes with the government have resulted from attempts to free him from jail.

More long running as an anti-state insurgency even than Boko Haram, but now far less dangerous, is the remnant force of what once was the Movement for the Emancipation of the Niger Delta (MEND). A decade ago it sponsored a secessionist entity based in the petroleum-producing Niger River Delta; for a few years it was a disrupting presence in the area, cut pipelines, attacked government installations and foreign-owned petroleum pumping facilities, kidnapped for ransom, and bunkered oil (siphoning it out of pipelines and selling it on the black market). MEND also engaged in ship hijacking in the Gulf of Guinea. Some of the last—piracy—resumed in 2018 and continued throughout 2019, with large tankers being taken and their oil cargo unloaded by version two of the Niger Delta Avengers and the Niger Delta Marine Force, successors to MEND.

When MEND began in 2006 it opposed the environmental destruction caused in its home territories by major foreign oil producers, and by the Nigerian federal government's willingness to facilitate the consequent exploitation and devastation of the peoples of the Delta by multinational petroleum concerns. Oil extraction activities destroyed the fishing livelihoods of many families in the Delta. MEND sought reparations for environmental degradation from the federal government and advocated secession so that local people could benefit from oil profits. The Ijaw, Ogoni, and Itsekiri peoples were the most affected; they formed the core of MEND.

The Avengers and the Marine Force come from the same areas and background. They, too, attempt to disturb oil production in the Delta and the shipping trade that takes Nigeria's petroleum overseas, now primarily to Europe and Asia. The Avengers campaign particularly against state governors in the Delta region whom they accuse of diverting funds meant for people like themselves. But both groups are also mercenaries, and profit from their taking of ships and cargos on the high seas. They also siphon fuel directly from pipelines, Mexican style.

In the same general area of southeastern Nigeria, another ongoing civil conflict pits communities in the Ebonyi and Cross River States against each other because of unresolved boundary disputes that have already caused killings and may, sometime soon, flare up again.

Burundi's Autocracy

Ever since Burundian president Pierre Nkurunziza defied his country's constitution and bulldozed his way to a third presidential term in 2015, ignoring local, African, and international opposition, the small state of Burundi, at the head of Lake Tanganyika, has been immersed in a brutal civil war. Nkurunziza's security operatives neutralize protestors brutally; opponents behave in guerrilla fashion, attacking police and military contingents and governmental installations. As many as 1,000 have lost their lives, 460,000 are internally displaced, and 600,000 have fled into neighboring (and safer) entities.

African Union and Ugandan attempts at mediation have failed. A UN mission to preserve the peace and an AU attempt to launch a similar mission were rejected. Burundi also has been the only African nation ever to withdraw from the jurisdiction of the International Criminal Court, but the ICC still continues an investigation into Nkurunziza's brutalities and could issue indictments.

Nkurunziza, a one-time high school teacher, is an autocrat who rules Burundi by fear. Yet he also has substantial support (as witnessed by the two elections before the illicit victory in 2015) from the majority Hutu. From 1993 to 2005, Burundi was beset by a violent civil conflict begun when the ruling Tutsi massacred Hutu and provoked that war. More than 300,000 Burundians lost their lives during those dozen years.

A rebel leader in the early civil war years, Nkurunziza was first appointed president by Burundi's parliament in 2005 and reelected in a rigged election in 2010. Subsequently, he managed legislatively to shrink the country's democratic space by targeting civil society, curbing press freedom, and restricting freedom of assembly. Ahead of the illegal 2015 balloting, security forces and his well-armed youth militia brutally repressed protest marches and other demonstrations, resulting in militant pushbacks and extended fighting ever since. Opponents, mostly furtively, have attempted to weaken the state and to deny Nkurunziza's legitimacy. A Pentecostal who participates in large-scale prayer crusades, he declared himself a "supreme traditional leader" in an attempt to justify his hold on the presidency. He further promoted a 2018 referendum that approved his plan to remain president until 2034, with intimidation by military forces and his militia securing that mandate. Protests and further violent clashes before and after the referendum propelled additional thousands to seek refuge outside Burundi, mostly in Tanzania, and even more to be displaced within Burundi itself.

Burundi's Nkurunziza fits the caricature of a "maximum leader"—someone who "subverts democratic norms, restrict[s] participatory processes, coerce[s] civil society, and override[s] such institutional checks and balances as may theoretically exist."[7] Nkurunziza has eroded judicial independence, harassed and repressed the free media, and turned the security forces into a praetorian guard. Nkurunziza, like so many African autocrats, years ago persuaded himself that the state and the riches of the state were his to appropriate. No wonder his subjects remain in revolt.

Civil war and the loss of foreign aid after the 2015 vote have reduced most of Burundi's previous educational and medical advances. Infant mortality has swelled and school completion results plummeted. According to the UN, 2.6 million of a total national population of 8 million Burundians lacked reliable access to food in 2018 and 2019. One-sixth of all children are chronically malnourished, stunting their growth and mental development. (Burundi is one of Africa's poorest countries, with an annual GDP per capita of about $770.) Despite Burundi's many humanitarian needs, Nkurunziza's government has harassed most relief agency and international NGO operations.

Until Nkurunziza relinquishes power or is overthrown by his externally based opponents and the guerrilla movement that tries to be effective within the country, Burundian standards of living will continue to deteriorate. Lives will be lost in clashes between security forces and insurgents and their civilian sympathizers. The resulting low-level civil conflict will persist for some time.

Comoros' Commotions

A winning referendum in 2018 in the Comoros, a three-island cluster off the coast of Mozambique, gave its autocratic leader the possibility of two more terms in office. It also ended the rotation of the presidency among each of the major islands. Azali Assoumani, president of the Comoros this time since 2016 (he was president from 1999 to 2001, after leading a coup) lords it over his fellow nationals from Moroni on the country's largest island of Grand Comore. The other two islands are Anjouan and Mohelli. Mayotte, yet another Comoran island, has opted to remain part of France, the former colonial power until 1975.

Assoumani closed his country's anti-corruption commission in 2016, probably because the rulers of the archipelago are steeped in all kinds of theft from their people. He suspended the tiny (800,000 people) nation's constitutional court in 2018. Later that year, masked gunmen seized control of the old town of Mutsamudu, on Anjouan, the second largest of the Comoran islands. Even on Grande Comore there were protests. Private radio stations were closed and more than one hundred supposed opponents arrested. Many hundreds have fled across the waters to Mayotte, and on to France.

Assoumani at the end of 2018 beseeched the national assembly to let him rule the islands by decree, without its help. The assembly refused. It also prevented the president from closing down the country's electoral commission on the eve of a presidential vote (for term two) in 2019. Clearly, Assoumani wants to rule without being hindered by his political allies as well as any opponents who may still dare to appear. Further demonstrations did nothing to dissuade him from acting undemocratically. Assoumani won more than 60 percent of the votes when the snap election was held in March, beating seven opponents.

The African Union has tried to mediate in Comoros, but, copying Nkurunziza, Assoumani refused to receive an AU delegation. (He has tried to cozy up to Russia and Saudi Arabia, having cut Comoran ties to Qatar and Kosovo.) In 2008, African Union forces from neighboring countries entered Grande Comore to end secession attempts by Anjouan and Mohelli, the islanders of which chafed under rule from Grande Comore—and still do.

Northern Mozambique

Since 2017, Islamists inspired by and probably funded by Somalia's al-Shabaab movement (despite the absence of confessed formal links) have perpetrated 173 armed attacks on towns and government installations in Cabo Delgado, Mozambique's northernmost province, just south of Tanzania. About 350 mostly civilians have lost their lives. This is a poor and neglected region, far away from Maputo, the country's capital in the nation's deep south. It is also an area in Mozambique with many Muslims and with strong ties to Muslims just across the Tanzanian line. Because of perceived discrimination, many Muslims in Cabo Delgado feel estranged from the national government. Unemployment is common, transport and other services are unreliable, and schooling opportunities and medical help are far less available than farther south. Yet this is also the part of Mozambique that could fairly soon yield a bonanza of oil and gas, from offshore deposits. (In 2019, rebels attacked a convoy carrying equipment and supplies to oil drillers. But as likely as those energy prospects are, the people of Cabo Delgado have so far benefited little. Thus, especially in the wake of damage from a deadly cyclone in April 2019, a host of long-simmering social grievances feeds discontent and provides fodder for the local version of the al-Shabaab insurgency.

Al-Shabaab in Cabo Delgado comprise a shadowy group of militants that emerged out of a youth brigade within the legally recognized Islamic Council of Mozambique. (One influential report names the insurgent group Ahlu Sunnah Wa-Jama.) In one small town, the youth brigade, calling itself al-Shabaab, attempted unsuccessfully to impose a strict version of the sharia code on local inhabitants, including a ban on the consumption of alcohol. Arrests followed in 2016, the youths retaliating by training militarily and (possibly) seeking external support. Most of the youths are Mwani, opposed to and marginalized by President Felipe Nyusi's Makonde ethnic compatriots.

In 2017, this transplanted or copycat al-Shabaab attacked another northern town and several surrounding communities. It has since made forays from its bush retreats against a number of other small northern outposts from the major city of Pemba northwards to Tanzania. Whether these insurgents are numerous and strong enough to deter the exploitation of the province's energy reserves, or to do more than attack a few villages from time to time, is not likely. But Boko Haram in Nigeria began just as haphazardly, and without much of a following.

In 2019, a cogent report prepared for the Center for Strategic and International Studies in Washington, D.C., argued against repression, the then current response to Cabo Delgado's troubles, and for much greater attention to and solving the grievances articulated by Ahlu Sunnah. If not, the report predicted, civil conflict levels in this district were sure to escalate.[8]

Cameroon's Conflict

Africa's newest major civil war embroils the northwestern and southwestern regions of Cameroon, the sections of Cameroon that border on southeastern Nigeria's Taraba, Benue, and Cross River states. Unlike the French speakers who populate most of the rest of Cameroon, the people in both of those western provinces speak English. They constitute a fifth of Cameroon's 24 million people and have long been discriminated against by the nation's majority, by President Paul Biya, its long-serving and often absent autocratic leader, and by the military and police forces that are loyal to Biya's thirty-eight-year regime.

Biya's Cameroon has long marginalized English speakers, especially in the nation's civil service, in the diplomatic corps, in the security services, and in terms of the provision of infrastructural improvements and schooling opportunities. English speakers have been compelled, they say, to assimilate into a dominant French culture. Biya, ruling from Yaoundé, in the French-speaking center of the country, concentrates the power and resources of the nation in majority areas, neglecting the Anglophone region, failing to pave its roads, construct bridges, erect proper schools, and more. The residents of Buea, the English-speaking region's major city, have long argued unsuccessfully for better services and for English-speaking officials to be sent to their region from Yaoundé.

In 2017, after police fired on Anglophone protesters, killing a number who had grown tired of the Francophone teachers, bureaucrats, and magistrates posted to their areas without being able to speak the region's language, aroused militants struck back. English-speaking Cameroonians had been complaining for years about the poor hand that English speakers had been dealt when the two Anglo-French separately administered UN Trust territories of Cameroon (once the German colony of Kamerun) had been bundled together in 1961. French and English are both official languages.

The Anglophone militants gained support throughout 2018 and their clandestine movement now numbers about 2,000. In 2018 and 2019 they engaged in hit-and-run assaults on governmental facilities. They destroyed bridges and blocked roads. The insurgents kidnapped French-speaking small-town officials and killed police officers. They declared that they were Ambazonians seeking to secede from the Cameroon proper. They created a flag and a website, and now attempt to end French-speaking Cameroonian control of their portion of the country, to be called Ambazonia.

Armed with homemade guns and, allegedly, taking instructions from English-speaking Cameroonian exiles in Nigeria, Europe, and North America, the Ambazonian rebels are hunted down by Israeli- and American-trained soldiers who constitute Biya's shock troops. Soldiers have burned homes and buildings in more than one hundred English-speaking villages, shooting and detaining civilians and sometimes executing hapless persons caught in the crossfires during their ruthless searches for separatists.

In town after town near the Nigerian frontier concrete houses and stores are riddled with bullet holes; many communities have been abandoned. The government also turned off the Internet in the Anglophone area for several months. Residents have fled their rubber, banana, and palm oil plantations, reducing the nation's agricultural output and impoverishing vast reaches of the Anglophone zone. (Cameroon's western forests provide abundant refuge for secessionists as, farther north in the country, they give cover to Boko Haram.)

As many as 1,000 separatists and civilians, and fewer than 100 security troops, were killed in the conflict in 2019, and more than 20,000 English speakers have fled into Nigeria and farther afield. More than 160,000 English speakers have lost their homes and are internally displaced within Cameroon.

Cameroon's state anti-separatist security force is stronger, better armed, and better trained than the secessionist shock troops. But those guerrillas have ample support within the Anglophone region, and can move back and forth across the porous Nigerian border.

Consternation in Chad

Idriss Déby, now president, swept across the northern desert from Libya in 1990 at the head of a wild west attack force of three hundred pickup trucks, captured N'Djamena, Chad's capital, and has since ruled his country as a repressive autocrat. He has appropriated much of the poor country's petroleum wealth and changed the constitution so that he can remain a virtual president for life until 2033.

In 2019, as several times since 1990, a new rebel group tried the same mad dash tactic from Libya in the hopes of unseating Déby. On this latest capture-the-flag occasion, however, French warplanes based in N'Djamena took to the air, strafed the pickup trucks, and left it to Déby's security forces to capture 250 combatants. The rebels were commanded from afar by Déby's long-estranged and long antagonistic nephew. But other attackers will doubtless try again to overcome Déby's grip on Chad at a time when French aircraft are not immediately on call. (Chad has never experienced a peaceful transfer of government, fair elections, or any of the other attributes of good governance.)

Western Sahara

A long-smoldering conflict on Africa's northwestern frontier could again become a live civil war if the Polisario Front, a nationalist movement dating from the 1970s, dares once more to contest Morocco for control of what was once the Spanish colony of Rio de Ouro, or Western Sahara, and the Polisario-proclaimed Sahrawi Arab Democratic Republic. The territory is still lightly populated, with an estimated 175,000 Sahrawis and the same number of Moroccan settlers living within the borders of the territory. Morocco, which occupied the colony after the Spanish colonizers pulled out in 1975, governs two-thirds of the vast sandy reaches of the former colony, has essentially annexed it to Morocco proper, and exploits underlying phosphate deposits and offshore fishing possibilities.

From refugee camps housing 30,000 exiled Sahrawis and from adjoining bases deep in the Algerian desert, the Polisario Front exerts its power mostly in the inhospitable one-third of the territory that Morocco has not occupied. The two contending forces are separated by a 2740-kilometer-long, 10-meter-high sand berm—the great wall of the Western Sahara.

Morocco promised thirty years ago to hold a referendum to decide the fate of the Western Sahara, but nothing ever happened. Polisario demands that the referendum, preferably worded with independence as an option, be held before the two sides can parley seriously. But Morocco is content, despite UN and U.S. requests and diplomatic visits and investigations, to bestow on its southern extension only a form of limited autonomy.

For years Morocco has sought to treat its control of Western Sahara as something accomplished and noncontestable. It has convinced thousands of Moroccans to move there by offering generous subsidies and demanding no taxes. The kingdom is also spending billions of dollars in the territory to win over locals, but impressing only a compromising elite. For years, the police have also repressed dissent and any embryonic pro-independence protests. Those who publicly support Polisario are denied jobs.

A UN peacekeeping mission, MINURSO, observes both sides and occasionally attempts to broker a sustainable peace. But Morocco annexed the Western Sahara as part of a patriotic crusade. Its military forces are also much stronger than the guerrillas of the Polisario Front. Even the African Union has given up attempting to pressure Morocco to free the Western Sahara; in 2017, it admitted Morocco to membership. But the UN still considers the Western Sahara as a "non-self-governing" entity.

For the near future, the Western Sahara will remain that way, a potential fifty-fifth African state. If the Polisario Front ever receives substantial arms and backing from the AU or significant African states, a civil war might break out. But no one wants to take on the Moroccans.

Other Incipient Conflicts

Much of the rest of Africa is largely free of serious conflict. However, western Uganda hosts a small separatist movement in and around the Ruwenzori Mountains. Troubles occasionally flare up there. The long family rule of the

Gnassingbé family in Togo has from time to time aroused protests, mostly from southerners. Those protests sometime turn violent. Mozambique's long-simmering hot war between Renamo and the ruling Frelimo political front is also mostly over, especially since the death of Afonso Dhlakama, its leader, in 2018. Tunisia is yet another rough spot, with infiltration of ISIS and AQIM militants almost inevitable, but not necessarily with the ability to foment insurrection against the state, now democratically governed.

The bitter wars in Côte d'Ivoire between north and the south appear over. So does civil war in Zimbabwe by opponents of the post-Mugabe rule of his former political party, now under the tight control of President Emmerson Mnangagwa, seem unlikely. Corrupt leadership and the presence of contested iron ore and bauxite riches in Guinea could produce protests and conflict. So could violence break out again in Guinea-Bissau, where drug smuggling prevails. Theoretically, the citizens of Equatorial Guinea could finally rise up martially against the kleptocratic family that has long ruled that petroleum-rich state. But these are all concerns for the future.

Ending Africa's Wars

Because of the continent's inherent volatility and, especially, its weak govern-ance, the potential for civil conflict erupting in one or more fragile states will always remain. So in Muslim regions it is possible that ISIS or al-Qaeda can join hands with discontented locals to spread zones of terror. In both instances, the remedies that minimize the likelihood of renewed arenas of civil war and terror include improved leadership and strengthened governance.

For all of the reasons advanced in Chapters II and III, countries governed well, and justly, do not go to war, harbor internal hostilities, or prove hospi-table to terror. If the Congo (Kinshasa) had not long ago become a corrupted, failed, weakly and maliciously governed polity, the probability of civil war would have been far less. Similarly, that conclusion holds for Mali, or even for superficially robust Nigeria. Somalia only spawned discontent and proved hospitable for movements of terror when governance almost entirely vanished and anarchy and warlordism took its place. The Central African Republic was always governed haphazardly, but more so when France relaxed its once strong grip on its finances and limited its hold on security. Then the race for resources began. The desire to create and go to war for Ambazonia stemmed, as discussed earlier, from a governance regime that strongly favored one side of a binomial equation. Good governance is defined as good governance for all constituents of a nation, not just for favored groups.

Middle classes cannot prosper in zones of conflict. As much of Africa becomes much more middle class in its social and economic attainments (see Chapter I), so will bourgeois preferences and aspirations more and more tend to drive politicians and electorates toward stability instead of confrontation. None of the top dozen or so polities on the Index of African Governance are about to be rent by civil war; those that are all fall much farther down the list, as do those places where conflict is plausible.

Rwanda, where interethnic conflict was persistent from independence from Belgium in 1960 to the genocide of 1994, now is peaceful despite still being populated by majority Hutu and a ruling minority of Tutsi. President Paul Kagame's stern administration has made it so. Kagame's government has introduced an effective rule of law, reduced corruption, improved schooling and public health outcomes, begun to modernize the state agriculturally and industrially, and guaranteed public order and personal security—but not freedom of press or speech, key elements of good governance. Incidentally, the new Rwanda has an expanding middle class, something that neighboring and ethnically congruent Burundi lacks.

As Africa becomes better educated and better governed, its proclivity to civil warfare will gradually recede. At least that is an optimistic prognosis.

VIII | Schooling for Growth

A FRICANS WANT TO learn. They seek educational advancement. They scramble for places in primary, secondary, and tertiary schools. They know, to a person, that as more and more are born and crowd relentlessly on the continent, educational accomplishments will separate those who get ahead and live well, from those who are left behind, scratching the soil or seeking unskilled ways to earn daily bread, posho, ugali, matoke, and the rest. The key to being selected for a formal sector job, and keeping it, is success in primary school, completing secondary school, and—if possible—receiving a university degree. Furthermore, to have any hope of rushing ahead of one's fellow nationals increasingly depends on schooling achievements and on gaining formal degrees, but also on amassing either professional or vocational knowledge and skills. This scramble will not be for the faint-hearted, nor for those who are less persistent and resourceful than their fellows.

Becoming a continent where working-age inhabitants are much better educated than in the present or the past will determine how well and how rapidly Africa, in this case particularly the peoples of Africa south of the Sahara, catch up in social and economic advances to their Asian and Latin American competitors. A high quality of schooling for Africans—or its absence—will decide the effectiveness and trajectory of Africa's growth. Very little else will be as important in securing African prosperity, African stability, and African peace and happiness.

Unfortunately for those who want only the best for Africa, the state of the African, especially the sub-Saharan African, educational establishment is very mixed, with pockets of real quality and large zones of weakness. Catering for increasing numbers of primary and secondary school children, as sub-Saharan Africa's median age hovers for the next three decades between 18 and 25, will present major ongoing challenges, especially in those countries where economies remain weak. So will training and employing effective teachers (and keeping them in the schools) tax many governments, especially in those places where budgets are shrinking or barely holding steady. Building and maintaining sufficient physical classrooms are a further problem, as are supplying textbooks and more modern learning materials.

Already, the World Bank concludes that increases in enrollment in primary school, to take one measure, have not brought about commensurate improvements in learning. Of 387 million pupils in primary school in 2018, a mere 56 percent will have achieved minimum proficiency levels by the time that they leave the first level of education. Students, says the Bank reasonably, should exit from primary school with competence in literacy skills, should be numerate, and should understand rudimentary science. It is no longer enough just to have been to school. The Bank reports that sub-Saharan Africa consequently has a "a severe learning crisis." If educational systems throughout the region fail to respond to the crisis, a "veritable disaster" will unfold across successive poorly educated and learning-forfeited cohorts.[1]

Too many African classrooms today are vastly overcrowded, sometimes with many fewer seats and desks than students; with cracked, scarred, or no blackboards, no chalk; and libraries that have few or no books. There is a common lack of computers, electricity, and lights. Overall, too many school systems are under-resourced, especially in the distant villages, but even in teeming city slums. Instruction is of uneven quality and, in a number of countries, even in South Africa, teachers arrive for their classes intermittently and haphazardly, leaving pupils too often to fend for themselves.

In corrupt jurisdictions, too, solving for national educational needs will be compromised as funds are diverted into personal pockets or to military or other priorities more glamorous than schools. Existing violent conflicts will also keep children from school, reduce their hours and days in classrooms, and distract them from the tasks of, and the personal obstacles to, learning. There will always more mundane constraints, too: a lack of electric, solar-powered, or kerosene light by which to read and study at home or after school; chores (for girls) such as fetching water from distant wells and (for boys) herding cattle, sheep, and goats. Getting an education has always competed with fundamental necessities and income production.

There will continue to be disparities in educational outcomes across political jurisdictions, among rich and poor countries, among Muslim and Christian areas, in and out of urban slums, and very much according to how well a nation-state is governed. Being well governed ensures at least some attention to building human resource capacity through learning. Having good governance (as in Chapter III) means, almost without exception, a close focus on improving educational offerings at all levels, and believing in and trying as much as humanly and fiscally possible to strengthen schooling and school performance.

But even some of the countries in Africa with good governance ratings and less corruption than their neighbors still continue to fail to tackle the single most important determinant of a nation-state's social attainments and economic growth prospects. As research in many continents has demonstrated abundantly, the education of girls through primary and secondary school, and if possible through university, alters national prospects directly in proportion to the percentages of eligible girls who attend and then complete schooling. As girls gain education, fertility rates per woman fall and overall population surges slump. The better educated they are, on average the fewer babies they have. As girls become well schooled, they become productive and contribute to a country's economic growth trajectory. With fewer mouths to feed and chase after, they become a significant part of the skilled or partially skilled labor force. Educating girls has a huge payoff. "Beyond its big effects on economic prosperity, it also leads to smaller family sizes, lower infant mortality, more stable families and communities, and likely lower levels of disease burdens like HIV."[2]

According to UNESCO, girls still lag behind boys in primary school enrollments by 10 percent. In 2017, there were about 17 million sub-Saharan African girls out of school, 10 million of whom will never enter a classroom. At the secondary level, for every ten boys enrolled, only eight girls begin secondary training. In some African countries such as Chad and the Central African Republic, only half as many girls as boys are enrolled in secondary school; in Latin America, more girls are enrolled at the same level than boys. Chad and Central Africa's deficient statistic rises to 65 percent in Angola, but that number is down from 76 percent in 1999.[3] Progress is not guaranteed.

Clean and easily available drinking water facilitates the schooling of girls. Even in urban areas, ready supplies of potable water mean that girls do not have to stagger with jugs and pails on their heads for miles in rural areas or for shorter but still difficult distances in cities and towns. Once they and their mothers can simply turn on a tap, going to school becomes a ready option. And then girls can be liberated to become schoolchildren instead of necessary cogs in families scraping by. Boys benefit, too, when they live in towns and do not have to herd animals. But then the availability of school places becomes the issue.

Adult Functional Literacy

Sub-Saharan African countries are much more literate than they were at the beginning of this century. The official UNESCO rates of literacy for the sub-continent now approach 70 percent—substantially less than Asia or South America, but nevertheless striking compared to 50 percent twenty years ago. Two offshore nations, the Seychelles and Mauritius, now approach almost full adult functional literacy, with about 94 percent of all adults being able to read and write. South Africans are equally literate. Botswana, on the mainland, and Cape Verde, another island nation, boast adult literacy rates of 87 and 84 percent, respectively. But in Nigeria, Africa's most populous nation-state, only 52 percent of its adults are literate. (Another recent study claims that "millions of Nigerians are half-educated, and over 60 million—or 30 percent—are illiterate."[4])

Ethiopia's functionally literate are 39 percent of the population. Poor, rapidly growing countries like Burkina Faso and Guinea count as few as 34 and 32 percent of adults, respectively, who can read and write. South Sudan, at 26 percent, and Chad, at 22 percent, include even fewer people who are functionally literate. Development, human and economic, is difficult if so few citizens can read and write. Economists and educators urge low-scoring African nations to mount all-out adult campaigns to bring their literacy rates up to at least 70 percent in order to drive development and industrialization (a path South Korea followed successfully in the 1950s).

In some countries even functional literacy does not translate into actual proficiency. In 2016, 93 percent of Kenyan and 83 percent of Ghanaian young people 15 to 34 years of age told investigators that they were fully literate. But, after being tested, only 65 and 47 percent, respectively, of those populations could in fact read or write. Older cohorts in both countries were even less literate. Table 8.1 provides national literacy rates for Africa.

Fully two-thirds of Africa's illiterates are women, a proportion that has held steady for the balance of this century. Only 70 percent of all young women (under 25 years of age) are literate. Half of all women in sub-Saharan Africa cannot read or write, handicapping their abilities to contribute significantly to the rise of African GDPs. The relatively high incidence of child marriage and early pregnancy outside of marriage contribute to these literacy deficiencies.

Literacy, however, is notoriously hard to measure accurately, especially in places with weak and underfunded statistical services and little experience calibrating literacy in traditional as well as imported languages. Moreover, in Africa literacy may not be a very good measure of learning or of any capacity to

TABLE 8.1 Africa's Functional Literacy Rates

Overall 70%

Country	Literacy Rate %
Seychelles and Mauritius	95%
South Africa	94%
Botswana	87%
Cape Verde	84%
Nigeria	52%
Ethiopia	39%
South Sudan	26%
Chad	22%

Two-thirds of illiterates are women.

absorb new information and concepts. After all, much of sub-Saharan Africa long transmitted cultural ideas and historical narratives orally, rather than in writing.

Improving Africa's schools and schooling outcomes depends, just like literacy measurements, on the collection and effective examination of basic data on enrollments, persistence (completion) rates, learning outcomes, teacher qualifications, teacher compensation, preparedness and actual teaching hours in classrooms, availability of textbooks and computers, and amounts expended per school and per school program. But little of these data are available in many African countries. Policy changes are therefore often based on limited statistics and more on anecdotal evidence (and anecdotal complaints) than on real numbers. Even rudimentary financial reports are rare. An informal survey carried out by the World Bank found that only a few countries compiled timely and reliable data on student assessment outcomes.

The Schooling Environment

Since 1990, sub-Saharan Africa has effectively universalized primary education. By 2015, the subregion's average primary gross enrollment ratio had increased from 68 percent to 98 percent, or from 63 million to 152 million pupils.[5] Millions of new teachers were employed. But that vast increase in opportunity and in bodies in school did not necessarily bring about a equivalent boost in learning.

A better measure of how well educated Africa now is, and an indicator of those places most in need of attention and remediation, is the overall school persistence rate by country, not just enrollment numbers. What percentage persisted, that is, completed the entire course of available elementary education? What percentage of that last number continued onto secondary school? What percentages of girls and boys persisted through secondary school?

Wherever these numbers are available, reliable, and up to date, we learn to what countries or to what sections of countries assistance should be allocated. If we want to emphasize economic, or social, advances, or both, we need to know the percentages of available young people who are being trained in some kind of school, no matter how rudimentary. With that knowledge, we can find ingenious ways to increase persistence rates so that greater percentages of a nation-state's population become educated and trained each year. Absent the statistics, we cannot reliably know where to put new funds or other kinds of support.

Striking, and disturbing, fewer Africans are completing their primary and secondary educational experiences now than twenty, thirty, and forty years ago (when the total numbers of those eligible and in school were far fewer). Even though more individuals than ever before are now attending and even graduating from primary school and secondary school, as percentages of eligible students within nation-states and throughout each of the countries of sub-Saharan Africa, those totals have steadily receded in this century. Gross enrollment rates in fourteen countries have even fallen. Kenya's enrollment numbers grew in this century, but places such as Liberia, Nigeria, and Uganda actually had fewer students than before in classrooms. Fifty million prospective pupils are not in school today. Completion rates since 1970 are plotted on the revealing graph in Figure 8.1.

Fewer sub-Saharan African students are persisting at both levels of schooling. If that trend continues during the likely population surge of this decade and the next, Africa's cities and towns will burst; they will contain the largest and least-educated collection of urban peoples on the planet. No other continent or assembly of nation-states has ever progressed while carrying the dead weight of so many unemployed or, just possibly, only partially skilled, contributors to a nation's productivity.

According to World Bank figures, in 2018 whereas 75 percent of eligible children in sub-Saharan African countries enrolled in primary school, only 55 percent persisted through to graduation from primary grades,

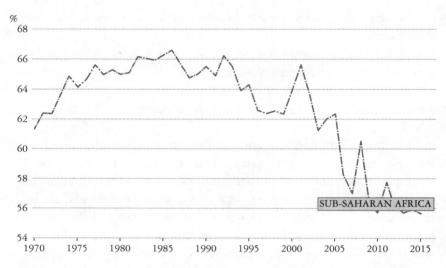

FIGURE 8.1 Africa's Primary School Overall Completion Rates, 1970–2015

10 percentage points lower than in 2000, and 1992. Especially challenged in this regard are eleven countries that the Bank calls "delayed" in meeting educational challenges, and thirteen that the Bank classifies as "emerging" and doing better. But those two groups are not performing the task of educating their citizens as effectively as a group of fourteen "established" countries such as Botswana and Cape Verde, and another group of eight "emerged" nation-states including the Comoros, Malawi, and Rwanda. Benin, Madagascar, Nigeria, and Zambia anchor the "emerging" group and Burkina Faso, the Central African Republic, Liberia, and Niger are in the fourth, lowest group.[6]

There are wide outcome differences, even in countries that share borders, peoples, languages, customs, and essentially similar colonial experiences. Kenya's persistence rate to grade 9 is 80 percent, Uganda's only 31 percent. Malawi's is only 16 percent. In West Africa, Côte d'Ivoire, Ghana, Nigeria, and Senegal all show persistence rates in primary school of 80 percent or more. But Burkina Faso only claims a 46 percent persistence rate. National persistence rates are shown in Figure 8.2, by country.

Students drop out of primary school because of the price of school fees and sometimes uniforms, lack of quality learning experiences, and sheer distance from a home to a school. Opportunity cost trade-offs are also significant: Does schooling contribute as much, in the here and now, to a family than helping with herding, washing, or other chores? Fully 46 percent of Malawian children said that they left their primary schools because of poor quality; 40 percent of Ugandans and 72 percent of Kenyans dropped out because fees were

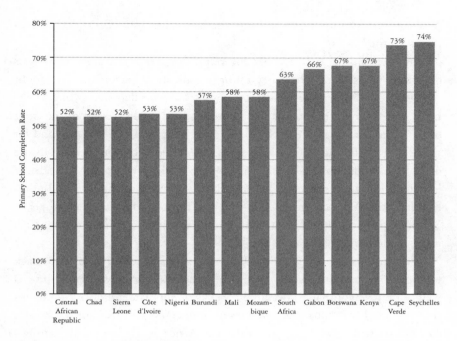

FIGURE 8.2 Africa's Primary School Completion Rates, by Country, 2018

too high. In Côte d'Ivoire, 75 percent of those who left before graduating from primary school said that they did so for other reasons—not because of fees, distances, poor quality, or their age (being too old).

Possibly one of the accelerants of these slides in attendance, persistence, and results is poor teaching, a quality deficit that has almost certainly been increasingly noticeable since the 1990s. In 2016, of the total of all primary school teachers, only 65 percent were certified, as compared to 85 percent in 2000. And only 43 percent of all primary school teachers were women, a factor which might negatively impact the numbers of girls who stay in school.

For all kinds of reasons, the African learning endeavor also suffers from the chronic absenteeism of teachers, even in prosperous places like South Africa. In some places, too, schools are staffed by "ghost" teachers—names of persons who draw salaries for a principal or some distant politician, but who do not exist. Corruption certainly enters the educational sector in this manner, in over-invoiced payments for improper textbooks, and for contracts to construct classroom buildings using shoddy materials. As a World Bank study comments cautiously: "The influence of rent-seeking and patronage in public administration as a whole has also had deleterious effects on the education sector."[7]

Another cause of both teacher and pupil discontent and slow learning is class size. Classrooms where beginning pupils are characteristically taught may have eighty or ninety students, some sitting on floors, standing at the back, and paying attention or not to lessons being delivered from the front of the room. In Malawi, the average size of classes in grade 1 is 150 and for grade 2, 125. Because of shortages of space, classes for younger pupils are often held outdoors. Classrooms that are too cold (in winter) and much too hot in summer are common. So are schools without washrooms and ablution facilities. Poor countries have much to improve upon in such respects. Without physical upgrades, teaching and learning continues to be much more challenging than ever before.

Curriculums are stodgy, too. Many teaching and lesson plans date back to the 1970s and imposing reforms on teachers who have long followed well-worn (even outdated) teaching paths is unpopular, and upsetting to entrenched teacher unions. But some revamping of older instructional methods and norms will have to be introduced if Africa is to capture student interest and upgrade learning. Some public-private educational experiments, and some purely local improvements, have been based on new curricula embedded in tablet computers distributed to teachers, and present on classroom computers employed in Africa's fortunate (mostly urban) teaching spaces. Such iterative technological advances will increasingly play a major role in strengthening primary and secondary school learning attainments. But so will an array of teachers with greater subject-matter knowledge; that characteristic is associated with significant and improved student learning achievements. What teachers know and how they teach is strongly correlated with how much children learn.

According to the World Bank, the countries that treat their teachers well and offer an environment and conditions conducive both to teaching and learning at the primary level are Eswatini, Mauritius, Botswana, Kenya, and Namibia, in that order. Conditions are far less salubrious in the Republic of Congo, Cameroon, Chad, Uganda, and Togo.

For learning, the language of instruction is relevant, too. Research findings strongly suggest that lower and middle primary pupils learn more and retain more of their instruction if they are taught and tested in their home languages, not the imported languages that they later need to learn in upper primary and lower secondary school. Burundi and Tanzania have strict home language instruction policies and, as a result, their students outperform their peers in neighboring countries on standardized tests. Ethiopia also uses local languages in schools, and its pupils also test more strongly than pupils taking the same test in other sub-Saharan African polities. But those three countries, and South Africa, are the only ones that privilege early year instruction primarily in a home language.

Testing and Spending

Burundi is an especially interesting case because, despite underperforming on several educational and governance metrics, its students test well. Possibly such a positive result reflects a single indigenous language coupled with a single imported language, classes that are much more reasonably sized than in neighboring countries, teachers trained at comparatively elevated levels, and unusually high levels of official support for teachers.

All of these prospective improvements ultimately emphasize the acquisition of basic knowledge and downgrade an earlier notion that average years of schooling provide a sufficient indicator of likely levels of learning. Now judgments about the quality of education in Africa are increasingly based on regional or global standardized assessment exercises. Overall, except for very high performing sub-Saharan African countries like Mauritius, only 50 percent of pupils in grades 1 through 6 in sub-Saharan Africa reached the absolute minimum level of basic learning. In a number of countries, only 25 percent of pupils did so. According to Early Grade Reading Assessment tests, 50 to 80 percent of second graders could not answer a single question based on the reading of a short passage in a local language. A large proportion of that sample could not even read a single word. About 78 percent of fourth graders in South Africa cannot read and understand a simple sentence, according to the *Economist*.

One of those measures is the Service Delivery Indicators reading test for the equivalent of fourth graders. Pupils score on the ability to read a sentence aloud. The Southern and Eastern Africa Consortium for Monitoring Educational Quality mathematics metric asks sixth graders to translate verbal information into arithmetical operations. On it, only a third of African sixth graders satisfied the "basic" category for reading and numeracy. The Trends in International Mathematics and Science examination for eighth graders (generally taken by the equivalent of ninth graders in Africa) requires knowledge of whole numbers and decimals.

Discouragingly, African scores on another widely employed international test, the Programme for International Student Assessment (PISA) for eighth or ninth graders, were much lower in 2016 than they were for comparable developing middle- and low-income countries across the globe. Even students in Botswana, Ghana, Mauritius, and South Africa, otherwise high-performing places, fared poorly. Only half of the sixth graders tested in Francophone countries were judged "sufficiently competent" in reading and mathematics. Overall, the World Bank concluded that in the mid- and late-primary years, sub-Saharan African pupils struggle for literacy; Ethiopia, Kenya, and Senegal were higher performers than Malawi, Mozambique, and Uganda, but—in general—fourth graders struggled with "foundational" skills and in five countries fewer than 10 percent of the pupils could read a paragraph. Sixth-grade Botswanans and fifth-grade South Africans scored well below their fourth-grade counterparts in Latin America and Morocco. Rurally based pupils also do less well, on average, than their urban or small town counterparts.

Additional funds could obviously bolster existing educational outcomes and be employed to prepare the entire schooling establishment for a doubling of school enrollees by 2050. But many African countries possess little free cash. In 2014, the median spending by African governments on primary education, per pupil, was just $208. For secondary schooling it was $412, well below comparable expenditure figures in South Asia of $451 and $665. Nearly all of those amounts for African spending were used to pay salaries (89 percent of the budget in Zambia), leaving little money for upgrading primitive classrooms and a tiny sum (less than 1 percent) for textbooks.

Foreign aid hardly helps because the amounts provided per pupil are low. In 2014 figures, these contributions range from $1 per person per year in such jurisdictions as Cameroon, the Republic of Congo, South Africa, and Togo, $2 in Nigeria, $3 in Uganda, $4 in the Democratic Republic of Congo, $6 in Kenya and the Sudan, $7 in Burundi, $9 in Mauritius, $10 in Ghana, $12 in Malawi, $14 in Rwanda, $16 in Ethiopia, up to $24 in the Seychelles, $34 in Namibia, and $40 in Botswana. But even those nation-states at the high expenditure end devote this external assistance less than they might to nurturing and schooling their younger, most formative, and most vulnerable citizens. (Families also often contribute to special school levies that are additional to government-supplied monies.)

Nearly all sub-Saharan African governments budget considerably more for primary education than for secondary schooling, with tertiary establishments receiving even less funding. And most of those funds are used to pay teachers, albeit most national budgets lack sufficient transparency to be sure. About 50 percent of expenditures on education is devoted to primary instruction, about 30 percent to secondary schooling, and 20 percent to universities and teacher training establishments, although the better-schooled nations spend more money on secondary than on primary schools. Additional budgetary attention to secondary school expansion would thus make sense across the board. Indeed, given Africa's jobs crisis and the pending explosion in youth numbers, many of the nations south of the Sahara ought to increase public spending per child on basic schooling. Unless they begin now to spend more on this and other educational sectors (possibly by reducing military budgets) they will be largely unable to educate a doubled or tripled student population between 2020 and 2050.

Progressing to Lower Secondary School

In 2015, roughly 53 million young people were enrolled in lower secondary schools throughout sub-Saharan Africa. Within the next ten years from 2020, another 47 million children will join that number as they leave primary school and enter the secondary ranks. A further 9 million could be added if existing dropout ratios are reduced severely, making a total of 108 million Africans who could attend lower primary schools annually from 2030 to 2050. These numbers obviously underscore Africa's compelling need for national investments in instructional buildings, texts, computers, teacher training, teacher retention, and teacher recruitment.

Although these enrollment numbers are certainly growing, and at least 66 percent of eligible sub-Saharan African children are in lower secondary school, up from 41 percent in 2000, those totals are still well below comparable figures for Southeast Asia, the world's second lowest performer; where 80 percent of children begin secondary schooling. Only a few African countries have achieved such high entrance numbers for their lower secondary schools.

But many of Africa's educational establishments have nevertheless shown remarkable gains in their gross enrollment ratios: Ethiopia increased from 17 percent to 56 percent between 2000 and 2014, Tanzania's percentages rose from 20 to 60 percent, Senegal's from 20 percent to 58 percent. Burundi's access went up from less than 10 percent to nearly 50 percent. But over the same period, three countries with universal primary education—Malawi, Uganda, and Zimbabwe—made no gains in available places for lower secondary school entrants. On average about 27 percent of the African young people who finish a grade 6 equivalent fail to continue onward, into lower secondary school (grades 7–9).[8]

These diminished outcomes for sub-Saharan Africa as a whole, and for some key countries, reflect the lack of access to secondary education for legions of African primary school graduates. Furthermore, it underlines the greater availability of schooling in urban as opposed to rural areas as well as the privileged access to secondary school of children from wealthier households (because of higher school fees at the secondary level). To lower this barrier, a dozen or so African countries have abolished fee-paying in state schools; increased enrollments followed almost automatically.

In some of Africa's polities gross enrollment ratios exceed 100 percent in cities and towns while remaining below 50 percent in or near the same nation's villages.[9] The limited availability of lower secondary school places in many countries hinders the already diminished enrollment of girls especially, as well as greatly disadvantaging students who reside at significant distances from such places of learning. Girls of that age need schools that have separate sanitary facilities. As many as half of Africa's lower secondary schools lack such amenities; their absence, and the scarcity of toilets and water in lower-secondary schools, often force girls to drop out.

A further barrier to seamless passages of pupils from primary to secondary school are school leaving examinations, even at the end of the equivalent of sixth grade. Test results compel many eligible students to drop out before entering the next level. Botswana and Ghana, among others, have abolished such examinations in favor of encouraging further training, especially of girls; total enrollments have greatly increased in such countries.

Upper Secondary Schooling

More than 66 percent of eligible students attend secondary school globally. In sub-Saharan Africa, only 34 percent are enrolled in lower and upper secondary schools (2016 statistics). That number varies enormously across the subregion: only 20 percent in Zambia and Niger; 27 percent in Mauritania, and 28 percent of Burkina Faso's eligible students are in secondary school, 30 percent in Madagascar, 35 percent in Côte d'Ivoire, 53 percent in Ghana (where cost deters many), 60 percent in Kenya, 76 percent in Botswana, 84 percent in Mauritius, and a hard to believe 98 percent in South Africa. Those are all 2017 numbers, from UNESCO.

The overall completion rate for sub-Saharan African upper secondary school students is 45 percent, much lower than in other regions of the world. Even in Ghana only 33 percent of enrollees graduate from secondary school. These low persistence to graduation rates in African secondary education reflect preferable opportunities outside of school, prohibitively expensive school fees even in government-managed entities, the need for students to support or assist their families, harassment by male teachers of female students, early pregnancies, and the lack of peer and family encouragement and support.

UNESCO also tells us that since 2002 the number of girls completing secondary school has risen from 86 to 91 per 100 boys (in 2016). We also know that each year of secondary schooling for girls reduces the likelihood of marriage before age 18 by five percentage points. Likewise, when the average secondary school enrollment rate is exceeded by 10 percent, the probability of war is reduced by 3 percent, a risk decline from 12 percent to 9 percent. The future of Africa south of the Sahara thus largely depends on its ability to increase secondary school persistence rates in an era of rapidly rising population numbers. Along with the social benefits just indicated, there are many more potentially beneficial results from boosting such numbers.

The Teaching Crisis

Enhancing the capabilities of sub-Saharan Africa's vast teacher workforce is at least one initiative that could boost primary and secondary learning outcomes throughout the continent. "The current stock of teachers in many countries comprises a mix of trained or untrained and qualified, unqualified, or underqualified teachers who have a modest and variable grasp of content knowledge and skills and teaching effectiveness," says a World Bank report.[10]

Ten percent of sixth grade instructors in key countries cannot do sixth grade math. More than 80 percent of Ghanaian primary school teachers and 65 percent of those guiding secondary school classes cannot read and write sufficiently to communicate significant knowledge. Only a third of all teachers in Tanzania and Kenya could answer appropriate pedagogical questions correctly. In Mozambique, Nigeria, and Togo, only a fifth of all teachers could likewise provide authoritative answers. No more than 33 percent of all teachers in a cross-section of African polities possessed sufficient knowledge to advise pupils adequately about their courses and their employment possibilities. To compound these concerns, in many countries the average sub-Saharan African pupil-teacher ratio is more than 45, nearly double what it would be in developed nations.

In terms of their classroom skills, World Bank surveys found that most teachers were accustomed to employ basic instructional techniques only. They wrote on blackboards, but assigned and reviewed little homework, and were largely unable to teach Socratically (by asking questions). Weak subject matter knowledge was common. Further, because of unimaginative teaching, student performance was less than it could have been.

Absenteeism is an even greater problem. From a low of 5 percent in Ethiopia to 43 percent in Mozambique, teachers prefer to avoid rural assignments, end-of-the-week classes, and any hard duties that might keep them away from urban pursuits and second jobs. Substitutes are rarely available or employed, so high numbers of classrooms in supposedly functional instructional buildings are frequently left unattended, with pupils forced to fend for themselves. Textbooks are often scarce, so under such combined circumstances, learning becomes unguided, haphazard or, occasionally, futile.

But just as there is no single "Africa" politically or demographically, so each of the national educational establishments has its own issues and problems. Burundi, despite its questionable political dispensation and political leadership, has schooled its young people better than expected; South African expenditures on schooling and learning outcomes, however, undershoot common expectations for one of Africa's more advanced and better led entities. Although a record 78 percent of the nearly 800,000 students who sat the national school leaving exam in South Africa in late 2018 passed, only 37 percent of those few (under 300,000) who took mathematics as a subject scored above a passing grade of 40 percent, a level which did not qualify them for university study in commerce, engineering, basic science, health sciences, and social sciences. An 80 percent pass in mathematics is required in such areas.[11]

To grow strong in an era of massive population increases, Africa desperately needs to educate its young people in technical subjects, but because of poor training and poor teaching, its output of such skilled secondary school graduates is sparse.

South Africa, for one, lags far behind smaller and less wealthy African countries in the manner in which it recruits only marginally qualified instructors, tolerates teacher absenteeism and incompetence, and fails to limit the power of unions that protect even woefully unqualified teachers.

Today's Africa has fewer trained teachers than it requires. As pupil numbers greatly increase, so this gap between demand and supply grows. But even with widespread wage unemployment, sub-Saharan African countries lack both training centers and sufficient potential tutors. Its pay scales for primary level teachers, especially, are 9 or more percent lower than those for comparably well-educated persons. (Many primary and secondary school teachers consequently hold second jobs, often in the gig economy or in farming, to which they may give better attention than their teaching responsibilities.) Competition for teachers with skills, especially in mathematics, science, technology, and imported languages, will grow and the continent's educational sector may be unable to retain its best instructors. For that reason, a World Bank report called for an overhaul of all national policies and methods regarding teacher recruitment, deployment, and personal support. It also asked for home language teaching; reduced teacher-student ratios; much better language training in secondary tongues; satisfactory texts; and a strengthened focus on upgraded management and planning.

Many national budgets in Africa are skewed against education. The world average is about 15 percent of total national budget expenditures. But South Sudan only allocates 1 percent to schools and schooling and the Sudan a full 3 percent while reserving at least 15 percent of its budget for its armed forces. Nigeria and Liberia spend only 7 percent of their totals on education, and Rwanda 11 percent. (Individual Nigerians and their families, however, spend as much as $514 million a year – an amount equal to a third of Nigeria's education budget – on schooling at several levels in the United States.)[12] South Africa, however, spends 17 percent of its total budget on educating its people and many of the stronger sub-Saharan African countries allocate comparable proportions of their budgets to improving schools. A continuing problem, of course, is that salaries and wages consume 80 to 90 percent of most national educational budgets.

Professional Knowledge and Improved Skill-Based Capacity Building

Providing better foundational knowledge acquisition for Africans is clearly critical if the nations of the continent are intent, as most are, on catching up with Asia and Latin America in terms of social and economic goods, standards of living, and human opportunities for their rapidly multiplying citizen numbers. That means stronger early capacity building, more students and more gender parity advancing through the secondary school years, better tested outcomes for secondary school leavers, and the kind of high-quality university training that contributes to an enlarged knowledge and skills base for this decade's maturing youths and their successors.

Unhappily, there is much to be accomplished to widen access to university (and to higher vocational training), and to ensure that university level endeavors meet the increasing learning aspirations of the students themselves and their sometimes fragile, sometimes more established, nations. More than 12 million Africans study in the sub-continent's universities. Yet, throughout all of sub-Saharan Africa, only 6 percent of potential enrollees (secondary school graduates) can find university places. A handful of the subregion's countries indeed send no more than 1 percent of their secondary school graduates on to university, mostly because of a lack of available openings.

These are the lowest gross enrollment tertiary education rates in the world by a factor of five, and a telling statistic testifying to the remaining educational gaps between sub-Saharan Africa and places like Southeast Asia, not to mention South America. North Africa boasts a similar ratio of 30 percent. Doubling sub-Saharan Africa's tertiary uptake to 12 percent might begin to address the sub-continent's overall skills deficit and, just possibly, respond to increasingly strident calls for advanced educational opportunities. Some of these university-trained graduates could also teach in the region's schools.

At the beginning of this century, Kofi Annan, secretary-general of the United Nations and a Ghanaian trained at universities in the United States, issued a clarion call: "The university must become a primary tool for Africa's development. . . . Universities can help develop African expertise; they can enhance the analysis of African problems; strengthen domestic institutions; serve as a model environment for the practice of good governance, conflict resolution, and respect for human rights; and enable African academics to play an active part in the global community of scholars."[13] Annan could have added that university training almost always speeds up the adoption of technological innovations and raises a nation's total factor productivity—its industrial and agro-processing capabilities. At the personal and household levels, advanced learning enhances employment opportunities and income-earning abilities while simultaneously raising a nation's economic growth prospects and standing in the world. The more completely learned and skilled a nation is, the more its citizens are going to enjoy good governance and freedom from civil war and terror. They will, likely, be richer and happier than their less fortunate peers.

Unhappily, Africa has not yet fully realized Annan's dream for his peoples and his continent. Sub-Saharan nations have risen in many ways, and a number are much more prosperous than they were when Annan spoke. But the universities themselves have neither come to occupy the place that Annan articulated for them globally nor have they, on the whole, contributed in easily measurable ways to the development and technological maturity of much of the sub-continent and its different peoples. For the most part, although important nationally and regionally, they occupy no greater place in the political and economic firmaments of their countries than they did when Annan issued his call. They educate about the same number of undergraduates as they did then (many Africans are primarily educated in overseas universities, before—not always—returning home), they swell the ranks of Africa's emerging middle class, they are avid consumers of Western ideas and goods, but they have entered the ranks of the political ruling classes in only a handful of countries. For the nations of Africa south of the Sahara, university education has been less transformative, so far, than Annan prophesied.

The universities themselves have, in many countries, fallen on hard times. Just as insufficient governmental funding handicaps quality improvements in primary and secondary schools, so universities—even in South Africa— are rarely now supported financially in the manner to which they were once relatively accustomed. There are substantial laboratory, library, and even classroom deficiencies throughout the continent's state-controlled and state-financed tertiary educational establishment. (Private colleges and universities, of which there are but a handful, are mostly church-related, and cater to a relatively limited student population, or are special and unique, as is Asheshi University in Ghana, a liberal arts institution.) Furthermore, the governments that fund nearly all of Africa's universities are not neces- sarily content that university education exists to enhance individual learning outcomes.

Many governments have always articulated that the role of a state-financed university is to produce human capital to serve the interests and fit the needs of the state. Knowledge for knowledge's sake is rarely promoted by national leaders in Africa even though the African Union officially announced an am- bitious and unexceptional goal for tertiary teaching institutions throughout the continent: actively to "promote science, technology, research, and inno- vation, to build knowledge, human capital, and [the] capabilities and skills to drive innovations."[14]

Among the many non-state controlled methods of remedying Africa's skills deficit and satisfying the aspirations of the legions of Africans who universities turn away is through on-line teaching efforts. Cyprus-based Unicaf University reaches at least 18,000 African students, many working adults. In partnership with American and British universities, it offers courses and mostly graduate degrees in business, education, and health management. Although it is a for profit endeavor, and its charges are com- paratively steep for Africa, Unicaf readily reaches out to the millions of Africans who are, or soon will be, under 25, and in quest of marketable learning certifications.

In a different mode, fully accredited American universities have started to establish outposts in Africa to provide openings for African undergraduates or research facilities for their own home-based students and faculty. Rwanda has attracted several, as have Kenya and South Africa.

Universities Rated

Given shortages of cash, pressure to teach as many students as possible, too few qualified instructors, unreliable Internet connectivity, interference from governments and political rulers, and restrictions in several countries on academic freedom, the learning environment in Africa's universities has suffered in the last twenty-five years. Only very few of Africa's 235 universities and college-type equivalents rank within the top 300 globally, according to ratings by the well-regarded *Times Higher Education World Rankings 2019*. In that year it put the University of Cape Town into 156th place, the most elevated standing of any African establishment of higher learning. Two other prominent South African higher education institutions, the University of the Witwatersrand and Stellenbosch University, were listed at the 200–250th and 300–350th levels, respectively. Makerere University in Uganda, once a top-flight learning center, was rated in the 600s and the University of Cairo in the 800s.

The widely followed Academic Ranking of World Universities metric, produced at the Graduate School of Education of Shanghai's Jiao Tong University since 2003, places Witwatersrand (201–300) before Cape Town (301–400), and also includes Pretoria and Stellenbosch (both 401 to 500). This evaluation system heavily favors research accomplishments. Hence other African universities failed to make this list of the top 500 learning establishments in the world in 2018. A third system, prepared at the University of Leiden's Centre for Science and Technology Studies, and focused largely on research output, in 2018 placed the University of Cape Town at number 395, the University of KwaZulu Natal at 418, the University of the Witwatersrand at 465, and Pretoria University at 468, just ahead of Kansas State University.

These international rating systems measure publishing performance, hence research accomplishments, and examine the number of citations attributed in reputable journals and indexes to faculty at each global institution. Africa, where most teaching and most university attention are devoted to undergraduates, performs poorly on that basis. Nonetheless, over the past decade, from a very low base the measurable share of world research output attributed to African universities has doubled. Only South Asian universities rate so low on the several scales, both geographical areas well behind East Asia, Southeast Asia, Latin America, and even North Africa and the Middle East.

Some of this published research weakness in Africa can be traced to the absence of students studying for advanced degrees; only the better South

African universities produce doctorates in any number. (A third of those are awarded to Africans from outside South Africa.) Moreover, many African universities, even those in South Africa, employ faculty themselves who are still finishing advanced degrees there or overseas. Funding for research is also difficult to obtain in African universities, even those that now rank faculty on the basis of their books and articles. Powerful as a drag on research productivity, too, some of the traditionally more advanced universities in Africa compel their staff to teach virtually around the clock and on weekends in order to accommodate the crush of students, and learners who still work full time.

In terms of comparisons within Africa, but on a somewhat different scale, a Spanish rating system, by the Consejo Superior de Investigaciones Científicas, annually ranks the globe's universities on their formal and informal scholarly attainments and issues a special listing of Africa's best one hundred institutions. Cape Town headed that list in 2018, as it had in all earlier ratings. The universities of Witwatersrand, Stellenbosch, Pretoria, KwaZulu-Natal, Cairo, Johannesburg, Nairobi, the Western Cape, the North West, South Africa (a distance-learning university), and Ibadan (number 12), in that order, follow. Makerere University is fourteenth on this list. Number 20 is Addis Ababa University in Ethiopia, with the University of Ghana next. The Kwame Nkrumah University of Science and Technology, also in Ghana and once ranked much more highly, is 32nd, the University of Khartoum 40th, the University of Mauritius 57th, and the University of Botswana 64th.

Those numbers correspond roughly to what could be considered the contributions to world knowledge from within African universities, a common measure of evaluating the quality of the world's higher educational establishments. (Teaching abilities are hard to measure everywhere, but the results of good teaching are—at least theoretically—accounted for in the results of research. Effective teaching, arguably, can best be done if faculty members are also engaged in cutting-edge scholarship.)

In that sense, a different study from a South African research center indicates that the University of Mauritius, Kwame Nkrumah University of Science and Technology, Makerere University, and Mbarara University of Science and Technology (also in Uganda) are, after the acclaimed South African institutions, the major research establishments in Africa. Moi University in Kenya also rates well. Mauritius was the only country, reported the same study, where, at both the national and institutional levels, "knowledge was seen as a key driver of development, and where the government and the higher educational institutions were in broad agreement about the role of universities."[15]

Mauritius' university has the distinction, too, of being located in a nation where teaching and research is focused, particularly, on training for science and technology. Undergraduate students in more established universities on the African mainland gravitate, in the traditional manner, to arts and humanities courses, demonstrating little desire to focus on the hard sciences or engineering. Furthermore, on a continent where for many years farming will remain a central pursuit and be essential for food security, African universities neglect this area of teaching and research. Sub-Saharan Africa's most important tertiary educational effort (unlike the original focus of America's land-grant universities) is devoted to preparing its students for employment in urban areas, little to innovating for rural development.

An evaluation by Nigerian academic leaders of the more than 160 universities, 128 polytechnics, and 177 colleges of education serving Nigeria, Africa's most populous country, reveals that cash shortages now and over many decades account for much of the weakness, and failure to perform, of that nation's tertiary educational establishment. The researchers reviewed the performance of tertiary institutions in comparative international perspective, finding that the Nigerian ones lag in virtually all respects.

Nigeria, in common with the rest of sub-Saharan Africa, has too few post-secondary places for its people. In 2017, upwards to 400,000 aspirants failed to find university places in Nigeria. The country, say the researchers, has only two universities good enough to rank in the top 1,000 of the higher education institutions of the world; South Africa counts nine and Egypt twelve.[16] Moreover, Nigerian universities produce only 44 percent of the research that South African universities manage to offer yearly, and only 32 percent of what comes out of Egyptian universities. Moreover, whereas the world average for governmental budgetary expenditures on research and development is about 1.77 percent of GDP, in Nigeria the percentage is 0.2. President Buhari's Nigerian government could decide to pump more funds into the higher education sector, and into supporting research more generally. If not, Nigeria's overall educational output could continue to fall farther behind the rest of Africa and the rest of the world.

The challenge of educating Africa's growing numbers of young persons beyond secondary school, and thus preparing them and their nations to upgrade the continent's essential knowledge base and its developmental prospects, will grow exponentially over the next three decades. Africa therefore needs more places in existing universities for secondary school graduates. It also requires universities capable of nurturing talent, fostering an atmosphere conducive to high-powered learning, and to imparting skills important to the twenty-first century. Doing so will depend upon visionary leadership in the universities, but also at national political levels. It will mean imaginative budgetary allocations, enhanced fee structures, the recruitment and retention of dedicated staff, and a student cohort that understands the critical role that students play in achieving Africa's new renaissance.

Vocational Training

That renaissance will only ensue when, in addition to marked advances in secondary and tertiary educational opportunities and performance, African countries provide more vocational training than has long been the norm. For decades, the critical need for artisanal work forces has been obvious. When Chinese companies construct Africa's roads and railways and try to hire local technicians, when domestic and foreign private concerns seek plumbers, electricians, IT gurus, mechanics, accomplished woodworkers, joiners, and even painters, and when African households require fundamental kinds of assistance, few accomplished African tradesmen are readily available.

There are vast ranges of occupations that will help to build African bridges to the future. Many African nation-states lack potential apprentices and experienced journeymen. South Africa consistently, as an example, is unable to fill 800,000 or more openings for artisans and skilled tradesmen each year. To close the gap, it has created Community Education and Training Centres to offer general tutoring and basic training in one or more critical need areas for otherwise unemployed (and unemployable?) young people. Senegal, which years ago recognized the same problem, is experimenting with mobile training units that tour that West African country and provide short courses in a variety of subjects and, presumably, impart immediately usable skills in smaller cities and towns. Morocco has a ministry of "Non-Formal Education" that specifically addresses these same issues. Rwanda's Skills Development Fund trains 6,000 young people a year. Some of the other countries of Africa also attempt to enhance skills acquisition via the Internet, through distance learning and similar methods. But only so much technical knowledge can be acquired that way; hands-on experience is essential, as exemplified by the European and Japanese apprenticeship models.

The number of unemployed in the formal sector is vast, especially in South Africa and Nigeria. Average formal underemployment levels across the sub-continent are about 40 to 50 percent. In South Africa alone, possibly 400,000 young people yearly under-perform on the secondary school leaving certificate examination and are forced onto the formal employment market without easily discernible employment qualifications. Yet there are numerous unfilled openings for engineers of all kinds, shoemakers, garment makers, electronic repair technicians, refrigerator specialists, jewelry makers, auto and aviation mechanics, and more. Agricultural productivity also requires technical assistance. Any firm in Africa that employs more than menial labor seeks skilled journeymen who have long been and still are in very short supply. Vocational training therefore makes good sense for almost every sub-Saharan African country.

The Southeast Asian tiger economies grew rapidly at the end of the last century and enjoyed vast demographic dividends in part because they educated young people who were about to enter their respective national wage forces. But they not only deepened and broadened the availability of university training. They also emphasized capacity building across several vocational sectors, hence upgrading productivity and the performance of their economies. In 1981, Singapore established a National Computer Board to train high tech workers, a successful initiative that helped to turn the city-state into an Asian Tiger. Adopting German and other European practices, Southeast Asian economies and South Korea focused successfully on apprenticeships and other methods of building capacity among emerging youths, school dropouts, and others who had little use for traditional tertiary educational paths. Vocational opportunities also need to be readily available for those, especially young women, who prefer to work with their hands rather than their minds. To date, too many African countries, even the bigger and wealthier ones, have neglected schooling for this important demographic. And too few have launched capacity building exercises in the IT area.

Where they have catered to the vocational-ready segment of the population, as in Ghana, there are still problems connecting the demand for well-trained technical persons with a supply of well-adapted and properly prepared graduates. Either because many technical and vocational training centers have been funded inadequately by governments because of obsolete, inadequate, or limited equipment, or because there are shortages of properly accredited instructors with practical and industrial experience, Ghanaian employers discovered that they could not rely on many such trainees. Unlike the experience in Southeast Asia, where employers worked very closely with the ministries responsible for strengthening vocational education, in Ghana and other African countries graduates of vocational training institutes have not impressed multinational and local employers with their proficiency or the thoroughness of their training. Nor have governments, attempting to advance industrial development and to take school-age young people off the streets, necessarily provided alternative paths of knowledge acquisition attractive to youths and convincing to those requiring well-prepared employees.

However it comes about, Africa cannot prosper in this and in coming decades without close attention to skill building of all kinds and at all levels. Catching up with the rest of the world and fully joining the global village will only occur when Africans themselves can advance technologically and in many other ways on their own, with donor assistance only for the least privileged countries. Political leaders need to plot a course of educational modernization capable of uplifting the national destinies for which they are responsible and thus equipping their countries to overcome the inevitably perilous demographic and urban challenges that lie immediately ahead.

Teacher Training

One of the keys to a possible revolution in the education of Africa, and to building a firm knowledge base among Africans, is renewed attention to the training of teachers, at all levels. To accomplish even modest objectives in this realm means increased expenditures on recruiting teachers from the upper echelons of African university graduates, retaining them, inventing or reinforcing stimulating teacher-training programs either as part of undergraduate university learning or in specialized post-graduate settings, and providing compelling continuing professional development for serving teachers. Current certifying methods produce woefully unprepared instructors.

As Ghana's president declared in 2018, "For us also to make a success of our nation, we must pay attention to teachers. It is only a crop of well-trained and motivated teachers that can help deliver the educated and skilled workforce we require to transform our economy." President Nana Addo Dankwa Akufo-Addo further said that the formation of capable human capital and significant economic developmental progress depends largely on teacher quality. That, he continued, was the strong lesson derived from the successes of Canada, Finland, Singapore, and South Korea.[17] After giving his speech, President Akufo-Addo announced that Ghana's three-year colleges of education (before 2012 plain teacher-training colleges) would become four-year bachelor-of-education-awarding university colleges within the University of Cape Coast. President Akufo-Addo made it clear that the intent of this significant shift was to make a first university degree a requirement for an instructional position at any level in Ghana's schooling system. And he promised an 11 percent pay rise, plus health insurance, to make schoolteaching an attractive profession.

Other African countries may be able to follow Ghana's lead. If not, capacity building for Africa's thousands of primary- and secondary-level teaching staffs will stagnate further. South Africa and Kenya have developed several initiatives in this regard and UNESCO, with Chinese backing, is undertaking to make innovative capacity-building innovations available in a number of the nations of sub-Saharan Africa.

South Africa, which has significant retention problems, once had 110,000 teachers in training in fifty stand-alone establishments, later reduced to twenty-five folded into universities. Three more were reopened in 2012. Now, just to replace teachers who leave each year, it must find 20,000 to 30,000 new teachers when its existing programs are only producing 8,000 or so fully accredited personnel annually.

Nigeria is attempting to provide more instructors for teacher training classes, many of which find single lecturers attempting to tutor 1,000 or more prospective teachers.

Kenya has faced similar stresses on its teacher training system and therefore upgraded teacher instruction at all levels, and emphasized access to information technology for all trainee teachers. It also reformed school curricula extensively to improve learning experiences. Previously, there was a significant gap between what trainee teachers were taught and what they were expected to instruct.

A British foundation is trying in Uganda and several other African countries to undo predilections among teachers for rote learning and repeated facts. Instead, it tries to encourage teachers to create cultures of personalized, interactive, almost Socratic learning techniques that can be experienced in specialized workshops and then introduced into classrooms. It shows teachers how they can cater to the different learning needs of children, and how standard chalk lectures and diagrams on a blackboard can be replaced by more innovative techniques.

UNESCO has attempted to boost teacher competence by holding more than one hundred workshops across the continent for more than 10,000 teachers. Working closely with thirty continental teacher-training institutions, UNESCO has also created more than 230 teaching service modules, seven online learning platforms, and three digital libraries—all intended to instill knowledge and motivate teachers to keep learning. Across Africa, UNESCO has installed an online learning management system that has 45,000 subscribers. In Namibia, the University of Namibia and UNESCO provide a chat forum so that teachers in far-flung sections of that country can communicate with one another to discuss methods and solutions capable of reinforcing progressive innovational instructional ideas.

These, and several other sub-continent-wide innovations, may help improve the questionable quality of the teaching profession in sub-Saharan Africa. So might the efforts of new attention to the problem in several influential African nations. If so, according to a critical Sussex University study, improvements cannot come too soon. Sussex found that teacher training programs in sub-Saharan Africa failed to prepare trainees adequately, especially for teaching English and mathematics in primary school. That gap was widened by stunted development of teachers once they had qualified. The preparation of teachers for Africa could be enhanced, the Sussex study said, by more content-rich exposure during training and by providing supervised exposure during the training period to actual classrooms, especially the large and overcrowded ones that are so much the African norm. Conventional methods used elsewhere are not necessarily appropriate for African classrooms.

Again, if the nations south of the Sahara expect to meet their national service expectations when primary and secondary school student numbers double between now and 2050, opening additional school buildings will hardly prove a sufficient response if the recruitment, upgraded training, and retention of teaching staffs is not made a priority at the highest levels of government. Other African nations would do well to emulate the forward-looking approach of Ghana's president.

Brain Drain

A very large proportion of Africa's professionals receive their advanced medical, science, arts, and humanities degrees overseas. Not all of these externally trained Africans return home to contribute to the uplift of their national fortunes. Moreover, many Africans trained in the continent's universities and research institutes quickly leave when they can for more supportive and more remunerative postings in Europe or North America. Africa's brain drain is real, of very long standing, and almost impossible to halt. The International Organization on Migration (IOM) defines "brain drain" sensibly as the "emigration of trained and talented individuals from the country of origin to another country resulting in a depletion of skills/resources in the former."[18]

As this brain drain accelerates because of policy weaknesses in the home countries, because of conflict, because of faltering economies, because of corruption and criminality, and because of insufficient prospects for advancement, so the losses of talent to Africa multiply. An outward flow becomes a torrent. When Zimbabwe endured multi-million percent inflation in the 2003–2009 period, 3 million or more able Zimbabweans decamped for South Africa, Botswana, Zambia, and Mozambique. If they were accredited professionals, they left home for the United Kingdom and Canada. Overland migrants are different from the brain drainers. They are usually the less skilled, but the general impulse to leave inhospitable terrain for more appealing pastures is much the same.

According to World Bank and other estimates, sub-Saharan Africa requires at least 1 million trained MDs, PhDs, engineers, surveyors, accountants, lawyers, and the like to meet its current skill and knowledge needs at a minimal level.

Instead, the IOM estimates that more than 100,000 well-trained professionals leave sub-Saharan African nations yearly. Three-quarters of that total have African degrees. The World Bank thinks as many as 46 million fully trained Africans will depart by 2050. If they have been schooled through an advanced higher degree in Africa, that is more the pity and more the loss.

Fully a third of all African scientists live and work outside of Africa. Half of all Ghanaian-trained physicians are permanently abroad. There are more Malawian nurses in London than in Malawi, more Zimbabwean midwives in the United Kingdom than in parlous Zimbabwe, and more Ethiopian physicians in Chicago than in Addis Ababa. Malawi can count only 17 nurses per 100,000 population while in European countries the ratio is 1,000 nurses per 100,000 people. Bringing "the missing" back would be ideal, but few are about to return, and fewer still are willing to come back and stay. Conditions are just not ripe, as yet, for such a hopeful return of the prodigal sons and daughters.

This hemorrhaging of professionals from the sub-continent has stripped the poorer countries of sub-Saharan Africa, and even some of the wealthier places, of any immediate hope that they can meet their own requirements for doctors, nurses, lawyers, engineers, tax specialists, and so on from within the ranks of their own nationals. Courageous and lonely outliers like Dr. Denis Mukwege, the 2018 Nobel Peace Prize winner from the eastern Congo, are unusual in their dedication, their resilience, and their willingness to serve their own peoples with little recompense and support. Each sub-Saharan African country harbors a few persons of similar selflessness, but many others that might have joined them have simply despaired, and fled.

The IOM avers that that exodus costs the unwitting sending countries upwards of $1 billion a year, a sum that exceeds all of the foreign aid that the same countries receive from generous donors annually. Hence, crudely but realistically, sub-Saharan Africa subsidizes the production of medical and other trained professionals for the developed, not the developing, world. That constitutes a serious brain drain, and is deplorable from many perspectives. But there may be a redeeming aspect or two.

Research by developmental and other economists reminds critics of the brain drain that those professionals who are well established overseas rarely forget their birth countries, or their original families. To the latter, they send remittances. The remittances annually to countries in sub-Saharan Africa are reckoned to total more than the amount of foreign aid that enters Africa over the same period. Remittances sent home by Nigerians top annual oil revenues. Remittances also repay many times over the costs of educating all of those individuals who have left their mother countries behind.

Furthermore, this specialized diaspora group includes a number of persons who give back even if they do not come back. That is, formally and informally both, they transfer knowledge back to their homelands either in person and directly, or amid small groups. They return to lecture, to demonstrate technological and medical advances, and even to set up research institutes. Some even teach in alternate semesters at a home university as well as a foreign one. A respectable argument may be made that those who are part of the brain drain phenomenon are not really lost to Africa; instead they are gone only temporarily. In fact, they assist the lands and peoples that they have left behind in material and capacity-building ways.

IX | Health and Wealth

Africa's current 1 billion or so residents are healthier than they have ever been thanks to medical science, special attention in several key countries to chronic disease remediation, and the efforts of several American philanthropic enterprises. Life expectancies are up and morbidity is mostly down, allowing Africans to work more productively, enjoy more leisure, and exert middle class pressures on their respective national governments. Daily life has become a little less brutish in a Hobbesian manner than it once was. There is more space and time now for the cultivation of progress socially, economically, and politically.

Those optimistic statements assume, however, that Africa will continue to build upon its current medical and public health accomplishments as population numbers soar in most of the sub-Saharan African nations. Just as the discovery and distribution of retroviral medicines turned HIV/AIDS from a fatal to a chronic disease, so new vaccines and other treatments may reduce the incidence of malaria and moderate the lethal spread of drug-resistant tuberculosis. Without such continued improvements, the doubling and tripling of sub-Saharan African populations could easily overwhelm fragile and understaffed medical and public health facilities and return many vulnerable countries and peoples to the parlous health state in which they floundered for so long.

The dangers of backsliding are real and imminent, especially since productivity advances are essential if Africa is to compete effectively against other developing regions and developing nations for incoming investments, for new jobs, and for the multiplier effects that emerge from increased wage earnings, more rewarding resource extractions, and expanding patterns of consumption. The health of the peoples of the continent is essential to its overall welfare.

It is harder to study intensively and do well in school if one is weakened by chronic diseases, by the fevers and chills of malaria, or by the accumulation of intestinal parasites. Building national knowledge bases becomes that much more difficult and problematic if too many schoolchildren are thus infected and suffering, and if their afflictions ultimately prevent them from persisting through primary school, entering secondary school, completing that educational level, and attending university. To prosper, sub-Saharan Africa must increase schooling opportunities so that its inhabitants can gain the credentials and knowledge to enable them to contribute meaningfully to societal transformation. Being well is essential. But how to achieve that improved wellness in the face of escalating population numbers, exploding cities, shortages of potable water, limited sanitation facilities, electricity failures, and many fewer physicians and nurses than are required, is a key question of our time, and one to which too few African political leaders pay much attention.

Life Expectancy

Average life expectancy is a crude but useful proxy measure for the health of a continent and a nation's people. Progress, limited or otherwise, from earlier times can be indicated. So can comparisons across the universe of African countries show which countries are working harder at improving their peoples' lives, or across the globe, and give African political leaders and health monitors targets at which to take aim.

Since 1960, when average life expectancies at birth in sub-Saharan Africa were about 48 years, that number has steadily risen to a 2019 figure of 61 years for men and 65 for women.[1] Overall deaths are many fewer than they were at the beginning of the century, which contributes to rising life expectancies. So do reduced childhood mortality, increasing incomes, better education, control of diseases, and health betterments of innumerable kinds add to the years of average life.

African numbers, however, are still considerably behind the world average of 74 for women and 70 for men in 2018. Furthermore, they are lower than average life expectancies at birth in Europe of 82 for women and 75 for men; of 81 for women and 77 for men in North America; in Latin

America, 79 and 73; and Asia, 74 and 71. Some selected countries show even greater disparities: Japan's average life expectancy for both genders is 85; for Singapore 83; for the United Kingdom's males it is almost 80, for females, 83. In Canada, life expectancy for women is 84, for men 80. In the United States, the comparable ages are 81 and 76. The latter age is also Morocco and Tunisia's life expectancy. Russia's average life expectancy is 72 years. For Egypt the magic number is 71, for Indonesia it is 70, for India it is 69. Haiti's number is 63.

Within sub-Saharan Africa, average life expectancies for men and women combined vary from only 52 in Sierra Leone, the Central African Republic, and Chad; 53 in the Côte d'Ivoire and Nigeria; 57 in Burundi; 58 in Mali and Mozambique; up to 63 in South Africa; 66 in Gabon; 67 in Botswana and Kenya; 73 in Cape Verde; and 74 in the Seychelles and Mauritius.[2] The wealthier, better-governed, and less corrupt countries thus produce elevated life expectancies compared to their sub-Saharan African peers. These uplifting results may stem from more attention over many years to public health issues in the selected countries, to heftier budgetary expenditures in those places, to the arbitrary incidence of particular diseases in one or more of the lower life expectancy polities, or to chance. But Botswana, with one of the highest HIV/AIDS incidences in the world per capita, still shows a relatively elevated life expectancy number compared to its neighbors. This improved figure doubtless represents that government's decision to spend more than the African norm on combating HIV/AIDS and a number of other health issues. Likewise, the low life expectancies for Sierra Leone, the Central African Republic, and Chad represent a collective comparative neglect of the public health sector in those countries, fewer hospitals and clinics, shortages of medical personnel, unconcerned leadership, civil combat, and unusually deficient nutrition.

If one spends x on health matters, according to a national budget, that need not mean that outputs resulting from x (the inputs) are particularly beneficial or improving of life expectancy results. That is why it is important to measure, as this chapter does, results in terms of disease prevalence reductions, maternal and child mortality rates, and life expectancy by region, by gender, and by ethnicity. In that manner it ought to be possible to diagnose and probe weaknesses, recommend immediate and longer-term remedies, and focus intensely on how to institute techniques and processes to strengthen a country's health sector performance and its effectiveness in reducing child and maternal mortality rates, eradicating dangerous diseases, and keeping its urban and rural peoples well.

Infant and Maternal Losses

From 1990 to 2018, sub-Saharan African countries cut their very high first-year fatality rate by more than half, from 110 per 1,000 live births to 52 per 1,000 live births. However, the global average for first-year mortality is 33 per 1,000 live births. That means that Africa still has work to do. Except for Afghanistan's high figure of 111 deaths in 1,000 live births, the globe's next twenty-four lowest performers, according to that statistic, are all in sub-Saharan Africa. The depressing list starts with war-ravaged Somalia and the Central African Republic at 95 and 86 per 1,000 respectively, continues with weakly-governed Guinea-Bissau and Chad at 85 per 1,000, and slides gradually upward through Nigeria, 70, Angola, 67, South Sudan and Zambia, 62, to Benin and Liberia, both 52 per 1,000. Pakistan is the next country on this list, followed by many of the remaining sub-Saharan African countries.

Interspersed, as this list continues, are a few non-African nations. Laos and Ethiopia both lose 49 under-one-year olds per 1,000; in Haiti and Lesotho the figure is 46; for Tanzania and India the number is 43. Among the better results, South Africa's under-one-year mortality rate per 1,000 is 31, as is Bangladesh's. Rwanda and Botswana are lower still, at 29. Cape Verde and Morocco show 21, and Egypt 19. China's number is 12 and the Seychelles and Mauritius are sub-Saharan Africa's best performers on this metric at a low of 10 first-year deaths per 1,000 live births. For comparison, the United States' result is 6, Canada's 5, and the overall European Union and United Kingdom number 4 per 1,000. Some of the Nordic countries and Singapore demonstrate even lower first-year death rates per 1,000. National infant mortality rates hint at the public health strengths and weaknesses of Africa's separate parts. Those numbers are shown in Figure 9.1.

Nigeria's overall number hides a revealing disparity. In the better-educated, wealthier south of the country, especially near its massive cities, only one in sixteen children die before they are 5 years old. But in Nigeria's massive north, where approximately half of the country's population lives, closer to one in five of all children perish sometime during the first five years.[3] To some extent, those disparities are very much a part of the African story. There is no one Africa, even within a nation.

The maternal mortality array of statistics per 100,000 (not 1,000) live births, another powerful health indicator, shows an equivalent disparity between developed and developing world results with the global average in 2017 being 216 per 100,000 live births and Africa's overall rate being 542 per 100,000, down from 965 in 1990, but still missing the Millennium Development Goal target of 205 by a wide margin. The official definition of

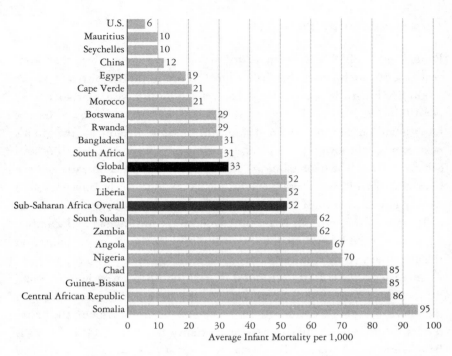

Country	Average Infant Mortality per 1,000
U.S.	6
Mauritius	10
Seychelles	10
China	12
Egypt	19
Cape Verde	21
Morocco	21
Botswana	29
Rwanda	29
Bangladesh	31
South Africa	31
Global	33
Benin	52
Liberia	52
Sub-Saharan Africa Overall	52
South Sudan	62
Zambia	62
Angola	67
Nigeria	70
Chad	85
Guinea-Bissau	85
Central African Republic	86
Somalia	95

FIGURE 9.1 Africa's Average Infant Mortality Rates per 1,000 Inhabitants, by Country, 2018

maternal mortality is: "the annual number of female deaths per 100,000 live births from any cause related to or aggravated by pregnancy or its management (excluding accidental or incidental causes). The MMR [maternal mortality rate] includes deaths during pregnancy, childbirth, or within 42 days of termination of pregnancy, irrespective of the duration and site of the pregnancy, for a specified year."[4]

Once again, sub-Saharan African countries are prominent as the worst performers globally in terms of maternal mortality rates. Sierra Leone is at the bottom end, as it has been for many years, with 1,360 deaths per 100,000. Following are such countries as the Central African Republic (882), Chad (856), Nigeria (814), South Sudan (789), and Somalia (732). These are all 2015 numbers and the Somali and South Sudanese outcomes may well have worsened because of intensified war conditions in 2017, 2018, and 2019.

South Africa's comparable maternal mortality number is 131, Botswana's 129, Morocco's 121, Tunisia's 62, Mauritius' 53, Cape Verde's 42, Egypt's 33, China's 27, the United States' 14, Singapore's 10, the UK's 9, Canada's 7, Japan's 5, Sweden's 4, and Iceland's 3. The full list is in Figure 9.2.

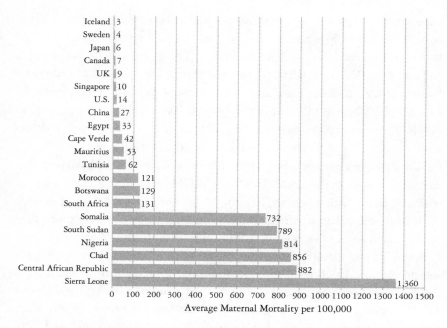

Iceland | 3
Sweden | 4
Japan | 6
Canada | 7
UK | 9
Singapore | 10
U.S. | 14
China | 27
Egypt | 33
Cape Verde | 42
Mauritius | 53
Tunisia | 62
Morocco | 121
Botswana | 129
South Africa | 131
Somalia | 732
South Sudan | 789
Nigeria | 814
Chad | 856
Central African Republic | 882
Sierra Leone | 1,360

0 100 200 300 400 500 600 700 800 900 1000 1100 1200 1300 1400 1500
Average Maternal Mortality per 100,000

FIGURE 9.2 Global and Africa Maternal Mortality Rates per 100,000 inhabitants, by Country, c. 2016

These raw statistics, and the infant mortality numbers, show clearly how unhealthy much of Africa is as compared to the rest of the world. That is less a reflection of African weaknesses and failures as it is a result of poverty, colonial neglect, paucity of clinical facilities and equipment, impaired national budgets since independence, palpable shortages of medically trained personnel, political leaders devoted to more rewarding policy pursuits, massive corruption, bitter civil conflict, and the severe tropicality of much of sub-Saharan Africa's environment, an overriding factor that climate change and global warming will only exacerbate.

Physicians and Nurses Needed

Given the enormous shortage in sub-Saharan Africa countries of traditionally qualified and degreed physicians, vast amounts of medical diagnoses, prescription writing, treatment, and even surgery are delivered by district assistants, nurses, local midwives, and other effective but less-formally credentialed health agents. For sub-Saharan Africa as a whole, there are only 0.19 physicians per 1,000 people, a number that will doubtless fall as population increases occur. For comparison, Austria has more than 5 medical doctors per 1,000; Switzerland, Sweden, and Germany more than 4; and the United States, the UK, and Canada about 3. The global average is about 1.2 and a figure of 2.28 medical doctors per 1,000 is the accepted global norm. Norway has 22 times as many as the sub-Saharan African average, Spain 26 times, Cuba 35 times more. Or, to employ the World Health Organization's (WHO) optic, sub-Saharan Africa is short about 2 million health workers now. (It has only 170 medical schools for its forty-nine countries' 1.3 - billion-strong population.) Per capita, Africa produces fewer physicians than any other region of the world. By 2035, WHO predicts that the subregion will have fallen farther behind, lacking 3.5 million trained health personnel.

Within sub-Saharan Africa, Gabon and South Africa count more than 5 physicians per 1,000, the Seychelles more than 4, and Mauritius almost 4. Botswana and Namibia almost reach the world minimum, with 2.7 medical doctors per 1,000 residents. São Tomé and Príncipe shows more than 2 and Angola, Eswatini, Nigeria, and the Sudan more than 1 physician per 1,000 residents. The remaining nations of sub-Saharan Africa are very short of medical doctors, with many having no more than 0.2 physicians per 1,000. Aside from Somalia, Burundi may have the fewest, 0.17 per 1,000. The Central African Republic shows 0.2; Ethiopia, Liberia, Madagascar, Malawi, and Chad 0.3; and Mali, Mozambique, and Côte d'Ivoire 0.4 physicians per 1,000. Or to express the ratios for Malawi in a more revealing manner, a single physician there serves 57,000 people. Uganda's ratio is a single medical doctor for every 11,000 residents. The complete list is in Figure 9.3.

When estimated numbers of nurses and midwives are added to these physician statistics, the Seychelles, Gabon, South Africa, and Mauritius show appealing ratios, but there are twenty African countries, with Niger and Sierra Leone at the very bottom, that benefit from only 0.05 personnel per 10,000 population. Delivering modern health care to a sub-continent that has 24 percent of world's disease burden, but only 3 percent of its health care workforce and about 1 percent of its financial resources, continues to be excruciatingly difficult.

Zimbabwe's 2019 disputes with government-employed physicians illustrate a further problem. Junior medical officers were on strike for a good proportion of the year, seeking significant pay boosts as the nation's currency and economic crises greatly lowered their living standards and fiscal weaknesses caused equipment breakdowns and shortages of basic medicines, sutures, and other essential supplies. Late in the year, senior medical personnel joined the strike of their juniors, and plunged Zimbabwe into a care calamity that was hardly alleviated by the government's decision to fire the striking doctors and attempt to recruit substitutes from other African countries and Cuba.

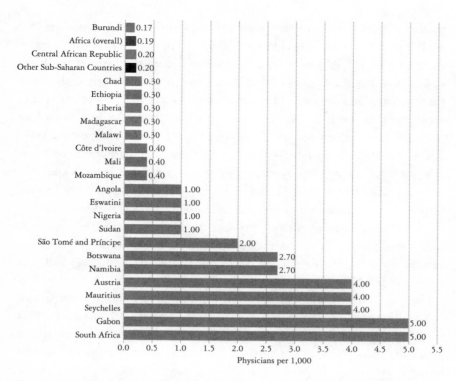

FIGURE 9.3 Percentage of Physicians in Africa per 1,000 inhabitants, by Country, 2018

One attempt to reduce the paucity of health workers trained specifically for African conditions and African problems is Rwanda's new University of Global Health Equity, run by the country's former minister of health and backed at the highest levels by the Rwandan government. Its students acquire medical degrees plus a required master's degree in "global health delivery," emphasizing the problems of providing high-quality public health care to underserved and infrastructurally compromised patients.

Tropical Impositions, Torrid Heat, and Water Scarcities

The nations located south of the Sahara face additional medical issues. Simply being located between the Tropics of Cancer and Capricorn, and being within reasonable distance of the equator, is correlated with slower economic growth (by almost 1 percent) than for nation-states situated in temperate climes. Those locations further influence productivity. Most of all, however, if a country is unavoidably tropical, it endures inescapable health challenges that are influenced by relatively close distances from the equator. Furthermore, if those tropically fixed places are also low-lying, as in the basin of the River Congo or along the coasts of West Africa, potential afflictions multiply in their lethality and ubiquity. Mosquito-borne malaria and yellow fever prefer such places. So do flies that carry parasites harmful to the eyes; snail-host parasites that feast on human livers; a variety of specialized cancers; HIV/AIDS; the hemorrhagic fevers such as Ebola, Lassa, and Marburg; infestations of worms; and varieties of dysentery. Epizootic (animal) diseases are also far more prevalent in tropical than in temperate zones. So are crop pests, like the locusts that swarmed into eastern Africa in early 2020.

A full forty-seven of Africa's fifty-four nations are irremediably tropical; to the south of the Sahara, only South Africa (minus a northern sliver) and Lesotho are completely excluded, and fully temperate. The lower halves of Botswana and Namibia escape being tropical, as well.

Simply being "hot," and also horribly humid, penalizes development and facilitates the emergence and growth of diseases and ill health. That is one reason why Prime Minister Lee Kuan Yew in 1982 air-conditioned Singapore, which lies on the equator. Economic research supports what he decreed intuitively. Tropical countries grow more slowly in terms of GDP (about 1 percent less) than their temperate cousins. And part of that lower economic growth stems from the health burden that tropicalness (high heat and intense humidity) bestows on countries that are both tropical and at sea level (Sierra Leone, Liberia, Côte d'Ivoire, Ghana, and on to southern Nigeria and Cameroon).

Cereal grains and the like also grow much more slowly in tropical than in temperate soils, and suffer more from crop and soil pests. (Plant respiration is higher and more costly for the plants in the tropics. And photosynthesis is harder.) Likewise, the torrid, damp surroundings that are so difficult for temperate-preferring crops are also much more deleterious to health outcomes than higher, drier, cooler zones of human habitation, some of which are found within the African tropics, at elevations trending toward a mile high. Johannesburg, Nairobi, and Addis Ababa are all at that level whereas Dakar, Monrovia, Cotonou, Abidjan, and Lagos are at sea level, and vulnerable to sea rises as well as to a mélange of location-related health afflictions.

Africa is liable to get even warmer than it now is, on average, and (as we learned in Chapter I) the impact of global warming on rainfall patterns and such hitherto well-calibrated weather phenomena as the inter-tropical convergence could make much of the already almost submerged segments of Africa hotter and wetter, and much more hospitable to irruptions of disease.

Children in most of sub-Saharan Africa will suffer the most. They are already vulnerable to malarial, diarrheal, and other common (and nevertheless killing) diseases and complaints.

Wellness in Difficult Surroundings

Neither village huts nor slum dwellings are conducive to good health. And unclean water for drinking and cooking compounds the misery. Only slightly more than half of all people living in sub-Saharan Africa (92 percent in North Africa) have ready access to clean water, even (sometimes especially) within cities where municipal water supplies are rarely available deep in the depths of slums. (And those crowded slums will grow apace with population increases, probably without today's modest number of water taps keeping pace.) Villagers traditionally have sent their girls and sometimes their mothers to fetch water from long distances, often several times a day with overflowing pails balanced on the heads of even the youngest females (but never males). Twenty-five percent of all Africans devote a minimum of thirty minutes daily to fetching water. Likewise only 30 percent of sub-Saharan Africans (90 percent of North Africans) enjoy proper sanitation facilities, especially in the mushrooming cities. (Sewerage is still inadequate in most of Africa's cities; it is not immediately clear how the African countries that are now doubling and tripling their city and town populations will be able to upgrade their sewage equipment and piping, including outflow treatment facilities, in a timely and effective manner.) Those cold statistical realities contribute to the spread of waterborne and other associated diseases. About 2,000 of Africa's children die every day (more than 750,000 per year) from diseases attributable to unclean water and insufficient sanitation. Over 60 percent of hospital beds in sub-Saharan Africa are occupied by patients suffering from ailments that stem from dirty water.

Naturally, too, as we have seen with infant and maternal fatality numbers, Africa varies enormously in the way fundamental health endowments are developed. Potable water—approaching 99 percent coverage—is easily available for residents of Mauritius, Botswana, and South Africa. Gabon and the Gambia also do well. Kenya's level is 63 percent. But only 52 percent of Congolese, 51 percent of Mozambicans, and 32 percent of Somali (8 percent in rural areas) can count on ready water. Even the oil-rich, despotically ruled country of Equatorial Guinea offers improved access to water to only 48 percent of its people.

Climate-induced bouts of persistent drought will make some of these numbers, especially across the Sahel, worse. So will the continued destruction or conversion (for housing and factories) of wetlands and mangrove swamps (both natural water purifying agents). But the major element will be the coming vast bulge in population numbers. That upsurge may overwhelm existing supplies of water, or at least make them far more costly than before. Some major cities, such as Harare, have already experienced chlorination crises. In that recent case, most of the entire city of 2 million people had to boil its water for months, or dig deep wells. Outbreaks of cholera and typhoid naturally followed.

Scarcities of water suitable for drinking and cooking, and the lack of experience in Africa of purifying and reusing waste water (only Windhoek, Namibia, has done so for decades), plus a reluctance so far to experiment with desalination, has made water availability a critical commodity inhibiting development and, when limited and scarce, a major threat to health and welfare. Even Cape Town went dry in 2018. Competition among countries in various parts of the world, and certainly in Africa, where whole peoples are so dependent upon water collection and use, can also lead to conflict, even to full-scale war.

To be healthy, Africans, especially children, also need adequate nutrition. Disease burdens intensify nutritional requirements and also facilitate the spread of epidemic and other maladies. It is no wonder that protein and micronutrient deficiencies, plus missing energy ingredients, accompany disease-caused morbidity and add significantly to the obstacles that Africans must surmount to live and to work, especially in tropical surrounds. Whole populations in a dozen African countries may be malnourished at any one time because of droughts, floods, crop failures, cash shortages, conflict, and the like. Visible kwashiorkor and marasmus in child populations, typically in the poorest or most embattled nations, are clear signs of malnutrition. For many years in this century a one-time bread basket such as Zimbabwe relied on World Food Program (WFP) assistance to feed as many as one-third of its residents. In late 2019, an official UN investigation reported that 60 percent of Zimbabweans (about 7.5 million persons) were "food insecure" and at risk of suffering "man-made starvation."[5] Similarly, in zones of persistent drought, as across the Sahel, the WFP feeds up to half of entire national populations. Those numbers sometimes reach 50 million or more. Reduced immunities that reflect malnourishment enable diseases to invade and flourish.

In 2018, before the cyclones, floods, and droughts of 2019, the Global Hunger Index reported even then that food shortages in the Central African Republic were "extremely alarming," were only "alarming" in Chad, Liberia,

Madagascar, and Zambia, and were "serious," the third category of concern, across much of the remainder of sub-Saharan Africa. Only Gabon, Ghana, Senegal, and South Africa had enough food to feed their people. In Zambia, for example, 40 percent of its children under 5 years of age were "stunted." Almost 50 percent of the entire population was "undernourished." Contrastingly, in Kenya, a country rated "serious," only 22 percent of the population was undernourished and only 23 percent of children were "stunted."

Africans naturally find it difficult to study and work, and resist diseases, if they are hungry, that is, if caloric intakes are below standard norms. Children are also weighed to see if they are below standard weights and heights for their age groups—hence the use of the term "stunted" to describe those who are below an appropriate norm.

The Heavy Weight of Disease

Of all the regions of the world, sub-Saharan Africa is unusually beset by disease. Fully 71 percent of the globe's disease burden from HIV/AIDS, tuberculosis (TB), and malaria falls on sub-Saharan Africa, where the number of health workers of all kinds on the ground only amounts to 4 percent of the existing global health workforce. That tiny cadre of mostly dedicated physicians, nurses, midwives, technicians, and orderlies tries, daily, to intervene effectively and humanely to diagnose, to treat, and then to commiserate with sufferers and their families. Overall, they are making progress despite budget shortfalls, national insolvencies, corruption, theft, and general despair.

More than 90 percent of all deaths worldwide from malaria occur in Africa. Nearly 70 percent of all people afflicted with HIV, and with AIDS, live in sub-Saharan Africa. About 25 percent of all fatalities from tuberculosis also take place in the sub-continent. Not only is the human impact of these several disease consequences, plus the calamitous incidence of pneumonia, punishing for the humans and their families, but this overall disease burden also has an immense socioeconomic impact in and on sub-Saharan African day-to-day life as well as its prospects for meaningful development. Malaria kills children and then systematically debilitates those who survive. HIV/AIDS and TB cripple people in what are supposed to be their most productive years. Unless these and other diseases are controlled effectively now, or very soon, members of the shortly to-be-born birth cohort will become less able to be schooled, obtain jobs, and work successfully. Businesses and governments already lose workers to premature death and find those who remain less productive than they once were because of the heavy disease burden that so many Africans carry. The human toll is immense. So is government and corporate business slowed because of these many illnesses, the lasting morbidity that often results from their incidence, and the prolonged treatments that are often necessary. As no less an activist as Bill Gates remarks, "When people aren't sick in bed, they can go to work or school."[6]

The world battled malaria and TB for centuries with little lasting effect, but the immense human toll of HIV/AIDS in the late 1990s, especially in Africa, injected a new urgency into global disease prevention and treatment efforts, again with a focus on Africa. Although the resources to fight these and other diseases have increased exponentially in this century, funding and attention remain mostly insufficient to ensure either eradication or widespread control. Infectious diseases are particularly challenging because remediation rarely means conquest. Even easily vaccinated-against maladies such as infantile paralysis (polio) and measles are revived if parts of populations (as in northern Nigeria and the Congo) resist, and evade the entreaties of public health workers.

Weak health systems further complicate the fight against disease, especially in sub-Saharan Africa. The shortage of health workers is a major obstacle in expanding treatment and prevention efforts. Health workers at all levels of delivery, the systems that they are dedicated to manage, the necessary equipment down to portable chilling boxes, basic supplies, fundamentals such as water and electric power, and the facilities that support such efforts, are never givens. In sub-Saharan Africa, particularly in its poorer parts, ensuring that all of these components exist is a necessity if infectious diseases are to be cured and better health care outcomes are to be realized.

That said, thanks to the Bill and Melinda Gates Foundation, the Carter Center, the U.S. government's PEPFAR initiative (the U.S. President's Emergency Plan for AIDS Relief), and help from several European and Japanese aid agencies, major advances against the key killing epidemics of Africa, and many minor but debilitating diseases, have been made in this century. Absolutely central to this effort have been the Global Fund (successor to the Global Fund to Fight AIDS, Tuberculosis, and Malaria); Gavi, the Vaccine Alliance; and the Global Polio Eradication Initiative, all generously supported by the Gates Foundation.

Millions of Africans have obtained access to antiretroviral medicines to combat HIV/AIDS, especially in the unusually hard-hit southern and eastern African regions where HIV-1 and HIV-3 killed 15 million people between 1990 and 2016 and now afflict about 25 million Africans. Botswana provides antiretroviral medicines free to its infected and vulnerable population. South Africa, after initially resisting the scientific understanding that HIV/AIDS was sexually transmitted, now makes antiretroviral treatments available to those among its population who are chronic sufferers. (The cost per patient for antiretroviral medications has also fallen dramatically.) Nevertheless, AIDS still kills. In 2018 alone, approximately 468,000 persons died from AIDS in sub-Saharan Africa. Yet, encouragingly, new transmissions of HIV are down 8 percent in West Africa and 30 percent in eastern and southern Africa.

Africa's killing maladies are many, of differing lethalities and frequencies.

Pneumonia, Diarrheal Disease, and Measles

Poverty and malnutrition (again common) weaken children and increase vulnerability, especially to the biggest destroyer of children—pneumonia. That malady yearly kills about 500,000 mostly sub-Saharan African children, fully half of all childhood deaths from pneumonia worldwide. More than 1 million adults also die of pneumonia. Globally, those deaths from pneumonia are more than all deaths from HIV/AIDS, diarrhea, and malaria combined, and the African proportions are much the same. Such killing fields exist despite the fact that pneumonia fatalities are often prevented in temperate and wealthier places by improved hygiene, reduced dwelling pollution (from open fires and the like), exclusive breastfeeding, and the availability of standard and inexpensive antibiotic treatments.

Diarrheal illnesses are additional killers, especially of very young Africans. These mostly waterborne diseases include dysentery, gastroenteritis, rotavirus, typhoid, and cholera, and are caused by fecal contamination. Like pneumonia, they are easily preventable through improved personal sanitary practices, the provision of enhanced access to sources of clean water, and upgraded disposal techniques using sewerage or fully functioning septic tanks. Nonetheless, in sub-Saharan Africa this bundle of diseases is a prime killer of children, and of many adults.

At least nine sub-Saharan African nations (Angola, Burundi, the Democratic Republic of Congo, Malawi, Mozambique, Rwanda, Zambia, and Zimbabwe) have all suffered twenty-first-century epidemics of one or more of these waterborne ailments. Zimbabwe's occurred because its government had run out of funds to purchase chemical disinfectants for municipal water supplies, and because its water mains had not been repaired for decades. More than 1 million people died across Africa during these several epidemic breakouts, possibly half of whom were children. Each year, about 120,000 persons lose their lives from cholera and 800,000 from various forms of dysentery. This second disease competes with pneumonia as the deadliest for Africa's children.

In Africa, measles is also destructive of young lives, primarily because of lapses in vaccination, vitamin A deficiencies (which multiply lethality), dangerous malnutrition, and failures to inoculate youthful populations. In poor countries with pools of unvaccinated people and limited access to experienced medical care, 10 percent of all children, compared to 1 percent in wealthier countries with fuller vaccination rates, risk contracting measles. Overcrowded refugee camps can suffer even higher fatality rates if measles arrives. Measles epidemics convulsed Malawi, Zambia, and Zimbabwe a decade ago, hit war-torn northern Nigeria more recently (because of rumors and resistance to vaccinations), and entered all twenty-six provinces of the Democratic Republic of Congo because of war and neglect. Over 310,000 people were infected by early 2020, with more to come before the epidemic runs its course. In excess of 6,000 died in four provinces in the eastern Congo alone, a much greater number than those who succumbed during the same year from Ebola.

In 2018, there was a major outbreak of measles in Sierra Leone in areas of the country that had not been reached for several years by vaccinators. In 2019, there were more than 118,000 cases in Madagascar, and at least 1,200 dead, thanks to very low vaccination rates. Across the waters separating that large island from the African mainland, a simultaneous cascading outbreak of measles occurred in central Mozambique after a disastrous cyclone flooded a large area that included Beira and its suburbs. All of these epidemics of measles were entirely preventable.

Another disease that spreads wildly in Africa, especially among children, is Group A *Netsseria meningitis*, the most prevalent African meningococcal infection. It erupts infrequently, but when it does it brings death to thousands across the northern belt from Senegal to Ethiopia. Mali, Burkina Faso, and Niger have suffered harsh epidemics. Fortunately, since 2010 more than 300 million persons have been vaccinated against the disease, and outbreaks are far less common. But boosters are needed to maintain immunity.

Malaria

There has been substantial progress in the enduring battle against malaria, as well, but more globally than in Africa. There, especially in tropical locations, the forward momentum that occurred before 2013 has not been sustained. Beginning in 2016, Africa south of the Sahara began to count more rather than fewer cases, possibly because of emerging resistance to the insecticides and medicines that had hitherto been effective. According to the World Health Organization (WHO) in 2019, nearly 200 million Africans contract malaria every year and approximately 425,000 of those many millions die.

Two-thirds of that number are children under 5 years of age, 800 of whom succumb each day, and rapidly, when parasites transmitted by mosquitoes swarm into their brains.

Fifteen of sub-Saharan Africa's forty-nine countries account for 80 percent of all African cases of malaria and 78 percent of all deaths. Nigeria leads this uncomfortable list, with nearly 20 percent of all fatal cases worldwide. Nigeria harbors a quarter of all malarial cases around the globe, and the number of its cases grew by more than 1 million in 2017 over 2016, possibly because Nigeria was spending less per capita on malarial prevention and care than ever before. The Democratic Republic of Congo, Burkina Faso, and Tanzania follow Nigeria, with between 11 percent and 5 percent of global deaths from malaria. The WHO praised better performances against malaria in Ethiopia and Rwanda, thanks to responsive leadership, and characterized those countries where malaria seems to be winning as having weak leadership, poor government, low public health budgets, and decades of erratic health sector management.

Because of the relative lack of anti-malarial success in the more populous parts of sub-Saharan Africa, malaria still decreases agricultural and industrial productivity, intensifies the probability of poverty, and increases the possibility of rural hunger and malnutrition because infections contracted during rainy seasons (when anopheles mosquitoes are active) result in farming inattention and losses. Because of malaria, sub-Saharan African nations forfeit an estimated $12 billion in economic growth, foreign investment, and tourism income each year, slowing average GDP rises by more than 1 percent. Moreover, malaria has direct costs in heavily impacted countries, possibly adding as much as 40 percent to public health expenditures. With global warming, mosquitoes carrying malaria may also fly further upward in elevation, onto the high plateaus in Ethiopia and farther up the great equatorial mountains of Tanzania, Kenya, and Uganda.

A vaccine against the parasite that is transmitted by female anopheles mosquitoes when they bite humans has been promised for decades, and may soon be tested and ready after trials in Ghana, Kenya, and Malawi. Meanwhile, insecticide spraying of village huts and even urban houses with a plant-based pyrethroid agent limits the ability of mosquitoes to linger in abodes before striking unsuspected victims. It also interrupts transmission of parasites from the mosquito vector to humans. Even more effective and inexpensive are bed nets saturated with mosquito repellent. Such bed nets prevent nocturnal mosquito bites and have proven remarkably effective, if employed consistently. And bed net costs have fallen substantially. The WHO also recommends treating pregnant woman and children with rounds of preventive medication, particularly necessary and effective during rainy seasons.

Moreover, antimalarial drugs such as artemisinin-combination therapy, much better than chloroquine, have successfully reduced malaria cases and deaths. But parasite-resistance to insecticides and drugs is a growing threat as these interventions continue to be scaled up.

To cope effectively with malaria, especially among children (who too often become dangerously ill before parents or health workers are aware of the danger) a further advance is a simple blood testing device, introduced to and tested in Zambia. This new method provides enough blood with a finger-prick; a quick diagnosis follows without the need for sophisticated laboratory analyses by trained technicians. A Ugandan has done this diagnostic innovation one better by inventing a device that beams light through a finger clip to detect infected red blood cells. The results appear quickly on a mobile telephone application, informing patients and health treatment workers whether or not a patient is, in fact, malarial.

A promising additional attack on malaria has also been tried in Zambia, where the use of a rectal suppository filled with artesunate has cut child death rates dramatically. Artesunate is a drug injected by better hospitals when children arrive in mortal danger. But rectal delivery puts artesunate straight into the blood system; Indian-made suppositories can easily be delivered to the patient by a village health worker or parent. Such a dosage can suppress sufficient parasites to prevent death and to provide time to move endangered children from rural clinics to district hospitals. Both Zambian trials were backed by the Gates Foundation.

Tested only in laboratories in London is an even more dramatic approach to malaria that, if proven in the field, could reduce malarial infections down to nearly nothing. Researchers at Imperial College say that they have edited the genes of female mosquitoes so as to render them incapable of reproduction, or of biting (and gathering and distributing parasites). Manipulating the DNA of caged *Anopheles gambiae* mosquitos (the main carriers of malaria) produced normal male insects and sterile females, and brought the trial population down to zero within six months. If this gene drive method works in the field, that would be the end of malaria as we know it. Africa and Africans would be the main beneficiaries.

Mosquitoes also transmit dengue fever and yellow fever, although the mosquito vector is usually of the different *Aedes aegypti* species. Neither dengue nor yellow fever poses as much of a threat to African health as does malaria. Dengue fever is found primarily in coastal eastern Africa, from Djibouti to Mozambique, and its symptoms are flu-like, and not usually fatal. Even so, children are more at risk, especially from the hemorrhagic variety, which does cause death. Furthermore, with global warming, more terrain (and more people living in such areas) will become exposed to dengue. (The Zika virus might also become more prevalent in Africa as a result of the same kinds of climatic changes.)

Yellow fever is present in thirty-two equatorial, more western African countries. A small percentage of victims suffer from high, malarial-like fever spikes, and from jaundice. In serious cases, yellow fever can damage the kidneys, liver, and heart. If it progresses to a hemorrhagic phase, patients bleed copiously from their eyes, mouths, and other organs; comas and death follow. As many as 25,000 Africans die from yellow fever yearly.

Ebola, Marburg, Lassa

The other dangerous hemorrhagic maladies have been much in the news in recent years. First, the rural and urban populations of Liberia, Sierra Leone, and Guinea, in 2013-2016, and then, in 2018–2020, people in the eastern reaches of the Democratic Republic of Congo suffered intensely from Ebola, an incurable disease. The Congolese epidemic caused at least 2,253 deaths before it subsided in 2020. The earlier West African epidemic caused 11,000 deaths from 30,000 infected cases.

Extremely difficult to treat before four experimental drugs were introduced in time to combat the Congolese outbreak, many patients still remained beyond reach and their relatives and contacts hard to vaccinate. Two American-made vaccines, in addition to promising antibody-based cures, are in use; the Ebola transmission sequence can now be interrupted if very carefully protected and heavily padded health workers are able to ring-vaccinate affected areas and others are able to introduce the experimental intravenous medicines successfully. More than 66,000 doses of the vaccines were administered in the Congo's North Kivu province alone, and a total of 255,000 overall in the Congo.[7] But doing so proved increasingly difficult in 2019, areas of the eastern Congo north of Goma and west of Beni. Militants who called themselves the Allied Democratic Forces obstructed and attacked World Health Organization workers. So did other rebels. At least one treatment center in the eastern Congo was razed by warriors; the Allied Democratic Forces, also killed at least 1,500 civilians before the end of 2019 in the eastern Congo Ebola area.(There was also an Ebola outbreak in the northwestern Congo that infected the city of Mbandaka.) The Ebola epidemic therefore continued for many more months than anticipated, and spread into Uganda and Tanzania, while Congolese by the hundreds lost their lives unnecessarily. In late 2019, GAVI announced that it would create a $178 million global stockpile of 500,000 of the new Ebola vaccines to prevent future outbreaks from spinning out of control, as the Congo epidemic did.

Scientists have isolated the Ebola virus in a tiny bat that is commonly found in West Africa and has relatives in Central Africa, where bats have long been suspected of hosting the Ebola virus. Previously, researchers discovered the Ebola virus in mouse-sized bug-eating bats (of the "greater long-fingered" variety) that roost inside houses in Sierra Leone. Africans eat bats, and touch them while preparing them for cooking fires, so the transmission route could be obvious.

Bats of several varieties also carry and transmit Marburg fever, one of the other two major African hemorrhagic diseases. The Marburg virus was specifically located in 2018 in a fruit bat (a much larger species) in Sierra Leone. However, Marburg outbreaks typically have occurred in Uganda and the northern Congo.

Lassa, the third unusual viral disease of Africa, is often transmitted by multimammate rat urine and feces. Outbreaks occur in Benin, Ghana, Mali, Nigeria, and a number of other coastal West African nations. Like Ebola and Marburg, the Lassa virus spreads easily, but more often rodent-to-human rather than human-to-human (after the first outbreaks). Nigeria, where Lassa was first identified in 1969 in the town of that name in the southeastern corner of Borno state, near the border with Adamawa state, has growing numbers of cases reported each year. In 2018, there were more than 600 cases across a broader range of the nation than ever before; 170 people died. In the first half of 2019, Nigeria reported more than 700 cases of Lassa fever in twenty-three states, with 90 persons dying. The persistence and spread of Lassa probably reflects increasing filth and garbage in Lagos and Nigeria's other swelling cities, giving rise to more rats carrying the pestilence. Additionally, whereas Nigerian states formerly coped with such disease outbreaks, now the federal government is in charge, and overwhelmed, despite the establishment of an all-Nigeria Centre for Disease Control. It is attempting to stem the proliferation of such rare diseases as Lassa as well as, in 2019, returned threats to health from yellow fever.

All three fevers present with a variety of flu-like symptoms and then progress to fatal bleeding from most orifices. The livers of Marburg victims fail and delirium occurs. Fortunately, all three of these catastrophic hemorrhagic diseases are as uncommon normally as they are devastating when they erupt, usually in rural settings. The West African Ebola epidemic, unusually and unexpectedly, was carried into the cities, originally from a rural part of Guinea, after the first cases appeared.

The Lungs and the Heart

Tuberculosis (TB) is much more common, highly contagious, and much deadlier than these fevers because of its presence almost everywhere in sub-Saharan Africa, especially in Nigeria and South Africa. It is a disease of congested cities and smoky village huts, especially among those who are poor and hungry. Globally, it is also a bigger killer than malaria and HIV/AIDS. It is the ninth leading cause of death worldwide, and the leading cause from a single infectious agent. In Africa about 2.5 million people fall ill yearly from the disease, a full quarter of the world's cases. About 1.7 million people across the world die yearly from tuberculosis, a quarter of them (417,000 in 2016) in Africa. A large proportion, once again, of those fatalities are of children. Africa also has the largest number of adults in the world who die because they are both HIV-positive and tubercular. In about 40 percent of African deaths, patients are HIV-compromised. Tuberculosis is the leading killer of those that are so infected. Having both diseases at once complicates the otherwise straightforward treatment regimes that keep most other forms of tuberculosis at bay.

Many of this latter HIV-TB group—500,000 strong in Africa—harbor a multi-drug-resistant form of the disease. That makes standard medications ineffective. According to the World Health Organization, this variety of tuberculosis constitutes a major health security threat. What happened, especially in South Africa and a few other African countries, is that standard anti-tubercular medicines were both abused and ingested only episodically. That led first to multi-drug-resistant forms of TB that fail to respond to standard first-line medications and are hence difficult and expensive to treat. Subsequently, and even more worrying, a more deadly strain of the disease labeled Extensively Drug-Resistant Tuberculosis emerged, especially in southern Africa. It responds to even fewer of the available remedies, including most of the otherwise effective second-line anti-TB drugs. Two new drugs and immunotherapy, however, seem to promise to retard TB's spread, especially among HIV-compromised persons. So do several therapies that are administered for one month instead of three to eight months. There is no proven vaccine as yet, but two new ones have produced positive results after extensive trials.

From the lungs to the heart: Little discussed in Africa, but surprisingly deadly, are the several diseases of the cardiovascular system. Often believed to be a rich world's complaint, heart-related problems are just as common, if not more so, in Africa. Although neither epidemic ranks among Africa's leading causes of death, African cardiovascular fatalities have increased by

81 percent since 1990. This rise has occurred primarily because of swelling populations (and there are more to come), aging (although that is decreasing, per capita), and fundamental epidemiological transitions. The age-adjusted mortality rate for sub-Saharan Africa has not, surprisingly, declined over the period from 1990. Stroke, unlike other parts of the world, is the major cardiovascular form of mortality. Ischemic heart disease is the second cause.

In recent years, there were more than 1 million cardiovascular-related deaths in sub-Saharan Africa, about 40 percent of all non-communicable disease deaths and 11 percent of deaths from all causes. More women are dying in this way than men, 512,000 to 445,000 in 2013. Rheumatic heart disease rates have also risen.

Cardiovascular disease increases are also going to be accompanied by other lifestyle change maladies that already reflect sub-Saharan Africa's comparative affluence and the emergence of a middle class. Higher blood pressures, higher blood sugars and diabetes, and obesity are now not uncommon; alcohol abuse is also common. Indeed, in late 2018, researchers in South Africa disclosed that for adults between ages 15 and 49 in sub-Saharan Africa in 2017, the leading causes of mortality were AIDS, tuberculosis, malaria, maternal disorders, and road injuries (mostly automobile accidents). For men in the same age group, interpersonal violence was an additional serious killer, followed in line by cirrhosis of the liver. Women were likely also to die from cervical cancer and breast cancer. For persons older than 50, the leading death causes were tuberculosis, heart attacks and stroke among men, and stroke, heart attacks, and TB among women. As the researchers concluded, "non-communicable diseases are . . . wreaking havoc . . . across the continent."[8]

Diabetes is also on the rise. About 20 million persons south of the Sahara have diabetes, a largely developed world condition that has migrated with modern dietary indulgences into Africa. More than 500,000 Africans are dying from diabetes each year, 76 percent of whom are under 60 years of age. With Africans becoming more urbanized and living longer, diabetes will likely become even more prevalent than it now is, and deadlier. Several researchers predict that by 2035, more than 41 million Africans will be diabetic, an increase that is higher than for any other region of the world. They also suspect the existence of many more cases of Type 2 diabetes, mostly affecting adults, that currently remain undiagnosed. Childhood or Type 1 diabetes is much less often seen in Africa.

Since diabetes is a new disease for Africa, patients usually become aware of their disease rather late in the process and therefore present with a cascade of complications. Many others remain undiagnosed and untreated until they begin to lose vision, suffer kidney damage or cardiovascular carnage, or need to amputate feet. Thus, as with the many other, better known diseases of Africa, diabetes inflicts a devastating impact on Africans and their families, and on national economies. Moreover, sub-Saharan African political jurisdictions are only now beginning to understand diabetes as a chronic health problem, and one that needs the kind of attention that TB and HIV/AIDS receive.

Things that Crawl and Slither

Plagues of worms and flies that live in human intestines and, according to the WHO, account for 40 percent of the tropical world's disease afflictions, also wreak havoc on the people of the sub-continent. Africa has a host of these unlovely infestations that impede everyday human activities and greatly hinder productivity. Most of them primarily affect rural dwellers, but with heavy migrations from villages to congested cities, even urban dwellers will no longer be immune from several of the debilitating diseases of the gut.

Foremost, because it affects vast numbers of Africans from the Sudan south to Malawi and Zimbabwe, and westward to Nigeria and Ghana, is schistosomiasis (bilharzia). Snails are the vector. They inhabit slow-moving freshwater behind new or old dams, in irrigation canals, and in quieter portions of even the biggest Rift Valley lakes. They host flukes or parasitic worms that leave the snails and head for unsuspecting humans who wade, wash, drink from, or swim in contaminated waters. The worm penetrates the skin of humans and migrates to a blood vessel, producing eggs on the go. The eggs follow the bloodstream into various organs, impairing growth and repair, and causing fevers and pain. Chronic schistosomiasis results in anemia, kidney lesions, stunting, cognitive impairment, and infertility. Until recently, the cure to repress flukes in the liver, kidneys, and spleen was painful, involving injections of antimony. Nowadays, fortunately, various less harsh antiparasitic worm killers work well. But 75 million Africans still contract schistosomiasis annually and 200,000 or so die each year from complications of the disease.

Next in order of lethality are the many soil-transmitted helminth plagues—roundworms, hookworms, and whip worms—found everywhere in the humid parts of Africa where sanitation is lacking and people walk, play, and become infected from contact. These worms produce abundant eggs in the human intestine; when the eggs are expelled in human feces and sanitation is poor or nonexistent, worm eggs end up contaminating both water sources and land around huts, and the cycle resumes. Typically, the infested human suffers from vitamin A deficiency, malnutrition, stunting, intestinal obstructions, and impaired learning. The WHO estimates that there are

300 million to 400 million cases of such helminthic diseases each year in Africa despite the relative ease of remediation.

Another nasty worm, a parasitic roundworm that is ingested by humans from stagnant water sources contaminated with aquatic fleas (copepods) or crustaceans carrying the worm's larvae, is responsible for dracunculiasis, or the disease of dragons, also known as guinea worm disease. Once inside a human abdominal cavity, the larvae multiply and become thread-like worms that are 2 to 3 feet long. These worms mature after a year inside and then produce new larvae that attempt to exit through large blisters on the affected person's lower extremities. Extracting the worms is painful and time consuming; at the exit site, intense itching and burning occurs. Obviously, this condition makes school attendance difficult and unlikely, inhibits work in the farming fields, and limits family care. Fortunately, again, most new cases of dracunculiasis are now curable at an early stage. Larvicide treatments and extensive use of introduced water filters have reduced annual cases from 3.5 million in northeast Africa, Mali, and Ghana to a mere eighteen in Africa in 2018, seventeen in Chad, ten in South Sudan, and one in Angola. The Carter Center, particularly, deserves credit for propelling such a striking fall.

Mosquitoes transmit lymphatic filariasis, or elephantiasis, another thin worm that blocks human lymphatic systems, swells limbs and breasts, hardens genitals and skin, and is distinctly disfiguring. Nigeria and the Democratic Republic of Congo have the most cases, a total for all of mostly western and central Africa of 30 million cases a year. Antibiotics can now cure many of those afflicted.

Flies spread a highly contagious bacteria to the eyes of West Africans, Ethiopians, and Sudanese who live where clean water is scarce. The trachoma bacteria cause a chronic, highly irritating inflammation of the mucous membranes of eyes. In time, with repeated visits by flies attracted to the trachoma infection, upper eyelids become scarred and blindness follows, more often in children and women than in men. Human contact also spreads trachoma; densely populated areas are breeding grounds for the disease. The populations of rural Ghana, Mali, Niger, and Nigeria have long suffered from trachoma, along with Ethiopians, Sudanese, and South Sudanese.

A third of all Ethiopians and nearly half of all Nigerian children once were afflicted by trachoma. But those numbers have fallen dramatically in recent years because of powerful antibiotics. In 2018, all of Ghana and two of Nigeria's thirty-six states were declared clear of trachoma; the Carter Center worked for many years with those governments and elsewhere to distribute effective antibiotics, build latrines, and educate affected populations on how to avoid the disease. Nearly 500,000 persons in the affected areas have also have had their eyesight restored through corrective surgery.

River blindness, or onchocerciasis, was once an equally destructive disease of the eyes transmitted by small black flies biting humans and releasing worm larvae into a host's bloodstream. There the larvae multiply and become tiny worms, causing inflammation, intense itching, ugly lesions, epilepsy, and loss of vision from damage to eye tissue. Death ensues in some cases, too. These pesky black flies live along fast-flowing rivers and streams mostly in West Africa and especially along Ghana's Volta River and the River Niger in Nigeria. Sharp reductions in the prevalence of onchocerciasis have occurred in Malawi and Niger. Fortunately, what once was another crippling African affliction is now controllable, again by the use of powerful antibiotics donated since 1986 by an American pharmaceutical firm. But 37 million Africans still remain at risk in 2020, with eradication predicted to be likely only in 2025.

Tsetse flies bite. They are large flies common in the savannah regions of East and Central Africa, and are one of the reasons why horses are rare in much of Africa south of Ethiopia and the Sudan. The tsetse fly bite transmits a parasite that conveys both equine encephalitis (swelling of the brain) and human trypanosomiasis (sleeping sickness). Before the turn of the twenty-first century, there were more than 300,000 African victims each year. Now, however, thanks to new combinations of drugs and heavy surveillance of affected areas by host governments energized by the World Health Organization, only about 1000 cases are reported each year. The remaining danger areas for sleeping sickness are in the conflict-encrusted parts of the Central African Republic and the Democratic Republic of Congo, where 70 percent of all cases occur.

Visceral leishmaniasis (kala-azar, or black fever) is little known but dangerous because when it spreads it does so among Africa's poorest and least medically savvy victims. It is a zoonotic infection spread from rodents by protozoa carried by female sand flies. When those tiny flies bite they inject parasites into cellular linings. Localized cutaneous ulcers result. Sometimes, and much more debilitating, the leishmania invade mucous membranes, the spleen, livers, and bone marrow, damage those organs, and cause acute peripheral neuropathy and death—all from a little bite of a sand fly.

Common in Africa at least from the eighteenth century, leishmaniasis has in recent years become more virulent because of immune weaknesses from HIV/AIDS. The sharing of unsterilized needles by intravenous drug users has also helped it to spread. The Sudan and South Sudan, Ethiopia, Kenya, Cameroon, Mali, Mauritania, and Burkina Faso have experienced especially heavy outbreaks of the least lethal version of this disease while the parts of Ethiopia and the Sudan that straddle the Blue Nile, and much of South Sudan, have seen major episodes of the more deadly visceral form of leishmaniasis. Treatment is difficult, and most medicines toxic.

Except for the very last, most of these worm and fly diseases of Africa have been tamed, largely through the philanthropic and imaginative leadership of the Gates Foundation, the Carter Center, the World Health Organization, UNICEF, the several global health NGOs saluted and funded by the Gates Foundation and several pharmaceutical companies. Keeping them at bay, and preventing the further spread of leishmaniasis, will depend on sensible political leadership and legislative approval of increased expenditures on the treating and caring for victims of these more specialized and localized diseases as well as those that catch the medical headlines.

Letting the Blind See

Already, public health and sanitation reforms, the administration of antibiotic doses, surgical interventions, and close attention to the mitigation of insect-carried ailments have restored sight to those who have lost it from attacks by bacteria, worms, and flies. But there are many more Africans who lose their eyesight from other causes, including the absence of qualified medical care. For example, to treat 112 million citizens of Ethiopia, which reports one of the highest rates of blindness in the world and where roughly 1.6 million inhabitants are blind (with another 3.6 million exhibiting low vision), only about 130 surgically competent ophthalmologists are available, most of whom live in Addis Ababa, far from potential patients. Fortunately, newly introduced methods of operating inexpensively and rapidly to replace the clouded lenses of affected Africans can relieve increasing numbers of individuals with acute loss of vision. Such cataract operations can now restore sight to millions of otherwise severely handicapped Africans.

Beginning only a few years ago, surgical techniques pioneered in India and Nepal and transferred to Africa by Americans, Australians, and borrowed Nepalese have extracted the clouded cataracts of thousands of blind Africans of all ages and replaced the old lenses with new, inexpensively manufactured, ones. The American Relief Agency for the Horn of Africa, from Minnesota, operates at district hospitals in the Sudan, where nearly 50 percent of all residents have distance vision loss. (Inhabitants of nearby countries such as Mali, Niger, the Central African Republic, and Somalia also show the same levels of sight impairment, and in many other sub-Saharan African jurisdictions citizens suffer from at least 25 percent distance vision loss, with

Botswana at the low end of the distribution with only 10 percent prevalence.) Cure Blindness, formerly the Himalayan Cataract Project, sponsors mass cataract removals and replacements in ten hospitals and five districts of Ethiopia. (Since 2008, Cure Blindness has restored vision to more than 37,000 Ethiopians and trained 148 local personnel to continue its work.)

Those cataract replacements initiatives are ongoing, and restorative. But it will take legions of cataract operations and the training of many indigenous ophthalmologists over many years for sight to be universally restored to Africa's blind. Fortunately, the techniques for doing so have been shown to work as well in Africa as in Asia. The lenses themselves can also be manufactured as affordably in Africa as in Asia. Doing so could bring the benefits of modern medicine and modern medical training and research directly to the most compromised African villager.

But sight problems in Africa go beyond surgical interventions that, from the patient's view, miraculously enable the blind to see. Specialists say that the largest cause of vision weakness is refractive error, often overlooked in Africa. Millions of children and adults consequently struggle to see blackboards or the insects that plague their daily lives. Access even to simple eyeglasses is often unavailable in rural, impoverished Africa despite the ease that comes with such an inexpensive public health addition. Five percent of a sample of Rwandans and 4 percent of a sample of South Africans endured poor sight from simple refractive error.

The Road to Better Health

This repair of a relatively inexpensive, but pervasive, humanly-damaging problem illustrates how much remains in the medical arena for African political leaders, ministers of health, civil society advocates, and influential donors and philanthropic organizations to fix with either comparative ease or immense difficulty. The longevity and freedom from disease outcomes of Africa are very much improved over what they were in 2000, but there is a great deal still to be accomplished. All ameliorations will strengthen productivity, enhance prosperity, and better the lives of many millions.

X | Technology Advances Africa

A FRICANS ARE EMBRACING many modes of modern technology in their race to advance economically and socially as far and as sustainably as Asians and Latin Americans. As many as two-thirds of the ballooning population of the continent owns or uses a mobile telephone to make calls, surf for news, answer questions, fill or drain their own bank accounts, place illegal sporting bets, contribute to worthy causes, connect with political allies, open their Facebook or Instagram accounts, conspire to organize protests, report extortionist overtures and other corrupt acts, collect election results, improve crop yields, obtain medical advice and treatment, and socialize. (Fully 48 percent of those hand held devices are produced by two Chinese companies.) Perhaps a third of all people also are regularly on a version of the Internet via computers, not handheld devices. In this now common manner, Africans are being incorporated relentlessly into the global village; they are tied to and abreast of the events of the world in a manner that was both unthinkable and untenable a few years ago.

Drones are delivering medicines. Satellites are providing critical information about crops, herds, and veterinary and human medical advances. Mobile telephones are being used as diagnostic devices. Medical practitioners are analyzing blood smears or other test results from afar. The Internet has become a distinct teaching tool, with at least a few countries ensuring that every school child has access to its lessons. Social media of all kinds have proliferated, for both good and ill, and sometimes to the annoyance of authoritarian regimes that prefer to cut the proverbial cord and censor free expression.

Africa's technological revolution is well underway, is transformative for human and economic development and greatly influences the conduct of politics. Where Africans were once relatively uninformed about the alternatives available to them in the spheres of political participation, economic path dependency, and social progress, now the glories of the World Wide Web, Google, Facebook, Instagram, WhatsApp, Twitter, and straightforward SMS have brought the globe's myriad opportunities and experiences to their urban and village dwellings. Amazon, Microsoft, and Huawei are all rolling out major data centers (cloud computing hubs) in South Africa and East Africa. The emergence of Africa's middle class is facilitated by this new technologically enabled knowledge. Even remote villagers are able to feel a part of something all-encompassing. Technology has expanded horizons, enlarged existing vistas, and provided a solid foundation for further innovative embraces of the global village in the decades ahead—when there will be many more young Africans to build upon such existing edifices. Things no longer fall apart.

Before new technological waves broke against African shores in this century, the continent was mostly stuck in a sclerotic analog universe. That was much more confining in the developing world, and especially in Africa, than elsewhere because landline telephonic capacity was limited, poorly maintained, and expensive. Before the arrival of 3G and 4G handheld devices, and the much later expansion of the Internet, most of Africa was effectively cut off from key global developments. Even television, hard to access outside cities, could not bridge the gap. Radio was the main medium of information, and it was too often government controlled. Only with the arrival of relatively inexpensive mobile telephones, first diesel and now solar-powered transmitting towers, the availability of SIM cards (making billing unnecessary), the arrival of high-capacity cables from Europe and Asia, and the consequent spread of broadband, could Africa begin to overcome its technological weaknesses and enter the global marketplace of ideas. That is where many of Africa's citizenries now are, well situated for further quantum vaults over long endured traditional barriers.

It's All Held in the Hand

Sub-Saharan Africa's 1.3 billion people own more than 444 million mobile telephones, half of which are up-to-date smartphones. But 747 million persons own SIM cards and therefore presumably use or borrow mobile telephones from time to time. Six new 4G networks launched in the first half of 2018. There are now 120 such networks in the region. New networks and cheaper smartphones are helping drive the transition to mobile broadband, but getting online is still more expensive in Africa than elsewhere in the world, with mobile devices and pay-as-you-go services still being costly. Nearly 90 percent of all sub-Saharan African households can connect to a mobile telephone network.

By 2025, 52 percent of all sub-Saharan Africans (about 634 million people) will own a mobile telephone. Nearly 300 million new subscribers will be online using their handheld instruments. But a full 1 billion Africans will own and use SIM cards. Moreover, mobile broadband coverage in sub-Saharan Africa will increase from 38 percent to 87 percent. Sixty percent of all mobile connections will be 3G or better, but 5G will only reach sub-Saharan Africa very gradually, and in limited areas.

One considerable obstacle to 3G and 4G coverage, and then eventually to 5G coverage with its more intense infrastructural requirements, is the difficulty of building, fueling, and servicing cell towers. Towers in remote regions are hard to reach and to supply with fuel; solar equipment should gradually improve the functioning and the diffusion of cell towers, without which even 3G coverage is spotty. Recognizing this problem and their obligation to keep their rural populations online along with urban residents, many sub-Saharan African nations have been building cell towers and then turning them over to private, even international, companies. Zimbabwe, for example, is constructing more than six hundred towers and base stations to improve connectivity in rural areas. Alphabet, Google's parent company, is partnering with Telkom Kenya to deliver mobile transmission service from untethered balloons designed to ride as high as 60,000 feet in the sky and relay messages to other balloons and to hitherto inaccessible Kenyan subscribers on the ground.

Mobile telephone technology raises economic productivity; lowers opportunity, transaction, and search costs; supports the possibility of greater general and government/citizen accountability and transparency; enables the better use of time; and much more. It empowers individuals and groups who hitherto were deprived by isolation, circumstance, and experience from maximizing their human potential or participating fully in the affairs of their towns and provinces. The sheer availability of even a low-capacity device unlocks vast amounts of previously unused creative power. As Africa's people numbers soar, the existence of a computer-like instrument held in the hand and a bigger version on the desk could enable an array of citizenries south of the Sahara, as well as to its north, greatly to overcome long-existing obstacles to economic and social progress.

Political and social change is also being facilitated by social media that only exist because of our era's technological revolution. The protests that were directed for months in 2019 at President Omar al-Bashir's despotic regime in the Sudan, and at elevated prices of bread and fuel, were sustained because of text messages on a large scale. Likewise, the vigorous effort to gain parity in Cameroon for Anglophone speakers, and protests there, were made possible by mobile telephone communications (until the state shut down the Internet). SMS texting brings disparate individuals together in a common cause, marshals crowds, and boosts the efficacy of anonymous leaders and groups against antagonistic states and their police and military enforcers.

More broadly, mobile telephones both generate and distribute the kinds of new and old information that create behavioral, social, economic, and even political progress. They can be utilized to protect human rights, correct breaches in civil liberties, ensure the fairness of elections, and improve the flow of commerce within cities and across the rural/urban divide. Armed with enhanced information, ordinary citizens can exercise the kinds of options that check state dominance and even enable emboldened civil society leaders to expose governance flaws. All of these varieties of new knowledge give less privileged members of society leverage versus the state or in opposition to concentrations of wealth, even at very local levels.

Mobile Money

Exploiting many of the unanticipated advantages of a mobile telephone has made operations common in the developed world, and long unavailable to Africans, readily accessible. When the two largest telephone provider networks in Africa, Orange and MTN, pooled their resources in 2019 to create Mowali, the largest aggregator of money transfers on the continent, numerous Africans could finally open bank accounts—online. Mowali potentially serves 300 million people in twenty-two countries, including Nigeria and South Africa, with their large subscriber bases. Mowali's big advantage is interoperability, the ability of users to send money between different mobile money accounts across different providers, something that was only previously available in Africa in Tanzania, Kenya, and Ghana. Whereas voice and data services were once the key generators of revenue for African telecom providers, now the big market is for money transfer services. Safaricom

(M-Pesa's East African host) was earning 28 percent of its revenues in that manner in 2019.

Mowali's major competitor is the much longer established M-Pesa, which dominates the East African market for moving money. M-Pesa, first in Kenya, pioneered creative solutions to financial problems common in the developing world. Realizing that Kenyans, and others like them, mostly lacked ordinary accounts in commercial banks and thus had no easy way of holding and moving cash, in 2008 M-Pesa's management team gradually opened its airwaves to such critical transfers. Funds equivalent to 20 percent of Kenya's annual GDP now move seamlessly along mobile telephone networks (especially M-Pesa's) as electronic banking transactions and money transfers (even across international borders). M-Pesa, hosted in the cloud, transfers funds from forty-five countries into Kenyan accounts.

M-Pesa also created M-Pesa 1 Tap in 2018 to allow its subscribers to use a card or a wristband connector to make secure and faster payments. M-Pesa partnered with Google to permit M-Pesa payments on Google's application store, a boon for Africans but also a first for global distribution sites. PayPal also accepts M-Pesa funds via M-Pesa's partner Safaricom. But perhaps even more forward-looking is M-Pesa's Bonga chat service. Its users can talk while sending and receiving money via the regular application. (M-Pesa also launched a ride-hailing company, and Songa, a music-streaming service paid through M-Pesa.)

M-Kesho, another Kenyan-originated service, deposits participant earnings in bank accounts that never existed in the pre-mobile telephone days. M-Kesho even enables banks to make loans to vetted customers. CurrencyFair cuts the costs of buying and selling currency and receiving remittances over older methods. Kenyan and Tanzanian mobile telephonic platforms permit the full transfer of cash anywhere much less expensively and reliably than the old Western Union method, the national postal services, friends, bus drivers, or even the Islamic hawala system. In Zambia, where only 25 percent of citizens have traditional bank accounts, Mobile Transaction International processes $2 million worth of payments a month, makes loans, and disburses cash aid from the World Food Program. When Zimbabweans ran out of physical cash in 2018 and 2019 in the form of locally produced faux money or American dollars, they began exchanging payments via mobile telephones. For too long, with the national banking system running on empty, that was the only method available to gain access to existing personal accounts. (Subsequently, the virtually bankrupt Zimbabwean government imposed a 12 percent tax on each mobile transfer.) In 2019, a Nigerian retail lending startup (backed by a Kenyan-based venture capital provider) became a fully operational digital bank, seeking to serve the 120 million or so adult Nigerians who have no formal bank accounts. Again in 2019, 135 live mobile money operations in thirty-nine sub-Saharan African nations served 122 million active accounts.

Mobile Food Production

Everywhere in sub-Saharan Africa, where prices on offer for agricultural produce were long available only within the markets themselves, seriously disadvantaging farmers and traders who crossed great distances to sell their sorghum, wheat, coffee, and avocados, text messaging capabilities now distribute such information easily and helpfully. TradeNet, in Ghana, matches buyers and sellers in four languages. Xam Marse ("know your market" in Wolof) offers real-time messages with the same kinds of critical information.

If you want to know how much your hens are worth today in Saint Louis or a village outside of Thies, or even in distant Kolda, you can obtain a text message from Xam Marse. Farmers in Niger and other countries can insert a coded text and instantly receive market price information. Congolese along that river can discover whether current manioc prices are conducive to a profitable sale. Tanzanians learn whether or not it makes sense to travel to far distant Mbeya, say, to sell surplus maize. Ugandans know, through similar means, how much their hands of bananas and plantains could bring in Soroti or Gulu, or even in Entebbe.

Furthermore, in the agricultural domain, the availability of mobile telephones permits advice to flow across the divide that once separated experts in capitals and regional towns from struggling, often less literate, small holders in rural areas. More than 8,000 cocoa farmers in Ghana, for example, and their counterparts in Côte d'Ivoire, receive practical information daily about preferred cultivation practices, crop disease prevention, post-harvest production and marketing ideas, farm safety, child labor avoidance, and health issues from the World Cocoa Foundation's CocoaLink.

A mobile layaway scheme in Kenya allows women to put money aside for the purchase of water pumps and other labor-saving devices by sending periodic micro-payments to an NGO that seeks to empower women. Even more quietly revolutionary, a University of Oxford team realized that since access to clean water was so essential to life and improved living standards in rural Africa, a method of improving the performance and durability of prosaic hand-pumps would contribute overall to development and directly to the welfare of women and girls. They attached an accelerometer to test pump handles in Zambia, connected it remotely to a laptop, and with the data obtained they invented and placed inside pump handles a small box containing an accelerometer, a microprocessor, a telecommunications chip, and a battery. That innovation enabled the Oxford team to monitor pump usage remotely in the Kwale region of southeastern Kenya, and to employ local technicians quickly to fix the pumps when they broke down (a relentless feature of heavily used water pumps) and thus maintain supplies of safe water. By so doing, the Kwale experiment (with 200 pumps) reduced the downtime of pumps (and the lack of water) to two days versus twenty in the pre-monitored era, thus making life easier and better for the women who fetch water. A basic algorithm on the microprocessor warns whenever there are problems with pump mechanisms or with the water depth in the wells.

Satellites photograph farms in Africa and provide valuable information about crops and likely crop yields. Planet Labs' satellite spies on the earth to track environmental alterations and to identify and manage ecological damage. Herders in Mali search for water for their cattle via satellite. Cocoa farmers in Ghana also employ satellite-guided precision information to guard over and improve the health of their trees. Machine-learning software analyzes images of cocoa farms taken in both visible light and in the near infra-red spectrum. The latter monitors the wavelengths that plants and trees reflect during photosynthesis, a proxy for health and potential productivity. This view generates recommendations such as more or less fertilizer, different kinds of pruning, and so on.

Best of all, a Ghanaian concern employs drones to fertilize farmers' fields. In Kenya, drones are being used to locate vast patches of invasive cactus, dangerous to elephants, that threaten to close off productive grazing lands.

Mobile Medicine

In the medical arena, where women have been particularly disadvantaged over decades and centuries, the text messaging and diagnostic capabilities of mobile telephones make it abundantly possible not only to spread helpful information and improve public health practices but to offer almost instantaneous analyses of blood samples, ear infections, and a host of other complaints that hitherto traditionally would have meant long treks to distant clinics and even on to district hospitals. Mobile telephones can be fitted to take and transmit blood pressures, monitor blood glucose and sugar levels, hear and send heartbeat sounds, and even—using photographic as well as texting capabilities—look at specific body lesions. They can be adapted to send samples showing potentially malarial blood. Indeed, a British inventor has designed a surface acoustic wave device, powered by a mobile telephone, that diagnoses malaria from afar. A Ugandan invented a way to beam light through a finger clip to detect blood infected with malarial parasites.

The little handheld computer that we call a mobile telephone can upload sufficient information to permit a fully trained physician or research specialist in a distant African city, or even overseas, to make telling diagnoses. Medicines and treatments can also be prescribed, especially in deprived rural areas where most morbid conditions are well known and susceptible to common forms of remediation. Such do-it-yourself medicine can mitigate the barriers of distance and local knowledge to provide effective care for some of the most vulnerable in African communities.

The possibilities are almost limitless. For example, otoscopes attached to mobile telephones can peer into ears and transmit images. A Connecticut firm has attached a handheld, battery-powered ultrasound device to a smartphone, permitting the examination in the field (with subsequent testing in Uganda and a dozen other African countries) of most internal organs and blood vessels and the clear identification of cancers, pneumonias, and other ailments. The same device can scan pregnant women to provide early information about their babies. Even stethoscopes can be attached in such a manner that a doctor in a capital city can hear heart murmurs and other complaints. These, and other similar kinds of innovative supplements to basic smartphones, ought to begin to reduce the profound health disparities that were discussed in Chapter IX.

Whereas in the not-so-distant past, illnesses outside of Africa's major cities were often diagnosed and treated late, if at all, now mobile telephone capabilities (growing all the time) permit entire countries to be tied to central hubs for scrutiny and potential medical fixes; relevant assurances and practical guidance can also be distributed with great ease to affected areas, even to whole nations.

Even beyond such sophisticated forms of telemedicine, all manner of which will benefit a physician- and nurse-deprived continent such as Africa, some day not too distant Chinese-pioneered methods of ailment diagnosis by means of artificial intelligence will come to Africa. A Chinese hospital in Guangzhou first trained its computers to associate specific kinds of patient-supplied and physician-verified information with common medical conditions, labeled and annotated those data, and then let its neural network loose on the resulting massive set of indicators. After instructing itself, the computer was able to recognize patterns and connect new symptoms to connections stored in its files. Fairly soon, the Guangzhou hospital claimed accuracy levels between 82 and 90 percent on a wide range of diagnoses. An ophthalmic practitioner in a San Diego hospital has used such deep learning methods with similar results. When this technique is brought to Africa it could prove a boon even more important than telemedicine and other kinds of remote links to national hospital centers.

Equally powerful, the messaging services of mobile telephones can improve the practice of public health in rural and even urban areas by reminding patients to take their medicines and retroviral pills at the right times (very important for tubercular sufferers) and to offer comfort and support to rural practitioners and patients. A text message can summon persons in need to clinics and can distribute alerts when epidemics and other crises occur. A flashing light on a mobile telephone reminds patients to see their physician or visiting nurse. A home care service in Kampala, Uganda, sends text messages at least twice a day reminding cancer, TB, and HIV/AIDS patients to keep appointments and ensure that they adhere to their medicinal delivery schedules. Rwanda distributes mobile telephones to thousands of community health workers so that they can keep tabs on pregnancies, send emergency alerts, call ambulances, and generally assist in the birth delivery process. In Ghana, counseling and encouragement delivered via text messages supports breastfeeding mothers soon after giving birth. A Ugandan endeavor alerts the wider public to medical issues and concerns. There is almost no end to the support that text messaging and other mobile telephone enabled assists can give to at-risk populations.

Fake medicines are common to Africa (and India). Afflicted Africans searching for generic or even prescribed cures often are gulled by unscrupulous entrepreneurs. That is why mPedigree is so important. It permits health workers and consumers in a number of African countries, including Ghana, Nigeria, Kenya, and Rwanda, to send text codes to a central hotline quickly to verify whether a supply of pills about to be purchased is or is not genuine. To meet roughly the same need, a Ghanaian entrepreneur created mPharma. It uses an electronic prescription system to track drug supplies at pharmacies and to negotiate lower prices directly with the suppliers, thereby ensuring reliable logistical chains. (After expanding widely in Ghana, in 2019 mPharma purchased a large East African drugstore chain, and moved its inventory methodology across the continent.) A Cameroonian pharmacist invented a portable device, True-Spec, that uses artificial intelligence to enable hospitals, pharmacies, and laboratories to verify within twenty seconds that drugs are genuine. Five teenage women in Nigeria created something similar (the Fake Drug Detector) to authenticate antibiotics and other pills that Africans purchase to cure their ills.

In sub-Saharan Africa, particularly, a paucity of road and rail connections, rutted roads when any exist, rains that wash out rural dirt roads, and sheer distances frequently turn good intentions into repeated failures. To transport vaccines where they are needed, in a hurry, and to ship vials of desperately needed blood plasma to distant clinics, almost always is a difficult, sometimes impossible, exercise in futility. That is why Zipline, a Californian company, has used a fleet of drones to take necessary supplies from Kigali, Rwanda's capital, to otherwise very hard-to-reach rural clinics. In nearly 9,000 flights, it has delivered blood for transfusions, and vaccines of all kinds. In Ghana, the same company takes vaccines where they are needed in the country's north. It has also dropped emergency rabies vaccines against dog bites, a constant African problem. UNICEF is perfecting a similar delivery model in Malawi. There is the further potential for drones piloted from any location in the world via satellite (and thus free from any ties to unreliable local networks) to provide almost anything a rural clinician needs quickly and inexpensively. The drones do not even need to land; they drop their payloads by parachute from about 100 feet up, and then return to base.

Conservation Drones' Air Shepherd program, based in Liverpool, maps and monitors biodiversity. In Africa, this NGO has attempted to discern and limit wildlife poaching. In South Africa and Malawi, its drones have cut attacks on elephant and rhino populations, simply by having eyes in the sky. They have also been used to deter elephants from raiding villages with particularly tasty food crops. Similarly, a Systematic Poacher Detection program uses artificial intelligence to train drones to discover suspicious activity. As readers shall see in the next chapter, poaching of big and small African animals remains a major problem for all of Africa, especially for the savannah region where most large mammals are accustomed to roam free.

In the educational realm, as adjuncts to schooling, mobile telephonic devices can be employed to teach and to reinforce reading and arithmetic skills, and guide homeschooling. Improving literacy in this manner can be done en masse, from a central location. So can primary schooling opportunities be enhanced if computers or mobile devices are utilized to their full effect, first for sounding out letters and much later for reviewing whole sentences and longer texts. Even the least literate young and older Africans can, in this manner, practice their letters and numbers, and later much more.

Strengthening Governance

In the political and governance spheres, mobile telephones (and enabled social media) are instruments of many uses. In addition to extending the ways in which citizens can mobilize to protest against inimical government policies, or raise issues using the mobile telephonic public platform to check or try otherwise to alter harmful actions of abusive or insensitive governments and their many appendages and sections, so responsible governments are able to inform constituents of their rights and obligations to each other via text messages and other alerts. Furthermore, governments can upload official rules and regulations to handheld devices, offering layers of transparency that were not readily available before the arrival of the Internet. Citizens, especially rurally based ones, were for too long kept in ignorance, purposely in order to give authorities enhanced power.

Once constituents know their rights, and expect governance performance and the delivery of essential political goods without too much difficulty, it makes sense—as many African administrations have agreed—to transfer the permitting and licensing process that frequently encourages extortion and corruption from a face-to-face engagement to one mediated entirely online. Indeed, the simplest and most direct use of modern technology to moderate or defeat petty corruption occurs when administrators eschew most, if not all, face-to-face contact between functionaries and constituents. If and when interactions between the state and its citizens are all carried out via user-friendly interfaces (preferably on mobile telephones), clients can secure birth certificates, marriage licenses, and all kinds of required documents without being asked for bribes or experiencing euphemisms like "help with school fees." In theory at least, putting all of these routine exchanges online should mean that all supplicants would be treated equally—by an algorithm or a computer program. Because none could be favored, no applicant could be speeded up or slowed down without breaching the rules guiding the computer, tasks that would be beyond the talents of most civil servants. Doing so removes the kinds of discretion that tempt bureaucrats to serve best those who provide a little extra for the man or woman behind the official grille. Applicants could also file for their permits and so on using just a number, not a name, making it that much more difficult for discrimination to occur.

When applications for permits and licenses are online and accessible from a mobile telephone, doing so saves constituents money and sometimes long travel times. It also upgrades the ease and efficiency by which a government serves its taxpayers and clients. Rwanda is now the easiest African country in which to open a business, partially because of its online capacity.

Where everything relatively routine is transferred to machine-moderated transactions that are overseen remotely and electronically, the ability of bureaucrats to discriminate against or for individuals would be reduced. This even-handed method of exercising authority can even be extended to the immigration hall, and to customs inspection facilities where categories and classes are in a few countries already reduced to algorithmic form so that officials are unable to manipulate the results to favor this or that commercial importer. Binomial decision-making is also being introduced as another method of reducing human discretion and involvement.

Mobile telephones (and dash cams) give citizens the ability to record and photograph abuses that should be reported to national ombudspersons (see Chapter V); to document such common lapses as potholed streets, missing traffic signs, or darkened street lights to responsible officials; and to portray the kinds of environmental infractions that bedevil much of Africa. In South Africa, such carefully collected evidence of ecological degradation has often led to remedial actions by municipal and provincial officials.

Africans use mobile telephones to report tragedies such as fires, floods, and bus and truck crashes, and they also alert authorities to terrorist attacks, to incursions by wild animals, and to the presence of poachers. But they have also been utilized in East Africa to mobilize public charitable responses. M-Pesa and similar services make it easy for subscribers to contribute small or large sums to those unfortunate countrymen who are struck by disaster.

The widespread availability of mobile telephone applications in Africa permits civil society—NGOs and citizens in groups or individually—to play a major role in combating corruption. The text messaging and photographic capabilities of such devices allow engagements with corrupt public servants to be documented and then quantified. Even if African authorities ignore or fail to act on such evidence when uploaded from numbers of telephones, the sheer ability to record and then present evidence of corrupt behavior by police, by bureaucrats, and even by politicians is empowering, and sometimes capable of reforming procedures and governmental actions. In East Africa, for example, Ushahidi ("Testimony") and Frontline SMS have been used to track human rights violations and violators, to note violent acts in real time, and to reveal breaches of security. Bribespot.com receives anonymous texts reporting bribes. In Nigeria, Tracka allows citizens to identify projects where state funds are being embezzled and misspent. BudgiT, yet another platform, allows citizens to unearth secrets embedded in national and state budgets and to discern whether official projects are real, and completed.

More dramatically, the possession of a mobile telephone and airtime gives concerned citizens an easy way of photographing or recording incidents of corruption. Indeed, because mobile telephone text reports of corrupt incidents can be aggregated, they provide one of the best ways of learning how much bribery takes place during a normal urban and rural day, how much is lost to extortion and other forms of petty corruption during an average month, and so on. If a government cares, it can also use the mobile telephonic investigative technique to reduce many kinds of small-scale influence peddling. Those same methods would not necessarily deter grand corruption, or reveal its extent, but mobile telephonic deployment at least could hamper the preying on citizens by policemen, inspectors of several kinds, and civil servant functionaries. Possibly the accumulation of reports about specific miscreants or places where corruption regularly occurs could lead to anti-corruption investigations and prosecutions, but too often the necessary political will is lacking in states deeply infected by corruption. Even so, releasing compendia of such reports to the media or otherwise publicizing them can have a salutary effect.

Dash cams—voice and video recorders mounted near drivers or more furtively in an automobile—are now being used to film traffic police shakedowns (a constant problem in many African countries) in real time. Resulting videos can be uploaded to YouTube, for widespread viewing and condemnation. In this manner mobile telephone self-documentations can help persuade culprits to restrain their breaches of the rule of law. Sometimes, of course, policemen and other officers of the state cause a ruckus when they realize that their illicit actions are being captured on video. But then those outbreaks can also be recorded, giving potential technological advantages to the (innocent) driver.

Kenya has long had an Indian-originated site to collect such text compilations. Ipaidabribe.com collects anonymous but telling accounts of bribe demanding and bribe giving. Together, in Kenya and elsewhere, the www.Ipaidabribe incidents reveal who is asking for and receiving bribes and other favors. Even if corrupt dealings are recorded after the fact, they are at least being documented. The bribee thus acquires agency through possessing a device. If the bribee is fortunate, too, his or her reports can lead to positive change.

Starting in 2011, Kenyans were invited to follow the Indian example and list their corrupt encounters with the police and with ministries and municipalities. Many thousands immediately sent texts describing how much they had paid and to whom, but, despite the sophistication of Kenyan mobile telephone users, within its first years only 7 percent of eligible Kenyans were reporting bribes on the local I Paid a Bribe site, possibly because of justifiable fears that their anonymity would not be maintained.[1]

"Not in My Country," another site, is specifically for reports of corruption in the Kenyan schools.

In 2013, two years after the Kenyan I Paid a Bribe website was installed—and after two years during which many millions in bribes (one estimate was that 125,584,333 Kenyan shillings, or about $1.3 million, had changed hands)—President Uhuru Kenyatta even launched an official website so that Kenyans could tell his government directly about bribery and graft. Citizens were invited to fill out online forms, upload photos or videos, and report corruption via text messages. They could do so anonymously, and by text message as well as on the web.

Capturing Bribes and Securing Elections

All accounts of corrupt behavior, both the taking and giving of bribes, are important. Quantifying helps to illustrate and strengthen the case against corruption more vividly than the accumulations of anecdotes. But verifying each incident is impossible; those who provide reports on I Paid a Bribe or other websites, especially including President Kenyatta's, may or may not be dishonest or have hidden agendas. But the mass of numbers over time reveals insights into the character and extent of corruption within countries and across those countries. Indeed, such an aggregation of incidents provides a formidable platform for remedial action.

But there is one critical aspect of corruption that these kinds of sites, as helpful as they are, cannot readily capture. Venal corruption or big-ticket corruption—the major scams—are not easily reported by individuals with direct knowledge of the vast amounts of shillings, pounds, euros, or dollars that have been paid to secure lucrative developing world opportunities, to facilitate arms transfers, and to gain access to profitable construction contracts. In some ways, lubricating or petty corruption constitutes low-hanging fruit; large-scale (venal) corruption is a much greater danger to the nation-state, to the economy, and to citizens. Different kinds of sleuthing are required to uncover the big frauds. Sometimes forensic accounting does so, sometimes individual whistleblowers unveil gross acts, and sometimes investigators from commissions or departments of justice zero in on accused individuals and corporations. If sufficient political will is available, exposures and prosecutions can follow. But the raw material mostly depends on information provided via the now common mobile telephone.

These are all promising beginning initiatives that help to impel transparency. But when smartphones in Africa get smarter and more powerful, so will such technological advances become more ubiquitous and less expensive. Their deployment will consequently make it possible for African governments to ferret out and fight corruption more directly, with citizen assistance. If the governments themselves are corrupt, then the same technological advances will permit civil society actively to unveil corrupt dealings. Financial transactions can be tracked and their shady versions highlighted.

Data mining, the inspection of big data, can also discover instances of grand corruption. The careful examination of municipal or national contracts, say, can discern patterns of probable fraud. Artificial intelligence, and carefully crafted algorithms, are beginning to unearth instances of likely high-level malfeasance. As civil societies, anticorruption investigative commissions, and concerned governments begin to use technological means in more sophisticated ways, so the opportunity for enhanced accountability and transparency will be available to more governments and institutions in Africa.

In roughly this manner, some administrations such as Mozambique and South Africa have unearthed payroll fraud, and purged the teachers or civil servants who were but names on spurious rolls. In Nigeria, investigators discovered evidence of serious money laundering by poring over property and company registers. In a complicated case in South Africa, large-scale judicial fraud was demonstrated when text messages between the several perpetrators were intercepted. Tax authorities now, if they wish, can search an international database to pinpoint the real owners of properties who are evading payments. As abundant data appear online, the more productive this process becomes.

In an additional area, mobile telephonic capabilities can also give citizens agency in defending themselves against state-orchestrated violence by persons or groups. It is hard for ordinary citizens to protect themselves against a powerful regime backed by implacable forces of security, but brutality against persons can at least be documented for later use, and sometimes for subsequent actions against the perpetrators of such injustices. Possessing a mere mobile telephone hardly helps prevent rapes and mass killings by warring gangs or official troops, but it can at least capture violations after the fact. Furthermore, it is possible that text messages from victims could warn others and serve eventually as evidence of criminal events that are hard, otherwise, to secure. Such detailed data, possibly even in real time, that directly implicate illicit behavior or retail attacks, say, by marauders, are much more valuable than general statements of concern.

Crowdsourcing is also employed frequently to reveal episodes of widespread violence by state-sponsored or warlord-employed vigilantes, often thugs loyal to an unpopular ruler. As helpful as crowdsourcing methods might be, however, large-scale SMS reporting to trained compilers can accomplish more by way of identifying the leading culprits, and enabling persuasive assessments of who threw the first rocks, say, and who fired first on the protesters. Retributive punishment and reparative compensation is more likely when careful documentation exists.

Contested national elections are another arena in which mobile telephones can play a decisive role. First, those who possess such instruments can report breaches of procedure and irregular behavior at or near polling stations or during the counting of votes. Second, mobile telephonic photographic records can verify unofficial results gathered at a large sample of the voting places to endorse or negate the so-called official counting of a disputed election. To a large extent that is what happened in the Democratic Republic of Congo in 2018–2019. Official observers attached to the Roman Catholic church in the Congo, as many as 40,000 of them, reported that one popular figure had in fact won the presidency overwhelmingly. But the official result gave the Congolese presidency to a rival, thus falsifying the Catholic observer outcome and denying evidence that had carefully been assembled by officials of the church.

The availability of SMS texting, confuting what happened in the Congo, provides reporting mechanisms that theoretically (if not in the Congo) reduces the reach of electoral manipulation and preserves the integrity of the vote, the count, and a legitimate result. Text messages can reveal acts of intimidation in the run-up to an election or at the actual polls themselves; infractions on election day itself; voter interference; the theft of ballots and ballot boxes, the stuffing of ballot boxes; and endless forms of interference that compromise the integrity of an election. Information gathered carefully by observers with their telephones can prevent falsified results, or at least make them more difficult to justify and announce.

The existence of clever handheld devices also makes it possible to ascertain the opinions of more and more Africans about matters of overriding concern, including issues affecting governance. Since so many Africans now use mobile telephones, Afrobarometer, which polls much of Africa frequently, can reach a broader sample of African respondents than ever before. So can in-country and many other local opinion-collecting operations. Africa and Africans are now connected to each other, to their governments, and to the world in ways that were hardly envisaged a decade ago.

In these many powerful ways the mechanism in one's palm or pocket can become an instrument of reform, even of probity.

The Internet

Africans living south of the Sahara access the Internet, and benefit from higher broadband speeds, largely via their mobile telephones. Desktop or laptop computer penetration usage is far less frequent, largely because of expense and because of the absence of ready sources of power. Until the second decade of the twenty-first century, too, the web was more difficult to reach than it became about 2015, when fiber optic sub-sea cables reached most parts of Africa from Europe and Asia, replacing expensive and balky satellite transmission systems. Still, parts of West Africa rely on Internet transmissions via high-voltage electrical lines and some countries such as Sierra Leone continue to be served by less bandwidth than would be available in a remote American rural town. Unsurprisingly, wherever in Africa the older methods of reaching broadband hubs remain, using the resources of the Internet is still very expensive and interminably slow. Two African Union initiatives—Uhurunet and Umojanet—were intended to link all African countries to each other and to the world. But both are works in progress.

In 2018, 72 million Nigerians, 44 million Egyptians, 31 million South Africans, and 28 million Kenyans were connected to the Internet. User numbers taper off rapidly in other African countries, but Morocco (22 million), Uganda (17 million), Ethiopia (16 million), and the Sudan (12 million) show reasonably high levels of penetration. In contrast, only 5 million Zambians, 3 million Rwandans, and 2 million Malawians use the Internet.

According to Huawei's 2018 Global Connectivity Index (GCI), of the seventy-nine countries rated, with the United States best connected with a score of 78 and Singapore second with 75, Egypt was the top-ranking African country, at 59th place, with a score of 34. The GCI measures demand and supply of broadband within a country, fixed broadband and mobile subscriptions, 4G coverage, overall investment, general affordability, and more than thirty other indicators of connectivity. Farther down the 2018 GCI list came Morocco (33) and Algeria (32). Kenya was next, in 68th place, with a score of 29. Ghana, Nigeria, Botswana, and Namibia immediately followed, in that order. Tanzania and Uganda were ranked 75th and 76th, with scores of 25 each. Ethiopia occupied 79th place, the last one, with a score of 23. No other sub-Saharan African nations were measured for connectivity in 2018.

On the 2018 version of the IMD World Digital Competiveness Index, where Singapore ranked first and the U.S. second, South Africa was listed in 47th place, of sixty-three nations examined. No other African country was rated. The index measures a country's "ability to adopt and explore digital technologies leading to transformation in government practices, business models, and society in general." The criteria were "knowledge, technology, and future readiness."

A third type of index is the Euler Hermes Digitalization Index, with 115 countries ranked in 2018 on the basis of a nation's ability "to provide the environment for businesses to thrive in the digitalization era." The Index purports to measure "the ability and agility of countries to help digital companies thrive and traditional businesses harness the digital dividend." On that largely corporate-friendly basis, South Africa (number 46) led Africa, with Kenya, praised for its digital infrastructure, at the 70th place, Egypt in the 80th position, and Nigeria at the 100th spot despite its large market. The United States was again first on this list, with Germany second, followed immediately by three other European countries.

What these three indexes show is that Africa is less fully digitized on the Internet than it is at the forefront of mobile telephonic substantive connectivity and accessibility. In 2018, only 24 percent of Africans were connected to the Internet, up from a mere 2.1 percent in 2005; compared to 44 percent across Arab-speaking states, Asia, and the Pacific; 66 percent in the Americas; and 80 percent in Europe. Compared to Singapore or Hong Kong, or even Chile, much of Africa is less advanced, if catching up with the other continents more rapidly in this decade than earlier. Its download and upload speeds are slower, too, especially in the rural areas where accessing the services of the web is often frustrating to the extreme. (Kenyans, an exception, enjoy the fastest data connection speeds in Africa and some of the fastest in the world.) However, many governments know that their taxpayers and voters expect central governments to bring connectivity closer to the standards of Asia and Europe. That is an ongoing objective.

Madagascar is one of Africa's surprising Internet commercial successes because of low wages, excellent French literacy, and relatively speedy Internet speeds. In 2019, more than two hundred business processing and outsourcing firms employed as many as 15,000 Malagasy workers, mostly in Antananarivo, the capital. Its main outsourcing competitor for the Francophone market was Morocco, with more firms and more employees. But Madagascar and Ghana (for English-speaking customers) are among the two sub-Saharan African states that successfully have entered the lucrative commercial processing and outsourcing business, thanks to the continent's emerging technological revolution.

Censorship

Too much of Africa also suffers from government denials of service. When Africans protest, or when there are elections that unpopular regimes fear will unleash antagonisms, the tendency in today's Africa is to disconnect the entire Internet. During Uganda's 2016 presidential election, the government restricted access to social media, justifying the cut as a security measure to avert lies and prevent the premature release of results before the government had massaged them appropriately. Benin did the same during its national parliamentary poll in 2019. Governments routinely wish to control the political narrative. But they often fail, interference with the Internet infuriating citizens and worsening relations.

Governments have to order providers to press the "off" button, or to throttle it back so that download speeds are impossibly slow, but those usually local commercial enterprises so far have obeyed such dictates from executive mansions. In early 2019, when there were riots in many of Zimbabwe's cities, its government told Econet to cut the cord (which it did). In the previous year, during the electoral contest in the Democratic Republic of Congo, President Joseph Kabila's unpopular outgoing regime also made local screens go dark. The Sudan, roiled in month-long active protests in 2019 against the harsh rule of President Omar al-Bashir, also shut down the Internet for weeks at a time. But the big blockers of the Internet in the second half of 2018 and the first half of 2019 were Chad (more than 300 days without the web and mobile telephone coverage), Cameroon (nearly 300 days, in order to prevent Anglophone protesters from communicating with each other and with their supporters), and Ethiopia (just shy of 200 days, presumably in order to keep the country calm as Prime Minister Abiy consolidated his rule and brought a number of separatist groups in from the cold). Somaliland, Togo, Sierra Leone, and South Sudan darkened their web access, too, but for much less time.

Chad is an exceptional case. Its approximately 400,000 users of social media and other web facilities have been blocked off and on since President Idriss Déby's disputed reelection in 2016. The government has also kept costs to join the Internet unusually high, even for Africa. (1 GB of data costs about €11. Globally, in many countries and regions the average price of a GB of data costs 2 percent of monthly incomes. In Africa, the most costly part of the world, with the lowest download speeds, the average charge is about 10 percent of monthly incomes.) Déby's regime presumably seeks to continue to control all flows of information in the sparsely settled and largely desert former French colony. Déby doubtless wants to make it much more difficult for Chadians to start or join movements against his government. And he certainly seeks to prevent communication between opponents in N'Djamena, the capital, and antagonists across or near the Libyan border who periodically attempt to raid government outposts and even surprise Déby and his security forces in the capital.[2] (See Chapter VII.)

In late 2019, Freedom House reported that of the sixteen African countries examined, only South Africa could claim Internet freedom. Kenya, Nigeria, Tunisia, and Malawi were close, in that order, but countries such as Angola, Uganda, Zambia, Morocco, Libya, Zimbabwe, Rwanda, and Egypt were distinctly unfree in this respect.[3]

Regimes under threat practice these access denials in order to interrupt the impact and reach of social media, and curb social media's ability to influence the unfolding of political events and political challenges within their jurisdictions. Doing so makes sense for nervous state houses and for their security forces. It means that they can once again exert (or seem to exert) hegemonic control over information. Protest movements thrive on shared knowledge; without SMS, WhatsApp (well employed in Africa), Facebook, YouTube, and the like, and even less-deployed Twitter, African protest leaders and their collaborators have much less agency, and much weakened abilities to collaborate.

Tanzania even licenses bloggers and charges anyone who manages to receive such permission $930 a year for the privilege. Those double blows constitute one of several attacks by President John Magufuli's government on free expression and opponents who employ the Internet to share their views. Uganda imposes a daily tax bite on social media platforms and popular messaging sites (like WhatsApp), and collects levies on mobile money transfers that reduce online usage considerably.

Cyber Security

Cyber security issues abound because most African countries to date have done little to counter potential external surveillance or to pursue technical and intrusive issues that could compromise the privacy of ordinary as well as governmental users. The Huawei company, China's largest telecommunications provider, in 2019 had built and therefore serviced 70 percent of all 4G network routing and transmission equipment on the continent. Huawei has also dotted compact cell towers across the continent to service its networks. Washington, which fears that China will use these installed networks for spying, wants African nations to purchase their future networks elsewhere. After all, when Huawei of China constructed the headquarters of the African Union in 2013, it embedded microphones in walls and desks throughout the building, and Chinese intelligence operatives then surreptitiously captured conversations for the next five years. Nevertheless, nearly all of Africa depends on Huawei, scoffing at any security concerns and risking American displeasure.

Other Chinese and Israeli concerns also sell varieties of digital surveillance equipment to African states so that they can watch over their own citizens in real time. The government of Zimbabwe, for example, signed a deal with the Chinese company CloudWalk to build a nationwide facial recognition system. Zimbabwe will use it to control its own citizens; the data will also flow back to China as a way of training its AI systems to recognize and track people from different ethnic backgrounds.[4]

The African Union's progressive convention on cybersecurity and the protection of personal data has only been accepted by ten of the potential fifty-four African signatories. Moreover, only twenty-three states have laws making privacy attacks or breaches illegal.

In fact, when concerned authoritarian regimes shut down the Internet for increasingly longer periods, when they attempt to control the entire digital economy by forcing subscribers to use their real names and to register their SIM cards, they demonstrate how much the Internet and social media have come to dominate, energize, inform, and become integral to the life of an estimated 90 percent of all urban Africans and perhaps 75 percent of all rural Africans. It is hard to imagine Africa, or any other earthly place, without meaningful connectivity between families, among colleagues, spanning whole nations, and, indeed, across the globe.

Maintaining Momentum

The little handheld device, occasional satellite instruments, and the much larger cables that connect continents and bring faster broadband have together propelled sub-Saharan Africans into the modern world in ways that would have been impossible in eras featuring only the telegraph, fax machines, landline telephones, and snail mail. Given the technical advances that this chapter has discussed (in the medical, agricultural, and governance arenas, among others), Africa is now well poised to join its planetary partners in improving lives for its swelling numbers of people, and for those many who will follow. Technology has made that progress possible.

Nonetheless, there is a caveat. As important as are technological innovation and improving Africa's competitiveness with the rest of the world, African expenditures on research and development lag behind the rest of the countries of the planet. That limits how fast Africa can catch up digitally and otherwise with Asia, Europe, and the Americas. On average, the rest of the globe spends 1.7 percent of GDP annually on research and development. South Asia spends only 0.7 percent, and Africa a woeful 0.4 percent of GDP on the same important area. There is much to be done.

Robotics

This chapter has said nothing thus far about the robotics revolution coming to Africa. Everywhere else in the world machines of some kind will substitute for human labor, and take on repetitive and other tasks that robots can do more efficiently and less expensively. This will increasingly be their role, especially in aging societies that now and for the foreseeable future will struggle to find willing labor—or any labor at all—for a variety of operations that once needed human attention. Much care for the elderly in societies like Japan will increasingly be offered by such machines. Keeping migrants out of the United States and Britain will mean the picking of many crops and the maintenance of citrus and other orchards by machines. But Africa will not experience similar shortages of labor in this century. With an abundance of young people envisaged for the next fifty or more years, and a median age that will not drop below 30 for much of the remainder of this century, robotic solutions will—except in some special circumstances in South African factories, mining, or on offshore oil and gas rigs—be a last resort in Africa, especially sub-Saharan Africa. Indeed, as the rest of the world turns to robots, Africa's terms of trade may recede unless it (and its political and economic leaders) can find ways of lowering its real costs of labor (see Chapter IV) and gaining competitiveness globally. Even as countries south of the Sahara have mastered mobile telephone technology and extended its uses to meet local needs, and just as part of Africa now competes with Asia in the call center and business processing arenas, so there will be few advantages for Africa to try to adapt robots to its continental needs—at least not yet.

The Rising Dawn

The digital revolution has swept over Africa. It will continue, even if some backward-thinking regimes attempt to repress social media or impose censorship. Fortunately, the digital information revolution is unstoppable. But the full potential of that revolution will only be released if the political leaders of Africa, especially sub-Saharan Africa, embrace it, exploit it for the betterment of their peoples, and refuse to try to deter or control what access to new knowledge will do to uplift whole populations.

XI | Africa's Vanishing Animals

A FRICA IS LOSING its animals. Many of the iconic fauna that are indelibly associated with Africa, and that attract so many local citizens and foreign tourists alike, no longer spread limitlessly across the vast savannahs of the mid-continent. Nor are many of the larger mammals of the unbroken forest often visible. Habitat loss, climate change, the pressure of humans searching for new pastures and agricultural fields, and this century's massive escalation of illegal poaching have all decimated the herds of elephants, the pods of rhinoceros, the prides of lion, and even the towers of giraffe that once browsed and foraged without much human interference. Even the lowly and secretive pangolin is being hunted ceaselessly to satisfy Asian demand.

The continued existence of all of these fauna, and even some specialized avifauna, is seriously at risk in the remainder of the twenty-first century. The numbers of the larger animals are all reduced from what they were as recently as 2000; worries about possible extinctions later in the century are not far-fetched. Since we know that Africa's human populations are exploding, and doubling or tripling in several of the savannah nations and even in a few of the forest countries, it is obvious that new generations will put renewed pressure on the land (even if most of the new peoples will gravitate to the continent's cities and towns). As the urban centers inevitably expand, so they will encroach upon lands used both for farming and by various mammals. Some will be able to adapt like the numerous serval that have taken up residence within the fenced perimeter of a massive synthetic fuels plant inside the city limits of Secunda, Mpumalanga Province, South Africa. Others will continue to raid village gardens, and infuriate long-suffering farming communities. But adaptation will have its limits and constraints; large and small fauna and human habitation can only coexist together without conflict in rare instances.

Water availability will prove limiting, as well. Animals need access to water. So do humans. There will inevitably be clashes that humans will win, driving animals farther away and into pockets of savannah or forest that humans rarely visit. Furthermore, animals depend as much on rainfall as most African tilled crops. With the onset of intensified global warming and weaknesses both in the Asian monsoons and the inter-tropical convergence system (see Chapter I), much of the savannah will be at risk of desiccating. Traditional water holes and watercourses will no longer remain reliable. Large and small fauna will have to move across the unyielding terrain in search of both water and pasture.

Poaching is also destroying today's animals and tomorrow's breeders. Few species numbers are increasing and, in the case of particularly valuable large mammals, poachers are literally killing as many as they can to meet Asia's demand for ivory, rhino horn, pangolin scales, and the like. Almost none of that enforced culling stays in Africa. But there is a long tradition, especially in the forest, of Africans harvesting large fauna for food, for bushmeat. In no African country are such slaughters now permitted, but the practice continues and also contributes to the loss of animals that is so prevalent in this century. Some of those killings, mostly of chimpanzees, monkeys, and bats, may have originally helped to spread zoonotic diseases from animals to humans, especially HIV/AIDS, and now Ebola and Marburg, the hemorrhagic diseases that stem from contact with bats (see Chapter IX).

Elephants and Rhinoceroses at Risk

Elephants, the planet's largest terrestrial animal, inhabit thirty-seven African countries. The savannah subspecies is more numerous and almost twice as large (about 13,000 pounds) as the forest subspecies. In both elephant subspecies their upper incisor teeth develop into tusks that continue to grow (if not disturbed) throughout their lifetimes. However, the savannah version's tusks curve outward while the forest variety has tusks that curve downward, possibly for digging purposes. Forest elephants are also darker than the savannah version; their skulls and skeletons are shaped differently. Both use their trunks equally to handle objects, feed themselves, and communicate (the last of which is also accomplished by deeply sounded voices). Because of poaching, forest elephant populations are declining at a more accelerated rate than the elephants that live on the savannah.

Africa in 1930 could count as many as 10 million elephants across more than fifty countries. In 2020, no more than 400,000 elephants remain, a decline (by one count) of 111,000 or more since 2006, or by 30 percent in the seven years from 2009. These great losses are due almost entirely to an epidemic of poaching.

As many as two-thirds of the remaining savannah elephants are in Botswana, home to more than 200,000 of the pachyderms, South Africa, Mozambique, and Namibia. Tanzania's elephant herd population declined from 110,000 in 2009 to 43,000 in 2014. Similar proportional losses have been noted in Zambia (where only 21,000 elephants remain), southern Angola, Kenya, Uganda, Chad, the Central African Republic, and South Sudan. The details of these decreasing elephant numbers are stark, as Table 11.1 shows.

Forest elephants primarily inhabit the basin of the Congo River, large sections of Gabon, Cameroon, and small areas in southern Burkina Faso and northern Benin. A proportion of the Namibian elephants stroll across stark desert terrain and the South Sudanese herds are often submerged in swampy, partially inundated, areas near the Nile River. Additionally, there are tiny populations of elephants as far northwest as northern Guinea and as far northeast as the northern and far eastern reaches of Ethiopia.

Clearly elephants are adaptable and resilient. They travel miles for water and to graze on the rough grasses, twigs, fruit, roots, bushes, and tree bark that are their main fodder. Elephants play a crucial role in Africa's savannah ecosystems as seed dispersers. Their dung recycles valuable nutrients and, by feeding on trees, they maintain the savannah's matrix of woodland and grassland and the biodiversity that it supports. Forest elephants' browsing habits

TABLE 11.1 Africa's Vanishing Elephants

- 1930 – 10 million elephants across 50 countries
- 2006 – 510,000 elephants in 37 countries
- 2019 – 400,000 elephants in 36 countries
- Botswana holds 200,000
- South Africa, Namibia, Mozambique 100,000?
- Tanzania – 39,000, down from 110,000 in 2007
- Zambia – 21,000
- Tusks (ivory) worth $5,000 per lb, in China

can reduce global warming, too, because of the carbon storage that occurs in the larger and harder trees that remain after they eat softwood and knock down smaller varieties. Paradoxically, when because of human population pressure and poaching threats elephants are confined to reserves and cannot roam freely, sometimes their numbers grow to exceed the carrying capacities of their demarcated lands. And then they need to be relocated or culled.

Elephants look after each other well, with matriarchs leading relatively large herds and bull elephants, especially younger ones recently pushed out of the herds by their mothers, roaming in smaller groups, or singly. On average, elephants live for fifty-six years in the wild. But as smart, as durable, and as resilient as they are, they fall unwitting victim to Africans working in gangs. The various local poaching accomplices across Africa are killing about 20,000 elephants a year, stripping the carcasses of their tusks, and leaving the rest of the slaughtered beasts for vultures, hyenas, and other scavengers of the savannah. Forest elephant populations are declining much more rapidly than savannah numbers, mostly because the authorities have been less successful in warding off poachers, and less protective generally of the elephants in those places. Also, in war-torn Congo, poachers have had a field day, slipping in between the contending militias, or joining with them to machine-gun elephants.

If anything, rhinoceroses are much more endangered than elephants. Until 2018, when poachers killed 892, Africa was losing more than 1,000 a year. Today the decade of slaughter leaves fewer than 25,000 white and black rhinoceroses in the wild, mostly in Botswana and Namibia, in South Africa and Mozambique, and—in fewer numbers—in Zambia, Tanzania, and Kenya. South Africa alone lost 1,028 rhinos to poachers in 2017. More than 7,000 have been killed since 2008. Undisturbed, they live between thirty-five and fifty years, on average.

Rhinoceroses are killed for their horns, or sometimes horns are stripped from live rhinoceroses, a much more dangerous operation for the poachers. Yet the horn itself is just a mass of keratin, the key component of human hair and fingernails. Admittedly, the horns are more than dense clumps of hair. They contain deposits of calcium and melanin, the calcium making the horn harder (for use by rhinoceroses as a weapon) and the melanin protecting the horn from the sun's harmful ultraviolet rays. Horns are similar in composition to horses' hooves, turtle beaks, and cockatoo bills. Rhino horns tend to curve backward, toward the eyes, because the keratin in front grows faster than the keratin in back. The outside of the horn is comparatively soft and can be worn down and then sharpened after years of use. And, paradoxically given the poaching frenzy, if a horn breaks off and is not sliced off, it can grow back gradually.

Black rhinoceroses are critically endangered. Only slightly more than 5,000 of the massive animals remain, half in Namibia. Large-scale poaching saw black rhino populations decline from around 70,000 individuals in 1970 to just 2,410 in 1995—a dramatic decline of 96 percent over twenty years. Fortunately, thanks to the persistent efforts of conservation programs across Africa, black rhino numbers have risen since then to a current population of between 5,042 and 5,458 individuals, and their range has increased.

Black rhinoceroses have narrow mouths and two horns, the front one from 20 to 51 inches in length and the rear one about 20 inches long. Black rhino horns are slightly larger than their white rhino counterparts. They are well adapted to arid and semi-arid terrain and can now be found in addition to Namibia in South Africa, Zimbabwe, and southern Tanzania. They have also been reintroduced to Botswana, Malawi, Eswatini, and Zambia.

White rhinoceroses are larger than black rhinoceroses, growing to 13 feet long and 6 feet from hoof to shoulder. White rhinos are so called because of their wider mouths (and a mistranslation from an Afrikaans word). In 1900 there were estimated to be 250,000 white rhinos. Now they number about 20,000 and are officially classified as "near threatened." Given the scale of killings earlier in this century, even those modest numbers represent an overwhelming conservation success story. The southern white rhinoceros has recovered from near extinction. Most live in South Africa and Namibia, with fewer individuals in Zambia. The northern white rhino has gone virtually extinct with the death of the last male in 2018 in Kenya.

Both the black and white rhinoceroses are herbivores. The black rhino eats trees or bushes because its long lips allow it to pick leaves and fruit from up high. The white rhino has a flat-shaped snout that lets it get closer to the ground to eat grass.

In Kenya, South Africa, Botswana, Namibia, and Zambia efforts to patrol national game parks and other areas against poachers have been vigorous in recent years, with some success in deterring attacks on the animals. Such conservation efforts have made the poaching business much more costly. But as important as vigorous anti-poaching efforts are to saving elephant and rhinoceros lives, with apprehension and punishment of miscreants to follow, the only way to end forever the killing of elephants for their tusks and rhinoceroses for their horns is to find various ways to squelch demand.

Asian Demand

With increasing prosperity in China and Southeast Asia, the primary world markets for elephant ivory, there has been increasing demand for what long ago was a commodity carved into ornaments and used for piano keys and similar products. But, since the 1990s, primarily Chinese, and Vietnamese and Malaysian, customers have sought to purchase carved-ivory ornaments and chopsticks as displays of wealth and status, and also for use in medicinal elixirs.

According to ancient wisdom, cancers can be cured and male sexual prowess enhanced by infusions of ground-up horn and ivory. Powder made from rhino horn is often added to food or brewed in a tea in the belief that the horns (and keratin) are a powerful aphrodisiac, a hangover cure, and treatments for fever, rheumatism, gout, and other disorders. Even though such outcomes have never been verified scientifically, many Asians still strongly believe in their efficacy. Alas, China has not yet embarked upon a campaign to educate consumers to dispel such myths about ivory and rhino horn, or even to inform potential customers of the prosaic composition of rhino horn. Nor has Vietnam.

Asians also value the aesthetics of ivory carvings, ownership of which enhances prestige and signifies wealth. China may hold as many as 100 tons of ivory carvings. The sizes of the Vietnamese and Malaysian hoards of carved figures are not precisely known, but they are likely to be but modest fractions of the Chinese total. Yemenis use rhino horn to produce traditional dagger grips.

Research done in China identifies women who live in smaller Chinese cities and possess medium-to-high incomes as the key modern purchasers of ivory. They are the supposed "die hard" buyers of ivory products. These women are apparently attracted to ivory because it is "rare and beautiful," carries cultural significance, and makes a good gift. Ivory, sometimes referred to as "white gold," clearly is a status symbol—a luxury product that people use to flaunt their wealth.

In Hong Kong, more than three hundred traders in 2019 held licenses allowing their stores to sell ivory legally. These were not backroom shops; many were situated on busy streets, open to regular street traffic. Some of the stores resembled expensive jewelry emporia, others were more haphazard in their displays. In both types of shop, the ivory on sale was hardly inexpensive.

A researcher remarked that China's rising middle class often parked their money in ivory. After all, "it never goes bad." Ivory is considered a smart way to spend money because it is both an investment and something that can be shown off. Collectors also regard well-carved ivory as akin to fine art in value and enjoyment.[1]

Ivory is worth $2,100 per kilogram, or about $5,000 per pound, in China, and somewhat more in Vietnam and Malaysia—the other big consumers— with rhino horn now worth as much as $12,000 per kilogram in Asia. At those prices, which are hardly realized by the actual poachers, or even by middlemen, there obviously is room for profit-taking at the end of the long logistical queue from Africa.[2] Local poachers in Africa usually work on consignment from African and Chinese middlemen, receiving a fraction of the overseas kilogram value of ivory and horn for their dangerous forays. Yet that fraction often represents the kinds of handsome incomes otherwise unavailable to rurally based African men and their families.

Effectively reducing the killing of African elephants and rhinoceroses thus depends more on curbing the foreign appetite for tusks and horn than on localized national endeavors to combat poachers. Although approaches from both angles are essential, it is the consumer lust for elephant ivory and rhino horn that propels illegal attacks on innocent herbivorous mammals across the savannahs and forests of southern, eastern, and even western Africa.

Catching Traffickers

Substantial quantities of ivory destined for China and trafficked by Chinese men and women have been seized in recent years in the ports and airports of Nigeria, Togo, Uganda, Kenya, Tanzania, Namibia, and South Africa. Cut-up tusks and horns have been detected in shipping crates, in regular luggage, and even in handheld packages. In early 2019, a Tanzanian judge sentenced a Chinese businesswoman dubbed "the ivory queen" to fifteen years in prison for attempting to smuggle 860 tusks or pieces of tusk belonging to 350 elephants, and worth approximately $5.6 million, out of the country. The perpetrator was the head of the Chinese-Africa Business Council of Tanzania and owned a popular restaurant in Dar es Salaam. She and two African co-conspirators were also convicted of running an organized criminal gang; her co-conspirators were sentenced to fifteen-year jail terms. All three were also required to pay fines amounting to double the value of the ivory, or to serve an additional two years incarcerated. In 2016, two Chinese men received an even stiffer sentence of thirty-five years in prison for attempting to smuggle ivory. In 2015, four male smugglers, also Chinese, each received twenty-year sentences for attempting to ship rhino horn to China. Even earlier, three Chinese "seafood" exporters were jailed and held for more than a year after being apprehended in Dar es Salaam, Tanzania's main port. They were trying to exit the country with seventy-six elephant tusks hidden under shellfish.

South Africa discovered a number of Chinese "tourists" traveling with hidden ivory and some horn. Namibia has deported a number of middlemen (and several women) for masterminding poaching syndicates. The suspects captured in Togo and Nigeria were relatively brazen about their illicit actions, possibly because bribing inspectors and customs officials had previously been successful. Ivory has also been intercepted in Hong Kong, en route to mainland China.

Corruption clearly plays an important role in facilitating poaching at the village level, where operators may pay local officials and policemen to look the other way. When the illicit goods are readied for shipment to China and Vietnam, the stakes grow larger and the payments commensurately grander. In Guinea, for example, the country's chief wildlife protector was ensnared by a West African organization of eco-activists and Interpol. He was successfully imprisoned for many years for corruptly trading in chimpanzees, bonobos, and gorillas. In Zambia, the official Anti-Corruption Commission in one year prosecuted 1,500 nationals for poaching and trafficking in big animal parts. The UN Office of Drugs and Crime explicitly reports that the illicit trade in rhino horns, elephant tusks, lion claws, and pangolin skins and scales could not exist without the kinds of corruption that encourages officials to look away when contraband crosses borders or passes through airports and harbors.

The Chinese Hoard

China sanctions thirty-six official ivory workshops. They are required to use ivory from existing and legal global stockpiles. All ivory sold in China is certified to have come from those sources. But the regulations are flouted daily, and cut-up tusks and raw ivory flow almost without hindrance every month into China. Chinese delegates to a Convention on International Trade in Endangered Species of Wild Fauna and Flora (CITES) meeting said that their commercial establishments required at least 200 tons of ivory yearly in order to satisfy internal demand. Ivory, after all, is a part of China's "intangible" cultural heritage and shutting it down is going to be a consuming work of decades. Banishing ivory carvers and their suppliers, they claimed, cannot be accomplished with a desultory wave, even in China.

Selling elephant ivory is banned in a number of countries, including the United States, where it is illegal to send even vintage pianos with ivory keys or oboes and bassoons with ivory mouthpieces across state lines without a permit from the U.S. Fish and Wildlife Service. China outlawed ivory imports in 2017 and Hong Kong followed in 2018 (but its ban will only take effect in 2021). China has burned piles of confiscated ivory and imprisoned a number of smugglers. Nevertheless, and although China is hardly unaware of how endangered elephants have become and how central China remains in the global pursuit of elephant tusks, it has refrained from launching educational campaigns to reduce demand. And in Japan, Thailand, Malaysia, Vietnam, Laos, and Myanmar, trafficking in elephants and rhinoceros parts is still legal, and potential conduits to China.

Chinese demand persists. In the ivory markets that remain open (either legally or due to lack of enforcement) in Asia, over 90 percent of the customers are estimated to hail from China. These ivory seekers can no longer legally purchase the goods they desire in their home country, but supplies are readily available just across national borders in Vietnam, Laos, and elsewhere. Furthermore, even though it is illegal to do so without a permit, carrying small amounts of ivory back home to China is not perceived as a risk.

As a counter to what happens at home, China has been attempting to assist especially East African countries and South Africa in their pursuit of poachers. Partnering with African conservation efforts, China directs overseas funding and training to wildlife ranger activities and other anti-poaching police efforts. With Chinese assistance and local control and major funding, several of these anti-poaching endeavors have been modestly successful in South Africa and Namibia but have yielded far less encouraging results in Zambia, Kenya, Tanzania, and Uganda.

Wild rhinoceroses have been protected in stockades deep in the bush, as in northeastern Zambia, and guarded extensively in South Africa, Namibia, and Botswana. But there is only so much that can be done on foot and in vehicles to safeguard animals. Drones are being used more and more to alert authorities to suspicious activities across the savannah and elsewhere, and to deter poaching simply by making surveillance a constant possibility. Using advanced technology, including drones, may indeed provide deterrents sufficiently powerful to stop poaching. But creating incentives for local rural communities to benefit more from anti-poaching than from poaching and bushmeat attacks is equally important. Without poachers being regarded as renegades by their own cohorts, little will change. Equally, what is needed to win the war against poaching, and gaining appreciation for the importance of preventing poaching, is greater budgetary support by governments. Very little is being expended directly in most African countries to make poaching more difficult and to capture poachers more readily. Politicians may be corrupted, and therefore reluctant to act firmly against poaching syndicates, but a lack of interest in the problem, and in conservation more generally, may be the real circuit breaker.

Giraffe, Zebra, and Antelopes

Unlike their taste for boiled-up tusks and horns, Chinese do not usually devour parts of the much more numerous ungulates that proliferate on the semi-arid, open woodlands of much of middle Africa. Nevertheless, the loss of their favored habitat, especially shrinking supplies of acacia trees, has helped to reduce giraffe numbers appreciably, from 165,000 in 1985 to 97,000 today. Zebra numbers are also declining, as are herds of some of the larger antelopes, such as eland and hartebeest.

The International Union for Conservation of Nature (IUCN) calls the dramatic plunge in giraffe numbers a "silent extinction." Illegal hunting (largely for bushmeat), civil wars in places like the Democratic Republic of Congo (where the okapi subspecies lives), South Sudan, and the Central African Republic, and habitat degradation caused by climate change and the eradication of acacia trees to make way for expanding agricultural settlements, have all contributed to the massive fall in giraffe numbers. Giraffe are also hunted locally for their tails, which become flywhisks, good luck bracelets, and strings on which beads are strung. Artists carve giraffe bones, which are exported to countries such as the United States.

Giraffe browse primarily on the leaves of acacia and mimosa trees, eat seeds and buds from the same trees, and consume hundreds of pounds of such herbivorous fodder each week.

Giraffe, obviously the tallest living animals in the world, may grow to be 18 feet high, with necks that are 6 feet long, 21-inch tongues, 25-pound hearts, lungs that can hold 12 gallons of air, and skinny legs equally as long as their necks. Males may weigh as much as 3,000 pounds, with somewhat shorter females weighing half as much. Unusually dense bone structures allow giraffes of both sexes to carry such great weights and still run as fast as 30 miles an hour across trackless savannah.

There are now four species and several subspecies of the animal we think of as a giraffe. Then there is the not nearly so tall okapi, its forest-dwelling brother with zebra-like stripes on its legs and chestnut or russet chests and backs. The four species of the giraffe proper include the southern giraffe (with subspecies identified as Angolan and South African), the storied northern giraffe or *Giraffa camellopardalis* (with subspecies called Kordofan, Nubian, and West African), the reticulated, and the Masai. The specie and subspecies differences may be seen in both the color and the pattern of varied patchwork squares that cover their skin, and also by facial markings.

Collectively, a posse of giraffe is a tower; often towers include ten to twenty members, led either by females or males. The shrinking size of these familial towers is indicative of the threatened or "silent extinction" status of giraffe, a conservation concern that alters somewhat according to geographical limits. The Kordofan and Nubian subspecies are both listed as "critically endangered." The reticulated giraffe is listed as "endangered." The West African and Thornicroft's subspecies (550 in the South Luangwa region of Zambia) are considered only "vulnerable," but still in danger. The Rothschild's (of Kenya) is regarded as "near threatened." Only the Angolan subspecies, with its strongholds in Namibia (more than 12,000), Botswana, and Zimbabwe, are doing well and are of "least concern." The Masai and South African giraffes were classified in late 2019 when the International Union for the Conservation of Nature updated its "red" list. It reported that the South African subspecies was doing well but that Masai numbers had plummeted and was now "critically endangered." There are now only about 5,000 northern and 16,000 of the reticulated varieties. Furthermore, because the four species do not mix, one species may head rapidly toward extinction without slowing its demise through interbreeding.

The plains of Africa from South Africa north to the Sudan are full of zebra, but one of its species and two subspecies persist in very low numbers. Plains or Burchell's zebra now number approximately 750,000. But Grevy's zebra, which once spread throughout the Horn of Africa from Eritrea and Djibouti to Somalia and Ethiopia, are now confined to a narrow segment of land along Kenya's northeastern border with Ethiopia. They are officially designated "endangered." Of 15,000 or so that once roamed in this largely arid area in the 1970s, only 2,600 remain. In South Africa and Namibia the Cape Mountain zebra population is down to 600 representatives, mostly near Cradock in the eastern Cape Province, and there are fewer than 13,000 of the closely related Hartmann's zebra in northwestern Namibia and southern Angola. The Cape Mountain subspecies is the smallest of the zebra, but it has the most stripes, including markings down to its ankles. Each zebra has distinctive individual striping patterns.

Sometimes Africans hunt zebra for their skins. But habitat loss is a much bigger threat to their range and, ultimately, their numbers. Zebra compete with livestock for water and with ranchers and farmers for land on which to browse for grass, seeds, and small shrubs. In the special case of Grevy's zebra, periodic droughts have dried up water holes and depleted available forage. These unavailabilities have also forced the remaining Grevy's to concentrate on the few enduring water sources, thus allowing zoonotic diseases to spread more readily.

Common eland, the largest and slowest antelope, are found in grasslands, mountains, acacia savannah, and specialized woodlands from Uganda to South Africa. The giant eland is mostly a West African animal that has lost territory in Côte d'Ivoire, Ghana, and Togo, but still has a toehold in the Central African Republic, Guinea, and northern Cameroon. But with expanding human numbers, eland (as zebra and giraffe) are being crowded out of their favored areas. In the last twenty years, common eland have lost 50 percent of their historic terrain and are now found only in parts of seventeen modern countries. Civil conflict has caused significant declines in Angola, Mozambique, Rwanda, and Uganda. Africans also hunt them for their tasty meat, which is especially prized and nutritious (as is eland milk).

The greater kudu is only slightly smaller than the common eland, but it is much faster and a better jumper over 6-foot-high farming fences. It is widely distributed across the lowland bushveld of southern Africa, with large concentrations in central and northern Namibia. The far less numerous lesser kudu are not as tall nor as weighty as the greater kudu. They inhabit eastern Africa, but have been and are being pushed out of favored lowland terrain by the expansion of human pastoral and farming activities. Consequently, they have retreated to dense woodland and thornbush thickets below 4,000 feet in elevation, and become nocturnal creatures forced to persist just outside of villages and towns. Kudu are susceptible to epidemics of rinderpest, a deadly disease that is found in cattle.

Also vulnerable mostly to habit loss and pressure from expanding human settlements are medium-sized antelopes such as the puku, a golden-brown-coated animal that glows in the sun, and lives preferably in flooded, but not waterlogged, plains in Angola, southern Tanzania, Zambia, Botswana, and along the eastern and southern peripheries of the Democratic Republic of Congo. Its relatively large ears are attuned to the sounds of large cats and human predators.

Two other medium-sized gazelles are named after the explorers Joseph Thomson and James Augustus Grant. There are 207,000 black-stripe flanked Thomson gazelles sprinting (at 40 miles an hour) and jumping across the open grasslands of southern Kenya and northern Tanzania. Brown, black-tailed Grant's gazelles, with a black-striped face, are larger and faster than Thomson's, and now number about 140,000. They can cruise at 50 miles an hour. Grant's prefer areas of shorter grass than Thomson's, and graze from the southeastern corner of South Sudan and the northeastern section of Uganda across much of northern and eastern Kenya and western and southern Somalia into northern Tanzania. Their survival has been greatly compromised by the raging civil wars in South Sudan and Somalia and their extension into Kenya. The meat of both small animals is highly valued by local Africans, as are their hides. Human predation, human population pressure, the expansion of farming settlements, and competition with Maasai, Turkana, Pokot, Karamojong, and other pastoralists has deeply limited room for Thomson's and Grant's gazelles to thrive. Consequently their numbers are decreasing, rapidly. The ICUN believes that Grant's, at least, will shortly be classified as "nearly endangered."

A very small antelope, the klipspringer, is found in isolated and mountainous terrain throughout eastern and southern Africa. Klipspringers are about 20 inches tall and are so named because they leap from rock to rock, always on the alert for leopards, caracals, black eagles, spotted hyenas, and humans. It is a nocturnal animal, for protection. A century ago it was hunted for its coarse fur, which made ideal stuffing for saddlebags. It eats flowers, small plants, lichen, and fruits and sometimes competes for territory with domestic goats.

Even smaller than a klipspringer is the dik dik, which stands up to 16 inches high and weighs up to 12 pounds. It lives in isolated pockets of arid land from the Horn of Africa, through the Kenyan and Tanzanian acacia savannah, to Namibia. The most populous is Kirk's dik dik, which live in those two eastern African countries. To its north are Guenther's dik dik, in Uganda and northern Kenya, Salt's dik dik, and the silver dik dik. The last is the smallest, weighing 5 pounds and inhabiting dense thickets in southern Somalia and in the acacia bush lands in southern Ethiopia. Salt's version is slightly heavier and longer and lives nearby in the desert and bush lands of the Horn of Africa, the Sudan, and Kenya. Guenther's stay in low, dense, thickets, preferring overgrazed and disturbed land where seeds, shrubs, and grasses are easily available. They are found on lava beds and sandy soils as well as acacia savannah. Guenther's dik dik are distributed across much of Somalia, the lowlands of Ethiopia, southeastern Sudan, northeastern Uganda, and northern Kenya. There is an isolated colony of Kirk's dik dik in northern Namibia, mostly inside the Etosha Game Park.

The Larger Cats

Conservationists estimate that about 200,000 lions roamed Africa a century ago. But now lions are extinct in twenty-six African nations and present in fifteen, often in small numbers. Lions only occupy 8 percent of their historic range. That includes savannah and woodlands from Guinea, Burkina Faso, Chad, South Sudan, and Ethiopia southward across the great plains of East Africa into southern Africa, with larger populations in Angola, Tanzania, and Botswana. But western African prides of lion are severely depleted. As a result, there may now be no more than 23,000 left in the wild. Or, say researchers, there could be as few as 16,000 and no more than an unlikely 30,000. The ICUN lists lions as "vulnerable."

Habitat loss has played a part in the loss of lions in recent years. So has competition from villagers preventively protecting their cattle and sheep, and themselves. Habitat loss consists of new physical developments, overgrazing by cattle and other ruminants, and the conversion of land to agriculture. Lions tend to retreat in the face of new settlements and farms; lions usually hesitate to tangle with humans. But as lions back off, lose some of their territory, and feel threatened, so the ecological balance of the African savannah is altered for the worse. Lions are critical to wildlife management. Their kills provide vital pickings for scavengers—hyenas, jackals, and vultures. If lions thrive, the others benefit and their prosperity multiplies down the chain of faunal, avifaunal, insect, floral, and grassland ecology. We need the king of the jungle to do well. But a major new and largely unanticipated threat to the survival of lions has suddenly appeared.

Lions are being poached in a serious manner for the first time. They are being killed so that their faces and paws can be hacked off and shipped along with rhino horn and elephant tusks to Asia. Mozambique, South Africa, Zimbabwe, Tanzania, and Uganda have all reported atrocities of this kind, and the wanton practice may also have spread to Kenya and Botswana. As it happens, it is far easier to poach lions (despite their feared reputations) than elephants or rhinoceroses. Lions scavenge, so poachers need only snare an antelope, poison the carcass, and wait. There are more poachers than game rangers, too. In one park in Mozambique there are at least a dozen separate poaching syndicates.

Once poisoned, the paws and face are easy to cut off the dead lion and are jointly worth about $2,000 to $4,000 to the poachers. In Asia, the claws and teeth become pendants and other forms of jewelry. On a regular Chinese online purchasing site anyone can order a lion tooth pendant for $126. Sometimes lion bones are also taken for use in traditional African religious ceremonies and magic or, shipped to Asia, as substitutes for increasingly rare tiger bones. Lion bones can be used to make (fake) tiger bone wine; it treats various ailments and is said to give drinkers "the strength of a tiger." But bones are harder to carry and smuggle than faces and claws. Transported to China, Vietnam, and Malaysia together with tusks and horns, these lion parts may just be another way of making money now that there are fewer rhinos and that the remaining rhinos are much better protected than before.

In one park in Kenya, conservationists are finding ways to attach radio broadcasting collars to local lions. That has two important uses. It alerts local villagers and cattle owners to a lion's presence and gives them time to protect their livestock and make sufficient noise to frighten away such predators. Additionally, it notifies especially trained Lion Rangers to help the villagers cope with the threat, and in that manner saves the lives of many lions.

Leopards can also be hunted for their claws and teeth, and for the same ultimate Asian uses. As elusive and often singular animals, they might be thought to be spared poaching and habitat loss, but leopards can also be tempted by poisoned carcasses and threatened by villagers who blame leopards for losses of sheep or goats. Leopards prefer to dine on impala, puku, and gazelles, or hares and mice, but if domestic stock are readily available, leopards are prepared to sample. The IUCN classifies African leopards as "vulnerable." Overall, there are about 700,000 leopards in thirty-five African nations, far less, and over fewer countries, than decades ago.

Leopards prefer to remain in rocky landscapes near dense bush and riverine forests, but they are sufficiently adaptable to seek out prey in desert environments. That is why they are found on Mounts Kenya and Kilimanjaro as well as across the savannah grasslands of East Africa, in West and Central Africa, and in southern Africa. Large numbers of leopards are found in Gabon and the Central African Republic, in Kenya and Tanzania, and across southern Africa from Angola and Namibia even into the coastal region of South Africa's Cape Province. Leopards further manage to cross into or live in suburban and urban environments, feeding on domestic as well as wild prey.

But, because of poisonings, some poaching, and retaliatory killings by aggrieved villagers, leopards are suffering along with so many of the other animals in this chapter with severe habitat fragmentation and the loss of, as well as the encroachment on, their territories by expanding human populations. They are sometimes hunted for their spotted skins, much valued in Asia, as well. The lonely, powerful, leopard, like the others, is forced to compete for space and comestibles not only with its usual rivals and enemies—lions and hyenas—but also with surging populations of humans. There are many more leopards now than lions and hyenas, as well as many of the smaller cats, but poachers and villagers may together become a growing threat to the survival of most leopards in Africa.

Cheetahs are much more threatened than leopards. Some scientists suggest that they are in imminent danger of extinction, although the IUCN only classifies the cheetah as "vulnerable." These researchers say that there are only

3,600 cheetahs (down from 15,000 in 1975) across their most established range area—Namibia, Botswana, Zimbabwe, and South Africa. Others estimate that there could be as many as 7,100 of this fastest mammal on earth in the four southern Africa countries mentioned and scattered into small pockets of Kenya and Tanzania. We know that their range and their numbers have been reduced down to 10 percent of what prevailed in the last century.

Where the South African, Namibian, and Botswanan borders converge, cheetahs still sprint after springboks, the southern African version of impalas. They hunt impalas proper in Kenya and Tanzania, too, where their numbers are much lower. Cheetahs are also found in Botswana's Okavango Delta, in Hwange and other game parks in Zimbabwe, in Etosha Park in northern Namibia, and in the lowlands of northern South Africa.

Everywhere, cheetahs are threatened by Africans protecting their livestock, by fearful villagers, and by lions and hyenas. Because of habitat loss, there has been severe inbreeding, which has limited the cheetah's reproductive success. Whether the higher or the lower number of cheetahs in the wild is accepted and verified, their numbers have fallen so low that extinction is clearly a possibility.

Pangolin

Chinese consumers also lust after the meat, scales, and other body parts of the four pangolin species that are found in Africa and rarely glimpsed by tourists or African farmers. Three of these four species of scaly anteaters live in the deep forests of Cameroon, the Central African Republic, Equatorial Guinea, Gabon, and the two Congos; the three tree-dwelling, white-bellied, and black-bellied pangolins each weighs as much as a small rabbit, up to 7 pounds. Temnick's ground-dwelling pangolin is much larger and heavier, weighing up to 25 pounds. It is found across the savannah in a dozen countries or more.

A pangolin is a very slow-moving anteater covered with hundreds of armored scales made of keratin. Nocturnal, it spends its life both searching for its favorite food, sometimes in trees swinging from long tails, but also keeping a low profile along the ground to avoid predators. Pangolin dig 90-foot long burrows and can even swim across rivers to escape attackers. They use their very long claws to tear apart insect nests. Then they feed by sticking tongues longer than their 19-inch bodies deep into the nests to acquire various kinds of ants and termites. Researchers estimate that a single pangolin can consume 70 million insects a year, thus helping to regulate insect numbers.

There may be even more than 600,000 pangolins ridding Africa of ants annually, and thus nothing to worry about. But we do not really know how many pangolins exist and, at the rapid rate that pangolin skins and scales are being seized at African ports, pangolins may soon be gone. They are among the most heavily trafficked wild animals in the world. Moreover, it is likely that customs and other port officials are blocking the export of but a tiny fraction of all pangolin shipped out of Africa, en route to Asia. One detailed study of one hundred areas in forested Africa over almost forty years discovered that at least 400,000 pangolin are hunted annually for their meat and for export. Asians are buying pangolin directly from local hunters in places such as Gabon.

The poaching process is dead easy. For millennia, when attacked, pangolin rolled up into a tight ball, protected by their impenetrable scales. That procedure worked until now against predator animals. But poachers simply pick up the conveniently arranged pangolin and carry them away to be killed. More than three hundred a day are killed.

Pangolin meat is considered a delicacy in southern China. (There are critically endangered Asian species, also.) Pangolin scales are prized as an ingredient in traditional Chinese medicines. When WildAid surveyed Chinese consumers, 70 percent believed that pangolin meat and other products could cure rheumatism and skin diseases if mixed into a wine or taken as a powder.[3] Pangolin penises possess aphrodisiacal properties, or so many Asians believe. All three products are easy to find in shops in Hong Kong, as well as in major mainland Chinese cities. Nearly 4 grams of pangolin scales were worth $38 in Hong Kong markets in mid-2019. Sometimes merchants grind the scales into powder, the better to avoid detection and the better to blend into medicinal soups.

In early 2019, Hong Kong custom officials found 800 pounds of pangolin scales secreted along with $1 million worth of purloined mobile telephones and digital cameras. The scales had a street value of about $300,000. A few months before, the same sleuths intercepted 9 tons of scales, the biggest haul ever recorded, on its way from Nigeria to Vietnam. In mid-2019, an even larger shipment was confiscated. Singaporean authorities discovered containers holding 14 tons of pangolin scales that came from Nigeria and were being transshipped to Vietnam. Specialists reckoned that 36,000 pangolin had to have been slaughtered to provide so many tons of scales.

Between 2013 and 2017, inspectors in Hong Kong—the gateway to southern China—confiscated 43 tons of pangolin carcasses and scales, representing probably tens of thousands of animals. They had arrived primarily from Cameroon and Nigeria. The UN Office of Drugs and Crime reported that the Hong Kong seizures represented almost 50 percent of the pangolin products confiscated globally in just three years earlier in this decade. The amounts of pangolin collected by the authorities doubled between 2017 and 2018. The traffic in pangolins is clearly massive, and profitable. And, in terms of the usual concerns for illegal ivory and rhino horn smuggling, pangolin commerce crawls under most radar.

In addition, deforestation in West and Central Africa has deprived pangolins of critical habitat; particularly affected are the semi-arboreal white-bellied pangolin and the fully arboreal black-bellied pangolin. As the pressure of population increases pushes Africans more and more into hitherto unexploited forest regions, or even more deeply into the grasslands, so the pangolin, as well as gazelle, giraffe, and big cats, find themselves crowded. This pressure, which will only worsen in coming decades, together with massive attacks on pangolin by poachers, can only drive slowly reproducing pangolin toward extinction.

Twenty-one million containers a day pass through Hong Kong's port, the fifth largest in the world. Inspecting even a fraction of those containers to discover pangolin scales or cut-up elephant tusks is a massive task, never to be accomplished. Thus, it is a testimony to customs and excise examiners, and other police agencies, that even a few shipments of African wildlife products have been discovered in and passing through Hong Kong. Those confiscations also indicate how much else must be coming from Africa that is never intercepted.

Moreover, Hong Kong has not been anxious to prosecute purveyors of illicit pangolin, or even traders in ivory. Low-level smugglers have been sentenced to a few weeks in jail and fined modest amounts. Possibly this laxness is explained by Hong Kong's reputation as a free port and as an economic entrepôt where very little trade is ever encumbered. Hong Kong regards itself as an open, rarely restrictive way station to China—the real market.

Donkeys

Chinese also consume African (and Asian and Australian) donkeys. Africa's long-used and abused beast of burden, the mainstay of rural transport in at least two dozen countries across the continent, is now in high demand in China. There is widespread fear in a number of African countries that if Chinese merchants keep bidding up prices offered for African donkeys, none will remain in five years or so. These are domesticated and hardly wild animals, but for centuries donkeys have been a fixture fundamental to upward mobility for indigenous subsistence farmers and traders. Indeed, donkeys were first domesticated long ago in Africa. Donkeys are adept at drawing heavy loads and are easy to handle. Ethiopia is estimated to have 7 million donkeys, more than any other nation across the globe. But, because of Chinese tastes and beliefs, African donkeys are now worth more dead than alive.

Thanks to strong new Chinese demand, new slaughterhouses for donkeys have been constructed, often financed by China, in Botswana, Ethiopia, Kenya, Namibia, and Niger. In some countries donkey hides fetch $500 each; a decade ago $100 would have been a welcome price.

In Kenya, the donkey population has fallen in the last decade by more than 30 percent, from 1.8 million to 1.2 million animals. There are three licensed slaughterhouses. In 2018 and 2019 they were butchering 1,000 or so donkeys a day to supply skins and meat to China. The returns at the slaughterhouses are so appealing that thieves are rustling donkeys and driving them to slaughterhouses; in Kenya, at least, there is a thriving black market in donkeys—all to satisfy Chinese tastes.

This intensified demand and the high prices that are now common in the donkey trade have driven governments such as Niger and Burkina Faso to ban the export of donkey skins. Twelve other African nations, including Botswana, Ethiopia, the Gambia, Ghana, Malawi, Mali, Nigeria, Senegal, Tanzania, Uganda, Zambia, and Zimbabwe, have also closed their specialized slaughterhouses or prohibited any sale of donkey hides or remains beyond their borders.

Nevertheless, China's import of donkey skins—a partial response to the halving of donkeys in China itself in the last decade—continues mostly unchecked. Curiously, most of the skins and other remains travel across the sea to end up in an otherwise unprepossessing eastern Chinese county called Dong'e, situated on the left bank of the Yellow River 60 miles upstream from Jinan, the capital of Shandong Province. That is where nearly all of the world's *ejiao*—a gelatin boiled down from donkeys—is now made from 4 million skins a year. Supposed curative powers once again drive demand. Consuming *ejiao*, billboards shout, will guarantee long lives, help persons lose weight, and boost energy. It is often prescribed to fix urinary, gynecological, cardiovascular, and other complaints, and has been a folk remedy for hundreds of years. It allegedly prevents cancer. As a blood tonic, it purportedly fixes anemia, removes acne, and improves libido. As a wellness product for the rising middle classes, it can be purchased as a face cream, as a candy, or even as a liqueur. The companies in Dong'e have brilliantly marketed this stewed extract of donkey into a health product with multiple beneficial benefits—all to the detriment of Africa.

Endangered Avifauna

Africa has no shortage of birds, and China is no more greedy for grey parrots and other "endangered" pet trade birds than Europe or America. Nonetheless, three dozen or so wild birds are currently "of concern" across Africa. Their habitats are shrinking, again because of human pressure and the effects of global warming. A few birds, like the grey parrot, are also captured in great number for the global pet trade. (That trade also takes live apes and other primates out of the wild in Africa for illicit sale to collectors.)

In addition to the grey parrots, among the notable birds showing serious declines in their abundance across large swathes of Africa are African penguins, white-backed vultures, two petrels, the black-browed albatross, Beaudoin's snake eagle, the black harrier, the African black oystercatcher, the African skimmer, and the black-crowned crane. A number of other birds, such as the Amani sunbird and the Abbot's starling of Kenya and Tanzania, the Albertine owlet of Rwanda and the Democratic Republic of Congo, two larks found in Somalia and another in South Africa, Bannerman's turaco and Bannerman's weaver in Cameroon, and Zambia's black-cheeked lovebird, are already limited to the territories listed, and are showing seriously reduced numbers because of shifting conditions and human interference.

Wild Africa under Threat

Poaching, rising human populations and expanding settlements, major alterations in rainfall and weather patterns, more high heat episodes, prolonged droughts, and a number of other unexpected changes in traditional natural conditions are greatly stressing wild animals as their living conditions become increasingly harsh. Animal and avifaunal population declines, which may have many causes, are in some cases, being accelerated in this decade, with much more to come.

The most important stressor of all, and the cause of greatest concern to the future of wild animals in Africa, is China's burgeoning prosperity, and the strengthened appetites of upper- and middle-class Chinese for products that have long been imported from Africa and are now coveted for their alleged medicinal properties or because of their status as symbols of wealth. Stopping the wanton killings of elephants and rhinoceroses, and even the slaughter of inconspicuous pangolin and the quiet donkey, requires reeducation and penalties on the demand side as well as intensified patrolling on the supply side. The disappearance of rhinoceroses, elephants, lions, cheetah, and even giraffe remains possible unless China and other Asian countries cooperate in bringing illicit trading in animal commodities to an end.

XII | Things Come Together: Achieving Greatness

T HINGS ARE COMING together in Africa, especially in sub-Saharan Africa. When Chinua Achebe wrote his pioneering, paradigm-setting *Things Fall Apart* (1959), and possibly of greater import for this book and for today, when he penned *A Man of the People* (1966) and *Anthills of the Savannah* (1987), Nigeria and the very young modern Africa were in fact falling apart. Colonialism and the disruptive demands that accompanied it had shattered the steady conceptual and spiritually receptive universe of indigenous Africa. Then, with independence in the 1960s, much of Africa gained control over its destiny but, as Achebe and others wrote bitterly, too many of its early leaders tossed freedom and liberty aside and immured Africans in the same kinds of clamped vises and ideological rigidities that had typified colonial rule. There were seventy-one military coups, abundant indigenous authoritarians, a preposterous Central African Empire, several crazed killers as leaders, profligate corruption, and too little economic development to benefit African peoples in the lost years between, 1970 and 1990.

Most of Africa discarded these dead-end performances in the 1990s, especially when Nelson Mandela's release from twenty-seven years of incarceration signaled the end of apartheid and the arrival of multi-party politics and open macroeconomic policies across the continent. Africa began to rise as, with China's surging demand for African primary commodities, it continued to grow throughout the first decade of this century. Even more recently, visionary and responsible leadership, stronger governance, the emergence of a significantly sized middle class, and the tying of much of Africa to the rest of the world via mobile telephones and the World Wide Web, finally reversed Achebe's doleful epitaph. Africans are achieving greatness, or are at least poised to do so in this century.

If careful readers of this book think that last sentence, and the title of this volume, are too optimistic (given population pressure, paucity of jobs, terror, war, and the rest), contemplating the resilience of Africa and Africans could provide abundant reassurance, as should the remainder of this chapter.

Admittedly, in order to ensure positive outcomes, Africans will have to tame the demographic tidal wave that threatens to bring vast numbers of young people into nearly all of their countries now, and for the next thirty-plus years. To meet this challenge effectively, schooling opportunities will have to expand and strengthen at the secondary and tertiary levels; technically skilled persons will need to become more numerous; and much more emphasis will have to be placed on capacity building for rapid economic growth. As people numbers surge, so crises will occur if employment possibilities expand too slowly, and without overcoming today's sclerotic production of jobs. As Chapter IV suggests, with intensifying urbanization, rural upheavals and massive in-migration, and with crushing pressures within the planet's largest cities, Africa's coming together will depend on successfully overcoming these and many other tough, but surmountable, obstacles.

Earlier chapters enumerated those hurdles: shortages of water, electrical generating capacity, capable roads and road networks; global warming and climate change; a hard-scrabble farming community that can no longer feed Africa (partly because of governmental policies and adverse climatic factors); a paucity of manufacturing; budgetary expenditures on soldiers and guns rather than butter and education; still worrying health outcomes; and sustained civil wars in a dozen states. This book's first chapter also emphasizes that because there are many Africas, not a single representative Africa, answers will have to come in many different guises that are responsive to the local circumstances and the varied leadership qualities and preferences of this state or that state.

Some of Africa's entities, in other words, will do better, be more resilient, adapt more rapidly and skillfully, and emerge from the supreme trials of this century stronger than now. Others, obviously, will perform less well because of deficiencies already discussed. In a few decades there may be two or three distinct new Africas. But the successful innovators will pull the others forward. Leadership will make most of the difference in outcomes.

Leadership

The key to turning these hard challenges into opportunities and sustained progress depends on vastly improved leadership and governance. Although twenty or so of Africa's fifty-four nations are still led by authoritarians and despotic kleptocrats, there are another twenty polities where the thoroughly democratic, public-interest-centered, responsible governance that has exemplified Botswana, Mauritius, Cape Verde, and the Seychelles since independence is now being emulated. Just as those countries are perceived as being comparatively noncorrupt for Africa, so Rwanda counts as a further anti-corrupt entity, and others, such as Benin, Ghana, and Senegal, and possibly Ethiopia, are joining their august ranks.

Transformational leadership of the kind that was pioneered by Sir Seretse Khama of Botswana and Sir Seewoosagur Ramgoolam of Mauritius, and then by Mandela when he became South Africa's first independent president, is now aspirational elsewhere, as personified by Prime Minister Abiy's relatively recent revamping of Ethiopia. Positive leadership of that ilk, in part responding to the preferences of an emerging middle class and in part reflecting Africa's newly-forged connections to the rest of the world's advanced nations, motivates better governance and thus improved human outcomes for Africa's people.

Because Africa still lacks a fully realized institutionalization of its political realm, with executives being much stronger than legislatures (Tanzania is a recent example) and with executives able to neuter or overwhelm the prerogatives of judicial establishments, the preferences and legitimacy of heads of state and heads of government matter much more than they do in Asia, Europe, or the Americas, where political institutions are long established and comparatively robust. So, as things come together, new leaders drive what is becoming Africa's renaissance. Consummate leadership, facilitating the beneficent outcomes that meet citizen needs and improve life chances for all, is a goal that now motivates many more African presidents and prime ministers than ever before. For their followers and the inhabitants of those countries, which are increasing in number, things are indeed coming together positively.

This is not to say that Africa has as yet reached Valhalla. But Africans on their handheld mobile telephones are able to send and receive money, deposit and withdraw from bank accounts, ascertain prices in markets, advise lactating mothers, transmit malarial blood specimens and images of injuries to distant physicians, report election results, and document corrupt dealings. The fact that Africans now have substantial connectivity and are able to employ their mobile telephones in a sophisticated manner is at least one measure of how far Africa has advanced in the last decade, and to what solid extent Africans have joined the global village—for good.

Africans are healthier than previously and their life expectancies are more elevated than in eras past despite the continued afflictions of malaria, HIV/ AIDS, tuberculosis, pneumonia, dysentery, and the sudden irruptions of Ebola and the other hemorrhagic maladies.

Insurgency

Terroristic movements still spread their fundamentalist tentacles, with mayhem following. But each of the main Islamist-inspired groupings, like Boko Haram and al-Shabaab, is being contained and the numbers of their militants and their territorial reach slowly diminished. Despite the American military pullback from the Sahel, and a consequent boost in the firepower of both al-Qaeda in the Maghreb and the Islamic State—plus more frequent raids on Malian, Burkinabe, and Nigerien outposts—local villagers and desert dwellers are not swelling their ranks. Smuggling of narcotics, cigarettes, and other commodities across the Sahara, or out of Somalia, still continues to finance the movements of terror, but authorities are very gradually beginning to interrupt such profiteering.

In addition to the Islamist-inspired attacks on African governments and peoples, several countries are still embroiled in costly internal conflicts that seem interminable, and often arise when ethnicities and other minorities within those states feel discriminated against, marginalized, and unheard. South Sudan and large sections of the Democratic Republic of Congo have for many years harbored such seemingly intractable hostilities. So has the Central African Republic. And now English speakers in Cameroon are seeking to secede from their French-speaking overlords, including a corrupt president who has served since 1982. Millions have been displaced because of these internal disputes, development prospects negated, and poverty and hunger intensified.

Even so, fewer Africans are getting killed in war, although the South Sudanese and the depredations of indigenous groupings in the eastern Congo may belie that affirmation. Episodes of carnage there are, but there is less blood-letting than before, and Africa's one interstate conflict has ended. Yet, in the Congo marauders have often interfered with health workers seeking to eliminate Ebola.

Governance

Africa has more and better governance than it had a decade ago. Many, but certainly not all African states are delivering fuller services to their citizens. Whereas several poor-performing political jurisdictions still provide little by way of good governance, and few services, many—more than ever—actually understand and accept the real needs of their constituents, and provide much of what is desired. The best leaders make sure that citizens are secure and safe, that they benefit from a robust rule of law, and that they genuinely participate in political and economic decision-making. Those responsible leaders further help citizens to prosper economically to the best of their personal abilities and act to give more and more educational opportunity and training to youthful citizens. In those better-led countries, the executive respects freedom of speech and assembly, freedom of the press and media, and freedom of religion. Elsewhere, especially in the despotisms, that is not the case. But the path forward to better governance everywhere in Africa is at least known, with social media highlighting potential citizen-satisfying improvements.

Corruption

Even corruption is receding. Petty corruption is probably as intense as it ever was, but fewer nations tolerate grand corruption—the willful siphoning of contracts and other large-scale economic enrichment opportunities in exchange for massive kickbacks—than in earlier decades. This is not to say that instances of kleptocracy are not as odious and venal as in times past, but the infamous days of Nigerian and Congolese thefts of billions and their laundering of the proceeds in Swiss and other banks have largely concluded. There is much more awareness than ever before of the dangers to citizens of wholesale official chicanery and misappropriation of national resources. South Africans, for example, are finally appreciating the full extent to which their state was captured and priorities distorted during the reign of President Jacob Zuma. The professionals who protest against corruption and everything else in the Sudan, in Algeria, in Cameroon, in Nigeria, in Zimbabwe, and in other countries express their abhorrence at what they have long endured. In Sudan, civil protestors even ousted a long-entrenched autocrat. When a new government in Zimbabwe ceased permitting police to shake down motorists at roadblocks, the populace cheered.

Democracy, or at least the rudiments of enhanced transparency and accountability, more independent judicial systems and fairer rules of law, and increasingly open political consultations, is now expected, even if not uniformly guaranteed. There are more meaningful elections and more contests that are free and fair despite the manipulated exercise in the Democratic Republic of the Congo in 2018 and questionable practices in the Nigerian, Comoros,' Guinea-Bissau, Malawian, and Namibian elections in 2019.

Nonetheless, although it is too soon to say that Africa has turned a decisive corner and that its politics will never again regress to the intolerant and fraudulent ways of yore, the new middle class and its acute concerns help to boost confidence. There are still ten presidents who hold office despite constitutional provisions that were meant to prevent staying indefinitely in office or beyond specified two terms. But much of Africa is nonetheless more mature politically than in the past. Different African peoples have much more voice than hitherto, and much more say about how they are ruled.

Toward Prosperity

But they and their political leaders inevitably have less to say about China. Its economic growth will as much as anything intrinsic to Africa determine how well much of Africa south of the Sahara, and even a few of the Maghrebi countries, thrive in the next several decades. If Chinese demand for African raw materials—for its petroleum, natural gas, cobalt, coltan, copper, ferrochrome, gold, iron ore, platinum, timber, and the rest—remains robust, then, and really only then, Africans will experience rising standards of living and more money in their individual and national pockets.

Those exports to China have enabled nearly all sub-Saharan African countries to obtain Chinese loans and Chinese refurbishing or constructing of railways, roads, hospitals, stadia, pipelines, and a variety of other infrastructural improvements, all of which have helped to vault Africa into the modern age. Similarly, the many hydroelectric dams that China is building or financing will greatly increase Africa's paltry energy supply, and help to bring steady light and power to Africa. Without Chinese money and expertise, and China's Belt and Road Initiative, Africa would be unable to provide facilities suitable for its aspirations and its citizens, and for today's modern age.

The new roads and installations, the towering dams, the schools and universities, the Chinese-constructed export processing zones, and much else have all helped more directly than European, American, Russian, Indian, or Japanese attention and trade to uplift Africans. Total trade between Africa and Europe and the United States is still larger annually than is trade between Africa and China. But China has more embassies than other countries, more military attachés, many scholarships, quite a few Confucius Institutes, numerous Mandarin teachers, and possibly 1 million new entrepreneurial residents.[1] (Chinese interlopers also sponsor animal poaching, primarily for elephant tusks, rhinoceros horn, lion claws, and pangolin scales, but also for donkey skins.) Just as in Ming times, China and Africa are deeply involved with one another. Without China, Africa's growth prospects would be diminished.

Underlying much of this book's examination of Africa's numerous challenges is an affirmation of the striking resilience of the peoples of the continent. Beset in earlier decades by checks on their freedom and barriers to fundamental economic growth, limited now by constrained opportunities for educational advancement, and still assaulted by difficult diseases, Africans remain resilient.

Resilience

With global warming has come uncertainty, unexpected rainfall patterns, devastating droughts, and colossal cyclones capable of dumping twenty-five inches of water in twenty-four hours on unsuspecting and unprepared areas like central Mozambique, southern Malawi, and mountainous eastern Zimbabwe. Such a catastrophic inundation occurred in early 2019 and will doubtless happen in some form or another in other parts of eastern Africa, where there were massive floods later in 2019. Or no rain at all will fall across the Sahel, causing great bouts of hunger. The low-lying coastal commercial capitals of most West African countries will also suffer from rising Atlantic Ocean levels. These climatic shifts will tax African resilience. Nevertheless, readers can expect that Africans will muster the know-how necessary to cope effectively with the population bursts that are just about to overtop their metaphorical levees, crowd their already congested cities, tax physical and social services, and create a potential demographic dividend. They and their leaders will also find imaginative ways to grow the foodstuffs that will be necessary, and import the rest. Africa's resilience will overcome any potential Malthusian moment.

Africa's political leaders will emerge to conquer the concatenation of difficult concerns that sharply challenge Africa in the remainder of this century. To repeat, things are coming together. Africa and Africans are achieving greatness.

As President Uhuru Kenyatta congratulated a singular Kenyan science teacher who won a $1 million global prize in 2019 for educating students supportively in a northern part of his country where drought and famine are common and school equipment is rudimentary, "You give me faith that Africa's best days are ahead of us, and your story will light the way for future generations."[2]

ACKNOWLEDGMENTS

This book draws on an adult lifetime's attention to Africa, with periodic visits to a range of countries and substantial periods of residence. But little could have been accomplished, even absorbed, without the significant guidance of a number of knowledgeable colleagues and political and official persons in numerous countries. I owe a very large debt of gratitude and respect to a vast community of perceptive Africanists at home and abroad and remain profoundly grateful as well to a daunting array of generous and wise friends across the length and breadth of the African continent (and in North America and Europe) for their insights, their penetrating observations and cautions, their moving hospitality, and their unfailing fellowship.

A few, alas, have passed, to use the African circumlocution, and therefore are not available to be reminded how greatly I still appreciate everything that they did over several decades to immerse me in the real Africa. Similarly unfortunately, I am unable to share the contents and the writing of this book with Joanna Hermione Hellicar Oakeshott, my late wife, who joined me in early journeys to West Africa before we traveled together throughout southern and eastern Africa. We worked together in the archives of Malawi, eating samosas from stalls below Zomba Mountain; followed different research paths in Lusaka, where she wrote about early childhood multiracial education; together drove the dusty earthroads of northern Zambia to interview our subjects and to visit with the much revered and politically prescient Sir Stewart Gore-Browne; jointly covered the early Malawian election victories by freedom fighters; and, much later, deepened our involvement with African politics in Nairobi and Kampala. It was on a subsequent visit to Nairobi, just after Jomo Kenyatta had been released from detention, that we spent much of a day with him. I sought his political views, especially of Mau Mau. But Mzee Kenyatta was far more interested in talking about banana cultivation with my wife, who had recently been investigating diseases of that tropical fruit. Her appreciation of everything African joined my own and is represented throughout the chapters of this book. She would have welcomed things coming together for Africa, as our three daughters and their husbands and children now do.

I am deeply grateful for the care that Margaret Hathaway and George Loft took to introduce me to their emerging Africa when I first landed in Central Africa at the very beginning of what became a delightful and engaging odyssey. Soon I was to meet Zambian politicians Harry Nkumbula, Simon Kapwepwe, and Arthur Wina. Before and after Arthur's early and much lamented death, I profited from many conversations with him and with his brother Sikota, sometime Speaker of Zambia's Parliament, and with President Kenneth David Kaunda, with whom my wife and I, and myself alone on numerous occasions over several decades, had telling conversations in Lusaka and in Cambridge, Massachusetts.

Learning about Africa, and sharing what I thought I knew with political science students at MIT; at Harvard Kennedy School; with young scholars in the Canadian universities of Carleton and Waterloo; with those mature minds who participated in three Older Wiser Lifelong Learners (O.W.L.L.) African politics courses; and with learned colleagues at a yearlong "African Challenges" seminar at the American Academy of Arts and Sciences, has fully informed and benefited this book's construction and presentation. So did years devoted to advising and helping a number of countries grow economically through the one-time Harvard Institute of International Development, where I worked particularly with Malawi and Mozambique, and briefly with the Kabila administration of the Democratic Republic of Congo. Devin Gattey, as a wise practicing physician with experience in Africa, kindly helped me to improve Chapter IX. Alex Kim deftly prepared the charts and graphics. David McBride edited this book with uncommon skill and deep understanding.

For their formative guidance and/or kind hospitality over time, in a variety of contexts and in cities and villages, in the bush as well as in capital cities, I recall with particular appreciation the collaboration and extraordinarily generous and formative multiple visits over many years with Denis and Noni Acheson, Tony and Libby Ardington, the late Finance Minister Aleke K. Banda, Finance Minister Tendai Biti, Dr. Selma Browde and the late Judge Jules Browde, Jenny and the Rev. Dr. Alex Boraine, Anne and Ambassador

Johnnie Carson, the late H. Masauko Chipembere, the late Dunduzu Chisiza, Mark Chona, Firle Davies, Sue Drummond Haley, Richard Hall, Judith Hawarden, Janet Heard, Tony Heard, Lady Francie and Sir Jeffrey Jowell, Professor Benson Kakoma, the late Foreign Minister Oscar Kambona, the late Simon Katilungu, Speaker Peter Katjavivi, Lishomwa Lishomwa, the late Jean and Ray Louw, Dr. Frances Lovemore, the late Governor and Vice-Chancellor Sir Richard Luyt, Vice-President Justin Malawezi, the late President Sir Ketumile Masire, President Festus Mogae, the late Lishomwa Muuka, the late President Julius Nyerere, Professor Hasu Patel, Benjamin Pogrund, Bennie Rabinowitz, Vice-Chancellor David Rubadiri, Penny and Clyde Sanger, Anne Sassoon, Professor Chris Saunders, Dr. Diana Seager, Justice David Smuts, Alice Storie, the late Helen Suzman, the late Prime Minister Morgan Tsvangirai, the late Ambassador John Willson, and the late Minister of Justice Eddison Zvobgo. Each of these formidable and accomplished politicians, diplomats, artists, editors, entrepreneurs, lawyers, and human rights advocates advanced my understanding of Africa, shared insights and vast knowledge, and made being in and with Africa uplifting and memorable. I hope that this book may be worthy of their friendship.

NOTES

I

1. But see Isaac Samuel, "The History of Writing in sub-Saharan Africa, Including the Most Notable Literary Works Written by African Authors about African History from the 2nd Century BC to the 19th Century AD," *Censored*, December 10, 2019, https://uncensoredopinion.co.za/the-history-of-writing-in-sub-saharan-africa-including-the-most-notable-literary-works-written-by-african-authors-about-african-history-from-from-the-2nd-century-bc-to-the-19th-century-ad/.
2. The United Nations counts fifty-four African nations. Some other entities include the Western Sahara, now essentially annexed to Morocco, and Somaliland, a fully-functioning polity denied recognition by the African Union, and therefore much of the rest of the world – giving Africa fifty-six designated political jurisdictions. Additionally, one could count the two Indian Ocean island dependencies of France: Reunion and Mayotte.
3. Pew Research Center, "Tolerance and Tension: Islam and Christianity in Sub-Saharan Africa," https://www.pewforum.org/2010/04/15/executive-summary-islam-and-christianity-in-sub-saharan-africa/.
4. Fraym Consulting's report, discussed in Yomi Kazeem, "What's the Best Way to Define Africa's Middle Class?" December 7, 2018, https://qz.com/Africa/1486764. (Fraym is based in Nairobi and McLean, VA.)
5. "World Population Prospects, 2019," https://population.un.org/wpp/2019.
6. Associated Press, "Water Shut Off in Zimbabwe Capital," *Boston Globe*, September 25, 2019.

7. Hilal Elver, quoted in Nyasha Chingono, "Zimbabwe on the Verge of 'Man-Made' Starvation, Warns UN Envoy," *The Guardian*, November 29, 2019, www.theguardian.com/global-development/2019/november/29/.

II

1. President Kennedy, speech, January 9, 1961, *Boston Globe*.
2. Fred Greenstein, quoted in obituary, *Boston Globe*, December 16, 2018.
3. President Kennedy, Inaugural Address, January 20, 1961, www.bartleby.com/124/pres56.
4. Daron Acemoglu and James Robinson, *Why Nations Fail: The Origins of Power, Prosperity, and Poverty* (New York: Crown, 2012), 116.
5. Rotberg, *Africa Emerges: Consummate Challenges, Abundant Opportunities* (Cambridge, UK: Polity, 2013), 191.
6. Quoted in Geoffrey York, "Foundation Unable to Handout Ibrahim Prize for Third Time in Six Years," *Globe & Mail*, October 15, 2012.
7. Acemoglu and Robinson, *Why Nations Fail*, 68.
8. Ellen Johnson Sirleaf, "Run, Women, Run," *Economist, the World in 2019*.
9. Khama, quoted in Thomas Tlou, Neil Parsons, and Willie Henderson, *Seretse Khama, 1921–1980* (Gaborone: Botswana Society, 1995), 252.
10. Quett Ketumile Joni Masire (ed. Stephen R. Lewis), *Very Brave or Very Foolish? Memoirs of an African Democrat* (Gaborone: Macmillan, 2006), 103.
11. Mandela, speaking in Katlehong, 1993, quoted in Stanley H. Greenberg, *Dispatches from the War Room: In the Trenches with Extraordinary Leaders* (New York: Norton, 2009), 145.
12. Mandela, the Rivonia trial, quoted in Anthony Sampson, *Mandela: The Authorized Biography* (New York: Knopf, 1999), 192.
13. Pascal Nyamulinda, quoted in Kristen van Schie, "The Kigali Paradox: How Did Rwanda's Capital Become Africa's Cleanest City?" *Mail & Guardian*, March 6, 2019.

III

1. Nic Cheeseman, "Both Democracy and Authoritarianism Are on the Rise in Africa," *The Conversation*, February 18, 2019, https://theconversation.com/both-democracy-and-authoritarianism-are-on-the-rise-in-Africa.
2. "Freedom in the World 2018: Methodology," *Freedom House*, https://freedomhouse.org/report/methodology-freedom-world-2018.
3. https://data.worldbank.org/indicator/VC.IHR.PSRC.P5. See also http://worldpopulationreview.com/countries/murder-rate-by-country.
4. https://freedomhouse.org/report/countries-world-freedom-2019; https://www.fraserinstitute.org/studies/human-freedom-index-2018. See also https://heinonline.org/HOL/LandingPage?handle=hein.journals/hurq32&div=20&i, for the Cigranelli-Richards Human Rights Dataset.

5. https://www.tralac.org/documents/resources/africa/2363-2018-ibrahim-index-of-african-governance-index-report/file.html. Unfortunately, this index of governance is now only issued every other year so there is no up-to-date listing for 2019. The numbers for the 2018 index hence reflect activity in 2017.

IV

1. Quartz Africa Weekly Brief (citing several academic studies), December 1, 2019. Africa+weekly@qz.com.
2. Yinka Adegoke, "Even Africa's Poorest Countries are Too Expensive to be the World's Next Manufacturing Hub," October 16, 2017, https://qz.com/africa/1102798.
3. Kim Cloete, "Africa's New Free Trade Area is Promising, Yet Full of Hurdles," World Economic Forum on Africa, Sept. 8, 2019, www.we.forum.org/agenda/2019/09.
4. https://www.reuters.com/article/us-zimbabwe-power-explainer/explainer-why-zimb; https://theodora.com/wfbcurrent/zimbabwe/zimbabwe_energy.htm.
5. Faith Birol, International Energy Agency, "World Energy Outlook," quoted in Brad Plumer, "Less Coal, More Wind: Energy Trends Shaping Climate Change," *New York Times,* November 13, 2019.
6. International Civil Aviation Organization, "Aviation Infrastructure for Africa Gap Analysis – 2019," www.icao.int/ESAF/documents/meetings/2019.
7. For the road statistics, see Axel Addy and Ratnakar Adhikari, "Africa's Infrastructure in Numbers." www.weforum.org/agenda/2017/07.
8. Kwasi Amoako Atta, Ghana's Minister of Roads and Highways, quoted in GhanaWeb, "It's a Shame that Only 23% of Our Entire Road Network is Paved," January 25, 2019, www.ghanaweb.com/ghanahomepage/newsarchive/.
9. Davies Adeloye, et al, "The Burden of Road Traffic Crashes, Injuries and Deaths in Africa: A Systematic Review and Meta-Analysis," *Bulletin of the World Health Organization,* 2016;94:510-521A. doi: http://dx.doi.org/10.2471/BLT.15.163121.
10. Landry Signé, "Africa's Consumer Market Potential," www.brookings.edu/wp-content/uploads/2018/12/; Yomi Kazeem, "What's the Best Way to Define Africa's Middle Class," December 7, 2018, https://qz.com/africa/1486764.

V

1. "Congestion Charging, Congo Style," *The Economist*, September 8, 2018.
2. UN Office on Drugs and Crime, "The Global Programme against Corruption," 3rd ed, 2004, chapter 1 (no pp).

3. "Lessons from Lusaka," *The Economist*, September 15, 2018.
4. Angelo Agrizzi, quoted in Norimitsu Onishi, "'Monopoly Money': Detailing Cash and Car Bribes to South African Leaders," *New York Times*, January 30, 2019.
5. James Hamill, "Why the ANC Itself Is the Chief Impediment to Ramaphosa's Agenda," *The Conversation*, December 14, 2018, www.theconversation.org.
6. Daniel Munkombwe, quoted in Linda Kasonde, "The Challenge of Leadership and the Poverty of Ambition," *African Leadership Institute Newsletter*, August 19, 2015.
7. Quoted in Raymond Fisman and Edward Miguel, *Economic Gangsters: Corruption, Violence, and the Poverty of Nations* (Princeton: Princeton University Press, 2008), 80.
8. Nelson Mandela, "Address by Comrade President Nelson R. Mandela to the International Federation of Newspaper Publishers Conference," Prague, May 26, 1992, http://Db.nelsonmandela.org/speeches/pub_view.asp?pg=item&itemID=NMS.
9. Memo of November 14, 2011, quoted in Lynsey Chutel, "A Search for Mozambique's Secret $2 Billion Debt Shows How the Global Banking System Aids Corruption," *Quartz Africa*, January 10, 2019, https//:qtz.com/Africa.
10. Quoted in Thomas Tlou, Neil Parsons, and Willie Henderson, *Seretse Khama, 1921–80* (Gaborone: Botswana Society, 1995), 49, 53.

VI

1. Heike Klovert, "The Chinese Builders Behind Africa's Construction Boom," *Der Spiegel Online*, November 28, 2019, www.spiegel.de/international/global societies.
2. AidData Center, College of William and Mary, cited in Mark Landler and Edward Wong, "Bolton Vows Bigger U.S. Role in Africa, but Goal is Countering China's Sway," *New York Times*, December 14, 2018.
3. Theo Neethling, "How Russia is Growing its Strategic Influence in Africa," *The Conversation*, February 6, 2019, www.theconversation.com/how-russia-is-growing-its-strategic-influence-in-africa.
4. The material in this paragraph draws upon, and the quotations are directly from, Stephanie Rupp, "Africa and China: Engaging Postcolonial Interdependencies," in Rotberg (ed.), *China into Africa: Trade, Aid, and Influence* (Washington, DC: Brookings, 2008), 77–78.
5. Michael Sata, quoted in *The Economist*, October 1, 2011.
6. Xi Jinping, speech to Beijing Summit of the Forum on China-Africa Cooperation (FOCAC), September 3, 2018, http://www.xinhuanet.com/english/2018-09/03/c_137441987.htm.

VII

1. Global Conflict Tracker, November 22, 2019, cfr.org/global-conflict-tracker/; Joe Penney, "Burkina Faso has Replaced Mali at the Epicenter of the Sahel's Security Crisis," November 27, 2019, www.qz.com/africa/1756917/.
2. Brittany Brown and Stephen Schwartz, quoted in Eric Schmitt and Charlie Savage, "U.S. Accelerates Shadowy Battle Against Shabab," *New York Times*, March 11, 2019.
3. Quoted in Adam Nossiter, "Helicopter Crash in Mali Kills 13 French Soldiers," *New York Times*, November 27, 2019.
4. Global Conflict Tracker, Nov. 27, 2019, cfr.org/interactive-globalconflict-tracker/.
5. Nicholas Kristof, "Marching Toward a Massacre," *New York Times*, January 17, 2019.
6. Amy Niang, "The CAR Provides Hard Lessons on What It Means to Deliver Real Justice," *The Conversation*, January 21, 2019, https://theconversation.com/the-car-provides-hard-lessons-on-what-it-means-to-deliver-real-justice-108947.
7. Rotberg, *Africa Emerges* (Cambridge, Polity, 2013), 74.
8. Emila Columbo, "Northern Mozambique at a Crossroads," December, 2019, https://csis-prod.s3.amazonAWS.com/s3fs-public/publication/191018.

VIII

1. Sajitha Bashir, Marlaine Lockheed, Elizabeth Ninan, and Jee-Peng Tan, *Facing Forward: Schooling for Learning in Africa* (Washington, DC: World Bank, 2018).
2. Ashish Jha, director of the Harvard Global Health Institute, quoted in Austin Frakt and Aaron E. Carroll, "Giant Strides Made in World Health, but Roadblocks Remain," *New York Times*, February 5, 2019.
3. www.brookings.edu/blog/africa-in-focus/2018/1/10/.
4. Omowumi Olabode and Steven Ekundayo, "Education in Nigeria Is in a Mess from Top to Bottom: Five Things Can Fix It," *The Conversation*, March 26, 2019.
5. The UNESCO definition of "Gross Enrollment Rate" is the "number of students enrolled in a given level of education, regardless of age, expressed as a percentage of the official school-age population..."
6. www.data.worldbank.org/indicator/SE.PRM.PRSLZS?
7. Bashir et al, *Facing Forward,* 51.
8. https://data.worldbank.org/indicator/SE.SEC.CMPT.LO.ZS?locations=ZG.
9. Net enrollment includes only children of the official school age, as defined by the national education system. Small discrepancies in the reported age of children may occasionally cause net enrollment rates to exceed 100 percent. Or, to be clear, the primary school net enrollment ratio (NER) is the share of

children of official primary school age that are enrolled in primary school; the NER cannot exceed 100%. The gross enrollment ratio (GER) is the share of children of any age that are enrolled in primary school.

10. Bashir, *Facing Forward*, 38.
11. Suellen Shay, "Matric Maths Pass Rate Poses Significant Challenge for Universities," University of Cape Town News, January 7, 2019, www.news.uct.ac.za/article/2019-07-01/.
12. Institute of International Education, cited in Quartz Weekly African Letter, December 1, 2019, Africa+weekly@qz.com.
13. Kofi Annan, "Information Technology Should Be Used to Tap Knowledge from the Greatest Universities to Bring Learning to All," August 3, 2000, www.unis.unvienna.org/unis/en/pressrels/2000/sg2625.html.
14. African Union, *Agenda 2063: The Africa We Want* (Addis Ababa: African Union Commission, 2015), 14.
15. Nico Cloete, Ian Bunting, and François van Schalkwyk, *Research Universities in Africa* (Somerset West: Mind in Africa, 2018), 20.
16. David Mba, "Nigeria's Universities are Performing Poorly: What Can Be Done About It?" *The Conversation*, March 11, 2019, https://theconversation.com/nigerias-universities-are-performing-poorly-what-can-be-done-about-it-112717.
17. President Akufo-Addo, quoted in Francis Kokutse, "University Level Upgrade for Teacher-Training Colleges," *University World News*, May 20, 2018.
18. Quoted in "Migration Data Portal," https://migrationdataportal.org/themes/diasporas.

IX

1. Erin Duffin, "Average Life Expectancy in Africa for Those Born in 2019," www.statista.com/statistics/274511.
2. https://data.worldbank.org/indicator/SP.DYN.LE00.IN?locations=ZG.
3. The Bill and Melinda Gates Foundation, Health Metrics Report, cited in Alicia Parlapiano, Josh Katz, and Margot Sanger-Katz, "Fewer of the World's Children Are Dying, But Many Remain at Risk," *New York Times*, September 18, 2019.
4. *The World Factbook*, 2017, https://www.cia.gov/library/publications/the-world-factbook/fields/353.html#XX.
5. Hilal Elver, UN special rapporteur on the right to food, quoted in Nyasha Chingono, " Zimbabwe on Verge of 'Man-Made' Starvation, Warns UN Envoy," *The Guardian*, November 29, 2019.
6. Bill Gates, "The Best Investment I've Ever Made," *Wall Street Journal*, January 19, 2019.

7. Associated Press, "Ebola Vaccine Stockpile Created," *Boston Globe*, December 3, 2019.
8. Charles Shey Wiysonge, "Lifestyle Diseases Could Scupper Africa's Rising Life Expectancy," *The Conversation*, November 26, 2018.

X

1. https://www.nation.co.ke/lifestyle/smartcompany/Paid-a-bribe-Just-click-here-and-let-everyone-know-/1226-1292134-f1klje/.
2. "Chad: Revelations on the Extent of Social Media Censorship—Internet sans Frontieres," https://internetwithoutborders.org/chad-revelations-on-the-extent-of-the-social-media-censorship/.
3. Freedom House, "Freedom on the Net, 2019," www.freedomonthe net.org/report/freedom-on-the-net/.
4. Amy Hawkins, "Beijing's Big Brother Tech Needs African Faces," Foreign Policy, July 24, 2018.

XI

1. See Charles Homans, "Crossroads of Traffic in Wildlife," *New York Times*, February 12, 2019.
2. Given the sharp fall in China's economic growth in 2019 and early 2020, these prices are out of date. Raw ivory in 2020 may be worth only $600 or so per kilogram, but at that price there is still a profit to be made by the middlemen who pay the poachers.
3. Cited in Tiffany May, "14 Tons of Pangolin Scales Are Intercepted," *New York Times*, April 9, 2019.

XII

1. Howard W. French, *China's Second Continent: How a Million Migrants Are Building A New Empire in Africa* (New York: Knopf, 2014), reviewed by Nicolas van de Walle in *Foreign Affairs,* November-December, 2014, 205.
2. Uhuru Kenyatta, quoted in "Kenyan Teacher who Helps Poor Wins $1 Million Prize," *New York Times,* March 25, 2019.

FOR FURTHER READING

There are many books and articles that will deepen an appreciation of all of the diverse subjects covered in this book. Not every topic has its own good synopsis, but many do. Equally, some topics have elicited a quantity of scholarly attention and publications. The select list that follows includes books of insight and value that are relatively recent—that were published within the last decade or so, and preferably within the past few years. It includes only books; relevant articles and research reports are too numerous to include here.

For a longer list than is provided here, and for older books on Africa, please see the bibliography to my *Africa Emerges* (which is listed below). That last bibliography also contains a number of country studies. For specialized publications on leadership and governance, please consult my *Transformational Political Leadership* and *On Governance* volumes, below. Anyone who seeks further references on corruption will find them in the bibliography to my *The Corruption Cure*, listed below, and in an updated form in the "further reading" part of my *Anticorruption* (Cambridge, MA: MIT Press, 2020).

For want of space, some of my own earlier writings on much narrower subjects concerning, for example, East African or South African politics or Zambian and Malawian political awakenings, are not listed here. Nor are very good older seminal books by African, American, British, and other scholars on particular countries such as the Democratic Republic of Congo, Mali, Ethiopia, and the like. Likewise, a number of fine older studies by anthropologists or educational experts are omitted. Particularly seminal books for the general reader are preceded by an asterisk.

References

Albaugh, Ericka A., *State-Building and Multilingual Education in Africa* (New York: Cambridge University Press, 2014)

Asserate, Asfa-Wossen (trans. Peter Lewis), *African Exodus Migration and the Future of Europe* (London: Haus, 2018)

Autesserre, Séverine, *The Trouble in the Congo: Local Violence and the Failure of International Peacebuilding* (New York: Cambridge University Press, 2010)

Baldwin, Kate, *The Paradox of Traditional Chiefs in Democratic Africa* (New York: Cambridge University Press, 2016)

Beyene, Atakilte (ed.), *Agricultural Transformation in Ethiopia: State Policy and Smallholder Farming* (Uppsala: Nordic Africa Institute, 2018)

*Bleck, Jaimie, and Nicolas van de Walle, *Electoral Politics Since 1990: Continuity in Change* (New York: Cambridge University Press, 2018)

*Bollyky, Thomas J., *Plagues and the Paradox of Progress* (New York: Council on Foreign Relations, 2018)

Boone, Catherine, *Property and Political Order in Africa: Land Rights and the Structure of Politics* (Cambridge: Cambridge University Press, 2014)

Branch, Adam, and Zachariah Mampilly, *Africa Uprising: Popular Protest and Political Change* (London: Zed, 2015)

Carmody, Pádraig, *The New Scramble for Africa* (Cambridge: Polity, 2011)

*Cheeseman, Nic, *Democracy in Africa: Successes, Failures, and the Struggle for Political Reform* (New York: Cambridge University Press, 2015)

Cheeseman, Nic, Eloise Bertrand, and Se'eed Husaini (eds.), *Oxford Dictionary of African Politics* (Oxford: Oxford University Press, 2019), online only

Chipkin, Ivor, Mark Swilling, Haroon Bhorat, et al., *Shadow State: The Politics of State Capture* (Johannesburg: Wits University Press, 2018)

*Collier, Paul, *The Bottom Billion: Why the Poorest Countries are Failing and What Can Be Done About It* (New York: Oxford University Press, 2007)

Du Toit, Fanie, *When Political Transitions Work: Reconciliation as Independence* (New York: Oxford University Press, 2018)

Elischer, Sebastian, *Political Parties in Africa: Ethnicity and Party Formation* (New York: Cambridge University Press, 2013)

*Frantz, Erica, *Authoritarianism: What Everyone Needs to Know* (New York: Oxford University Press, 2018)

French, Howard W., *China's Second Continent: How a Million Migrants Are Building a New Empire in Africa* (New York: Knopf, 2014)

Guest, Robert, *The Shackled Continent: Power, Corruption, and African Lives* (Washington, DC: Smithsonian, 2004)

Hagmann, Tobias, and Filip Reyntjens, *Aid and Authoritarianism in Africa: Development without Democracy* (London: Zed Books, 2016)

Hansen, Stig Jarle, *Horn, Sahel, and Rift: Fault-Lines of the African Jihad* (London: Hurst, 2019)

Harper, Mary, *Everything You Have Told me is True: The Many Faces of Al Shabaab* (London: Hurst, 2019)

Heilbrunn, John R., *Oil, Democracy, and Development in Africa* (New York: Cambridge University Press, 2014)

Hino, Hiroyuki, Arnim Langer, John Lonsdale, and Frances Stewart (eds.), *From Divided Pasts to Cohesive Futures: Reflections on Africa* (Cambridge: Cambridge University Press, 2019)

Ibhawoh, Bonny, *Human Rights in Africa* (New York: Cambridge University Press, 2018)

Jerven, Morten, *Africa: Why Economists Get It Wrong* (London: Zed, 2015)

Juma, Calestous, *Innovation and Its Enemies: Why People Resist New Technologies* (New York: Oxford University Press, 2016)

Karekwaivanane, George Hamandishe, *The Struggle over State Power in Zimbabwe: Law and Politics since 1950* (New York: Cambridge University Press, 2017)

LeVan, A. Carl, *Contemporary Nigerian Politics: Competition in a Time of Transition and Terror* (New York: Cambridge University Press, 2019)

Lyons, Terrence, *The Puzzle of Ethiopian Politics* (Boulder: Rienner, 2019)

*Mills, Greg, *Why Africa Is Poor: and What Africans Can Do About It* (Johannesburg: Penguin, 2010)

Morrell, Robert, Fran Collyer, Raewyn Connell, and Joao Maia, *Knowledge and Global Power: Making New Sciences in the South* (Johannesburg: Wits University Press, 2019)

Morse, Yonatan L., *How Autocrats Compete: Parties, Patrons, and Unfair Elections in Africa* (New York: Cambridge University Press, 2019)

Mueller, Lisa, *Political Protest in Contemporary Africa* (New York: Cambridge University Press, 2018)

Nyabola, Nanjala, *Digital Democracy, Analogue Politics: How the Internet Era Is Transforming Kenya* (London: Zed, 2018)

Obadare, Ebenezer, *Pentecostal Republic: Religion and the Struggle for State Power in Nigeria* (London: Zed, 2018)

*Okonjo-Iweala, Ngozi, *Fighting Corruption Is Dangerous: The Story Behind the Headlines* (Cambridge, MA: MIT Press, 2018)

Paller, Jeffrey W., *Democracy in Ghana: Everyday Politics in Urban Africa* (New York: Cambridge University Press, 2019)

Pierce, Steven, *Moral Economies of Corruption: State Formation and Political Culture in Nigeria* (Durham, NC: Duke University Press, 2016)

Roessler, Philip, *Ethnic Politics and State Power in Africa: The Logic of the Coup–Civil War Trap* (New York: Cambridge University Press, 2016)

Roessler, Philip, and Harry Verhoeven, *Why Comrades Go to War: Liberation Politics and the Outbreak of Africa's Deadliest Conflict* (New York: Oxford University Press, 2016)

Rotberg, Robert I., *Africa Emerges: Consummate Challenges, Abundant Opportunities* (Cambridge: Polity Press, 2013)

*Rotberg, Robert I., *The Corruption Cure: How Citizens and Leaders Can Combat Graft* (Princeton: Princeton University Press, 2017)

Rotberg, Robert I., *Transformational Political Leadership: Making a Difference in the Developing World* (Chicago: University of Chicago Press, 2012)

Rotberg, Robert I. (ed.) *On Governance: What It Is, What It Measures, and Its Policy Uses* (Waterloo, ON: CIGI, 2015)

Smuts, David, *Death, Detention and Disappearance: A Lawyer's Battle to Hold Power to Account in 1980s Namibia* (Cape Town:Tafelberg, 2019)

Stearns, Jason K., *Dancing in the Glory of Monsters: The Collapse of the Congo and the Great War of Africa* (New York: Public Affairs, 2011)

Taoua, Phyllis, *African Freedom: How Africa Responded to Independence* (New York: Cambridge University Press, 2018)

Williams, Paul D., *War and Conflict in Africa* (Cambridge: Polity, 2011)

Wrong, Michela, *It's Our Turn to Eat: The Story of a Kenyan Whistleblower* (London: Fourth Estate, 2009)

INDEX

China (*cont.*)
  critically important to Africa, 94–96, 142–146
  concessional lending, 151–152
  corona virus, 143
  dam building, 146–147, 160
  debt, 147–148
  demand for animal products, 276–277
  despots and dictators, 152, 161
  domestic engine of growth, 142–143
  donkeys, 288–289
  environment, 159
  financial aid to Africa, 149–150
  fishing in Senegal, 157
  human rights in Africa, 161–162
  humanitarian aid, 151–152
  hydro power, 297
  imports problem, 159–160
  infrastructure building, 297
  in Ghana, 160
  infant mortality, 145
  investment in Africa, 146
  ivory, 278–279
  jobs, 155–156
  leader visits to Africa, 149
  liberation movements, 152
  Mandarin teaching, 154
  media, 154
  medical aid, 150
  mining labor, 155–160
  mobile telephones, 248
  neo-imperialism, 154–155
  no interference policy, 149, 161
  pangolins, 286–287
  peacekeeping, 150, 153
  poaching and antipoaching, 278–279, 284, 290
  prosperity and Africa, 142
  public health, 151
  railways, 160
  race relations, 154–158
  safety regulations, 156
  schooling, 151
  scholarships, 151
  seeking minerals, 144–145
  seeks oil, 144
  shoddy work, 160
  soft power, 154, 298
  state control of aid, 150–151
  supply of military hardware, 152–153
  teachers for Africa, 151
  television, 154
  trade, 143
  traditional medicinal beliefs, 255, 284.
Chirundu, Zambia, 160
Chissano, President Joaquim, 41–42
Chokwe, people, 4
Cholera, 3, 26, 232, 235
Christians, in Africa, 5–7, 16, 21, 58, 73, 171, 177, 179, 181–183, 185. See also Faiths.
  schooling, 195–196.
Chrome, 11, 94–95, 143. See also Ferrochrome.
Church of England, 6. See also Anglicans.
Church of Rome, 6
Cirrhosis of the liver, 242
Cities, 14, 19, 23, 24–25, 27, 28, 60, 104, 112, 271, 298
  disease, 240
  fertility, 22
  growth of, 293
  sanitation, 231
Civil Code, the, 73
Civil service, 13, 53–54, 125
Civil society, role of, 43, 63, 74, 185, 259,
Civil War. See Conflict, civil
Civil wars, 16, 72–73, 81–83, 90, 174–193, 295
  casualties, 177
  causes of, 174–178

Data, objective, 78
De Beers Mining Corporation, 46
De Klerk, President Frederik W., 50
Deaths
  disease, and terrorism, 167
  from cardiovascular disease, 241
  from diabetes, 242
  from dysentery, 235
  from Ebola, 239–240
  from Lassa, 240
  from malaria, 236–238
  from schistosomiasis, 243
  from yellow fever, 239
  in Burundi, 185
  in Cameroon, 190
  in Central African Republic, 181–183
  in civil war, 16, 72, 164–165, 175, 177, 295
  in South Sudan, 180
  in Sudan, 179
  road accidents, 115
Déby, President Idriss, 41, 190, 266–267
Deeper Life Bible Church, 6
Delaware, 105, 127
Deliberative democracy, concept of, 44
Demand, Asian, for animal products, 271–287, 291
Democracies, defective, 63
Democracy, 7, 32, 36, 42, 43, 44, 45, 47, 51, 55, 56, 57, 59, 61–84, 185, 294, 297
  electoral, 64–65
  liberal, 64–65
  representative, 68
Demographic dividend, concept of, 17, 23, 30–31
Demographic issues, xiii, 18–23. See also Population, increases.
Deng Ziaoping, 31
Dengue fever, 238–239
Denmark, 72, 122
Density, 17–19, 20, 51

Department of Justice, US, 127
Derg, of Ethiopia, 57–58
Desalination, 232
Deserts, of Africa, 1
Despots and despotism, 41, 149, 152, 161
Development, and literacy, 197
Dhlakama, Afonso, 192
Diabetes, 242–243
Diagnostic, of governance, 78–79
Diamonds, 11, 37, 38, 44, 46–47, 82, 86, 88, 91–93, 96, 128, 129, 153, 156, 177–178, 182
Dictators, 28, 39, 44, 81
Dik-dik, 283
Dinka, people, 179–180
Discretion, and corruption, 258–259
Discrimination, as a cause of conflict, 174–177, 179, 188–190, 295
Disease, animal, 103. See also zoonotic disease.
Disease, from mosquitoes, 230
Disease, plant, 103
Division of Population, UN, 18, 20, 21–22
Djibouti, 57, 66, 82, 96, 146, 148, 150, 153, 168, 169, 238, 281
Djotodia, President Michel, 181
Doctorates, in Africa, 213, 220–221
Doing Business, 54, 75, 98,
Dong'e, county, China, 289
Donkeys, 288–289, 298
  value, 289
Donors, dependence on, 78, 80, 89
Dracunculiasis, 244
Drones, 53, 175, 257
  against al-Shabaab, 169
  antipoaching, 279
  AQIM, 172
  medical deliveries, 248
  helping farmers, 254–255
  in Agadez, 173
  use of against terrorists, 166

Oman, 5
Ombuds Offices, 132–133
Omo River, 111
Online education, 215
Onchocerciasis, 245
Online deregulation, 258–259
Online learning, 213
Ophthalmologists, shortage of,
    246–247, 256
Opinion, public, 6, 263
Opium, 168
Opportunity, economic, 13
Oral transmission of culture, 198
Orange River, 111
Orange, mobile phones, 251
Oranges, 92, 103, 143
Organization for Economic Cooperation
    and Development (OECD), 152
Organization of African Unity
    (OAU), 10
Organization of Islamic Courts,
    Somalia, 167
Oromo Liberation Front, 57
Oromo, people, 4–5, 19, 58
Orthodox Catholics, 6
Ostentation, and leadership, 33, 45
Otigba Computer Village, 116
Otoscopes, and mobile phones, 255
Ougadougou, Burkina Faso, 24, 175
Outputs, not inputs, 78
Outsourcing, consumer, 265–266
Owlet, Albertine, 290
Oxford, University of, xii, 43, 253–254
Oystercatcher, Black 290

Pakistan, 18, 19, 93, 98, 168, 225
Palladium, 92, 143
Pangolin, 143, 286–287, 298
    poaching, 287
    scales, value, 287
Paris, France, 127
Parliamentary systems, 66–67. See also
    Legislatures.

Parrots, Grey, 290
Participation, Political, 74–75
Parties, political, 59, 65–66, 84
Parties, role of, 68–69
Pastoral peoples and pastoralism, 5, 7,
    16, 101–103, 172, 283
Patriarchy, in Africa, 40
Patronage, political, 42–43, 68
Peace dividend, the, 50
Peacekeeping
    in CAR, 181–183
    in conflict, 55, 72, 150, 153,
        164, 180
    in Western Sahara, 191
Peculation. See corruption
Pedagogy, in schools, 201–202
Pemba, Mozambique, 188
Penguins, 290
Pentecostalism, 6, 58–59, 185
People, "my", 8
People, smuggling, 16
PEPFAR (U. S. President's Emergency
    Plan for AIDS Relief), 234
Persia, 2. See also Iran
Persistence (Completion) Schooling
    Rates, 11–12, 199–201
Persistence, in secondary school,
    205–207
Personnel, medical, 255
Peru, 173,
Pesticides, 103
Pet trade, 290
Petrels, 290
Petroleum. See oil
Pew Research Center, 6, 60
Phantom projects, and corruption,
    130–131
Pharmaceuticals, 94, 148
Pharmaceuticals, fake, 256–257
Philippines, the, 6
Phosphates, 191
Physician numbers, 220. See Numbers
Physicians, per capita, 78

Public Procurement Commission (Liberia), 55
Public Protector, in South Africa, 133
Public Trust, abuse of, 120
Puerto Rico, 72
Puku, 282, 285
Puntland, 168

Qaddafi, President Muammar al-, 166
Qaeda, al-, 82, 167–179. See also AQIM
Qat, 93,
Qatar, 187
Quinces, 103

Racism, by Chinese, 155–158
Radio, 134–135, 249
Rail lines, 9, 57, 76, 112, 114, 146–147, 160
Railways, Botswana, 114–115
Railways, Nigeria, 114–115
Rain, and rainfall, 27–28, 30, 110, 172, 230–231, 272, 298. See also climate change
Ramaphosa, President Cyril, 32, 50
Ramgoolam, Prime Minister Sir Seewoogasur, 39, 140, 294
Ransoming, incidence of, 168, 182, 184
Rape
  CAR, 181–183
  South Sudan, 180
  war, 72, 177, 262
Rats, and Lassa, 240, 245
Rawlings, President Jerry John, 39
Reconciliation, and Mandela, 50–51
Red Sea, 1, 57, 144, 146, 150, 179
Red tape, 54, 97
Redistribution of resources, 27
Referendum, and Western Sahara, 191
Religion, 5–7, 175. See also Faiths
Remittances, from diaspora, 221
Renamo, Mozambique, 192
Renewable energy, 107–108, 110

Rent seeking, and corruption, 28, 62, 87, 91, 108, 177, 201–202
Reporters Without Borders, 134
Representative democracy, 68
Republic of Congo. See Congo, Republic of
Research, and development 269
Research, in African universities, 213–214
Resilience, 3, 17, 293, 298
Resource avarice, 178, 182–183
Resource Curse, the, and corruption, 46, 129–130
Resources, competition for, 177–180
Resources, primary, 11
Retroviral medicines, 256
Rheumatic heart disease, 242
Rhino horn, 288, 298
  medicinal properties, 276
Rhinoceros, numbers of, 274–275
Rhinoceroses, 143, 273–275, 277, 279, 290–291,
Rhodesia, xii
Rice, 2, 28, 151
Rift Valley, 1, 2, 43
Rinderpest, 282
Rio de Ouro (Western Sahara), 190–191
River blindness, 245
River transport, 114
Rivers, of Africa, 1
Rivonia trial and Mandela speech, 49
Road injuries, 242
Roadblocks, and extortion, 125
Roads
  accidents on, 115
  China, 147
  network, 113–114
  paved and unpaved, 76, 104, 112, 293
Robben Island, South Africa, 48–49, 51
Robotics, 269–270
Roman Catholic Church, in Congo, 263
Roman Catholicism, 6

Roman Empire, the, 2
Romania, 92
Roosevelt, President Franklin D., 34
Rotavirus, 235
Rotberg, Dr. Nicola S. D., xiii
Rubber, 55, 93
Rugby, 51
Rule of Law Index, 73
Rule of law, 10, 13, 45, 50, 52, 62, 64,
    73–75, 80, 84, 98, 118, 137, 140,
    193, 296–297
Russia, xiv, 6, 42, 70, 82, 108, 142,
    144, 149, 152–154, 168, 171–
    172, 187, 224, 297
  Central African Republic, 153, 182
  Madagascar, 153
  trade with Africa, 153
Ruwenzori Mountains, 191–192
Rwanda University of Global Health
    Equity, 229
Rwanda, 9, 15, 17, 20, 32, 34, 37,
    40–42, 51–55, 66, 69–70, 81, 83,
    87–88, 93, 98–99, 101, 106, 108,
    110–111, 113, 122, 132, 139, 148,
    162, 193, 200, 209, 211, 224, 235,
    257, 282, 290. See also Kagame.
  anticorruption methods, 132–133
  business, 258
  contraception, 31
  demographic dividend, 31
  family planning, 31
  health, 256
  infant mortality, 225
  Internet, 264, 267
  malaria, 237
  skills development, 215
  vision loss, 247

Saakashvili, President Mikheil, 53
Safaricom, 251–252
Safety, 71–73
Sahara, desert, 3, 5, 16, 165–166, 172–
    173, 178, 295

Sahel, and drought, 232
Sahel, the region, 1, 5, 28, 103, 165–
    179, 172–173, 236, 295, 298
Sahrawi Arab Democratic Republic, 67,
    190–191
Sahrawi, people, 190–191
Saint Louis, Senegal, 253
Salafism, 166, 173. See Islam
Sall, President Macky, 39, 147
Salt, 2
Samburu, people, 5
San Diego, 256
Sand, mining, 159–160
Sango, language, 63, 181
Sanitation, 223, 231–231, 240, 243,
Santos, President Eduardo dos, 41, 123,
    130, 161
São Tomé and Príncipe, 15, 67, 87,
    122, 224, 228–22
Sassou Nguesso, President Denis,
    37, 127
Sata, President Michael, 158
Satellites, and information, 248, 257
Satellites, and water, 254
Saudi Arabia, 93, 143–144, 168, 187
Schistosomiasis (Bilharzia), 243
School Certificate, in South Africa, 11
School fees, impact of, 206
School provisions, 77
Schooling, 11, 193–221, 293
  absenteeism, 208
  cities, 199
  class size, 207, 209
  computers, 202
  constraints, 298
  corruption, 124–125
  disease, 223
  drop out rates, 200–201
  expenditures on, 214
  fertility, 196
  foreign aid, 204
  girls, 207
  impact on fertility, 21,